BEST Solution
Guaranteed •••

NCERT EXEMPLAR

Problems – Solutions

Biology 11th

Author
Anubhuti Jain

ARIHANT PRAKASHAN (Series), MEERUT

卐 **Administrative & Production Offices**

Regd. Office

'Ramchhaya' 4577/15, Agarwal Road, Darya Ganj, New Delhi -110002
Tele: 011- 47630600, 43518550

卐 **Head Office**

Kalindi, TP Nagar, Meerut (UP) - 250002
Tel: 0121-7156203, 7156204

卐 **Sales & Support Offices**

Agra, Ahmedabad, Bengaluru, Bareilly, Chennai, Delhi, Guwahati, Hyderabad, Jaipur, Jhansi, Kolkata, Lucknow, Nagpur & Pune.

卐 **PRICE** ₹275.00

卐 **PO No. :** TXT-59-T069007-1-26

Published by Arihant Publications (India) Ltd.

For further information about the books published by Arihant, log on to www.arihantbooks.com or e-mail at info@arihantbooks.com

Follow us on   

PREFACE

NCERT Exemplar Problems, published by the NCERT, are designed to provide students with a diverse range of quality questions in formats such as Multiple Choice Questions, Very Short Answer Type Questions, Short Answer Type Questions, and Long Answer Type Questions, catering to varying levels of difficulty.

These problems are essential for success in school and board exams, as well as competitive exams like engineering and medical entrances. Regular practice with these problems prepares students to tackle challenging questions effectively.

This book, **NCERT Exemplar Problems-Solutions Biology 11th**, offers precise and detailed solutions to all the questions in the NCERT Exemplar Biology textbook. Each solution is complemented by explanatory notes and authentic explanations, enabling students to deepen their conceptual understanding and enhance their analytical skills.

Key features

- **Thinking Process** Provides simple steps to approach and solve the question, clearing up any confusion.
- **Concept Insight** Explains the main ideas and concepts needed to answer the questions correctly.
- **Mistake Alert!** Points out common mistakes students might make and helps them avoid these errors.

I hope this book proves to be a valuable resource, aiding students in their academic journey and leading them to great success.

Author

CONTENTS

***Note(*)** These Chapters have been deleted from latest NCERT.*

Chapter

01

The Living World

Multiple Choice Questions (MCQs)

Choose the correct answer from the given four options in the following questions.

Q. 1 As we go from species to kingdom in a taxonomic hierarchy, the number of common characteristics

(a) will decrease (b) will increase

(c) remain same (d) may increase or decrease

Ans. ***(a)*** Lower the taxa, more are the characteristic that the members within the taxon share. So, lowest taxon share the maximum number of morphological similarities, while its similarities decrease as we move towards the higher hierarchy, *i.e.*, class, kingdom.

Q. 2 Which of the following 'suffixes' used for units of classification in plants indicates a taxonomic category of 'family'?

(a) – Ales (b) – Onae (c) – Aceae (d) – Ae

Thinking Process Biological classification of organism is a process by which any living organism is classified into convenient categories based on some common observable characters. The categories are known as taxa (PL) (Sign-taxon)..

Ans. ***(c)*** The name of a family, in plants always end with suffixes **aceae**, *e.g.*, Solanaceae, Cannaceae and Poaceae. The other options are incorrect because **Ales** suffix is used for **'order'** while **onae** and **ae** suffixes are not used in any of taxa.

Q. 3 The term 'systematics' refers to

(a) identification and study of organ systems

(b) identification and preservation of plants and animals

(c) diversity of kinds of organisms and their relationship

(d) study of habitats of organisms and their classification

Thinking Process The planet earth is full of variety of different forms of life. The number of species that are named and described are between 1.7-1.8 million. As we explore new areas, new organisms are continuously being identified, named and described on scientific basis of systematics, laid down by taxonomists.

Ans. ***(c)*** The word systematics is derived from the Latin word *'Systema'* which means systematic arrangement of organisms. Linnaeus used *'Systema Naturae'* as a title of his publication. Systematics deals with the diversity of an organisms and their relationship at every level of classification.

Q. 4 Genus represents
(a) an individual plant or animal
(b) a collection of plants or animals
(c) group of closely related species of plants or animals
(d) None of the above

Ans. *(c)* **Genus** comprises a group of closely related species which has more common characters in comparison to species of other genera.

Q. 5 The taxonomic unit 'Phylum' in the classification of animals is equivalent to which hierarchial level in classification of plants.
(a) Class
(b) Order
(c) Division
(d) Family

Ans. *(c)* **Division** includes classes with few similar characters in group of organism and is equivalent to 'Phylum' in animals.

Q. 6 Botanical gardens and zoological parks have
(a) collection of endemic living species only
(b) collection of exotic living species only
(c) collection of endemic and exotic living species
(d) collection of only local plants and animals

Ans. *(c)* **Botanical gardens** and **zoological parks** have a collection of endemic and exotic living species and they are used to restore depleted population, reintroduce species, *i.e.*, to build and restore degraded habitats.

Q. 7 Taxonomic key is one of the taxonomic tools in the identification and classification of plants and animals. It is used in the preparation of
(a) monographs (b) flora
(c) Both (a) and (b) (d) None of these

Thinking Process Correct identification of any living organism is important in biological classification and nomenclature. It requires some reference of already named and classified organism to check their similarity and dissimilarity with newly discovered organism.

Ans. *(c)* **Taxonomic keys** are tools that help in identification of organism based on the specific characters, which are used in the preparation of monograph and flora.

Q. 8 All living organisms are linked to one another because
(a) they have common genetic material of the same type
(b) they share common genetic material but to varying degrees
(c) all have common cellular organisation
(d) All of the above

Ans. *(b)* All living organisms share common genetic material, *i.e.*, DNA but with variations, *e.g.*, bacteria have double stranded circular DNA chromosome (one in number) while in highly evolved eukaryotic cells of plants and animals DNA organised as chromatin (many chromosome) with in the nucleus.

Q. 9 Which of the following is a defining characteristic of living organisms?

(a) Growth (b) Ability to make sound
(c) Reproduction (d) Response to external stimuli

Ans. *(d)* **Response to external stimuli** or to the environment in which an organism lives, is the most important characteristic of any living organism, besides growth and reproduction.
Growth and ability to make sound are some properties that can also be observed in non-living things. While virus (which is not included under living organisms) also show growth and reproduction. Hence, these options are not true.

Q. 10 Match the following and choose the correct option.

Column I		Column II	
A.	Family	1.	*tuberosum*
B.	Kingdom	2.	Polymoniales
C.	Order	3.	*Solanum*
D.	Species	4.	Plantae
E.	Genus	5.	Solanaceae

Codes

	A	B	C	D	E		A	B	C	D	E
(a)	4	3	5	2	1	(b)	5	4	2	1	3
(c)	4	5	2	1	3	(d)	5	3	2	1	4

Ans. *(b)* Given matching represent the taxonomic classification of potato plant. The correct matching is as follows

Family – Solanaceae
Kingdom – Plantae
Order – Polymoniales
Genus – *Solanum*
Species – *tuberosum*

Very Short Answer Type Questions

Q. 1 Linnaeus is considered as Father of Taxonomy. Name two other botanists known for their contribution to the field of plant taxonomy.

Ans. **Carolus Linnaeus** (1707-1778), a Swedish botanist is regarded as Father of Plant Taxonomy. He published his work in book *Genera Plantarum* in 1737. Two other botanists known for their contribution to plant taxonomy are **G Bentham** and **Joseph Dalton Hooker**. Both are famous for their work on classification of plants based on natural characteristics.

Q. 2 What does ICZN stand for?

Ans. ICZN stand for **International Code of Zoological Nomenclature**. It ensures that scientific name assigned to any animal has only one name and will be recognised by that name all over the world by scientific community.

Q. 3 Couplet in taxonomic key means ....

- **Concept Insight** The renowned taxonomist have already named and classified a good number of known biological objects. Their character and phylogeny have already been documented and is available for further reference to help in the identification of newly discovered biological objects.

Ans. In taxonomic key couplet is a pair of contrasting characters used as a tool for identification of newly discovered organisms.

Q. 4 What is a monograph?

Ans. Monograph is a detailed study or writing work on a particular taxon, *i.e.*, family or genus. It takes into account the descriptive features and characters of an organism or species. A monograph is made by reviewing all of the present species with in a group. Whenever an organism is discovered and needs to be placed in a particular taxon, the monographs are reviewed.

Q. 5 *Amoeba* multiplies by mitotic cell division. Is this phenomena growth or reproduction? Explain.

Ans. *Amoeba* multiplies by simple mitotic cell divisions giving rise to two daughter amoebae. Here, the process is synonymous with reproduction, *i.e.*, increase in number.

Q. 6 Define metabolism.

Ans. **Metabolism** is total sum of all biological reactions occurring in any living cell, which are absolutely controlled by enzymes. These reactions are of two types breaking down reactions (catabolism, *e.g.*, cellular respiration) and synthesising reactions (anabolism, *e.g.*, photosynthesis).

Q. 7 Which is the largest botanical garden in the world? Name a few well known botanical gardens in India.

Thinking Process A botanical garden is dedicated to collection, cultivation and display of wide range of plants labelled with their botanical names. Try to find out International and National Botanical Gardens.

Ans. The largest botanical garden in the world is Royal Botanical Garden (RBG) Kew, London. Some well known botanical gardens in India are:

(i) Indian Botanical Garden, Sibpur, Kolkata.

(ii) Lloyd's Botanical Garden, Darjeeling.

(iii) Botanical Garden of FRI, Dehradun (UK).

(iv) National Botanical Garden (NBG) Lucknow, UP.

Short Answer Type Questions

Q. 1 A ball of snow when rolled over snow increases in mass, volume and size. Is this comparable to growth as seen in living organisms? Why?

Thinking Process Think about living and non-living objects around you. Try out to make differences between them. Living organisms grow, have metabolism and respond to external stimuli and also reproduce. These characteristics are not shown by non-living objects.

Ans. Growth in biological terms is the characteristic feature of all living organisms. It relates to increase in size by accumulation of protoplasm in the cell thus results in increase in size of the cell. Whereas increase in number of cell by cell division results is the growth of an individual organism (internal growth).

Snow is an inanimate (non-living) object, while rolling over snow, it gathers more snow on its surface thus (external growth), it increases in size by physical phenomenon but not by biological phenomenon. So, this growth cannot be compared to that seen in living organisms. Therefore internal growth is the defining feature of living organisms.

Q. 2 In a given habitat we have 20 plant species and 20 animal species. Should we call this as 'diversity or biodiversity'? Justify your answer.

Ans. In a given habitat, there are 20 plant species and 20 animal species. This exhibit the biodiversity of that given habitat because **diversity** refers to variation in a broad term and can be applied to any area. Whereas **biodiversity** is a degree of variation of life forms within a specified area.

Q. 3 International Code of Botanical Nomenclature (ICBN) has provided a code for classification of plants. Give hierarchy of units of classification, botanists follow while classifying plants and mention different 'suffixes' used for the units.

Thinking Process There are 1.7-1.8 million known living organisms in the world, out of which there are 422,000 known species of plants.
ICBN provides the scientifically agreed principles and criteria for identification, classification and scientific nomenclature, discuss taxonomic hierarchy while classifying any plant.

Ans. ICBN has specified certain rules and principles is order to facilitate the study of plants by botanists. It helps in correct positioning of any newly discovered organism through proper identification and nomenclature.

Given below is the taxonomic hierarchy, which is used while classifying any plant with their suffixes.

Kingdom–Plantae

Division–phyta

Class–ae

Order–ales

Family–eae/ceae

Genus–First name of organism usually carrying Latin word and written in italics, starts from capital letter.

Species–Second word of scientific name, also written in italics, starts from small letter.

Q. 4 A plant species shows several morphological variations in response to altitudinal gradient. When grown under similar conditions of growth, the morphological variations disappear and all the variants have common morphology. What are these variants called?

Ans. These variants are called **biotypes**. It is a group of genetically similar plants that exhibit similarity when grown in same environmental and geographical conditions. The same environment provide similar abiotic factors like soil, pH, temperature, etc.

When grown in two different geographical regions, they are exposed to different abiotic characters thus, it affects their growth and development leading to changes in their external morphological features but, they have the same genetic constitution.

Q. 5 How do you prepare your own herbarium sheets? What are the different tools you carry with you while collecting plants for the preparation of a herbarium? What information should a preserved plant material on the herbarium sheet provide for taxonomical studies?

Thinking Process Herbarium is a collection of preserved plant specimen, which are often used as reference material in describing plant taxa.

Ans. For preservation of plant material on a herbarium sheet the following tools and steps are required to be followed.

Tools Digger and pruning knife, sickle with long handle, vasculum, polythene bags, magazines or newspapers, blotting papers, plant press, field notebook, herbarium sheets, glue, labels, small transparent polythene bags.

One can prepare herbarium sheets by cutting papers of size 29×41.5 cm $(11\frac{1}{2} \times 16\frac{1}{2})''$.

The preparation of a herbarium specimen required following steps

(i) **Collection** of plant or plant parts.

(ii) **Pressing** It involves the spreading and pressing of collected specimen over a newspaper so as to preserve its all parts.

(iii) **Drying** It involves the drying of the specimen between the folds of newspaper.

(iv) **Poisoning** Antifungal (dipping in 2% $HgCl_2$) and pesticidal (DDT) treatment of the dried specimen.

(v) **Mounting** It involves mounting of the specimen over a herbarium sheet.

(vi) **Labelling** and **identification** of the dried specimen are the last steps, while preparing a herbarium sheet.

Tools/equipments required for the collection of herbarium specimens are as follows

(i) A tin or aluminium container of $50 \times 30 \times 15$ cm size.

(ii) Collection bags/plastic/polythene bags.

(iii) Digger for digging roots.

(iv) Magnifying lens of at least 10X magnification.

(v) Field note book.

A preserved plant material on the herbarium sheet may provide information about the family, genus, species, date of collection, area of collection, etc., for taxonomic studies.

Q. 6 What is the difference between flora, fauna and vegetation? *Eichhornia crassipes* is called as an exotic species, while *Rauwolfia serpentina* is an endemic species in India. What do these terms exotic and endemic refer to?

Ans. The difference between flora, fauna and vegetation are as below

Flora	Fauna	Vegetation
Flora refers to the plant life occurring in a specific region at a particular time, typically consisting of the naturally occurring, indigenous and native plant species.	Fauna is total number of animals found in a particular region at particular time.	It refers to the plant forms of region. It is broad and general term used for a plant forms, which does not include particular taxa or any botanical characteristics.

The terms exotic and endemic refers to

Exotic Species	Endemic Species
Any species of a plant living in any other place except its native place is said to be **exotic species.** *e.g., Eichhornia crassipes* is native of Amazon basin but it was introduced in India, so it is an exotic species in India.	Endemic species are restricted to a particular area, *e.g., Rauwolfia serpentina* is found only in India.

Q. 7 A plant may have different names in different regions or the country of world. How do botanists solve this problem?

Thinking Process Single plant may be known by many common names in a region or even universally or single name may be given to many plants. Think the importance of scientific method of identification, nomenclature and classification of plants.

Ans. There is a need to standardise the naming of living organisms such that a particular organism is known by the same name all over the world. Botanists have solved this problem by setting International Code for Botanical Nomenclature (ICBN).

Scientific naming ensures that each organism has only one name in any part of the world. ICBN ensures that a name is not been used for any other organism.

Each scientific name has two components the generic name and the specific epithet. This system of naming is called **bionomial nomenclature** given by **Carolus Linnaeus**. *e.g.,* mango has the scientific name *Mangifera indica* and for potato is *Solanum tuberosum*.

Q. 8 Brinjal and potato belong to the same genus *Solanum*, but to two different species. What defines them as separate species?

Thinking Process Genus (plural genera) is a taxonomic rank used in bionomial nomenclature. It comprises of a group of related species sharing few common characters. Discuss common characters of *Solanum* exhibited by brinjal and potato.

Ans. *Solanum* is the largest genus of flowering plants which includes few economically important plants, *e.g.*, potato, tomato, tobacco and brinjal. These plants share common morphological features related to vegetative and reproductive structures.

So, they have the same common name of genus-*Solanum*. the main criterion for defining them as two different species because they cannot cross, reproduce or inter breed and produce fertile offspring. Potato and brinjal can not cross each other, so they are identified as different species.

Q.9 Properties of cell organelles are not always found in the molecular constituents of cell organelles. Justify.

Ans. The properties of cell organelles are not always found in the molecular constitutents of cell organelles. For example, ribosome are non-membrane bound cell organelle, that are a site for protein synthesis. It is made up of proteins and *r*RNA. If these components are separated, individually, they cannot perform the process of protein synthesis. Therefore, the molecular constituents alone do not fully define the function of the organelles.

Q. 10 The number and kinds of organism is not constant. How do you explain this statement?

Thinking Process Change is law of nature. Nothing is constant or forever in the world. There are approximately 5-7 million living organisms of which nearly 1.2-1.5 million have been scientifically described. Apply the role of sexual reproduction and evolution in evolving a new species. Simultaneously factors like environmental threats, loss of habitat, etc., are continuously depleting the different life forms.

Ans. The number and kinds of organism is not constant, due to several dynamic factors that influence the existence of life forms on earth. These factors include:

Mechanisms for adding new organisms by

(i) Sexual reproduction
(ii) Mutation
(iii) Evolution

Mechanisms for reducing the number of organisms are

(i) Environmental threats
(ii) Loss of habitat
(iii) Anthropogenic activities

Long Answer Type Questions

Q.1 What is meant by living? Give any four defining features of life forms.

Ans. The living organism exhibit distinctive characteristics, which are as follows

(i) **Growth** All living organisms grow in size as well as in number. Plants show growth throughout their life whereas animals grow only up to a certain growth period after which growth ceases.

(ii) **Reproduction** The process of reproduction is essential for the continuity of life on earth. Every organism whether unicelluar or multicellular gives rise to an individual of its own kind. Lower organisms usually reproduce asexually, *e.g.*, *Hydra,* fungi, yeast, etc.

Sexual reproduction is found in advanced group of organisms, which involves two parents. In *Amoeba* growth and reproduction however is synonymous.

(iii) **Metabolism** There are thousands of enzymatically controlled reactions occurring in all living cells. These include synthesising (anabolic) and breaking down (catabolic) reactions. Hence, it is the most important characteristic of living organisms.

(iv) **Response to stimuli** Consciousness and response to stimulus are the defining property of all living organisms. Plants respond to light, water and temperature. Unicellular organisms also sense their environment and respond accordingly.

(v) **Cellular organisation** The cellular organisation of the body is the defining feature of life forms. Cells work together in hierarchial manner : group of cells make tissues, tissues make organs, organs make systems, organ systems when work in co-ordination form an individual.

So, we can say living organisms are self replicating, evolving and capable of responding to external stimuli.

Q.2 A scientist has come across a plant, which he feels is a new species. How will he go about its identification, classification and nomenclature?

Ans. Newly discovered plant can be identified with the help of taxonomic keys, herbaria, monographs and preserved plant specimens.

The scientist has to study the morphological and anatomical characteristics of the plants and compare these characteristic features with these similar information available in the scientific literature and after that he can determine the exact systematic position of the plant and name it according to the rules of binomial nomenclature and fix its systemic position.

Q.3 *Brassica campestris* Linn.

(i) Give the common name of the plant.

(ii) What do the first two parts of the name denote?

(iii) Why are they written in italics?

(iv) What is the meaning of Linn written at the end of the name?

Ans. *Brassica campestris* Linn.

(i) Common name of the plant is mustard.

(ii) The first part of the name denotes the generic name and the second part of the name is specific epithet or species name of the plant.

(iii) According to ICBN, all scientific names are comprised of one generic name followed by a species name, which have to be written in italics always. It is a rule of bionomial nomenclature or if not to be written in italics, both genus and species names should be underlined separately.

(iv) Linn means Linnaeus was the first to discover the plant. He identified, named and classified the plant, so credit is given to him by adding suffix 'Linn', after the scientific name *B. campestris* Linn.

Q. 4 What are taxonomical aids? Give the importance of herbaria and museums. How are Botanical gardens and Zoological parks useful in conserving biodiversity?

Ans. The taxonomical aids are the tools which help in identification, classification and naming of a newly discovered organisms (plant or animal).

It could be in the form of preserved **document** like **herbaria** or **specimen** kept at museums for future reference or scientific institutions. Other aids can be in the form of written document like **monograph, taxonomic keys, couplets,** etc.

A newly discovered organism found can be studied while comparing it with living plants and animals living in protected areas like Botanical gardens, Zoological parks, etc.

Botanical gardens helps in conservation of plants by

(i) Growing important local plant species and keeping record of them.

(ii) Growing and maintaining rare and endangered species.

(iii) Supplying seeds for different aspects of botanical research.

Zoological parks also contribute in conserving biodiversity by

(i) Providing natural environment and open space to animals, particularly wild species.

(ii) Keeping them safe from predators ensuring their protection, food and shelter.

(iii) Providing home to different native and exotic wild animals.

(iv) Involving in the rescue of endangered species.

(v) Facilitating breeding of animals and releasing them free.

Thus, both botanical gardens and zoological parks play an important role in conservation of biodiversity.

Q. 5 Define a taxon. What is meant by taxonomic hierarchy? Give a flow diagram from the lowest to highest category for a plant and an animal. What happens to the number of individuals and numbers of shared characters as we go up the taxonomical hierarchy?

Ans. A **taxon** is a scientific term used to refer to the different categories of classification in taxonomy.

Taxonomic hierarchy is the serialwise or orderly arrangement of taxonomic categories or rank.

Given below is the flow diagram of taxonomic hierarchy from lowest to highest category for a plant and an animal.

Taxon	Plant	Animal
Species It is a group of individuals with similar morphological characters, which are able to interbreed and produce individuals of their own kind.	*e.g., Solanum nigrum* (brinjal) and *Solanum tuberosum*. Here *nigrum* and *tuberosum* are two species of *Solanum* genus.	*e.g.*, The genus *Panthera* includes species *leo* (lion) and *tigris* (tiger).
Genus It is the first higher category above the species level. It is a group of species, which are related and have fewer characters in common as compared to species.	*e.g.*, Family–Solanaceae comprises of genus *Solanum*.	*e.g.*, Felidae comprises of genus *Panthera* (lion, tiger) and *Felis* (cats)
Family It includes one or more genera differentiated from others related families by certain characteristic differences (both vegetative and reproductive).	*e.g.*, Order Polemoniales comprises families like Solanaceae and Convolvulaceae	*e.g.*, Order-carnivora include families like Felidae (cats), Canidae (dogs, foxes), Ursidae (bears) etc.
Order It is an assemblage of families resembling one another in few characters. These characters are less similar as compared to characters of many genera placed in a family.	*e.g.*, Dicotyledoneae consists of order-Rosales Polemoniales, Sapindales, Ranales, etc. on the basis of floral characters.	*e.g.*, Class-Mammalia includes order Chiroptera, Marsupialia, Rodentia, Cetacea, Carnivora.
Class Represents organisms of related orders.	Found only in flowering plants, *i.e.*, Monocotyledoneae and dicotyledoneae.	Comprises of related orders, *i.e.*, class–Mammalia
Phylum/Division It includes different classes having a few common characters.	Division is used in plants.	Phylum is used in animals, *e.g.*, Chordata includes classes like Pisces, Amphibia, Reptilia, Aves and Mammalia.
Kingdom This is the highest category of classification, which includes all organisms that share a set of distinguishing common characters.	*e.g.*, Kingdom-Plantae	*e.g.*, Kingdom-Animalia.

As we move up in the taxonomic hierarchy the number of shared characters decreases and the number of inviduals increases.

Q. 6 A student of taxonomy was puzzled when told by his professor to look for a key to identify a plant. He went to his friend to clarify what 'key' the professor was referring to? What would the friend explain to him?

Ans. Identification of a plant is a scientific process. One must study the plant's general morphological characters habitat, time of flowering, etc., For identification Several reference materials are available in the form of taxonomic keys. The 'key' the professor is referring to is a taxonomic, key which helps in identifying plants based on their characteristics.

This concept of key was introduced by Carolus Linnaeus. Separate taxonomic keys are required for each taxonomic category. Keys are analytical in nature and are used as reference to help in identification of a newly discovered plant.

Q. 7 Metabolism is a defining feature of all living an organisms without exception. Isolated metabolic reactions *in vitro* are not living things but surely living reactions. Comment.

Ans. Metabolism is the sum of all synthesing (anabolic) and breaking down (catabolic) reactions. These are highly specific and enzymatically controlled reactions, which take place inside all the individual cells of unicellular or multicellular organisms. These are infact the basis of life. These reactions help an organism to grow, reproduce, maintain homeostasis and respond to stimuli.

While, isolated metabolic reactions *in vitro* (outside a living organism) can still occur, they are not considered living processes because they takes place outside the context of a living organism. Although these reactions are crucial to life, they require the full biological context-such as enzymes, energy sources, and cellular organisation-to function meaningfully as part of an organism's metabolic network. Without this context, such reactions cannot be classified as "living", even through they are biologically significant.

Thus, isolated metabolic reactions are indeed biological reactions but are not considered "living" without the structure and context of a whole organism.

Q. 8 Do you consider a person in coma-living or dead?

Ans. **Consciousness** is a defining property of all living organisms. A coma is profound or deep state of unconsciousness lasting more than six hours, in which person can not be awakened, fails to respond to stimuli, like light or sound.

Although the person is still breathing and may have some brain activity, they are considered "brain dead" if the brain's function cease. In this case, the person is often referred to as being "living dead", as they are no longer able to function consciously despite having vital signs.

Q. 9 What is the similarity and dissimilarity between 'whole moong daal' and 'broken moong daal' in terms of respiration and growth? Based on these parameters classify them into living or non-living?

Thinking Process Daal as a whole grain is a seed of a leguminous plant. Seed is a miniature plant, which when given suitable conditions, germinate and develop into a plant. Discuss structure of a seed viability and process of germination in terms of metabolism and growth.

Ans. The similarity and dissimilarity between whole moong daal and broken moong daal are as follows

S.N.	Whole Moong Daal	Broken Moong Daal
1.	Whole moong dal is an intact seed of a plant.	It is not an intact seed.
2.	It germinate, when all the suitable conditions are provided.	Unable to germinate as vital seed part such as embryo and cotyledons are destroyed.
3.	During germination, it resumes metabolic activity.	Unable to resume metabolic activity.
4.	The enzyme activated during germination hydrolyse stored food in the cotyledons.	Broken seed will imbibe water, enzyme will get activated but will not lead to growth.
5.	Uses oxygen and respire as a result emits CO_2.	Because of destruction of embryo, no respiration, so no CO_2 emission.
6.	As seed resumes active metabolism the embryo gives rise to plumule (shoot) and radicle (root).	No such growth seen, but broken daal has nurishment value for human as its cotyledons have stored food material rich in protein.

So, we can conclude that broken moong daal does not have viable embryo so does not germinate and does not show any metabolism and growth, but it has great nutritive value as it has good amount of protein and minerals.

Q. 10 Some of the properties of tissues are not the constituents of its cells. Give three examples to support the statement.

Thinking Process Cell is structural and functional unit of life. Cellular organisation of the body is the defining feature of life forms which involves interactions at molecular, cell, tissue and organ level in a living organism.

Ans. In multicellular organisms, tissues are formed by the coordinated action of multiple cells. The properties of tissues often differ from the properties of individual cells. Here are three examples.

1. **Digestive function of the stomach and intestine** The digestive function of the stomach and intestine is a coordinated activity of various cell types, including epithelial, muscle and glandular cells. Individual cells do not perform the entire digestive function; it requires the co-operation of multiple cell type.
2. **Neural control in the nervous system** The nervous system, which controls body functions, involves the interaction of various types of neurons and glial cells. Individual neurons do not provide the co-ordination and control needed for complex nervous system functions.
3. **Muscle contraction in muscular tissue** Muscle tissue generates movement by coordinating the action of many muscle cells.
   A single muscle cell can not perform the entire movement process; it requires the collective contraction of many cells to produce macroscopic movement.

In each case, tissue exhibit properties that individual cells do not possess, demonstrating the complex, integrated function of tissues within multicellular organisms.

Chapter

02 Biological Classification

Multiple Choice Questions (MCQs)

Choose the correct answer from the given four options in the following questions.

Q. 1 All eukaryotic unicellular organisms belong to

(a) Monera (b) Protista (c) Fungi (d) Bacteria

Ans. *(b)* **Protista** is a group of all unicellular eukaryotic organism include both plants and animals. The organisms included in this group are either photoautotrophs, heterotrophs or parasites.

On the other hand **Monera** includes prokaryotic unicellular organisms that lack a nucleus *e.g.,* Bacteria. **Fungi** are eukaryotic but are mostly multicellular (except for yeast which is an unicellular organisms).

Q. 2 The five kingdom classification was proposed by

(a) RH Whittaker (b) C Linnaeus (c) A Roxberg (d) Virchow

Ans. *(a)* RH Whittaker (1969), an American taxonomist proposed the five kingdom classification which includes.

(i) Monera (ii) Protista

(iii) Fungi (iv) Plantae

(v) Animalia

Whereas, C Linnaeus developed two kingdom classification, *i.e.,*

(i) Kingdom–Plantae (ii) Kingdom–Animalia.

Virchow is associated with the discovery of cell theory.

Q. 3 Organisms living in salty areas are called as

(a) methanogens (b) halophiles

(c) heliophytes (d) thermoacidophiles

Ans. *(b)* Organisms living in salty areas are called as halophiles. The name halophiles is originated from the greek word that means 'salt loving'.

Whereas, **heliophytes** are the plants that grow best in sunlight and cannot survive in salty conditions.

Methanogens are the archae bacteria that produces methane as a metabolic by products in anaerobic conditions. They live in the rumen of catlles.

Thermoacidophiles are archaebacteria thriving under strong acidic environments and high temperatures, but can not tolerate high salt concentrations around them.

Q. 4 Naked cytoplasm, multinucleated and saprophytic are the characteristics of

(a) Monera (b) Protista
(c) Fungi (d) Slime moulds

Thinking Process Protoplasm is the living content of a cell that is surrounded by plasma membrane. Naked cytoplasm refers to the cytoplasm that is devoid of cell wall and possess a membrane of mucous or slime hence called naked cytoplasm.

Ans. ***(d)*** **Slime moulds** are saprophytic protists, moving along the dead leaves engulfing organic material. These are multinucleated and do not possess cell wall and have naked cytoplasm.

Whereas, **Monera** are prokaryotes, which include all bacteria. These do not contain naked cytoplasm, **Protista** are a group of eukaryotic organisms, that bear a well-defined membrane around cytoplasm, may be uni or multinucleated **Protista** may have cell wall or mostly not and **fungi** lack naked cytoplasm. Their cell has well-developed cell wall made of chitin.

Q. 5 An association between roots of higher plants and fungi is called

(a) Lichen (b) Fern (c) *Mycorrhiza* (d) BGA

Ans. ***(c)*** ***Mycorrhiza*** is the symbiotic association of fungus with roots of a higher plants like gymnosperms and angiosperms.

The fungus is dependent on plants for food and shelter, while the plants are benefitted by the fungal hyphae as they are involved in absorption of water and dissolved minerals present in the soil debris and makes it available to the plants.

Whereas **lichens** are the symbiotic association between algae and fungi. **Ferns** are group of plants, belong to pteridophytes like other vascular plants and **BGA** is blue-green algae with a prokaryotic cell are not involved in mycorrhizal associations.

Q. 6 A dikaryon is formed when

(a) meiosis is arrested
(b) the two haploid cells do not fuse immediately
(c) cytoplasm does not fuse
(d) None of the above

Ans. ***(b)*** Dikaryon is a cell containing two nuclei. This results when the cytoplasm of two somatic cells fuse but their nuclei do not fuse immediately. Meiosis does not lead to this condition.

Q. 7 Contagium vivum fluidum was proposed by

(a) DJ Ivanowsky (b) MW Beijerinck (c) Stanley Miller (d) Robert Hooke

Ans. ***(b)*** **M.W. Beijerinck** proposed *Contagium vivum fluidum* means contagious living fluid. This phrase was first used to describe virus, and underlined its characteristic in escaping from the finest mesh available. Virus is a latin word which means poison.

DJ Ivanowsky was a Russian Botanist who discovered the filterable nature of viruses and one of the founder of virology.

Stanley Miller was a Jewish American chemist experimented on **origin of life.**

Robert Hooke was the first to study and record cells using his primitive microscope.

Q. 8 Association between mycobiont and phycobiont are found in

(a) *Mycorrhiza* (b) root
(c) lichens (d) BGA

Ans. ***(c)*** **Lichens** are dual organisms which have a permanent symbiotic association of fungus and an alga.The fungal partner is called mycobiont and the algal partner is called phycobiont.

Mycorrhiza is an association of fungus with roots of plants but not with an algae, while **BGA** is blue green alga a member of Monera having a prokaryotic cell and are not involved in this type of symbiosis.

Q. 9 Difference between virus and viroid is

(a) absence of protein coat in viroid, but present in virus
(b) presence of low molecular weight RNA in virus, but absent in viroid,
(c) Both (a) and (b)
(d) None of the above

Ans. ***(a)*** Virus contains DNA or RNA as genetic material and a protein coat, whereas viroids have no protein coat, but only have RNA of low molecular weight. This is the reason why viroids are carried inside viruses. *e.g.*, Hepatitis-D is a viroid that is carried in the capsid of Hepatitis-B virus.

Q. 10 With respect to fungal sexual cycle, choose the correct sequence of events.

(a) Karyogamy, plasmogamy and meiosis
(b) Meiosis, plasmogamy and karyogamy
(c) Plasmogamy, karyogamy and meiosis
(d) Meiosis, karyogamy and plasmogamy

- **Concept Insight** The fungal sexual cycle involves the fusion of two compatible haploid hyphae in a process called plasmogamy, leading to a dikaryotic ($n + n$) stage. This is followed by karyogamy, where the nuclei fuse to form a diploid nucleus ($2n$), which immediately undergoes meiosis to produce genetically diverse haploid spores (n). These spores germinate under favorable conditions, ensuring genetic variation and survival; and the structures involved in spore formation (*e.g.*, asci in Ascomycota, basidia in Basidiomycota) are key to fungal classification.

Ans. ***(c)*** Plasmogamy means fusion of protoplasm and karyogamy means fusion of nucleus. These two events lead to the formation of zygote ($2n$), which is diploid undergoes meiosis to restore the haploid state.

Q. 11 Viruses are non-cellular organisms, but replicate themselves once they infect the host cell. To which of the following kingdom do viruses belong to?

(a) Monera (b) Protista (c) Fungi (d) None of these

Ans. ***(d)*** In five kingdom classification of Whittaker, non-cellular organisms like viruses and viroids are not mentioned. Viruses did not find any place in classification since they are not truly 'living' and are non-cellular.

Monera includes all unicellular prokaryotes *e.g.*, bacteria in which viruses cannot be included.

Protista and **Fungi** include eukaryotic, cellular organisms, so viruses do not belong to these groups.

Q. 12 Members of Phycomycetes are found in

(i) Aquatic habitats
(ii) On decaying wood
(iii) Moist and damp places
(iv) As obligate parasites on plants

Choose from the following options.

(a) None of the above (b) (i) and (iv) (c) (ii) and (iii) (d) All of the above

Thinking Process Phycomycetes is a lower group of fungi which shows diversity in its habitat Mostly are saprophytes and only few are parasites.

Ans. *(d)* Phycomycetes are the members of fungi that can thrive well on dead and decaying wood as saprophytes. These prefer to live in moist and damp places and need water for the movement of zoospore and sexual gametes.

Few members of Phycomycetes are obligate parasites like *Phytophthora infestans* causing late blight of potato and *Peronospora viticola* causing downy mildew in grapes.

Very Short Answer Type Questions

Q. 1 What is the principle underlying the use of cyanobacteria in agricultural fields for crop improvement?

Ans. Cyanobacteria are used in agricultural crop improvement because of their ability to fix atmospheric nitrogen and make it available to the plants. This process improves the yield of the crops and also reduces the cost of application of nitrogen fertilisers. *e.g., Anabaena* and *Nostoc*.

Q. 2 Suppose you accidentally find an old preserved permanent slide without a label. In your effort to identify it, you place the slide under microscope and observe the following features

(a) Unicellular
(b) Well-defined nucleus
(c) Biflagellate one flagellum lying longitudinally and the other transversely

What would you identify it as? Can you name the kingdom it belongs to?

Thinking Process Identification, classification and nomenclature is based on the morphological characters of an organism. One has to study the characters very throughly, by taking the help of taxonomy.

Ans. Based on the above characteristics features as the organism can be identified as dinoflagellate.

Q. 3 How is the five kingdom classification advantageous over the two kingdom classification?

Ans. The five kingdom classification, proposed by RH Whittaker is based upon cell type, body organisation (unicellular, multicellular), nutrition (autotrophic, heterotrophic) cell well and nuclear membrane.

So, it is more useful as compared to two kingdom system of classification which does not distinguish between prokaryotes and eukaryotes and no other kingdom except plantae and animalia are identified.

Q. 4 Polluted water bodies have usually very high abundance of plants like *Nostoc* and *Oscillatoria*. Give reasons.

Ans. Polluted water bodies possess high algal growth due to the presence of nutrients such as nitrogen and phosphorous. These nutrients increase the rapid growth of water plants, *i.e.*, algae especially *Nostoc* and *Oscillatoria*, etc., and result in colonies. These colonies are generally surrounded by a gelatinous sheath and further leads to the formation of blooms in water bodies.

Q. 5 Are chemosynthetic bacteria autotrophic or heterotrophic?

Ans. Chemosynthetic bacteria are autotrophic because they are capable of oxidising various inorganic substances such as nitrates, nitrites and ammonia and use the energy released for their ATP production. So, they are autotrophs and not heterotrophs.

Q. 6 The common name of pea is simpler than its botanical (scientific) name *Pisum sativum*. Why then is the simpler common name not used instead of the complex scientific/botanical name in biology?

Ans. The common or vernacular names changes with the change in place, causing confusion regarding the identification of specific specimen, whereas scientific names are in Latin and are universally accepted and understood.
Hence, scientific names are preferred over the common vernacular names.

Q. 7 A virus is considered as a living organism and an obligate parasite when inside a host cell. But virus is not classified along with bacteria or fungi. What are the characters of virus that are similar to non-living objects?

Ans. Viruses are considered as living when they are inside a host cell, but when they are present outside a host they are referred to as non-living due to their

(a) inert nature

(b) inability to reproduce

(c) lack of cellular organisation

(d) inability for growth and cell division

These characters potraited by viruses make them identical to non-living organisms. Viruses are considered as a connecting link between living and non-living organisms.

Q. 8 In the five kingdom system of Whittaker, how many kingdoms are eukaryotes?

Ans. In the five kingdom classification given by Whittaker four kingdom belongs to eukaryotes (*i.e.*, Protista, Fungi, Plantae and Animalia) except for the kingdom–Monera that belongs to prokaryotes.

Eukaryotic organisms are those that possess

(i) An organised nucleus (with nuclear membrane).
(ii) Possess double envelope system
(iii) Presence of cell wall (except in animal cell).
(iv) Membrane bound organelles are present.

Short Answer Type Questions

Q. 1 Diatoms are also called as 'pearls of ocean', Why? What is diatomaceous earth?

Thinking Process Discuss cellular composition of diatoms and formation of 'diatomaceous earth.

Ans. Diatoms and desmids are included under the group Chrysophytes, in the kingdom–Protista. These are the main producers in the ocean. They prepare food not only for themselves but also for the other life forms in the ocean. This is the reason they are also called as 'pearls of ocean. Body of diatoms is covered by siliceous shell known as frustule.

'Diatomaceous earth' is the accumulation of large deposits of indestructable siliceous cell wall of diatoms that forms a siliceous covering extending for several hundred metres over billions of years. The material obtained from these deposits is used in polishing and filtration of oils and syrups.

Q. 2 There is a myth that immediately after heavy rains in forest, mushrooms appear in large number and make a very large ring or circle, which may be several metres in diameter. These are called as 'fairy rings'. Can you explain this myth of fairy rings in biological terms?

Thinking Process Discuss the mycilial structure in *Agaricus* and its soil borne nature.

Ans. The fruiting bodies in *Agaricus* known as basidiocarps form a concentric ring like structure from the mycelium present in the soil. These basidiocarps resemble button in shape and develop to form a ring like-structure.

This fairy ring structure in *Agaricus* is often associated with enhanced plants productivity in the surrounding soil. These rings are infact fruiting bodies of this fungus and the diameter of this fairy ring increases every year due to spread of mycelium.

Q. 3 *Neurospora* an ascomycetes fungus has been used as a biological tool to understand the mechanism of plant genetics much in the same way as *Drosophila* has been used to study animal genetics. What makes *Neurospora* so important as a genetic tool?

Ans. *Neurospora* fungus was selected to be a very good tool in genetics because it can be grown easily under laboratory conditions by providing 'minimal medium' containing inorganic salts, carbohydrates source and vitamin (such as biotin).

Also under X-ray treatment the mutations can be easily introduced in the fungal cells and meiotic division can be easily seen. Which make it an invaluable organism for studying genetics.

Q. 4 Cyanobacteria and heterotrophic bacteria have been clubbed together in eubacteria of kingdom–Monera as per the 'five kingdom classification' even though the two are vastly different from each other. Is this grouping of the two types of taxa in the same kingdom justified? If so, why?

Thinking Process Discuss the cellular composition of cyanobacteria and heterotrophic bacteria that make them introduced in eubacteria.

Ans. Although the two are vastly different from each other. They still bear some common characters, on the basis of which they are introduced in eubacteria of kingdom–Monera. These characters are as follows

(i) Both are prokaryotic organisms.
(ii) Both the groups lack well-defined nucleus.
(iii) DNA (genetic material) lies freely in the cytoplasm.
(iv) They possess 70 S type of ribosomes.
(v) Both lack membrane-bound organelles.

Q. 5 At a stage of their cycle, Ascomycetes fungi produce the fruiting bodies like apothecium, perithecium or cleistothecium. How are these three types of fruiting bodies different from each other?

Thinking Process Discuss the type of fruiting bodies formed by Ascomycetes fungus and differentiate accordingly on the basis of there structures.

Ans. **Ascomycetes** consist of sporangial sac called asci. Asci (singular-ascus) may occur freely or get aggregated with dikaryotic mycelium to form the fruitification called ascocarps. The fruitification formed by asci are like

(i) **Apothecium** is a cup-like structure, *e.g.*, *Peziza*. Where the asci are arranged in a hymenium (a layer of spori-producing cells).

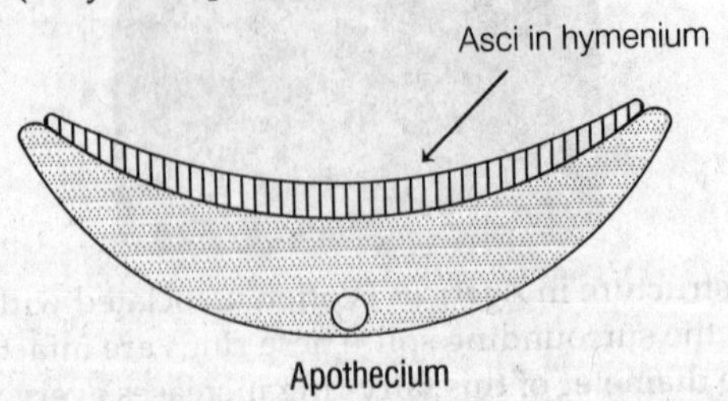

Apothecium

(ii) **Perithecium** flask-shaped, *e.g., Neurospora* with a small opening at the top where the spores are released.

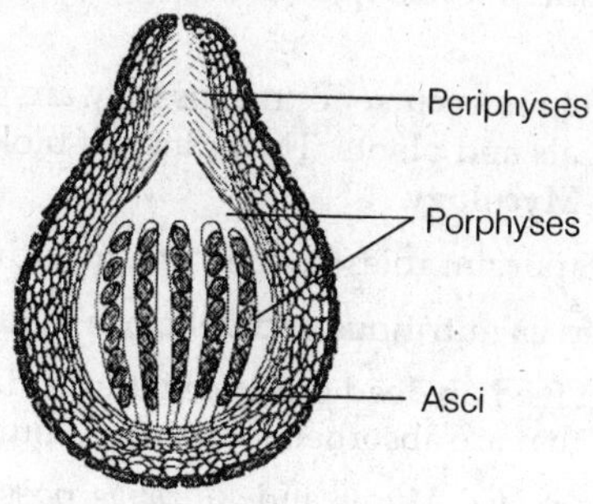

Perithecium

(iii) **Cleistothecium** closed with a slit, *e.g.,* Penicillium where the asci are enclosed within a thick wall and only open when the fruiting body break down.

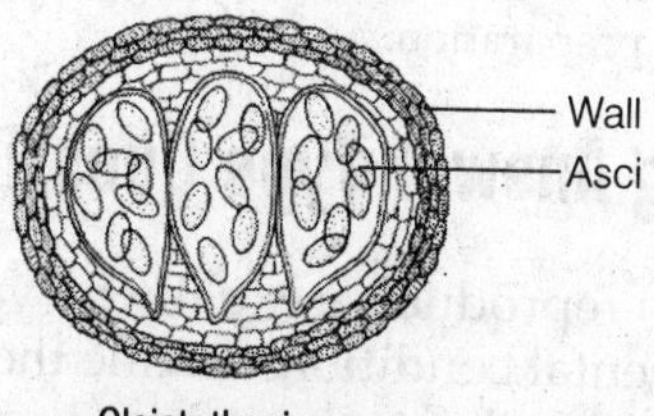

Cleistothecium

Q. 6 What observable features in *Trypanosoma* would make you classify it under kingdom–Protista?

Thinking Process Discuss cell structure of *Trypanosoma* also discuss its different strain in brief.

Ans. On the basis of locomotary organ *Trypanosoma* is included under flagellated protozoans. It resembles with Protista on the basis of following characters

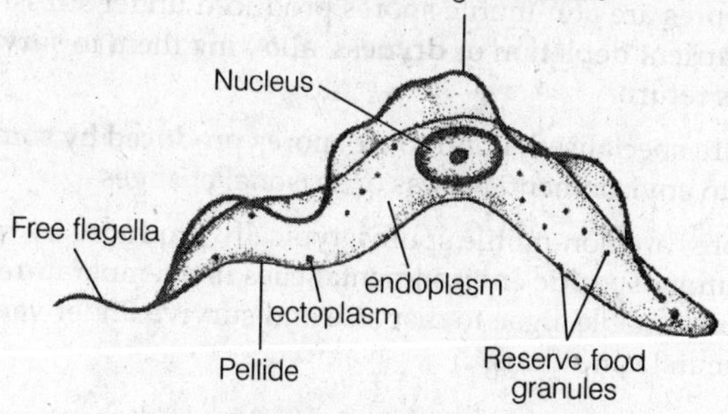

Trypanosoma gambiens

(i) Possess unicellularity.
(ii) Possess asexual reproduction, *i.e.,* by binary fission.
(iii) Possess centrally located nucleus and also contain an prominent nucleus endosome.
(iv) Reserve food material is in the form of granules, such characters possessed by *Trypanosoma* made it to be included under kingdom–Protista.

Q. 7 Fungi are cosmopolitan, write the role of fungi in your daily life.

Thinking process Discuss the role of fungi, with respect to its economical importance to humans.

Ans. Fungi are cosmopolitan in occurrence means they are present in air, water, soil over and inside animals and plants. The branch of biology dealing with the study of fungi is known as **Mycology**.

Fungi play several important roles in daily life, including:

(i) Few fungi are used as nutritious and delicious food. *e.g., Agaricus compestris.*

(ii) Saprophytic fungi feed on dead organic matter and breaks complex substances into simple ones, that are absorbed by plants as nutrients.

(iii) Some fungi like *Absidia, Mucor* and *Rhizopus* possess soil binding properties and make the soil suitable for cultivation by improving its fertility.

(iv) They also provide pest-resistance, *e.g., Empusa, isaria, farinosa,* etc.

(v) Yeast (*Saccharomyces*) has the property of fermentation, thus it is used in alcohol and dough preparation.

Long Answer Type Questions

Q. 1 Algae are known to reproduce asexually by variety of spores under different environmental conditions. Name these spores and the conditions under which they are produced.

Ans. Algae reproduce asexually by various types of spores, depending on environmental conditions which are as follows

I. **Sporangia** are structures that release spores like zoospores or aplanospores, typically produced in favorable conditions for growth, such as abundant nutrients and suitable environmental factors.

II. **Zoospores** are motile, flagellated spores that can swim toward favorable environments, often produced in aquatic habitats.

III. **Aplanospores** are non-motile spores produced under stressful conditions, such as nutrient depletion or dryness, allowing them to survive until better conditions return.

IV. **Conidia** are specialised, non-motile spores produced by some algae in response to environmental stress or seasonal changes.

V. **Carpospores** are non-motile spores, typically produced by red algae and are released under specific environmental cues like temperature or light changes. These spores enable algae to disperse and survive under varying environmental conditions.

Mistake Alert! *Be careful to include examples relevant to all the categories–food, chemicals, medicines and fodder double-check that each organism is appropriately classified as algae or fungi, as confusion between them can occur.*

Q. 2 Apart from chlorophyll, algae have several other pigments in their chloroplast. What pigments are found in blue-green, red and brown algae that are responsible for their characteristic colours?

Ans. In addition to chlorophyll, algae contain various pigments that contribute to their characteristic colours. The pigments found in **blue-green, red**, and **brown algae** are as follows.

1. **Blue-green algae** (Cyanobacteria):

   Phycocyanin This pigment gives blue-green algae their characteristic blue colour. It absorbs red and orange light, complementing chlorophyll's absorption of blue and red light.

   Chlorophyll *a* The main pigment for photosynthesis, which gives these algae a greenish tint in combination with phycocyanin.

2. **Red algae** (Rhodophyta):

   Phycobilin (Phycoerythrin and Phycocyanin) Phycoerythrin is the main pigment responsible for the red colour in red algae, absorbing blue and green light, while phycocyanin adds a blue colour.

   Chlorophyll *a* and *d* These pigment is also present in red algae, but its green color is often overshadowed by the red pigments.

3. **Brown algae** (Phaeophyta):

   Fucoxanthin This pigment imparts a brownish colour to brown algae and is responsible for absorbing light in the blue and green regions of the light spectrum, complementing chlorophyll's role in photosynthesis.

   Chlorophyll *a* and *c* are both present, with chlorophyll *a* being the primary pigment involved in photosynthesis, capturing light energy, while chlorophyll *c* assists in light absorption.

Q. 3 Make a list of algae and fungi that have commercial value as source of food, chemicals, medicines and fodder.

Ans. Algae

Approximately 70 species of marine algae are used for food, chemical and medicinal purpose. Some of these are as follows :

Medicines	Chemicals	Food
Corollina-capable in curing worm infection	Phycolloids include agar, carrageenan and funori.	*Porphyra* (flower), *Rhodymenia* (pulse), *Chondrus* (Trishmoss).
Polysiphonia-exhibit antibacterial property.		*Rhodymenia* (sheep's weed) is also used as fodder
Carrageenan is an coagulant, obtained from red algae.		
	Alginic acid It is a phycocolloid obtained commercially from *Laminaria, Macrocystis*	*Laminaria, Alariam Macrocystis, Sargassum* are used as food in many countries.

Medicines	Chemicals	Food
Sodium laminarin sulphate from *Laminaria* act as a anticoagulant.	*Nerocystis, Fucus, Sargassum*, etc. used as salts in obtaining emulsions (ice-creams, ointments, toothpasts, cosmetics, creams, etc)	The edible brown algae are used as fodder.
Ascophyllum and *Laminaria* bears antibiotic properties. *Durvillea* has vermifuge properties.		
Antibiotics can be extracted from *Chlorella* and *Caulerpa* (Green algae).	*Chlamydomonas, Chlorella, Scenedesmus* play an important role in sewage oxidation.	*Ulva, Caulerpa, Enteromorpha, Chlorella* can yield food rich in lipids, proteins, vitamins and minerals.

Fungi

The role of fungi was established in early-history; yeast have been used in making of bread and alcohol since, the beginning of agriculture. The discovery of penicillin, marked the beginning of a new approach to microbial diseases in human health.

More recent approaches include the application of hydrophobins to surfaces leading to biocompatibility of implants and to emulsion formation improving drug delivery.

Products of fungi in medicine, chemicals and food are

Medicines	Chemicals	Food
Penicillin (*Penicillium notatum* and *P. chyrso genum*), used as an antibiotic	*Aspergillus niger, Trichoderma,* and *Mucor* are used in production of citric acid.	Fermentation-*Aspergillus oryzae* yeast-*Saccharomyces cerevisiae*
Griseofulvin (*P. griseofulvum*) used as an antifungal drugs.		Cheese production by *Penicillium camemberti* and *Penicillium roqueforti*
Baccatin-A (*Gibberella baccata*) used as a precursor of anticancer drug.	*Aspergillus niger* and *P. purpurogenum* in production of gluconic acid.	Colour of foods - by *Monascus purpureus*
Ergotine (*Claviceps purpurea*), clavicin (*Aspergillus clavatus* Flavin (*A. flavus* and *A. fumigatus*).	*P. glacums* and *A. gallomyces* forms gallic acid	

Q. 4 'Peat' is an important source of domestic fuel in several countries. How is 'peat' formed in nature?

Ans. Peat forms in waterlogged areas like bogs and marshes where the accumulation of plant material exceeds its rate of decomposition. In these environments, the water saturation slows down the decomposition process by limiting oxygen, which is essential for microbial breakdown.

As a result, plant remains, such as mosses, grasses and shrubs, start to accumulate over time. The organic matter partially decays, forming a thick, spongy material called peat. Over thousands of years, peat layers build up, eventually compacting and transforming into a source of fuel. Peat serves as an important domestic fuel in some regions, especially when dried.

Q. 5 Biological classification is a dynamic and ever evolving phenomenon which keeps changing with our understanding of life forms. Justify, the statement taking any two examples.

Ans. Classification has been a centre aspect of biology ever since Linnaeus, providing a frame work on which existing knowledge can be organised and predictions about unknown entities can be made.

However the basis of biological classification has gone through a series of upheavals over the past three centuries, from being considered a plan in mind of the creator, to the neutral assessment of over all similarities, to a reflection of evolutionary niches and finally to a phylogenetic mapping of the tree of life. For example in two kingdom classification there are two groups, *i.e.*, Plantae and Animalia.

These groups are made on the basis of structural and cellular difference like plant possess cell wall, central vacuole, whereas animals lack cell wall and central vacuole but the drawback in this system classification is that eukaryotic and prokaryotic organisms like *Euglena*, bacteria and fungi are not included in this kingdom classification.

Such organisms later added in three kingdom classification under kingdom–Protista Finally in 1969, Whittaker proposed five kingdom classification.

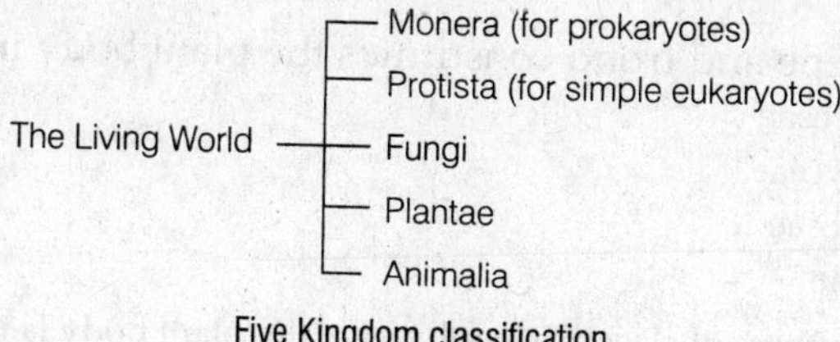

Five Kingdom classification

These changes in classifications are done on the basis of increase in understanding regarding organism by the advancements made in scientific techniques and by observing minute detailing that has led this classification more accurate and scientifically correct, reflecting evolutionary relationships rather than merely structural similarities.

Chapter

03 Plant Kingdom

Multiple Choice Questions (MCQs)

Choose the correct answer from the given four options in the following questions.

Q. 1 Cyanobacteria are classified under

(a) Protista (b) Plantae

(c) Monera (d) Algae

Thinking Process Cyanobacteria are also known as blue green algae. These are primitive prokaryotes.

Ans. *(c)* Cyanobacteria are classified under kingdom Monera, which exclusively includes all forms of bacteria. All bacteria are prokaryotes and do not have well-defined nucleus and other cell organelles.

The other options Protista, Algae and Plantae include eukaryotic and unicellular or multicellular organism.

Q. 2 Fusion of two motile gametes which are dissimilar in size is termed as

(a) oogamy (b) isogamy

(c) anisogamy (d) zoogamy

Ans. *(c)* Sexual reproduction in which the gametes are not similar in shape, size and structure, is called anisogamy. *e.g., Chlamydomonas.*

On the other hand oogamy is the fusion of large female gamete (oospore) with small male gamete. Isogamy is the fusion of similar gametes in size and structure. Zoogamy is sexual reproduction of animals.

Q. 3 Holdfast, stipe and frond constitutes the plant body in case of

(a) Rhodophyceae

(b) Chlorophyceae

(c) Phaeophyceae

(d) All of these

Ans. *(c)* In the members of class–Phaeophyceae, the plant body is usually attached to the substratum by a holdfast and has a stalk called stipe and a leaf like photosynthetic organ called frond.

Q. 4 A plant shows thallus level of organisation. It shows rhizoids and is haploid. It needs water to complete its life cycle because the male gametes are motile. Identify the group to which it belongs to

(a) pteridophytes
(b) gymnosperms
(c) monocots
(d) bryophytes

Ans. *(d)* **Bryophyta** is a group of plants which have gametophytic (haploid) thalloid body. The motile male gamete are produced in special male reproductive structure called antheridia. These gametes need thin film of water to move and reach to the female reproductive organ called archegonia. Whereas, plants form monocots and gymnosperms do not need water for fertilisation. Pteridophytes need water for fertilisation but they have true roots.

Q. 5 A prothallus is

(a) a structure in pteridophytes formed before the thallus develops
(b) a sporophytic free-living structure formed in pteridophytes
(c) a gametophyte free-living structure formed in pteridophytes
(d) a primitive structure formed after fertilisation in pteridophytes

Ans. *(c)* **Prothallus** is usually a gametophytic stage in the life cycle of a Pteridophyte. Spore germinates to form a prothallus, it is short-lived inconspicuous heart shaped structure. The prothallus bears rhizoids and sex organs, (archegonium and antheridium).

Q. 6 Plants of this group are diploid and well adapted to extreme conditions. They grow bearing sporophylls in compact structures called cones. The group in reference is

(a) monocots
(b) dicots
(c) pteridophytes
(d) gymnosperms

Ans. *(d)* **Gymnosperms** include medium sized trees or tall trees and shrubs. Leaves of these plants are well adapted to withstand extremes of temperature, humidity and wind. Reproductive organs are usually in the form of cones or strobili.

The male cone are made up of microsporophyll and female cones are made up of megasporophyll. The presence of sporophyll (micro and megasporophyll) shows the development of seed habit but seeds develop from naked ovule and are not covered.

Other examples are incorrect because monocots and dicots belong to angiosperms which have covered seeds. Whereas, pteridophytes are not adapted to the above mentioned conditions.

Q. 7 The embryo sac of an angiosperm is made up of

(a) 8 cells

(b) 7 cells and 8 nuclei

(c) 8 nuclei

(d) 7 cells and 7 nuclei

Ans. *(b)* Embryo sac in angiosperm is a female gametophyte. It contains 2 synergids, 1 egg cell, 3 antipodal cells and 2 polar nuclei (present in central cell. So an embryo sac of angiosperms is made up of 7 cells and 8 nuclei.

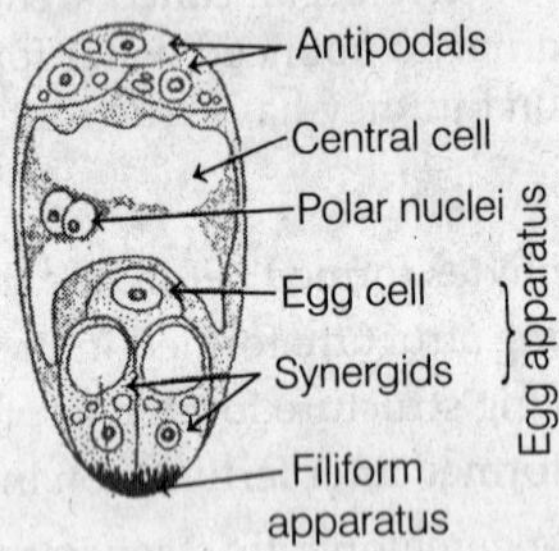

Structure of female gametophyte of an angiosperm

Q. 8 If the diploid number of a flowering plant is 36. What would be the chromosome number in its endosperm?

(a) 36

(b) 18

(c) 54

(d) 72

Thinking Process The ploidy of an angiospermic plant is $2n$. Reduction division (meiosis) occurs at the time of gamete formation to produce male and female gametes, *i.e.*, pollen and egg cell. The double fertilisation is feature of angiosperms, related to the ploidy of endosperm.

Ans. *(c)* **Endosperm** is a product of triple fusion. One male nuclei (n=18) fuses with diploid secondary nucleus ($2n$=36), forming a triploid structure ($3n$=54). So, ploidy of endosperm is ($3n$) and chromosomes number in endosperm is 54.

Q. 9 Protonema is
(a) haploid and is found in mosses
(b) diploid and is found in liverworts
(c) diploid and is found in pteridophytes
(d) haploid and is found in pteridophytes

Thinking Process Mosses and liverworts are simplest terrestrial plants evolved from algal ancestors. Protonema is one cell thick, filaments structure developed in early developmental stage of bryophyte which resemble with filamentous algae.

Ans. *(a)* Protonema is a haploid structure that forms during the germination of spores in mosses. It is a one-cell thick filament that develops into the gametophyte.

Q. 10 The giant redwood tree (*Sequoia sempervirens*) is a/an
(a) angiosperm
(b) free fern
(c) pteridophyte
(d) gymnosperm

Ans. *(d)* *Sequoia sempervirens* is a gymnospermic plant. Gymnosperm is a group of plants having thick, woody, branched stems. These plants also have some xeric adaptations which help them survive in adverse climatic conditions.

The other examples are incorrect because **pteridophytes** is primitive plants no tree is included in this. **Ferns** are included in pteridophytes. **Angiosperms** have covered seeds, unlike gymnosperms.

Very Short Answer Type Questions

Q. 1 Food is stored as floridean starch in Rhodophyceae. Mannitol is the reserve food material of which group of algae?

Ans. The members of Phaeophyceae (brown algae) store mannitol as a reserve food material.

Q. 2 Give an example of plants with
(a) haplontic life cycle
(b) diplontic life cycle
(c) haplo diplontic life cycle

Ans. (a) **Haplontic life cycle** It is exhibited by *Volvox*, *Spirogyra* and *Chlamydomonas*. The dominant photosynthetic phase in these plants is gametophytic phase which develops from a haploid spores after a mitotic cell division of zygote.

(b) **Diplontic life cycle** is found in gymnosperms and angiosperms. The dominant phase is diploid sporophyte plant develop from zygote. Example-*Fucus*, *Sargassum*, etc.

(c) **Haplodiplontic life cycle** It is an intermediate conditions exhibited by bryophytes and pteridophytes. Here, haploid gametophytic stage alternates with diploid sporophytic stage.
Example-*Polysiphonia*, *Ectocarpus*, etc.

Q. 3 The plant body in higher plants is well differentiated and well-developed. Roots are the organs used for the purpose of absorption. What is the equivalent of roots in the less developed lower plants?

Ans. Rhizoids acts as the equivalent of roots in lower plants (bryophytes and pteridophytes). The tissue system in these plants is not differentiated into true leaf, stem and roots as it is found in higher plants (gymnosperm and angiosperm).

Q. 4 Most algal genera show haplontic life style. Name an alga which is
(a) Haplo diplontic
(b) Diplontic

Thinking Process In plants both haploid and diploid cells can divide by mitosis. This ability leads to the formation of different plant body—haploid or diploid. Haploid plant body produces gametes by mitosis. This plant body is called as gametophyte.

Ans. (a) Haplo diplontic type of life cycle is exhibited by *Ectocarpus*, *Polysiphonia* and *Kelps*. Here, diploid sporophytic phase alternate with haploid gametophytic phase.

(b) In *Fucus*, the main plant body is sporophytic and it shows diplontic type of life cycle.

Q. 5 In bryophytes male and female sex organs are called .... and ....

Ans. In bryophytes the male sex organ is antheridium and female sex organ is archegonium.

The gametophyte (n) in bryophyte bears the sex organs in the form of **antheridium** (male) which produce flagellate male gamete known as antherozoids.

They need thin film of water to swim and reach female reproductive organ (archegonium). Archaegonium is female part which has single egg cell. Both these reproductive parts are borne on specialised branches anthridiophores and archegoniophores.

Short Answer Type Questions

Q. 1 Why are bryophytes called the amphibians of the plant kingdom?

Thinking Process Amphibians can live their life in water as well as on terrestrial habitat. Think of plant and animal species that can live this mode of life.

Ans. Bryophytes are called the amphibian of plant kingdom because they are group of primitive plant that can live on land but depend on water for movement of male gametes called antherozoids to reach archegonium (female organ having egg cell) so that fertilisation can take place. Hence, although they can survive on land,they require water for reproduction.

Q. 2 The male and female reproductive organs of several pteridophytes and gymnosperms are comparable to floral structures of angiosperms. Make an attempt to compare the various reproductive parts of pteridophytes and gymnosperms with reproductive structures of angiosperms.

Ans. The comparison is given below :

Reproductive Organ	Pteridophytes	Gymnosperms	Angiosperms
(i) In Male	Antheridia	Pollen cones	Stamen (consist of anther and filament)
(ii) In Female	Archegonia	Ovules	Pistil (consists of stigma, style and ovary)

- The antheridia of pteridophytes are similar to the anther of angiosperms in their role of producing male gametes, though they differ in structure. The pollen cones in gymnosperms are also similar to the anthers of angiosperms in function, as they both produce pollen.
- The archegonia in pteridophytes and ovules in gymnosperms are similar to the ovules in angiosperms, as they both contain the egg cell. The female reproductive organs in all these plants are involved in egg production and fertilisation.

The structures are as given

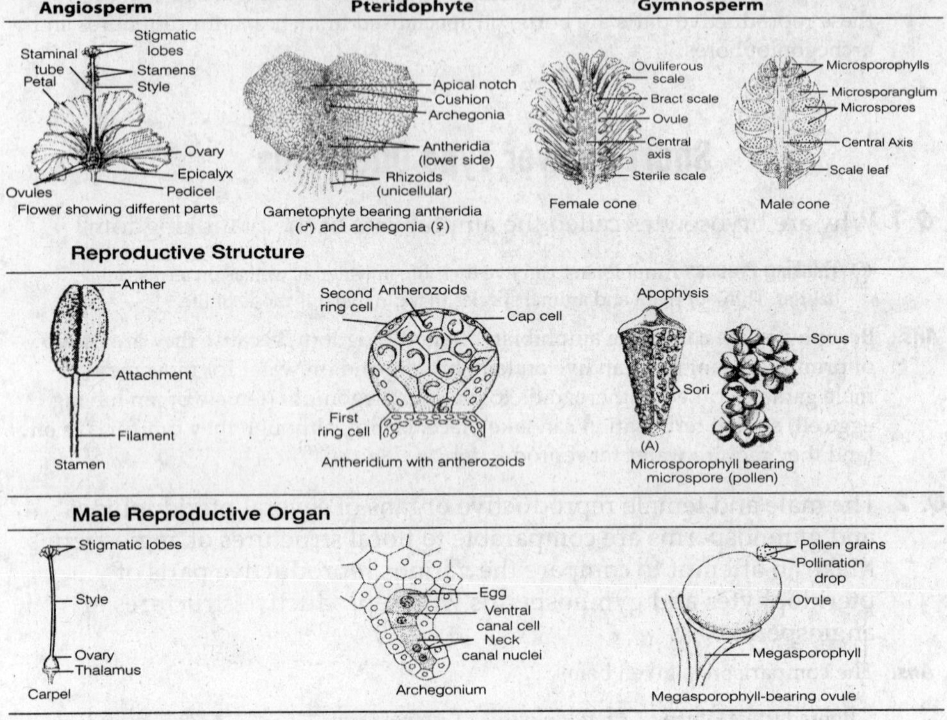

Female Reproductive Organ

Q. 3 **Heterospory, *i.e.*, formation of two types of spores—microspores and megaspores is a characteristic feature in the life cycle of a few members of pteridophytes and all spermatophytes. Do you think heterospory has some evolutionary significance in plant kingdom?**

Thinking Process Formation of two types of spores is an evolutionary advancement of sexuality in plant over primitive form of plants .

Ans. Heterospory is production of two types spores of different sizes and sexes by the sporophytes of land plants.

Smaller spores are microspores which germinate into male gametophyte while larger spores are megaspores which develop into female gametophyte.

In evolution of plants, pteridophytes are considered as intermediate between bryophytes and gymnosperms. All bryophytes are homosporous while all gymnosperms are heterosporous. The heterosporous condition is considered an advancement as, it promotes sexual dimorphism and facilitate cross fertilisation.

Primitive or earlier pteridophytes where homosporous but later pteriodophytes are heterosporous *e.g., Dryopteris* and *Pteris* are homosporous while *Selaginella, Salvinia* are heterosporous.

Q. 4 How far does *Selaginella* one of the few living members of Lycopodiales (pteridophytes) fall short of seed habit?

Ans. **Seed habit** refers to the differentiation of spores into microspores and megaspores and their dependence on the parent sporophyte for the nutrition. These features have been considered as the essential requisite for formation of seed, which are the characteristic of spermatophyte.

The evolution of heterospory and seed habits in *Selaginella* is evident from the following characters

(i) Reduction to a single functional megaspore per sporangium.
(ii) Retention and germination of megaspore within megasporangium
(iii) Development of protective layer and nutritive tissue called tapetum.
(iv) Formation of embryo sac within the sporangium.
(v) Modification of distal end of megasporangium to capture pollen grain.
(vi) Pollination and siphonogamy.
(vii) Temporary suspension of growth of embryo (dormancy period). Despite these features being similar to the seed habit, *Selaginella* does not have fully developed seeds, as the megaspore is eventually released and germinates externally. Therefore, it falls short of seed formation, which is fully realised in gymnosperms and angiosperms.

Q. 5 Each plant or group of plants has some phylogenetic significance in relation to evolution *Cycas*, one of the few living members of gymnosperms is called as the 'relic of past'. Can you establish a phylogenetic relationship of *Cycas* with any other group of plants that justifies the above statement?

Thinking Process Similarity between phylogenetic characters of two plants shows that advanced group of plants have evolved from the primitive one.

Ans. *Cycas* often referred to as a "relic of the past" because it exhibits several primitive characteristics, linking it to both pteridophytes (ferns and their relatives) and early gymnosperms. The following evolutionary traits of *Cycas* show its relationship with pteridophytes

(i) Slow growth typical of early vascular plants.
(ii) Shedding of seed when the embryo is still immature (similar to the behaviour of early seedless plants).
(iii) Little secondary growth and manoxylic wood means more ground tissue (parenchymatous) with small number of xylem tracheids.
(iv) Leaf like megasporophylls.
(v) Flagellate sperms even when pollen tube is present.
(vi) Persistent leaf bases.
(vii) Circinate venation (means young leaf is tightly coiled so that the tender growing tip of leaf is protected within a coil).
(viii) Arrangement of microsporangia is distinct and archegonia are present within the female reproductive organs.

Q. 6 The heterosporous pteridophyte show certain characteristics, which are precursor to the seed habit in gymnosperms. Explain.

Thinking Process Presence of seed and woody stem is the characteristic feature of gymnosperms. The development of seed plants have evolved from few plants like *Selaginella* (pteridophyte) whose life cycle clearly shows the development of seed habit. Compare the life cycle of this pteridophyte with *Cycas*.

Ans. Heterospory, *i.e.*, production of two types of spores smaller microspores and larger megaspore was first reported in *Selaginella* a pteridophyte. In *Selaginella*, the smaller microspores are destined to produce male gametophytes and the larger megaspores develop to female gametophyte.

The male gametophyte produces male gametes, whereas the female gametophyte produces archegonia and also provides nourishment to the developing embryo.

The phenomenon of heterospory, thus lead to the production of gametophyte, *in situ* germination of spores, retention of megagametophyte in the megasporangia and finally to the seed development. Thus, the heterospory in *Selaginella* forms the foundation for seed habit in gymnosperms.

Q. 7 Comment on the life cycle and nature of a fern prothallus.

Ans. The life cycle of fern (*Dryopteris*) clearly shows the alternation of generation. The gametophytic stage (n) alternates with the sporophytic stage ($2n$) figure given shows its complete life cycle.

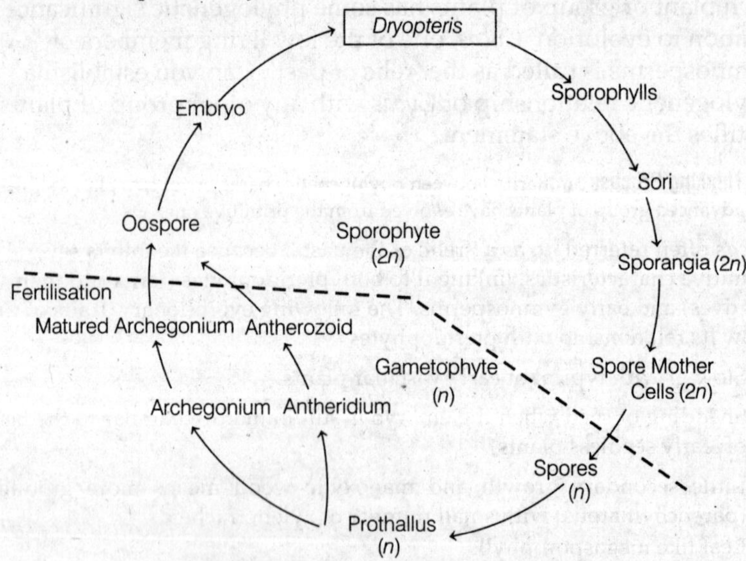

Diagrammatic representation of the life-cycle of fern

Prothallus The prothallus of the fern is multicellular, free-living, thalloid, haploid and autotrophic structure. It develops from the spores produced by sporophyte after reduction division. These spore germinate to form a germ tube with an apical cell and forms a filament of 3-6 cells and one or two rhizoids at the base which later develops into gametophytic plant.

The prothallus bears both male and female reproductive organs *i.e.*, **antheridia** and **archegonia** respectively. Fertilisation occurs when sperm swim through water to reach the egg, leading to the formation of a diploid zygote that develops into a new sporophyte, completing the life cycle.

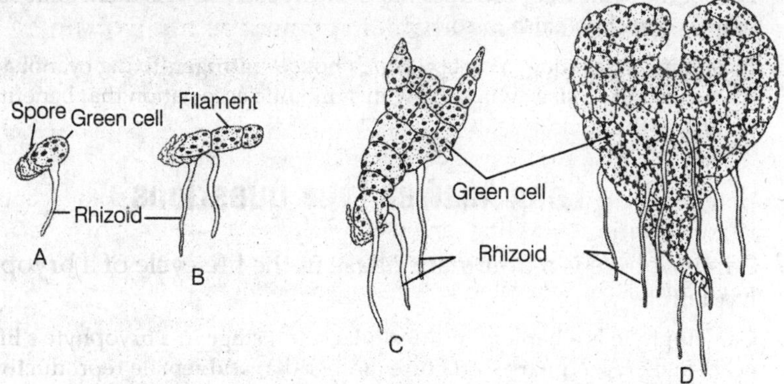

Different stages in the germination of a spore and development of prothallus

Q. 8 **How are the male and female gametophytes of pteridophytes and gymnosperms different from each other?**

Ans. The male and female gametophytes of pteridophytes and gymnosperms different from each other in the following ways

Male Gametophyte of Pteridophyte	Male Gametophyte of Gymnosperm
A distinct male gametophyte is present, but is typically small and dependent on the parent plant.	A male gametophyte is always present and form from a pollen gain.
It contains an antheridium.	An antheridium is not found.
Male gametes are flagellated.	Male gametes are non-flagellated.
Male gametes reach the female gamete by swimming through a thin film of water.	Male gametes reach the female gamete through a pollen tube. Water is not required.

Female Gametophyte of Pteridophyte	Female Gametophyte of Gymnosperm
A distinct female gametophyte is always present but may be small.	A distinct gametophyte is always present.
It is independent and free-living	Female gametophyte does not leave the parent plant.
It is not enclosed is an ovule.	It is enclosed inside an ovule.

Q. 9 **In which plant will you look for mycorrhiza and corolloid roots? Also explain what these terms mean?**

Thinking Process Symbiosis is a phenomenon of interaction of two living organisms in such a way that both the associated partners derive some benefit from each other so that both co-exist and flourish well.

Ans. *Mycorrhiza* (*from Greek Myco* = fungus, *rhiza* = roots) is a symbiotic association between fungus and the roots of vascular plants. The fungus colonises the roots of the host either intra or inter cellularly. It helps in the nutrient absorption from soil for the plant. Mycorrhizal associations are present in conifers, like *Pinus, Cedrus, Abies* and *Picea.*

Coralloid roots develop in cycads, such as *Cycas*. It is produced in clusters at the base of the stem and protrudes out over the ground. It is dichotomously branched and greenish in colour.

It contains algal zone in cortex. which houses nitrogen-fixing cyanobacteria like *Anabaena* and *Nostoc*, which grow in symbiotic association that benefit both the plant and the algae.

Long Answer Type Questions

Q. 1 Gametophyte is a dominant phase in the life cycle of a bryophyte. Explain.

Ans. Gametophyte is a haploid multicellular adult stage in a bryophyte's life cycle. It bears male reproductive structure (antheridia) and female reproductive structure called archegonia, which produce haploid gametes antherozoids (male gamete) and egg cell (female gamete) respectively. In mosses, liverworts and hornworts the gametophyte is a dominant form and thus most familiar phase of life cycle of the bryophyte.

The moss gametophyte originate from a haploid spore. Initial phase of growth forms protonema in moss. Protonema is creeping and short lived. The protonema further develops into a main plant body of bryophyte which is thallus like prostrate and erect, attached to substratum by unicellular or multicellular rhizoids. They may possess root like, leaf like or stem like structures.

Q. 2 With the help of a schematic diagram describe the haplo-diplontic life cycle pattern of a plant group.

Ans. **Haplo-diplontic life cycle** (is also referred as diplo haplontic, diplo biontic or dibiontic) shows **multicellular** diploid and haploid stages as depicted in the following figure.

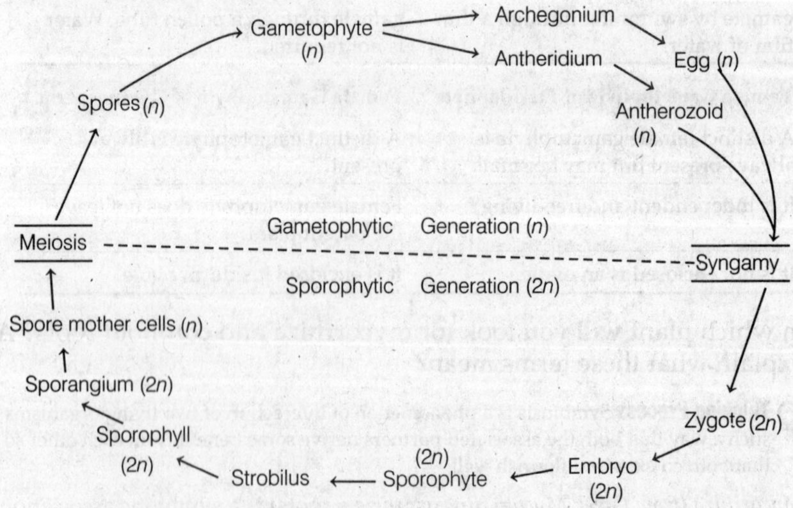

Schematic diagram representation of life cycle of a pteridophyte (homosporous one) haplo-diplontic type of life cycle

Life Cycle of a Pteridophyte The life cycle of a pteridophyte consists of two morphologically distinct phases

(i) The gametophytic phase (ii) The sporophytic phase

These two phases come one after another in the life cycle of a pteridophyte. This phenomenon is called **alternation of generation**. The gametophyte is haploid with single set of chromosomes. It produces male sex organs (antheridia) and female sex organs (archegonia).

(i) The antheridia may be either embedded or projecting type. Each antheridium has single layered sterile jacket enclosing a mass of antherozoids.

(ii) The archegonium are flask-shaped, sessile or shortly stalked and differentiated into globular venter and tubular neck.

(iii) The archegonium contains large egg, which is non-motile.

(iv) The antherozoid after being liberated from antheridium, reaches to the archegonium and fuses with the egg and forms a diploid structure known as zygote.

(v) The diploid zygote is the first cell of sporophytic generation. It is retained inside the archegonium and forms the embryo.

(vi) The embryo grows and develop to form sporophyte which is differentiated into roots, stem and leaves.

(vii) At maturity the plant bears sporangia, which encloses spore mother cells.

(viii) Each spore mother cell gives rise to four haploid spores which are usually arranged in tetrads.

(ix) The sporophytic generation ends with the production of spores.

(x) Each spore is the first cell of gametophytic generation. It germinates to produce gametophyte and completes its life cycle.

Q. 3 Lichen is usually cited as an example of 'symbiosis' in plants where an algal and a fungal species live together for their mutual benefit. Which of the following will happen if algal and fungal partners are separated from each other?

(a) Both will survive and grow normally and independent from each other.

(b) Both will die

(c) Algal component will survive while the fungal component will die.

(d) Fungal component will survive while algal partner will die.

Based on your answer how do you justify this association as symbiosis?

Ans. ***(b)*** Both will die, Lichen is a symbiotic association between an alga and a fungus, where both live together for their mutual benefit. If both are separated from each other then they will die. In turn the fungus holds water, provides protection and offer an ideal habitat for to the alga. The alga in turn supplies carbohydrate food for the fungus. If the alga is capable of fixing nitrogen (*e.g.*, *Nostoc*), it supplies fixed nitrogen to the fungus.This kind of mutual interdependence helps lichens to grow on dry, barren rocks, where the other plants fail to exist. Morever, the algae or the fungi alone cannot grow in such places. Thus, both the partners cannot survive without each other.

Q. 4 Explain why sexual reproduction in angiosperms is said to take place through double fertilisation and triple fusion. Also draw a labelled diagram of embryo sac to explain the phenomena.

Thinking Process Double fertilisation and triple fusion is characteristic feature of all angiosperms. This process represent an advancement in sexual reproductions.

Ans. An angiospermic plants are sexually reproduces by the formation of male and female gametes. The male gamete is a pollen which contain two male nuclei and female gamete is egg cell produced in ovule (female gametophyte).

The pollen grains germinate on the stigma of a flower and the resulting pollen tube grows through the tissues of stigma and style and reach near the egg apparatus. The two male gametes are discharged within the embryo sac. One of the male gamete fuses with the egg cell to form a diploid zygote. This fusion is known as **fertilisation** or **syngamy**.

The second male gamete fuses with the diploid secondary nucleus and forms the triploid Primary Endosperm Nucleus (PEN). This fusion is known as triple fusion.

Because of the involvement of two fusion, this event in angiosperms is termed as **double fertilisation.** The zygote then develops into embryo and PEN develops into endosperm which provides nourishment to the developing embryo.

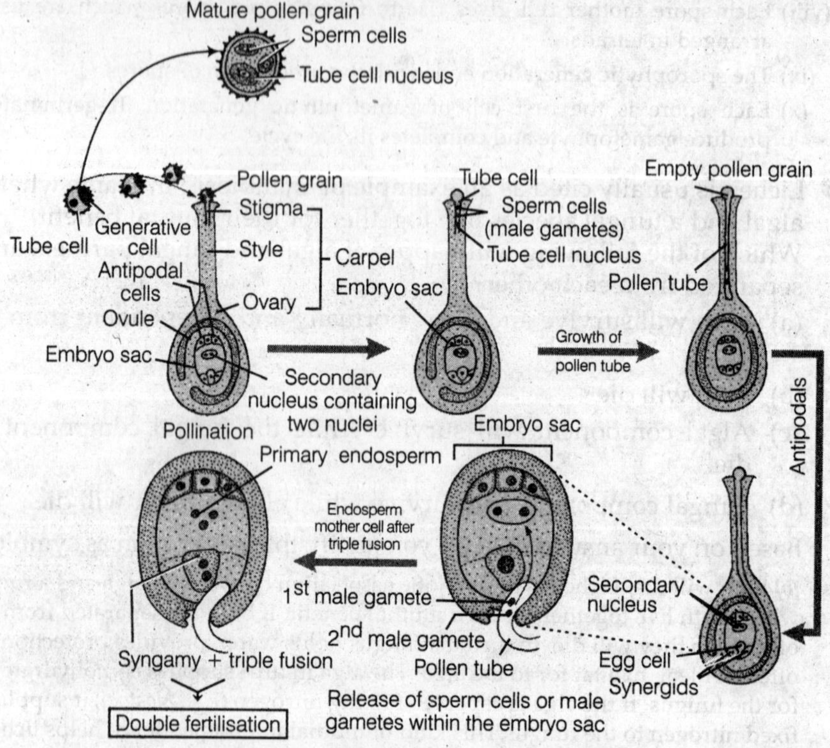

The process of fertilisation and double fertilisation

Q. 5 Draw labelled diagrams of

(a) Female and male thallus of a liverwort.

(b) Gametophyte and sporophyte of *Funaria*.

(c) Alternation of generation in angiosperm.

Ans. (a)

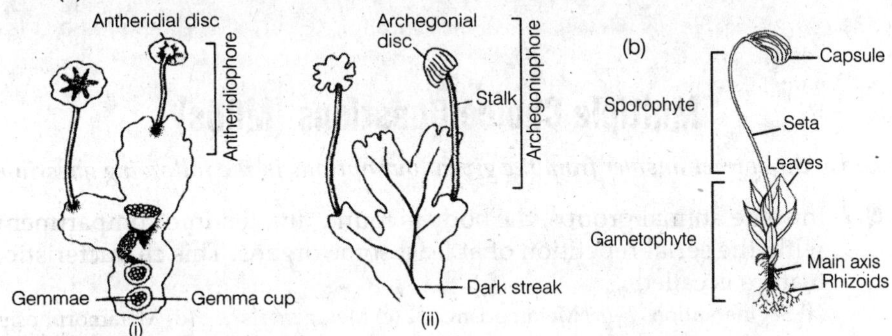

Liverworts (i) Male thallus of Marchentia polymorpha
(ii) Female thallus of Marchentia polymorpha

Funaria
(gametophyte and sporophyte)

(c)

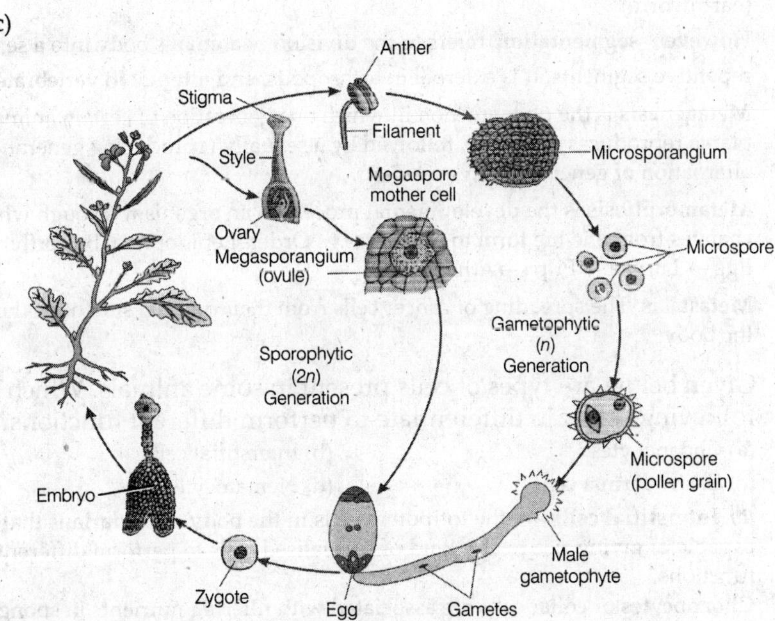

Life cycle of an angiosperm showing alternation of generation

Chapter

04 Animal Kingdom

Multiple Choice Questions (MCQs)

Choose the correct answer from the given four options in the following questions.

Q. 1 In some animal groups, the body is found divided into compartments with the serial repetition of at least some organs. This characteristic feature is called

(a) Segmentation (b) Metamerism (c) Metagenesis (d) Metamorphosis

Thinking Process Compartmentalisation of body of multicellular organisms is an evolutionary advancement over lower group of animals. Various kinds of organisms show these features.

Ans. *(b)* **Metamerism** is the division of animal body, externally and internally into segments with a serial repetition of at least some organs, *e.g.*, annelids (earthworm).

However, **segmentation** refers to the division of animal's body into a series of repetitive segments. It is external in arthropods, and internal in vertebrates.

Metagenesis is the phenomenon in which one generation of certain animals and plants reproduces asexually, followed by a sexually reproducing generation, *i.e.*, alternation of generation (*e.g.*, *Obelia*).

Metamorphosis is the developmental process in an organism through which it changes from one life form to another (*e.g.*, Order–Lepidoptera, Butterfly : Egg $\rightarrow$ Larvae $\rightarrow$ Pupa $\rightarrow$ Adult).

Metastasis The spreading of cancer cells from their original site to another part of the body.

Q. 2 Given below are types of cells present in some animals. Which of the following cells can differentiate to perform different functions?

(a) Choanocytes (b) Interstitial cells

(c) Gastrodermal cells (d) Nematocytes

Ans. *(b)* **Interstitial cells** are the totipotent cells in the body of cnidarians that are capable of giving rise to any kind of specialised cells to perform different functions.

Choanocytes or collar cells are associated with filtering nutrients in sponges.

Gastrodermal cells are specialised cells that form the inner layer of the body wall in the cnidarians, lining the gut and involved in digestion, but they do not differentiate into other cell types.

Nematocyst are specialised stinging cells in cnidarians which contain nematocysts (capsules that release toxins) and are primarily used for defense and capturing prey.

Q. 3 Which one of the following sets of animals share a four chambered heart?

(a) Amphibian, Reptiles, Birds
(b) Crocodiles, Birds, Mammals
(c) Crocodiles, Lizards, Turtles
(d) Lizards, Mammals, Birds

Ans. ***(b)*** Crocodiles, birds, mammals have four-chambered heart.

In reptiles **heart** is usually three chambered with an exception crocodiles, which possess four chambered heart.

In **birds** and **mammals** heart is four chambered and there is a complete division of interventricular septum in ventricles. Whereas, **amphibians** possess a three chambered heart in which the ventricles are not divided hence, two atria and one ventricle is present.

Q. 4 Which of the following pairs of animals has non-glandular skin?

(a) Snake and frog
(b) *Chameleon* and turtle
(c) Frog and pigeon
(d) Crocodile and tiger

Thinking Process Skin is the soft outer covering in vertebrates. This is made up of more than one layer of cells. In some organisms, the epidermal cells possess certain modifications which help in protecting the organs against harsh environment.

Ans. ***(b)*** *Chameleon* and turtle belong to class–Reptilia and possess dry and non-glandular skin with scales,

Frog, pigeon and tiger possess modifications in their skin according to adaptations in their respective habitats.

Frog has mucous glands, pigeon has oil glands located in hind limbs and the tiger has sweat and sebaceous gland.

Q. 5 Birds and mammals share one of the following characteristics as a common feature.

(a) Pigmented skin
(b) Pneumatic bones
(c) Viviparity
(d) Warm blooded body

Ans. ***(d)*** Warm blooded animals can maintain constant body temperature, irrespective of the surrounding environment, *i.e.*, their body temperature is fixed. Warm blooded body is the common characteristic feature in birds and mammals. This characteristic was first evolved in higher reptiles, birds and mammals acquire this feature from higher reptiles during evolution.

Pigmented skin is the adaptive feature in mammals, and is not present in birds. Pneumatic bones are found only in birds as their flight adaptation. These reduce body weight for flight. **Viviparity** is shown by mammals and not by birds as they are oviparous, *i.e.* lay eggs. (Exception – Platypus, an egg laying mammal).

Q. 6 Which one of the following sets of animals belong to a single taxonomic group?

(a) Cuttlefish, jellyfish, silverfish, dogfish, starfish
(b) Bat, pigeon, butterfly
(c) Monkey, chimpanzee, man
(d) Silkworm, tapeworm, earthworm

Ans. ***(c)*** Monkey, chimpanzee and man belong to a single taxonomic group, *i.e.*, mammals, because all of them possess the following characters

(i) Milk producing mammary glands.
(ii) Two pairs of limbs.
(iii) Presence of external ears.
(iv) Viviparity.
(v) Skin possessing hair.

Whereas,

Animal Group	Taxonomic Group
Cuttle fish	Phylum–Mollusca, Class–Cephalopoda,
Jelly fish	Phylum–Cnidaria
Silver fish	Phylum–Arthropoda, Class–Insecta, Order–Zygentoma,
Dog fish	Phylum–Chordata, Class–Chondrichthyes, Super class pisces
Starfish	Phylum–Echinodermata, Class–Asteroidea,

Animal Group	Taxonomic Group
Bat	Phylum–Chordata, Class–Mammalia
Pigeon	Phylum–Chordata, Class Aves
Butterfly	Phylum–Arthropoda, Class–Insecta, Order–Lepidoptera

Animal Group	Taxonomic Group
Silkworm	Phylum–Arthropoda, Class–Insecta, Order–Lepidoptera
Tapeworm	Phylum–Platyhelminthes, Class–Cestoda
Earthworm	Phylum–Annelida, Class–Oligochaeta

Q. 7 Which one of the following statements is incorrect?

(a) Mesoglea is present in between ectoderm and endoderm in *Obelia*
(b) *Asterias* exhibits radial symmetry in adults
(c) *Fasciola* is a pseudocoelomate animal
(d) *Taenia* is a triploblastic animal

Ans. ***(c)*** Statement given in option (c) is incorrect because, *Fasciola* lacks body cavity hence, it is an acoelomate.

Mesoglea is an undifferentiated layer and is a characteristic of diploblastic and triploblastic animals present along with ectoderm and endoderm.

Symmetry in which the body can be divided into two equal identical halves from any plane passing through the central axis as shown by Asterias (adult from) is called radial symmetry.

Taenia is a triploblastic animal, it possesses three germinal layers, *i.e.*, ectoderm, endoderm and mesoderm.

Q. 8 Which one of the following statements is incorrect?

(a) In cockroaches and prawns excretion of waste material occurs through Malpighian tubules

(b) In ctenophores, locomotion is mediated by comb plates

(c) In *Fasciola* flame cells take part in excretion

(d) Earthworms are hermaphrodites and yet cross fertilisation take place among them

Thinking Process Malpighian tubules are the blind end tubules that arise at junctions of midgut and hindgut and are excretory in function. Green glands are a pair of excretory organs in some crustaceans, that open at the base of each antennae.

Ans. *(a)* The statement given option in (a) is incorrect because Malpighian tubules are excretory structures in most of the insects, including **cockroach**, but green glands perform excretory functions in **crustaceans** like **prawns** while rest statements are correct.

Q. 9 Which one of the following is oviparous?

(a) Platypus (b) Flying fox (bat) (c) Elephant (d) Whale

Ans. *(a)* Platypus is an oviparous mammal, as it reproduces by laying egg. This is the unique characteristics among mammals, and the vast majority give birth to live young ones. It belongs to small group of egg-lying mammals known as monotremes.

Rest all three animals, *i.e.,* flying fox, elephant and whale are viviparous mammals and giving birth to young ones.

Q. 10 Which one of the following is a non-poisonous snake?

(a) Cobra (b) Viper (c) Python (d) Krait

Thinking Process Poison in snakes is a highly modified form of saliva, which contains zootoxins (toxin of animal origin), which may cause the immobilisation and killing of prey. It also defends snakes from any threat.

Ans. *(c)* Except Python, all other snakes are highly poisonous in nature. Python kills its prey by constriction of their body not by venom.

Q. 11 Match the following list of animals with their level of organisation.

	Division of Labour		Animals
A.	Organ level	1.	*Pheretima*
B.	Cellular aggregate level	2.	*Fasciola*
C.	Tissue level	3.	*Spongilla*
D.	Organ system level	4.	*Obelia*

Choose the correct match showing division of labour with animal example.

	A	B	C	D
(a)	2	3	4	1
(b)	2	4	3	1
(c)	4	1	2	3
(d)	1	4	3	2

- **Concept Insight** Living organisms are organised from cells, the basic units of life, which form tissues. Tissues combine into organs, organs work together in organ systems and all systems together create an entire organisms.

Ans. ***(a)*** A-2, B-3, C-4, D-1

Pheretima possesses organ system level of organisation.
Fasciola possesses organ level organisation.
Spongilla possesses cellular aggregate level organisation.
Obelia possesses tissue level organisation.

Q.12 Body cavity is the cavity present between body wall and gut wall. In some animals the body cavity is not lined by mesoderm. Such animals are called

(a) Acoelomates (b) Pseudocoelomates (c) Coelomates (d) Haemocoelomates

Thinking Process Germ layer gives rise to all the organs and tissue of the fully formed individual. On the basis of germ layer, animals can be divided as

(i) **Diploblastic** Body cells are arranged in two layers, outer ectoderm and internal endoderm with mesoglea.
(ii) **Triploblastic** Three germ layers *i.e.*, ectoderm, mesoderm and endoderm, give rise to different tissues, organ and organ system of an organism.

Ans. ***(b)*** When body cavity is not completely lined by the mesoderm and is present in the form of scattered pouches between ectoderm and endoderm, this type of body cavity called **pseudocoelomate**, *e.g.*, roundworm.

Acoelomates the animals in which coelom is completely absent as, *e.g.*, flatworms, sponges, stenophers and cnidarians.

Coelomates have their body cavity lined by mesoderm and hence have true coelom, *e.g.*, annelids, molluscs, arthropods, etc.

Haemocoelomates are the animals in which body cavity is filled with haemolymph, *e.g.*, arthropods, molluscs.

Q. 13 Match the Column I with Column II and choose the correct option.

Column I	Column II
A. Porifera	1. Canal system
B. Aschelminthes	2. Water vascular system
C. Annelida	3. Muscular Pharynx
D. Arthropoda	4. Jointed appendages
E. Echinodermata	5. Metameres

Codes

	A	B	C	D	E		A	B	C	D	E
(a)	2	3	5	4	1	(b)	2	5	3	4	1
(c)	1	3	5	4	2	(d)	1	5	3	4	2

Ans. (c) A-1, B-3, C-5, D-4, E-2.

The body of porifera (sponges) is organised in such a way, that it form a complex system of pores and canals called canal system. This system helps in regulating the flow of water within them *e.g.*, *Sycon*.

Aschelminthes possess muscular pharynx *e.g.*, *Ascaris*.

Annelids possess metameric, segmentation in body *e.g.*, earthworm.

Arthropods possess jointed appendages in each segment of their body *e.g.*, cockroch.

Echinoderms possess water vascular system or ambulacral system *e.g.*, *Asterias* or starfish.

Very Short Answer Type Questions

Q. 1 Identify the phylum in which adults exhibit radial symmetry and larva exhibit bilateral symmetry.

Ans. Symmetry refers to the arrangement of body parts in an organism along a plane or around an axis.

In Phylum Echinodermata, the adult echinoderms are radially symmetrical but their larvae exhibit bilateral symmetry.

Q. 2 What is the importance of pneumatic bones and air sacs in Aves?

Ans. Birds possess light weight bones that contain internal spaces filled with air. These are called **pneumatic bones**. They help in reducing their body weight, which is an adaptation for flight.

Highly specialised lungs with specialised air sacs are an additional feature that give adaptability to birds needed for flight (*e.g.*, bald eagle, pigeon).

Q. 3 What is metagenesis? Mention an example which exhibits this phenomenon.

Ans. **Metagenesis** is the phenomenon in which one generation of certain plants and animals reproduce asexually, followed by the sexually reproducing generation. Both the forms are diploid in metagenesis hence, it is the false alternation of generation.

Coelenterates exhibits **metagenesis** (*e.g.*, *Obelia*) where polyp form alternates with medusa in its life cycle.

Q. 4 What is the role of feathers?

Ans. Feathers are the epidermal growth that forms distinctive outer covering or plumage in birds.

Feathers serves a variety of roles like

(i) They help in creating airfoil shape for wings, providing lift and help in flight.

(ii) Feathers helps in maintaining body temperature.

(iii) Feathers play a vital role in mating by providing secondary sexual characteristices. The colour and markings of feather determine the attractiveness of mate.

Q. 5 Which group of chordates possess sucking and circular mouth without jaws?

Ans. Class–Cyclostomata is comprised of living jawless fishes. Their mouth is circular and lack jaws, hence they are also called Agnathans (jawless). It functions as a sucker and is surrounded by tentacles (*e.g.*, lampreys and hagfishes). These animals also possess retractable chitinous teeth.

Q. 6 Give one example each for an animal possessing placoid scales and that with cycloid scales.

Ans. An example of an animal with placoid scale is shark, while an example of an animal with cycloid scales is common carp.

Q. 7 Mention two modifications in reptiles required for terrestrial mode of life.

Ans. There are certain characters acquired by reptiles for the terrestrial adaptations.

Two of them are

(i) Their body is covered by dry and cornified skin and epidermal scales or scutes.

(ii) Fertilisation is internal.

Q. 8 Mention one example each for animals with chitinous exoskeleton and those covered by a calcareous shell.

Ans. Every living organism maintain a proper shape, size and structure. In multicellular lower organisms the shape of body is maintained by certain biological materials like **chitin** and **calcium substances. Chitinous exoskeleton** is the characteristic feature of arthropods. (*e.g.*, cockroach, termite, wasp) whereas, **calcareous shell** is present in molluscs (gastropods). (*e.g.*, snail and slugs).

Q. 9 What is the role of radula in molluscs?

Ans. The radula is a special rasping structure found in many **molluscs**. It is used to scrape and scratch the food and to create depressions in rocks which molluscs use as their habitat.

The radula bears many rows of tiny teeth that are replaced as they wear down. *e.g.*, *Limplet* is a marine invertebrate that uses its radula to create home by boring a shallow hole in the rock.

Q. 10 Name the animal, which exhibits the phenomenon of bioluminescence. Mention the phylum to which it belongs.

Ans. The phenomenon of production and emission of light by an organism as a result of chemical reaction in which chemical energy is converted to light energy is called **bioluminescence.**

Pleurobrachia from phylum–Ctenophora, exhibits bioluminescence.

Q. 11 Write one example for each of the following in the space provided.

(a) Cold blooded animal ....

(b) Warm blooded animal ....

(c) Animal possessing dry and cornified skin ....

(d) Dioecious animal ....

Ans. (a) ***Crocodilus*** (crocodile) is a cold blooded animal. (Cold blooded means those who cannot regulate their body temperature).

(b) ***Elephas maximus*** (elephant), (mammal) is warm blooded animal. (Warm blooded animals can regulate their body temperature.

(c) ***Testudo*** (tortoise) bears dry cornified skin covered with scales.

(d) ***Ascaris*** (roundworm) is dioecious *i.e.*, males and females are distinct (unisexual).

Q. 12 Differentiate between a diplobastic and a triploblastic animal.

Ans. Animals in which the cells are arranged in two embryonic layers, an external ectoderm and an internal endoderm are called diploblastic animals (*e.g.*, Coelentrates). While those animals in which the developing embryo has a third germinal layer, *i.e.*, **mesoderm** lying between the **ectoderm** and **endoderm** are called **triploblastic** animals. (*e.g.*, Chordates).

Q. 13 Give an example of the following

(a) Roundworm
(b) Fish possessing poison sting
(c) A limbless reptile/amphibian
(d) An oviparous mammal

Ans. (a) Roundworm – ***Ascaris***

(b) Fish possessing poison sting – ***Trygon***

(c) A limbless reptile/amphibian – ***Ichthyophis***

(d) An oviparous mammal – **Duck billed platypus.**

Q. 14 Provide appropriate technical term in the space provided.

(a) Blood-filled cavity in arthropods ....

(b) Free-floating form of cnidaria ....

(c) Stinging organ of jelly fishes ....

(d) Lateral appendages in aquatic annelids ....

Ans. (a) **Haemocoel** is the blood-filled cavity in arthropods containing haemolymph.

(b) **Medusa** is a form in cnidarians in which the body is shaped like an **umbrella** which can float freely in sea water

(c) **Nematocysts** are capsules of specialised cells **in cnidarians** which act as a paralysing sting.

(d) **Parapodia** are the paired unjointed lateral outgrowth in annelids bearing chaetae.

Q. 15 Match the following.

	Animals		Locomotory Organ
A.	*Octopus*	1.	Limbs
B.	Crocodile	2.	Comb plates
C.	*Catla*	3.	Tentacles
D.	Ctenoplana	4.	Fins

Ans. **A.** → (3) **B.** → (1) **C.** → (4) **D.** → (2)

(a) ***Octopus*** Tentacles are the appendages in invertebrates that are used for grasping food and for locomotion.

(b) **Crocodile** Limbs are used for locomotion, and swimming.

(c) ***Catla*** Fins are means of locomotion and are used to generate optimum thrust thus controlling the subsequent motion.

(d) ***Ctenoplana*** Comb plates are locomotory organs formed by strong cilia with fused bases.

Short Answer Type Questions

Q. 1 Differentiate between

(a) Open circulatory system and closed circulatary system.

(b) Oviparous and viviparous characteristic.

(c) Direct development and Indirect development.

Ans. Differentiation between these are as below

(a) Open Circulatory System	Closed Circulatory System
In this type of circulation, blood flows in spaces called sinuses and the cells and tissues are directly in contact with the blood *i.e.*, nutrients and gases are exchanged directly. *e.g.*, arthropods (grasshopper, cockroach), gastropods (snail).	In this type of circulation, blood is circulated *via* a series of vessels (arteries, veins and capillaries). *e.g.*, annelids (earthworm) and vertebrates (birds, primates etc).

(b) Oviparous Animals	Viviparous Animals
Oviparity is expulsion of undeveloped eggs rather than live young ones. The eggs are laid and the embryos develop outside the maternal body.	Viviparity is retention and growth of fertilised egg within the maternal body until the young one is capable of independent existance.
Animals that lay eggs are called oviparous. *e.g.*, fishes, reptiles, amphibians, birds, in sects and monotremes (mammals that lay eggs).	Animals which give birth to their young ones and are called viviparous animals. *e.g.*, mammals.

(c) Direct Development	Indirect Development
Direct development is the type of development in which there are no larval/nymphal or other intermediate stages in life cycle between the egg (or birth) and the adult (*e.g.*, mammals)	Indirect development is mostly observed in lower animals. The adult individuals lay eggs, which develop into the adult after passing through few to several larval nymphal stages. (*e.g.*, echinoderms, arthropods).

Q. 2 Sort out the animals on the basis of their symmetry (radial or bilateral): Coelenterates, ctenophores, annelids, arthropods and echinoderms.

Ans. Body symmetry is the arrangement of body parts in different region and directions of the body plan. In radial symmetry, body of an individual can be divided into equal halves by any plans passing through the longitudinal axis. *e.g.*, Coelentrates, Ctenophores, Echinoderms as adults. In bilateral symmetry, body can be divided into two equal halves when the plane passes through the median longitudnal or saggital axis. *e.g.*, Annelids, Arthropods

Radial symmetry

Bilateral symmetry

Mistake Alert! *Make sure to focus on the adult forms of the animals when categorizing their symmetry. Specifically, echinoderms (like starfish and sea urchins) have radial symmetry in their adult stage, but they actually have bilateral symmetry during their larval stage. it's important not to mix up the symmetry of their larvae with that of the adults.*

Q. 3 There has been an increase in the number of chambers in heart during evolution of vertebrates. Give the names of the class of vertebrates having two, three or four chambered heart.

Ans. (a) **Two chambered heart** is present in organisms like pisces. It consists of one atria and one ventricle and only deoxygenated blood flows in the heart, and oxygenation of blood occurs in gills and from gills oxygenated blood is distributed to all parts of body.

(b) **Three chambered heart** develops after the division of atrium into right and left halves as in amphibian and reptiles. The oxygenated and deoxygenated blood gets mixed slightly, in single ventricle. Crocodiles, thus having four-chambered heart.

(c) **In four chambered heart** both the atrium and ventricle are divided into two halves and thus no mixing of oxygenated and deoxygenated blood occurs. *e.g.*, birds and mammals.

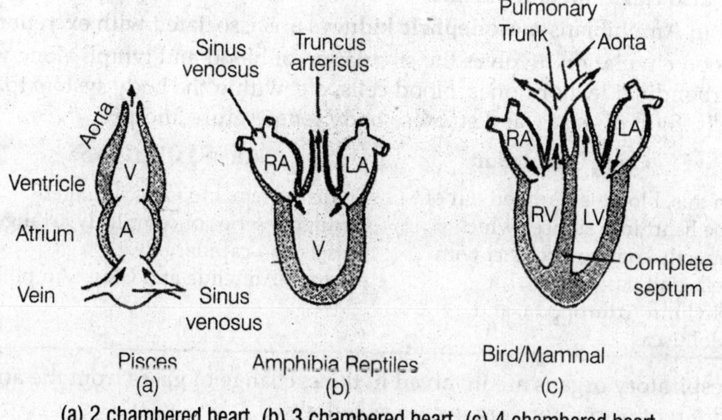

(a) 2 chambered heart, (b) 3 chambered heart, (c) 4 chambered heart

Q. 4 Fill up the blank spaces appropriately

Phylum/Class	Excretory Organ	Circulatory Organ	Respiratory Organ
Arthropoda			Lungs/Gills/ Tracheal System
	Nephridia	Closed	Skin/Parapodia
	Metanephridia	Open	
Amphibia		Closed	Lung

Ans.

Phylum/Class	Excretory Organ	Circulatory Organ	Respiratory Organ
Arthropoda	Malpighian tubules	Open	Lungs/Gills/ Tracheal System
Annelida	Nephridia	Closed	Skin/Parapodia
Mollusca	Metanephridia	Open	Gills
Amphibia	kidney	Closed	Lungs

Excretion involves the elimination of metabolic waste products from the animal body. Different organs are involved in the process of excretion in different animals.

(a) **In Arthropods**, the Malpighian tubules remove excretory products from haemolymph.

(b) **In Annelids,** the excretory organ occurs as segmentally arranged, coiled tubules called nephridia

(c) **In Mollusca**, excretion occurs by paired structures called organ of Bojanus also called **metanephridia.**

(d) In Amphibians **mesonephric** kidneys are associated with excretion.

Blood circulation involves the circulation of blood and lymph along with oxygen, carbondioxide, hormones, blood cells, etc, within the body system to nourish cells, fight diseases, and stabilise body temperature and pH.

Open Circulation	Closed Circulation
In this, blood is pumped out of the heart into sinuses which directly comes in contact with cells and tissues, *e.g.*, phylum–Arthropoda, and Mollusca.	In this system, blood is circulated through a series of complexly arranged vessels and capillaries *e.g.*, phylum–Annelida and Class–Amphibia.

Respiratory organs are involved in the exchange of gases from the atmosphere. Different respiratory organs are as follows

(a) Lungs/gills/tracheal system in arthropoda and molluscs.

(b) Skin in annelids. (c) Lungs and skin in amphibian.

Q. 5 Match the following

A. Amphibia	(1) Air bladder
B. Mammals	(2) Cartilaginous notochord
C. Chondrichthyes	(3) Mammary glands
D. Osteichthyes	(4) Pneumatic bones
E. Cyclostomata	(5) Dual habitat
F. Aves	(6) Sucking and circular mouth with out jaws.

Ans. **A.** → (5) **B.** → (3) **C.** → (2) **D.** → (1) **E.** → (6) **F.** → (4)

A. **Amphibians** possess **dual habitat**, *i.e.*, they are found in both aquatic and terrestrial habitats. Their larvae is completely aquatic while adult live in terrestrial as well as in aquatic habitat

B. **Mammals** have **mammary glands** which produce milk to feed their young ones. The mammary glands are enlarged exocrine modified from sweat glands and are functional in female mammals.

C. **Chondrichthyes** have the **cartilaginous rod** (notochord) in the juvenile stage which is gradually replaced by cartilage.
D. **Osteichthyes** have **air bladder** which is a vesicle or sac containing air,
E. **Cyclostomes** possess **sucking** and **circular mouth** without jaws which is surrounded by tentacles and the tongue bears teeth. ***e.g.*, lamprey and hagfish.**

F. **Aves** have light weight bones with internal spaces filled with air called **pneumatic bones** and modified lungs with specialised air sacs. These are the adaptations which enable birds to fly.

Q. 6 Endoparasites are found inside the host body. Mention the special structure, possessed by these and which enables them to survive in those conditions.

Ans. The endoparasites such as *Taenia solium* and *Fasciola hepatica* (liver fluke), etc., are found inside the host body, and survive due to the presence of certain adaptations. Special adaptations possessed by endoparasites are as follows

(i) They use anaerobic mode of respiration and the gaseous exchange is through general body surface.
(ii) These organisms bear additional organ for the attachment to the host. *Fasciola hepatica* possesses **acetabulum** or **posterior sucker** for the attachment. *Taenia solium* posses **hooks** and **suckers** for the attachment with the host.
(iii) Reproductive organs are well developed. They are generally, hermaphrodite and self fertilisation is common in them.
(iv) A thick tegument (body covering) is present which is resistant to the host's digestive enzymes and antitoxins.
(v) Absence of locomotary organs.
(vi) Tapeworms lack digestive organs because digested and semidigested food of the host is directly absorbed through their body surface.

Q. 7 Match the following and write correct choice in space provided

	Animal		Characteristics
A.	*Pila*	(1)	Jointed appendages
B.	Cockroach	(2)	Perching
C.	*Asterias*	(3)	Water vascular system
D.	*Torpedo*	(4)	Electric organ
E.	Parrot	(5)	Presence of shell
F.	Dog fish	(6)	Placoid scales

A. .... B. ....
C. .... D. ....
E. .... F. ....

Ans. A. → (5) B. → (1) C. → (3) D. → (4) E. → (2) F. → (6)

A. **Pila-Presence of shell** Shell in *Pila* is an elongated structure which consists of a tubular whorl coiled around a central axis called columella. The main function of shell is to provide protection from harsh conditions.

B. **Cockroach-Jointed appendages** Presence of jointed appendages along with segmented body is the characteristic feature of arthropods (e.g., spiders, bees, crabs etc).

C. **Asterias-Water vascular system** It is the unique and characteristic feature in echinoderms. This system acts as a hydraulic system, composed of canals connecting numerous tube feet. It is very important as it helps Asterias (sea star) to move as well as to catch food. Respiration also takes place, through, water vascular system.

D. **Torpedo-Electric organ** *Torpedo* are unique organisms, having two large kidney shaped electric organs. These organs are capable of generating high voltage electric shocks.

E. **Parrot-Perching** Birds with feet adapted to hold onto tree branches are perching birds. The *Passeriform* birds are true **perching birds** with four toes, three directed forward and one backward.

F. **Dog fish-Placoid scales** Placoid scales are tough scales that cover the skin of elasmobranchs (dog fish, sharks and rays). They are covered with hard enamel. The function of these scales is to protect against predators.

Q. 8 Differentiate between

(a) Open and closed circulatory system
(b) Oviparity and viviparity
(c) Direct and indirect development
(d) Acoelomate and pseudocoelomate
(e) Notochord and nerve cord
(f) Polyp and medusa

Ans. *For (a), (b) and (c) refer to Q. 1*

Acoelomate	Pseudocoelomate
(d) Animals without a coelom are called as acoelomates *e.g.*, sponges, cnidarians, ctenophores and flatworms.	Animals in which body cavity is derived from the blastocoel of the embryo are called pseudocoelomates. *e.g.*, roundworms.

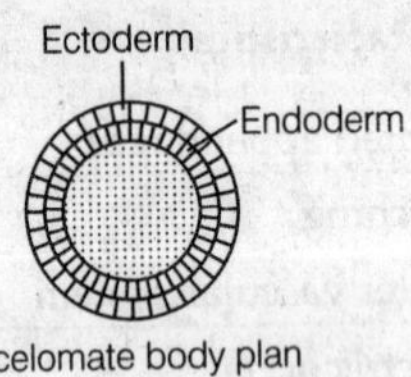

Acelomate body plan

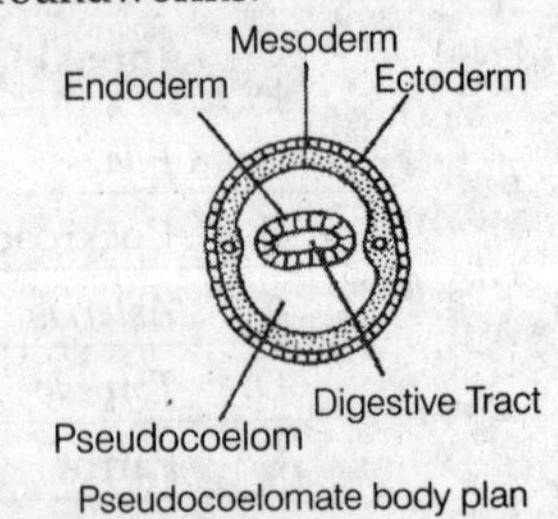

Pseudocoelomate body plan

Notochord	Nerve Cord
(e) Notochord is the flexible rod like structure which lies lengthwise dorsally to the gut and ventrally to the neural tube	Nerve cord is the solid strand of nervous tissue forming a part of central nervous system, especially in invertebrates.
Vertebrates possess it at the early stage of development. But it is gradually replaced by the vertebral column in adults.	A dorsal nerve cord and exist in all chordates in embryonic stage that develops into the central nervous system i.e. Brain and spinal cord in adults
It is a part of skeleton system	
In adults vertebrates, notocord is replaced by vertebral column.	

Polyp	Medusa
(f) Polyp is sessile and cylindrical form in *Aurelia.*	Medusa is umbrella shaped and free swimming form in *Aurelia.*
Polyp produces medusa by reproducing asexually	Medusa forms polyp by reproducing sexually.

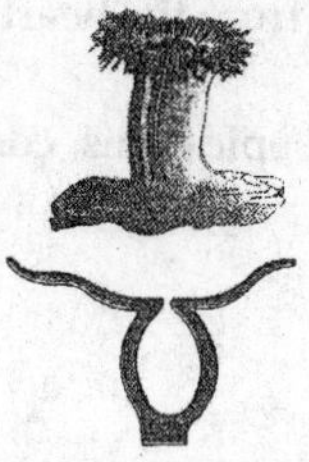

Polyp in *Aurelia*

Medusa in *Aurelia*

Q. 9 Give the characteristic features of the following citing one example of each

(a) Chondrichthyes and ostichthyes

(b) Urochordata and cephalochordata

Ans. Characteristic features of different classes mentioned are as follows

(a) **Chondrichthyes**

(i) These are marine animals with a streamlined body.

(ii) Body has a cartilaginous exoskeleton and the skin is tough due to the presence of minute placoid scales.

(iii) These animals are predatory.

(iv) Due to the absence of air bladder they have to swim constantly to avoid sinking.

(v) They are cold blooded animals *e.g., Scoliodon* (dog fish), *Pristis* (saw fish).

(vi) Some of them possess electric organs and poison sting (*e.g., Torpedo* and *Trygon*).

Osteichthyes

(i) These animals are found in both habitats, *i.e.,* marine and freshwater. They bear a bony endoskeleton.

(ii) Body is streamlined, posseses four pairs of gills covered by an operculum on each side.

(iii) Skin is covered by cycloid or ctenoid scales.

(iv) Presence of air bladder provide buoyancy to the body.

(v) Heart is two chambered.

(vi) Sexes are seperate, fertilisation usually external, oviparous animal with direct development.

e.g., Marine- *Exocoetus* (flying fish), *Hippocampus* (sea horse); Freshwater- *Labeo* (rohu).

(b) **Urochordata**

(i) In urochordates, notochord is only present in larval tail and disappears in adults. They show retrogressive metamorphosis.

(ii) They contain a tough outer covering called tunic.

(iii) Persence of pharyngeal slits during some stage of the life cycle and a muscular, post-anal tail is the characteristic features in urochordates. *e.g., Salpa, Ascidia, Doliolum.*

Cephalochordata

(i) Cephalochordates are exclusively marine animals.

(ii) The notochord in cephalochordates extends from the heart to tail region and is persistent throughout the life.

(iii) Body-wall shows one cell thick, non-ciliated epidermis, connective tissue, striated muscle and parietal peritonium.

(iv) Fertilisation is external

e.g., Branchiostoma (Amphioxus or *Lancelet).*

Q. 10 Mention two similarities between

(a) Aves and mammals (b) A frog and crocodile

(c) A turtle and Pila

Ans. (a) **Similarities between aves and mammals**

(i) The members of both groups are homeotherms, *i.e.,* warm blooded. They are able to maintain constant body temperature.

(ii) Heart is completely four chambered.

(b) **Similarities between frog and crocodile**

(i) The members of both the groups are poikilotherms, *i.e.,* they lack the capacity to regulate their constant body temperature. They are cold blooded animals.

(ii) Frog and crocodile are oviparous animals.

(c) **Similarities between turtle and Pila**

(i) In both animals, body is covered with dry and cornified skin. In turtle, the epidermal covering is known as scales whereas in case of Pila, it is known as calcareous shell.

(ii) Both animals are oviparous.

Q. 11 Name

(a) A limbless animal

(b) A cold blooded animal

(c) A warm blooded animal

(d) An animal possessing dry and cornified skin

(e) An animal having canal system and spicules

(f) An animal with cnidoblasts

Ans. (a) *Ichthyophis* does not possess limbs.

(b) *Scoliodon* (dog fish) is a cold blooded animal.

(c) *Columba* (pigeon) is a warm blooded animal.

(d) *Naja naja* (snake) possesses dry and cornified skin.

(e) *Sycon* (sponge) possesses canal system and bear spicules.

(f) *Obelia* bears cnidoblast.

Q. 12 Give an example for each of the following
(a) A viviparous animal
(b) A fish possessing a poison sting
(c) A fish possessing an electric organ
(d) An organ, which regulates buoyancy
(e) Animal, which exhibits alternation of generation
(f) Oviparous animal with mammary gland

Ans. (a) **A viviparous animal** is the one in which development of young ones is direct, and the offsprings are nourished internally. for example **humans**.

(b) **A fish possessing a poison sting** is *Trygon* (sting-ray). Which is found on its tail. The poison released is strong enough to stun an animal.

(c) **A fish possessing an electric organ** is *Torpedo* (electric ray). Electric organ in *Torpedo* is located in its large round pectoral fin which is just behind the eye. Large *Torpedo* can generate an electric current of up to 200 volts, which is strong enough to kill a fish.

(d) **An organ, which regulates buoyancy** is **air bladder** present in class–Osteichthyes. (e.g., Exocoetus, Catla).

(e) **Animal exhibiting alteration of generation** is *Obelia* of phylum–Cnidaria. It has two distinct body forms called polyp and medusa are present. Polyp is sessile and cylindrical whereas medusa is umbrella shaped and free swimming form. Polyp produces medusa asexually and medusa forms polyps sexually (*e.g., Obelia).*

(f) **Oviparous animal with mammary gland** is *Ornithorhynchus* is the mammal which lays egg and also bear mammary gland, which is a characteristic feature of mammals.

Q. 13 Excretory organs of different animals are given below. Choose correctly and write in the space provided.

	Animal		Excretory Organ/Unit
A.	Balanoglossus	1.	Metanephridia
B.	Leech	2.	Nephridia
C.	Locust	3.	Flame cells
D.	Liver fluke	4.	Absent
E.	Sea urchin	5.	Malpighian tubule
F.	Pila	6.	Proboscis gland

A. .... B. ....
C. .... D. ....
E. .... F. ....

Thinking Process Metabolism in body leads to the formation of waste that can affect body's vital organs so it has to be removed from body. Different classes of organisms possess different types of excretory organs to eliminate the byproduct of metabolism.

Ans. A. → (6) B. → (2) C. → (5) D. → (3) E. → (4) F. → (1)

A. **Balanoglossus-Proboscis glands** This gland present in front of central sinus and excretes brown granules.

B. **Leech-Nephridia** It helps in osmoregulation and excretion.

C. **Locust-Malpighian tubules** These tubules open into gut and help in excretion.

D. **Liver fluke-Flame cells** They are specialised cells in Platyhelminthes which helps in osmoregulation and excretion. These are also called protonephridia.

E. **Sea urchin-absent** Specialised excretory organs are absent in sea urchin.

F. ***Pila*-Metanephridia** It is a type of excretory organs or nephridia found in many types of invertebrates such as annelids, arthropods, and molluscs (in molluscs nephridia is also known as Bojanus organ).

Long Answer Type Questions

Q. 1 Give three major differences between chordates and non chordates and draw a schematic sketch of a chordate showing those features.

Ans. The major differences between Chordates and Non-chordates are as follows

	Chordates	Non-Chordates
1.	A notochord is present at some stage in the life cycle of a chordate.	Notochord is not present at any stage in the life cycle of a non-chordate.
2.	Gill-slits are present in the pharynx either in embryo or in adult organism.	Pharyngeal gill slits are absent.
3.	Tail is present at some stage in the life of the chordate.	Tail is absent in non-chordates.
4.	Heart is ventrally located.	Heart (if present) is dorsally located.
5.	Central nervous system is dorsal and hollow in chordates.	Central nervous system in non-chordates is solid and ventrally located.

Schematic sketch illustrating important characters of chordates is shown below

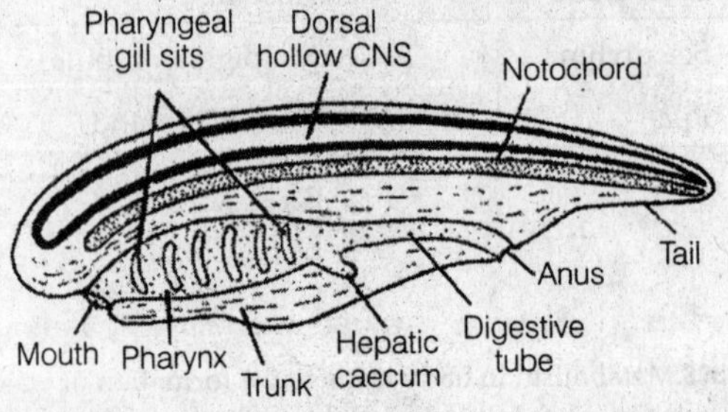

Q. 2 What is the relationship between germinal layers and the formation of body cavity in case of coelomate, acoelomates and pseudocoelomates?

Ans. All adult multicellular organisms typically possess a concentric arrangement of tissues in the body. These tissues are derived from the three embryonic cell layers called **germinal layers.**

(i) The outer layer is the **ectoderm**, the middle layer is the **mesoderm** and the innermost layer is the **endoderm**.

(ii) Endoderm layer is associated with the formation of the stomach, colon, liver, pancreas, urinary bladder and other vital organs in an organism.

(iii) Mesoderm forms the main structural components of the body like the skeletal muscles, the skeleton, the dermis of the skin, connective tissue, etc.

(iv) Ectoderm is associated with the formation of CNS, eye lens, ganglia, nerves and glands.

(v) The body cavity that is lined by mesoderm is called **coelom**, and the animals possessing coelom are called as **coelomates**. *e.g.*, phylum–Annelida, Mollusca, Arthropoda, Echinodermata, Hemichordata and Chordata.

(vi) In some organisms, body cavity is not lined by mesoderm, instead mesoderm is present in the form of scattered pouches between ectoderm and endoderm, Such body cavity is called **pseudocoelom** and animals possessing it are referred to as **pseudocoelomates** *e.g.*, ***Ascaris***.

(vii) The animals in which there is complete absence of body cavity are called **acoelomates**. e.g., Platyhelminthes.

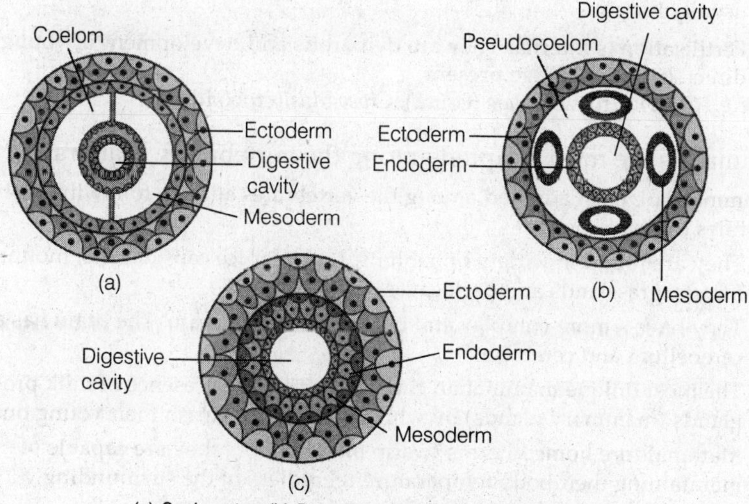

(a) Coelomate, (b) Pseudocoelomate and (c) Acoelomate

Q. 3 Comment upon the habitats and external features of animals belonging to class–Amphibia and Reptilia.

Ans. Amphibia

(i) They possess dual life as they can live in aquatic as well as terrestrial habitat. They are ectothermic (cold blooded).

(ii) They are tetrapods (4 limbs) which facilitate movement on land except Ichthyophis (a limbless amphibian).

(iii) Their limbs are evolved from the pectoral and pelvic fins.

(iv) Skin is thin, covered by mucus remain moist, also serves as an accessory source oxygen.

(v) They are both gill and lung breathers. Usually gills appear in th larval stage and are replaced by lungs in the adult stage.

(vi) They possess three chambered heart with two atria and one ventricle.

(vii) Fertilisation is mostly external, females are oviparous.

(viii) Larva is a tadpole, which undergoes metamorphosis. *e.g.*, Rana (frog), *Necturus* (mud puppy), *Salamandra* (salamander).

Reptilia

(i) In reptiles, crawling and slithering mode of locomotion is found.

(ii) They are mostly terrestrial animals and their body is covered by dry, and cornified skin, epidermal scales or scutes.

(iii) Lungs are well developed and present in all stages of life.

(iv) Toes possess claws.

(v) Appendages are well adapted for the movement on land.

(vi) Heart possesses a partially divided ventricle and 2 atria.

(vii) They lay amniotic eggs which are incubate on land.

(viii) They are poikilothermic or cold blooded animals. Temperature is regulated mechanically and not metabolically, by moving in and out; of heat source usually the sun.

(ix) Fertilisation is internal They are oviparous and development of young ones is direct. (no larvas stage present)
e.g., *Chelone* (turtle), *Naja* (cobra), *Crocodilus* (crocodile).

Q. 4 Mammals are most adapted among the vertebrates. Elaborate.

Ans. Mammals are most adapted among the vertebrates and the following features justifies this statement

(i) They are found in variety of habitats, *i.e.*, polar ice caps,deserts, mountains, forests, grasslands and dark caves.

(ii) They have a more complex and better-developed brain. The brain has a large cerebellum and cerebrum.

(iii) The most unique mammalian characteristic is the presence of milk producing glands (mammary glands) by which mammals nourish their young ones.

(iv) Mammals are homeotherms (warm blooded), *i.e.*, they are capable of maintaining their body temperature regardless of the surrounding environment.

(v) They possess oil secreting glands (sebaceous glands) and sweat glands (sudoriferous glands) in the skin.

(vi) They possess two pair of limbs, that are well adapted for walking, running, climbing, burrowing, swimming and flying.

(vii) Fertilisation is internal. They show viviparity with few exceptions like oviparous mammals *e.g.*, *Ornithorhynchus* (platypus) and the development is direct. Examples of viviparous are *Macropus* (kangaroo), *Rattus* (rat), *Canis* (dog), *Delphinus* (common dolphin), *Panthera tigris* (tiger), etc.

Chapter 05

Morphology of Flowering Plants

Multiple Choice Questions (MCQs)

Choose the correct answer from the given four options in the following questions.

Q. 1 Rearrange the following zones as seen in the root in vertical section and choose the correct option.

A. Root hair zone B. Zone of meristems
C. Root cap zone D. Zone of maturation
E. Zone of elongation

Codes

(a) C, B, E, A, D (b) A, B, C, D, E
(c) D, E, A, C, B (d) E, D, C, B, A

Ans. *(a)* **Root Cap Zone** protective covering at the root apex, secretes mucilage to soften the hard soil for the growth of root.

Zone of Meristem region of actively dividing densely packed cells resulting into root growth.

Zone of Elongation divided cells grow in size and elongate increasing the length of root. They cannot divide further.

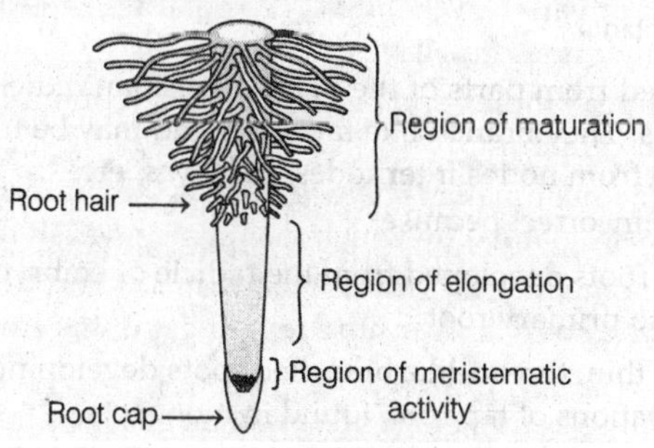

The regions of the root

Root Hair Zone root hair arises and grow in this region, helps in water and mineral absorption from the soil.

Zone of Maturation the cells of root at this region are fully differentiated and mature, performing different functions of root.

Q. 2 In an inflorescence where flowers are borne laterally in an acropetal succession, the position of the youngest floral bud shall be

(a) proximal
(b) distal
(c) intercalary
(d) Any where

Thinking Process The arrangement of flower on the main axis of the plant is called inflorescence. Think of the different kind of flower arrangement. How do the plants put up their flower to attract the pollinating agencies?

Ans. ***(b)*** In racemose inflorescence, younger flowers are born at the apex or distal end while older flowers are at the base, this type of succession is acropetal succession. Thus, the position of youngest floral bud would be distal.

Q. 3 The mature seeds of plants such as gram and peas, possess no endosperm, because

(a) these plants are not angiosperms
(b) there is no double fertilisation in them
(c) endosperm is not formed in them
(d) endosperm gets used up by the developing embryo during seed development

Thinking Process Gram and peas are dicot plants belonging to angiosperms. All angiosperms bear seeds. During seed development inside the embryo sac, embryo needs nourishment for its development. It is provided by endosperm. It is a product of triple fusion ($3n$) ploidy.

Ans. ***(d)*** Endosperm is a nourishing tissue of seed which provide nourishment to the developing embryo either before or after germination. In gram and peas, the endosperm is consumed during the development of seed. So, seed is non-endospermic, *i.e.*, endosprem is not present in the mature seed.

Q. 4 Roots developed from parts of the plant other than radicle are called

(a) tap roots
(b) fibrous roots
(c) adventitious roots
(d) nodular roots

Thinking Process As the seed germinates, it gives rise to plumule and radicle. Radicle develops into root system. Other plant parts also can give rise to roots depending upon the need of the plants.

Ans. ***(c)*** Roots developed from parts of the plant other than radicle are called adventitious roots. They branch like tap roots and may be underground or aerial, and may develop from nodes internodes on leaves, etc.

Other options are incorrect because

Tap roots are the roots developed from the radicle of embryo and persists and grows directly into primary root.

Fibrous roots are thin, thread-like branched roots developing from base of stem. These are modifications of tap root, found in monocots.

Nodular roots are also modifications of tap roots in which roots and its branches develop small or large swelling called nodules. They help in nitrogen fixation.

Q. 5 Venation is a term used to describe the pattern of arrangement of

(a) floral organs
(b) flower in infloresence
(c) veins and veinlets in a lamina
(d) All of them

Ans. *(c)* **Venation** The veins are the part of leaf which possess vascular tissues, *i.e.*, xylem and phloem. They are meant for the conduction of water, minerals and food to and fro in the leaf. The special arrangement of veins and veinlets in a leaf is called as **venation**.

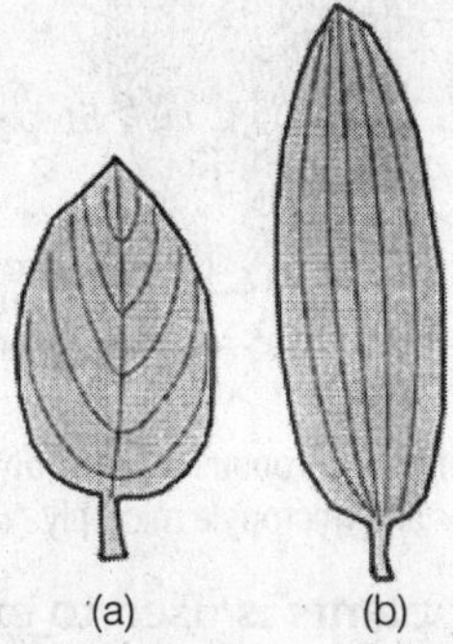

Venation in leaves (a) Reticulate venation (dicot leaf)
(b) Parallel venation (monocot leaf)

Q. 6 Endosperm, a product of double fertilisation in angiosperms is absent in the seeds of

(a) Coconut (b) Orchids (c) Maize (d) Castor

Ans. *(b)* Orchid seed is a non-endospermic seed, *i.e.*, endosperm is absent in it. Endosperm is a nourishing tissue present in the seed which nourishes the developing embryo. In orchid seed endosperm is absent because it is used up during the time of seed development. Nourishment for germinating seed is provided by the food material present in cotyledons.

Rest of the options are examples of endospermic seeds.

Q. 7 Many pulses of daily use belong to one of the families below.

(a) Solanaceae (b) Fabaceae
(c) Liliaceae (d) Poaceae

Ans. *(b)* **Fabaceae** is a subfamily of Leguminosae which was earlier called Papilionoideae. Plants of this family are the source of pulses and edible oils. Pulses are rich in protein content.

Q. 8 The placenta is attached to the developing seed near the

(a) testa (b) hilum (c) micropyle (d) chalaza

Thinking Process Placenta is a special tissue by which ovule is attached to the ovary. It has a special kind of arrangement in the ovary which is called placentation.

Ans. *(b)* The placenta is attached to the developing seed near hilum. It is the scar located near the edge where seed breaks from stalk or funiculus, *i.e.*, connecting the seed with fruit wall and placenta.

Rest of the options are incorrect as

Testa is the outer most covering of seed, **micropyle** is a small opening in seed coat through which water enters into seed and **chalaza** is a tissue where nucellus and integument are joined.

Nutrients from the plant travel through vascular tissue in the funiculus and outer integuments through the chalaza into the nucellus.

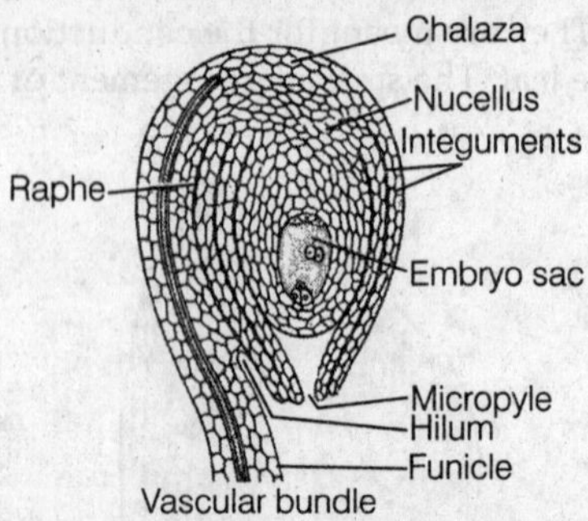

Detailed structure of an anatropous ovule showing chalaza, hilum and micropyle microply

Q. 9 Which of the following plants is used to extract the blue dye?

(a) *Trifolium* (b) *Indigofera* (c) *Lupin* (d) *Cassia*

Thinking Process Dyes are the secondary metabolites of certain plants and are important economically.

Ans. **(b)** *Indigofera tinctoria* and *T suffruticosa* are the two plants belonging to the family–Fabaceae that produce blue indigo dye.

The other options are incorrect as

Trifolium is used as fodder.

Lupin is an ornamental plant.

Cassia is a shrub usually grown on the road side as an ornamental plant.

Q. 10 Match the following columns.

Column I		Column II	
A.	Aleurone layer	1.	Without fertilisation
B.	Parthenocarpic fruit	2.	Nutrition
C.	Ovule	3.	Double fertilisation
D.	Endosperm	4.	Seed

Codes

	A	B	C	D		A	B	C	D
(a)	1	2	3	4	(b)	2	1	4	3
(c)	4	2	1	3	(d)	2	4	1	3

Ans. **(b)** A-2, B-1, C-4, D-3

It is the correct sequence of the options in the two columns.

Aleurone layer surrounds the tissue of monocot seeds. It is morphologically and biochemically distinct from seed. It is a proteinaceous layer (surrounding the endosperm and separating embryo) which provides nutrition and helps in germination.

Parthenocarpic fruits are seedless fruits, which develop without the fertilisation of egg cell present in the ovule of the plants.

The ovule contains the female reproductive unit, *i.e.*, embryo sac that develop into a seed after it is fertilised.

Endosperm is formed during the process of double fertilisation by the fusion of one male gamete with the two polar nuclei at the centre of the embryo sac.

Very Short Answer Type Questions

Q. 1 Roots obtain oxygen from air in the soil for respiration. In the absence or deficiency of O_2, root growth is restricted or completely stopped. How do the plants growing in marsh lands or swamps obtain their O_2 required for root respiration?

Thinking Process Every plant cell require O_2 for cell respiration. The air present in between the soil particles is used up by the roots. The plant growing in water logged conditions do not get O_2 form the soil so they evolve some other mechanism to get it.

Ans. The roots of the plants (*e.g., Rhizophora*) growing in marshy/swamp areas become negatively geotropic. They grow vertically upwards in air, above the soil level and respire through specialised roots called respiratory roots or pneumatophores.

Q. 2 Write floral formula for a flower which is bisexual, actinomorphic pentamerous sepal petal stamens free with ovary syncarpous, superior, trilocular with axile placentation.

Ans. **Floral formula** is a formula by which we can describe the flower by using some symbols. The various symbols describing the above given conditions are as follows

(i) Bisexual ⚥ (ii) Actinomorphic ⊕

(iii) Sepals five K_5 (iv) Petals five C_5

(v) Stamens A_6 (vi) Tricarpellary ovary G_3

(vii) Syncarpus $G_{(3)}$

(viii) Trilocular (ix) Axile placentation 

Floral formula would be ⊕ ⚥ $K_5 C_5 A_6 \underline{G}_{(3)}$

Q. 3 In *Opuntia*, the stem is modified into a flattened green structure to perform the function of leaves, (*i.e.*, photosynthesis). Cite two other examples of modifications of plant parts for the purpose of photosynthesis.

Thinking Process Photosynthesis is performed by green parts of the plants (mainly leaves). Think of plants in which this function is performed by other plant part except leaf. It has to be green and contain chlorophyll pigment.

Ans. *Opuntia* is a xerophytic plant, in which leaves are modified into spine to reduce the rate of transpiration and the leaves do not perform the photosynthesis at all.

So function of photosynthesis in *Opuntia* plant is performed by stem which is thick fleshy and flattened structure containing chlorophyll and stores food. It is known as phylloclade.

Sometimes, the stem, (*i.e.*, about one internode long) modifies into a leaf like structure to carry out photosynthesis, as in *Asparagus*. They are present in axil of scale leaves while true leaves are reduced to scales or spines.

Similarly in some plants, roots become assimilatory as in the case of and *Tinospora*. These roots grow outside the soil, develop chlorophyll in them and perform photosynthesis.

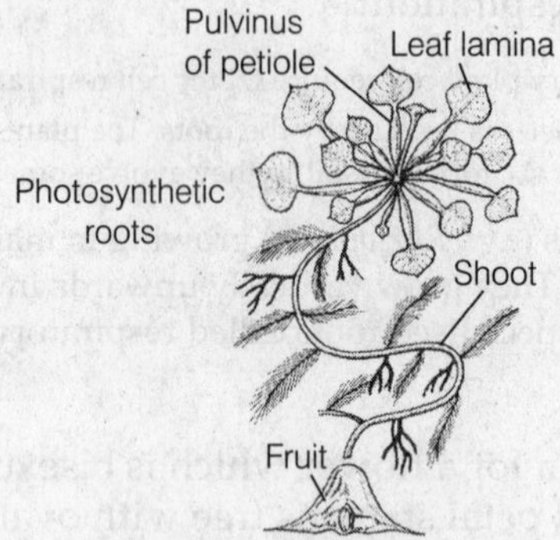

Assimilatory roots of *Trapa*

Q. 4 In swampy areas like the sunderbans in West Bengal, plants bear special kind of roots called ....

Thinking Process There are many plants that can grow in swamp areas like water lily, cypress trees, etc. sunderbans have halophytic mangroove forest.

Ans. **Pneumatophores Roots** are the organs meant for the absorption of water and minerals from the soil. Cells of roots require O_2 to respire. In swampy areas, soil does not have air, so no O_2 is available to them.

In such cases, roots come out of the soil shows negative geotropism and breathe after coming in contact with air, *e.g.*, *Rhizophora*. Such roots are called pneumatophores respiratory roots.

Q. 5 In aquatic plants like *Pistia* and *Eichhornia*, leaves and roots are found near ....

Ans. In *Pistia* and *Eichhornia*, which are floating plants, the stem is like a runner, where it branches to form leaves at the apex and roots below. The roots are found near the surface of water as both the plants are hydrophytes.

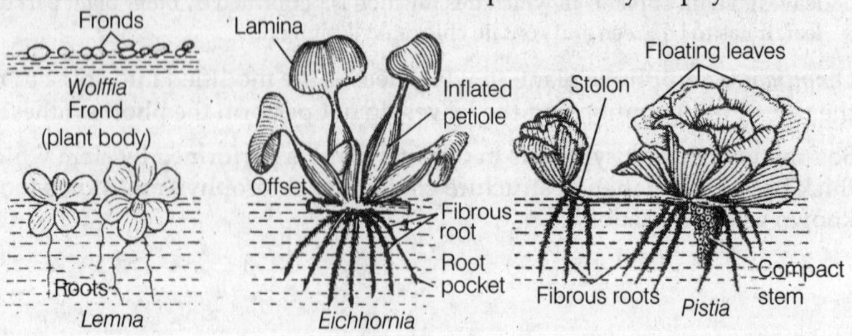

Free floating plants

Q. 6 Reticulate and parallel venation are the characteristic of .... and .... respectively.

Ans. **Dicot and monocot plants** All dicot plants have reticulate venation (*i.e.*, veinlets forms network) except in *Calophyllum*, whereas all monocot plants have parallel venation (veins run parallel to each other within a lamina) with the exception of *Alocasia and Smilex*.

Q. 7 In epigynous flower, ovary is situated below the ....

Ans. In epigynous flower, ovary is situated below the thalamus (inferior) while the other whorls of flower like sepals, petals and androecium grows above the ovary (superior), *e.g.*, carrot, guava, *Cucurbita*, sunflower, etc.

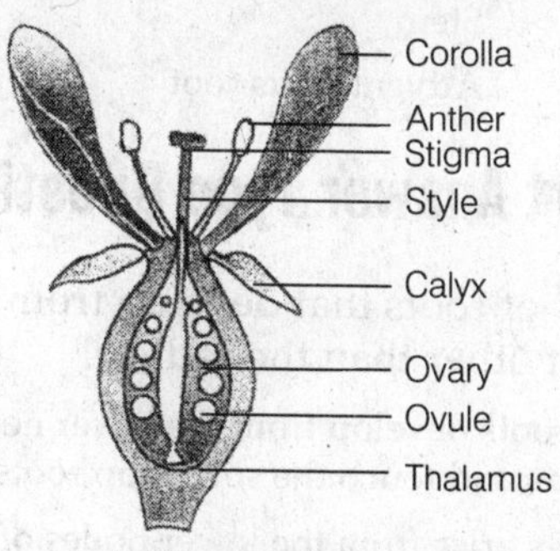

Epigynous flower

Q. 8 Add the missing floral organs of the given floral formula of Fabaceae.

% ⚥ $K_{()} \ldots C_{()}\ A_{(9)+\ldots)}\ \underline{G}$

Ans. The floral formula of Fabaceae family is

= %⚥ $K_5\ C_{1+2+(2)}\ A_{(9)+1}\ \underline{G}_1$

Floral character of Fabaceae shows bisexual, zygomorphic, petals-five, gamosepalous, corolla-petals 5, consists of a posterior standard, two lateral wings, two anterior ones forming a keel, androecium, ten diadelphous, gynoecium-superior, ovary monocarpellay.

Q. 9 Name the body part modified for food storage in the following

(a) Carrot ....
(b) *Colocasia* ....
(c) Sweet potato ....
(d) *Asparagus* ....
(e) Radish ....
(f) Potato ....
(g) Dahlia ....
(h) Turmeric ....
(i) *Gladiolus* ....
(j) Ginger ....
(k) *Portulaca* ....

Ans. (a) Carrot — Tap root

(b) *Colocasia* — Stem-(corm)

(c) Sweet potato — Root

(d) *Asparagus* — Adventitious root

(e) Radish — Root

(f) Potato — Stem

(g) Dahlia — Adventitious root

(h) Turmeric — Stem

(i) *Gladiolus* — Stem

(j) Ginger — Stem

(k) *Portulaca* — Adventitious root

Short Answer Type Questions

Q. 1 Give two examples of roots that develop from different parts of the angiospermic plant other than the radicle.

Ans. In banyan tree, prop roots develop from the lower nodes of stem of banyan tree. They grow downwards and touch the soil. Prop roots are meant for support.

In sugarcane, stilt roots arise from the lower nodes of stem and enter the soil to provide strength to the plant. These roots also protect the plant against strong winds.

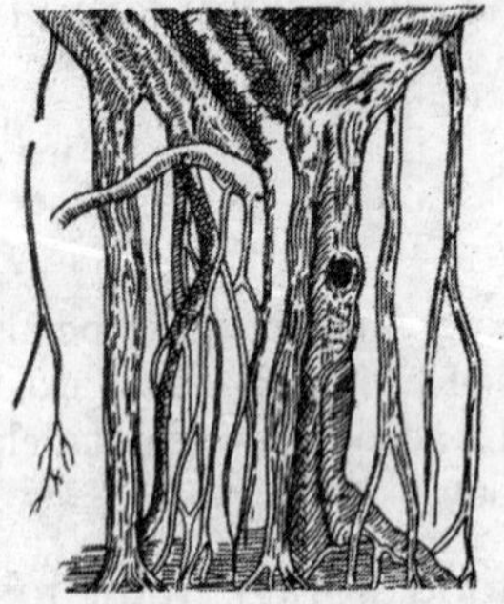

Prop roots of banyan

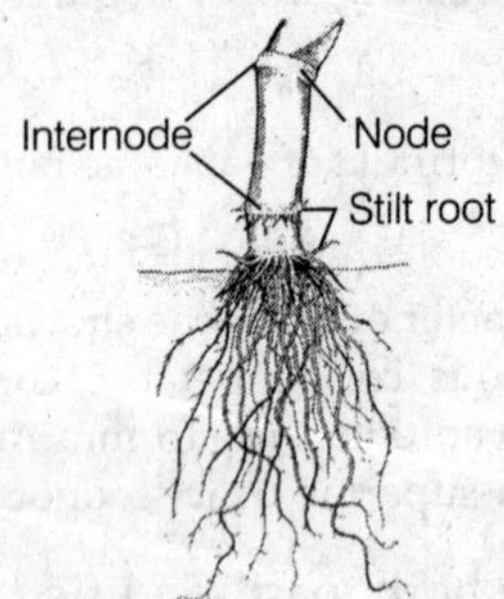

Stilt roots of sugarcane

Q. 2 The essential functions of roots are anchorage and absorption of water and minerals in the terrestrial plant. What functions are associated with the roots of aquatic plants. How are roots of aquatic plants and terrestrial plants different?

Thinking Process Aquatic plants grow where plenty of water is available. These may be free floating, submerged, attached floating or attached emergent hydrophytes. Their roots possess several aquatic adaptations.

Ans. Usually the terrestrial roots show a branched network that helps in anchorage and absorption of water and minerals from soil to the plant.

In aquatic plants, roots show modifications that deviate from their normal function. *e.g.*, in plants like *Trapa, Tinospora* the roots are green and highly branched to increase the photosynthetic area, whereas in plants like *Jussiaea*, they get inflated due to air and project out of water so to help the plant in floating and exchange of gases.

Difference between roots of aquatic plants and terrestrial plants are as follows

Aquatic Plants	Terrestrial Plants
Roots may be absent, *e.g., Wolffia*. If roots are present they are not well developed. Usually thin adventitious roots are present.	Roots are well developed with root cap and root hairs and branches.
Vascular strands are poorly developed.	Vascular bundles are well developed.
Modified to carry out photosynthesis food storage and exchange of gases.	Provide anchorage and help in absorption of nutrients from soil.

Q. 3 Draw diagrams of a typical monocot and dicot leaves to show their venation pattern.

Ans. Venation is the pattern of distribution of veins and veinlets in the lamina of leaf. It is different in monocot and dicot leaf.

Monocot leaf	Dicot leaf
The veins run parallel to each other within a lamina. It is called parallel venation.	Veins and veinlets form a network in the lamina. It is called reticulate venation.
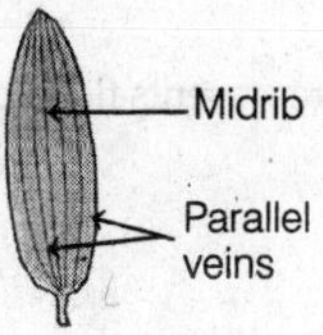 Midrib Parallel veins	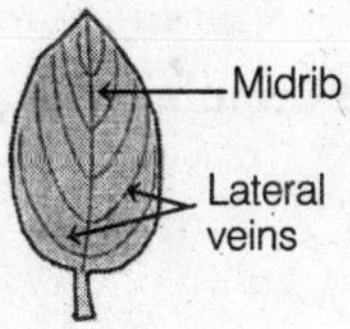 Midrib Lateral veins
Parallel venation, *e.g.*, grasses, wheat, maize, etc., (usually found in monocots).	Reticulate venation, *e.g., Hibiscus*, bean, pear etc., (usually found in dicots).

Q. 4 A typical angiosperm flower consists of four floral parts. Give the names of the floral parts and their arrangements sequentially.

Ans. The four floral parts of typical angiospermic flower are

Calyx It is the outermost whorl of the flower and members are called calyx or sepals. These are usually green and are protective in function (in bud stage).

Corolla It is composed of petals, usually bright coloured to attract insects for pollination.

Androecium It is composed of stamens, the male reproductive organ. Each stamen has stalk or filament and anther (containing pollen sac and pollen grains).

Gynoecium It is the female reproductive part and made up of one or more carpels. Each carpel has stigma, style and ovary.

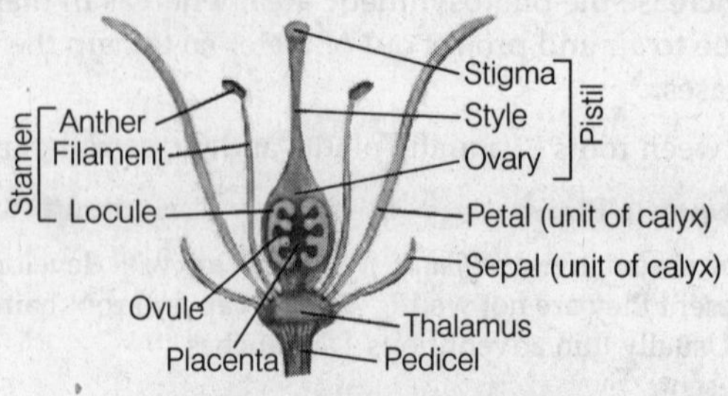

L.S. of flower showing different whorls

Q. 5 Given below are a few floral formulae of some well known plants. Draw floral diagrams from these formulae.

(i) $\oplus$ ⚥ $K_{(5)}\ C_{(5)}\ A_5\ \underline{G}_{(2)}$

(ii) $\oplus$ ⚥ $K_{(5)}\ C_{1+2+2}\ \overline{A}_{(9)+1}\ \underline{G}_1$

(iii) $\oplus$ ⚥ $K_5\ C_5\ A_{5+5}\ G_{(5)}$

Ans. (i) **Floral Formula** $\oplus$ ⚥ $K_{(5)}\ C_{(5)}\ A_5\ \underline{G}_{(2)}$ represents flowers of Solanaceae family.

(ii) **Floral Formula** $\oplus$ ⚥ $K_{(5)}\ C_{1+2+2}\ A_{(9)+1}\ \underline{G}_1$ represents flowers of Fabaceae family.

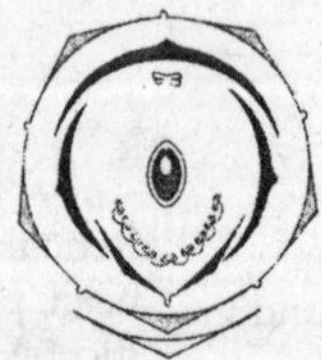

(iii) **Floral Formula** $\oplus$ ⚥ $K_5\ C_5\ A_{5+5}\ \underline{G}_{(5)}$ represents flowers of Malvaceae family.

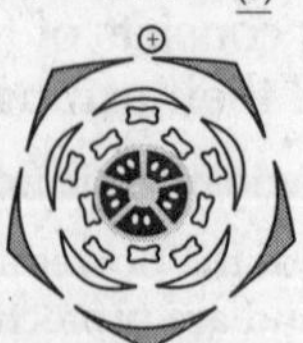

Q. 6 Reticulate venation is found in dicot leaves while in monocot leaves venation is of parallel type. Biology being a 'Science of exceptions', find out any exception to this generalisation.

Ans. Reticulate venation is a characteristic of dicots and parallel venation is of monocots. But few exceptions are also seen in this generalisation parallel venation is also found in dicot plants, *e.g., Calophyllum, Corymbium*, etc., and reticulate venation is also found in monocot plants such *Alocasia, Smilax*, etc.

Q. 7 You have heard about several insectivorous plants that feed on insects. *Nepenthes* or the pitcher plant is one such example, which usually grows in shallow water or in marsh lands. What part of the plant is modified into a pitcher? How does this modification help the plant for food even though it can photosynthesise like any other green plant?

Ans. In insectivorous plant, *e,g., Nepenthes,* the leaf lamina gets modified in the form of pitcher and anterior part of petiole coils like **tendril** which keeps the pitcher in a vertical direction. Posterior part of the petiole remains flattened like a leaf. The apex of lamina forms a lid. Pitcher contains digestive enzyme which digest the trapped insects. All these modifications and adaptation are developed to make up the nitrogen deficiency in the plant because these plants are found in N_2 deficient soil, (such as marshy or swamp soils)

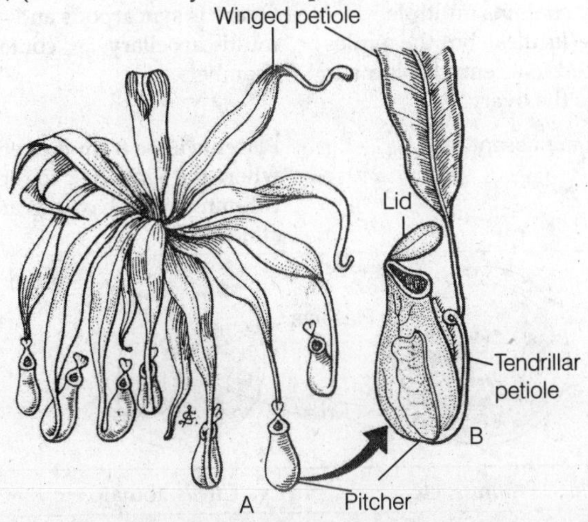

Nepenthes : pitcher shaped leaf

Q. 8 Mango and coconut are 'drupe' type of fruits. In mango, fleshy mesocarp is edible. What is the edible part of coconut? What does milk of tender coconut represent?

Ans. Mango and coconut are drupe fruits. They develop from monocarpellary superior ovaries and are one seeded. It is differentiated into outer thin epicarp, middle fleshy mesocarp and the stony endocarp.

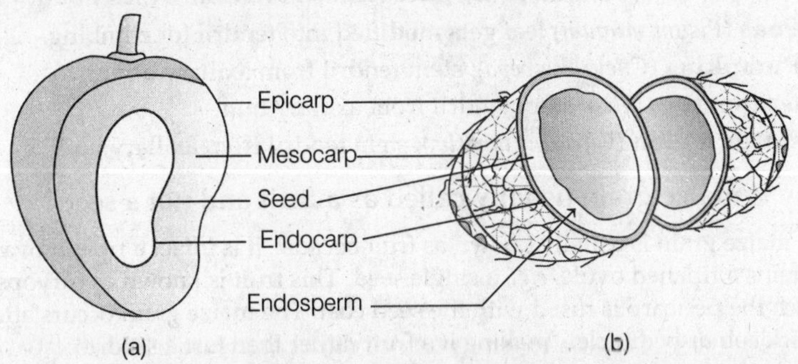

Parts of fruit (a) Mango (b) Coconut

The edible part of coconut (*Cocos nucifera*) is endosperm. The milk of tender coconut represents the free nuclear endosperm. in liquid form. Later it gets deposited along the walls of endocarp and forms edible flesh.

Q. 9 How can you differentiate between free central and axile placentation?

Ans. Placentation is the arrangement of ovules on the walls of ovary with the help of special kind of tissue called placenta. Plants show different types of placentation, free central and axile are among them.

They have the following differences

Free Central Placentation	Axile Placentation
The ovary contains multiple chambers (locules), but the ovules are attached to a central column or axis inside the ovary.	Ovary is syncarpous and multi-carpellary, *i.e.*, contain many chambers.
The septa are absent.	Placenta arise from the central axis where the septa fuse to form axile column to which ovules are attached.
e.g., Dianthus, Primrose, etc,	*e.g., Citrus*, tomato etc.

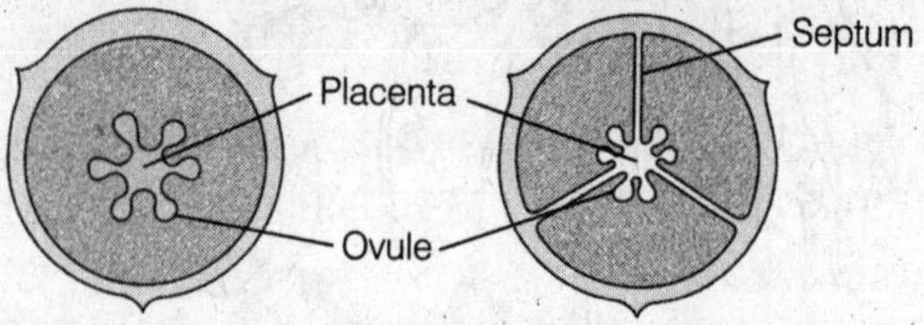

Q. 10 Tendrils are found in the following plants. Identify whether they are stem tendrils of leaf tendrils.

(a) Cucumber
(b) Peas
(c) Pumpkins
(d) Grapevine
(e) Watermelon

Ans.

(a) **Cucumber** (*Cucums sativus*), have stem tendril from axillary bud.
(b) **Peas** (*Pisum sativum*) leaf gets modified into tendril for climbing.
(c) **Pumpkins** (*Cucurbita pepo*), stem tendril from axillary bud.
(d) **Grapevine** (*Vitis*), stem tendril from axillary bud.
(e) **Water melon** (*Citrullus lanatus*), stem tendril from axillary bud.

Q. 11 Why is maize grain usually called as a fruit and not a seed?

Ans. The maize grain is usually known as fruit because it is infact a ripend ovary which contains a ripened ovule, *e.g.*, a single seed. This fruit is known as caryopsis in which the pericarp is fused with the seed coat. The maize grain occurs attached to a thick cob or peduncle, , making it a fruit rather than just a seed.

Q. 12 Tendrils of grapevines are homologous to the tendril of pumpkins, but are analogous to that of pea. Justify the above statement.

Ans. **Homologous Organs** are organs that have similar origin but they differ functionally. Axillary bud of stem gives rise to tendril in both grapevine and pumpkins so they have same origin, *i.e.*, homologous, whereas **analogous organs** are organs having different origin, but perform same function. The tendril of pea arises from the leaf and helps the plant to climb.

Hence, the origin of pea tendril is different but, its function is similar to the tendrils of grapevines.

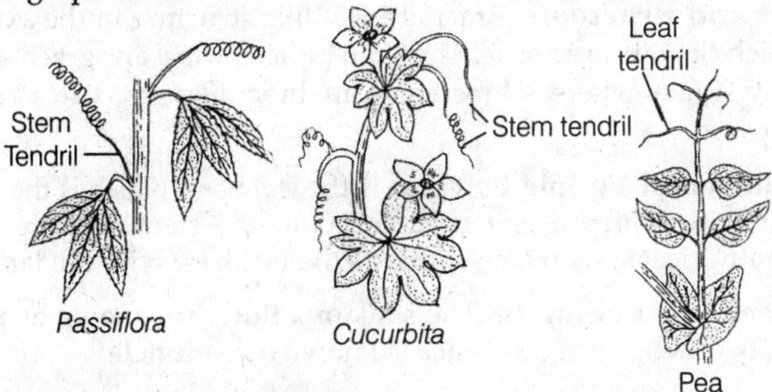

Q. 13 Rhizome of ginger is like the roots of other plants that grows underground. Despite this fact ginger is a stem and not a root. Justify.

Ans. **Rhizome of Ginger** is a type of underground modification of stem which grows horizontally, underground and bear nodes, internodes and scaly leaves and buds, which gives rise to aerial shoots.

The adventitious root arises from the lower surface of nodes. It is not a root because root does not have nodes and internodes. Further the rhizomes do not perform the function of roots, *i.e.*, anchorage and absorption, rather serve as reservoirs for storage of food. All these characteristics support the fact that ginger is a stem and not a root.

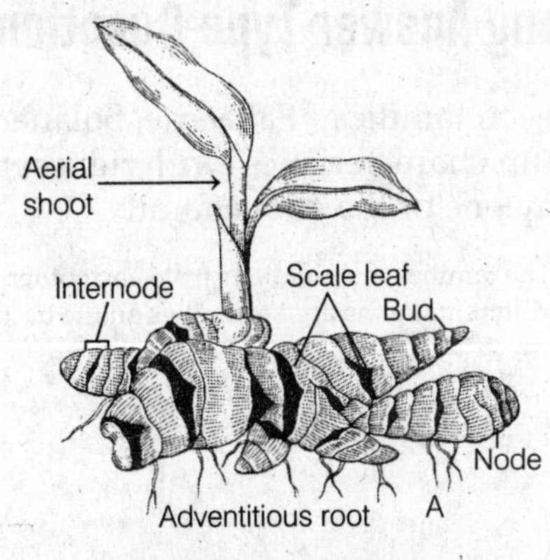

Rhizome of ginger

Q. 14 Differentiate between

(a) Bract and bracteole

(b) Pulvinus and petiole

(c) Pedicel and peduncle

(d) Spike and spadix

(e) Stamen and staminode

(f) Pollen and pollinium

Ans. (a) **Bract and Bracteole** Bract is a leaf like structure in the axil. *i.e.*, at the base of which flowers are borne. They can be small or scaly, green and coloured and usually single, whereas **bracteoles** are bract like structures borne on the stalk of a flower.

(b) **Pulvinus and Petiole** Pulvinus is the leaf base, which is the proximal swollen region with which a leaf is attached to the stem. **Petiole** is cylindrical or sub-cylindrical stalk which connects the leaf base with the lamina.

(c) **Pedicel and Peduncle** The stalk of a flower is known as **pedicel**, whereas the stalk of whole inflorescence is known as **peduncle**.

(d) **Spike and Spadix** In **spike inflorescence**, the flowers are sessile that develop on an elongated peduncle in acropetal succession, *e.g.*, *Adhatoda*. The peduncle is non-fleshy. The **spadix inflorescence** is like spike, but it is covered by one to a few large bracts called **spathes, *e.g.*, *Colocasia*.** The peduncle is fleshy and its opical portion is naked, *i.e.*, without flowers.

(e) **Stamen and Staminode** The male reproductive organs or microsporophylls of a flower are called **stamen**. A fully sterile underdeveloped or abortive stamen is called a **staminode** , *e.g.*, *Verbascum*.

(f) **Pollen and Pollinium** Microspore of an angiospermic flower is known as **pollen**. It is haploid, whereas a mass of pollen grains from the same anther constitute the **pollinium** as in *Calotropis*.

Long Answer Type Questions

Q. 1 Distinguish between families - Fabaceae, Solanaceae, Liliaceae on the basis of gynoecium characteristics (with figures). Also write economic importance of any one of the above family.

Thinking Process The families mainly differ from each other in their reproductive structures. Try to differentiate the above families on the basis of androecium and gynoecium.

Ans. The difference between the three families on the bases of charateristics of Gynoceium are as follows

Gynoecium Characteriseies	Fabaceae	Solanaceae	Liliaceae
Carpels	Monocarpellary free, single	Bicarpellary Syncarpous	Tricarpellary syncarpous
Ovary	Superior unilocular	Superior bilocular (2-4 locules in tomato)	Superior
Ovules	Margin in two alternate rows	Many in each locule	Trilocular
Placentation	Marginal	Axile	Axile
Style	Bent, single	Simple	Simple but may be united or separate
Stigma	Simple and capitate	Simple and lobed	Free or fused, trilobed
Floral formula	Br % $K_{(5)}$ $G_{1+2+(2)}$ $A_{1+(9)+1}$ $\underline{G}_1$	-Br ⊕ $C_{(5)}$ G 5 A_5 $\underline{G}_{(2)}$	Br ⊕ P_{3+3} A_{3+3} $\underline{G}_{(3)}$
Examples	All pulse, sunhemp, *Trifolium*	Potato, tomato, brinjal, datura, etc	*Asparagus*, colchine, tulip

Economic Importance of Fabaceae

Plants of this family are the sources of pulses and edible oils. Dye is extracted from *Indigofera* which is a plant of this family. It serves as a source of various other products like fibres (sunnhemp), fodder (*Sesbania* and *Trifolium*), ornamental (lupin, sweet pea) and medicine (multiathi).

Q. 2 Describe various stem modifications associated with food storage climbing and protection.

Thinking Process Stem is the aerial part of plant bearing nodes, internodes, buds, flowers, fruits and seeds. Besides these functions and forms, under special conditions, it gets modified and perform many functions, *e.g.*, storage, protection and climbing. Search out different forms of stem and its modified forms performing variety of functions.

Ans. The various stem modifications are as follows

Stem	Modification of Stem for Storage of Food
Rhizome	In this case the stem becomes underground *i.e.*, rhizome and grows horizontally, stores food material. It bears nodes, internodes and buds which give rise to aerial shoots, *e.g.*, ginger, banana, turmeric. **Rhizome of ginger**
Corm	Stem is underground, grows vertically and bears nodes as well as internodes *e.g. Colocasia.* **Corm of *Colocasia***
Bulb	In this case, the stem becomes underground, the internode is shortened in such a way that the leaves are condensed and these leaves become thick and fleshy and store food material e.g.,-onion. **Tunicated bulb of and L.S. of bulbs**
Tuber	This is also a special kind of stem modification, which arises at the tips of special narrow underground branches. They have nodes, internodes apical buds, scale leaf in the form of ridge. They gave no. of eyes which represent nodes. It is meant for storing food material, *e.g.*, potato **Tuber of potato**

Stem	Modification of Stem for Storage of Food
Stem tendrils	**Modification of Stems for Climbing** These are found in cucurbits and grapevine. The axillary buds of the stem become elongated and spirally coiled and twine around a support for the plant to grow as the stem is weak and herbaceous.
Stem thorns	These are modified stem that present in the axil of leaf or apex of stem performing the function of either climbing or defence, *e.g., Duranta, Calamus* and also reduce transpiration.

Q. 3 Stolon, offset and rhizome are different forms of stem modifications. How can these modified forms of stem be distinguished from each other?

Ans. **Stem modifications** Stem gets modified in different forms like stolon, offset and rhizomes. These can be distinguished from each other in the following manner

Stolon	Offset	Rhizome
The stem is a creeper that grows along the surface and helps in vegetative propagation. It is a long distance runner with longer and thicker internodes. Horizontal branches arise from the internodes, *e.g.,* strawberry *Colocaica.*	It is like a small runner of one internode long, but inter nodes are shorter and thicker sub-aerial modification where the lateral branches develops from the stem. Lateral branches have short internodes where each node bears a rosette of leaves and adventitious roots *e.g.,* Aquatic plants like pistia and *Eichhornia.*	These are underground stem grow horizontally bear nodes and internodes, scaly leaves, axillary buds and roots arising from nodes e.g.,Ginger, banana, turmeric. They are modified to store food in plants.

Stolon

An offset of *Eichhornia*

Rhizome of ginger

Q. 4 The mode of arrangement of sepals or petals in a floral bud is known as aestivation. Draw the various types of aestivation possible for a typical pentamerous flower.

Ans. The mode of arrangement of petals or sepals in a flower bud with respect to the members of the same whorl or with each other is known as **aestivation**.

It is of following types

Valvate Margin of adjacent petals or sepals touch each other, but do not overlap, *e.g.,* mustard (*Brassica*).

Twisted Regular overlapping of petals or sepals occurs in which margin of one petal overlap with the adjacent next one petal, *e.g.*, China rose (*Hibiscus rosa sinensis*).

Imbricate There are five petals arranged in such a way that one petal is completely external and one petal is completely internal, three petals are partially external and partially internal, *e.g.*, *Cassia, Callistemon, Caesalpinia.*

Quincuncial There are five sepals or petals of which two are completely out and two are completely inside, while one is partially external and partially internal *e.g.*, *Cucurbita* (Cucurbitaceae).

Vexillary It is the characteristic aestivation of corolla of family - Papilionaceae, in which corolla (petals) are papilionaceous.

The largest petal overlap the two lateral petals (wings), which in turn overlap the two smallest anterior petals (keel) *e.g.*, *Artobotrys, Polyalthea, Pisum.*

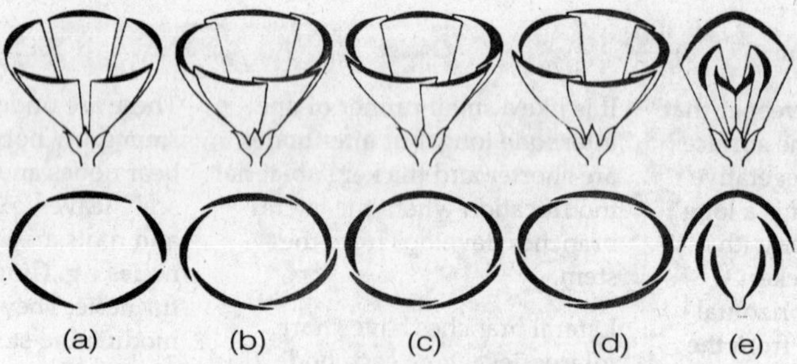

Different types of aestivation of calyx and corolla (a) Valvate, (b) Twisted, (c) Imbricate, (d) Quincuncial and (e) Vexillary

Q. 5 The arrangement of ovules within the ovary is known as placentation. What does the term placenta refer to? Name and draw various types of placentations in the flower as seen in T.S. or V.S.

Ans. **Placenta** is a flattened, cushion like tissue in the ovary where one or more ovules are attached.

The various types of placentation seen in the flowers are described in the following table

Type of Placentation	Description with example	Diagram
Marginal	There is a single placenta which develops along the junction of two fused margins, *e.g.*, pea.	
Axile	Mutlicarpellary, syncarpous gynoecium, inward growth of carpel's margin forms a multicarpellary condition that contains an axis in the centre. Placenta arises from central axis bearing ovules. *e.g.*, *Solanum*, China rose.	

Type of Placentation	Description with example	Diagram
Parietal	The number of placenta corresponds to number of fusing carpels. Sometimes the ovules bearing placenta grow inward to form false septa and thus ovary becomes bilocular (*e.g.*, mustard) and trilocular *e.g.*, *Curcurbita*	
Free central	The ovary is unilocular and ovules are borne on the central-axis and not connected to the ovary wall by septum. *e.g.*, *Dianthus*, Primrose.	
Basal	The ovary is unilocular and the single ovule is borne at the base of the ovary attached by a single placenta, *e.g.*, sunflower, wheat.	

Q. 6 Sunflower is not a flower. Explain.

Ans. Sunflower is not a flower, but it is a kind of inflorescence called **capitulum** in which the receptacle is flattened. It bears numerous sessile and small florets. The youngest floret is in the center and oldest lies at the periphery. Whole cluster of florets gets surrounded by bracts, known as **involucre**.

(i) **Ray Florets** Arranged on the rim of receptacle having distinct yellow and strap shaped petals. These florets are female, sterile and are always zygomorphic and may be arranged in one or more whorls.

(ii) **Disc florets** Grouped in the center, bisexual and actinomorphic.

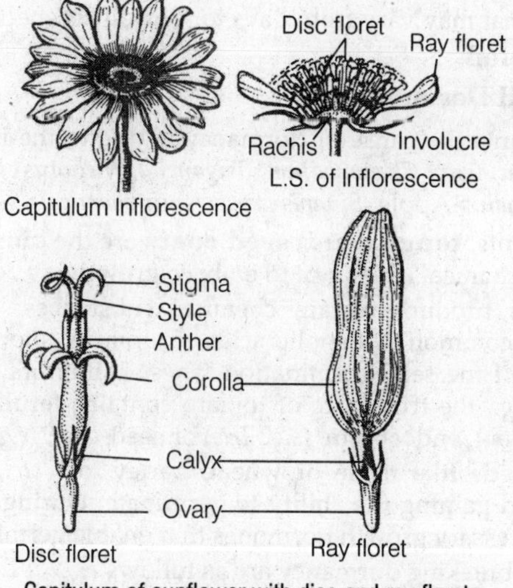

Capitulum of sunflower with disc and ray florets

Q. 7 How do you distinguish between hypogeal germination and epigeal germination? What is the role of cotyledon(s) and the endosperm in the germination of seeds?

Ans. Difference between hypogeal germination and epigeal seed sermination are as follows

Hypogeal Seed Germination	Epigeal Seed Germination
Rapid growth and elongation of epicotyl.	Rapid growth and elongation of hypocotyl.
Cotyledons remain inside the soil.	Seed cotyledons emerge above the soil level.
Cotyledons remain non-green, non photosynthetic.	Cotyledon becomes green and photosynthetic
e.g., maize, rice	*e.g.*, castor, beans

Hypogeal germination

Epigeal germination

Role of Cotyledons and Endosperm Cotyledons and endosperm contain reserved food materials. When seed imbibes water, enzymes get activated, hydrolyse reserve food material and makes it available for the germinating seed.

Q. 8 Seeds of some plants germinate immediately after shedding from the plants while in other plants they require a period of rest before germination. The later phenomena is called as dormancy. Give the reasons for seed dormancy and some methods to break it.

Ans. Dormant seeds remain under non-germination conditions only for a specific period of time that may vary from days to years. This specific period is called **dormancy period**.

Causes of Seed Dormancy

(a) In many plants the cause of dormancy is due to the impermeability of seed coat to water, (*e.g.*, *Chenopodium, Trigonella, Meliotus*) or *oxygen* (*e.g.*, *Brassica alba, Pyrus malus*-Apple, *Sinapis arvensis*) or *chemicals*, (*e.g.*, *Xanthium*)

(b) In many plants, **tough** (hard) **seed coats** are the cause of dormancy as they provide mechanical resistance to embryo growth, *e.g.*, *Capsella, Lepidium*.

(c) Some seeds produce certain chemical substances, such as abscisic acid (ABA,most common), phenolic acids, coumarin, short chain fatty acid, etc. which inhibit the seed germination. These inhibitors may be present inside the fruit, (*e.g.*, the fruit juice of tomato contains ferulic acid), in the embryo (*e.g.*, *Xanthium*), endosperm, (*e.g.*, *Iris*) or seed-coat, (*e.g.*, *Cucurbita*)

(d) Shedded seeds like those of wheat, barley, oat *etc.*, need an interval for ripening and gaining the ability to germinate. During the interval, the seeds produce necessary growth hormones that enable germination.

Methods of breaking dormancy are as follows

(i) Inactivation of growth inhibitors by heat or cold treatment.

(ii) Mechanical abrasions weaken the tough and impermeable seed coat.

(iii) Microorganisms present in the soil weaken and decompose hard seed coat.

(iv) Washing away of inhibitors by rain or irrigation water.

(v) Maturation of embryo.

Chapter 06

Anatomy of Flowering Plants

Multiple Choice Questions (MCQs)

Choose the correct answer from the given four options in the following questions.

Q. 1 A transverse section of stem is stained first with safranin and then with fast green following the usual schedule of double staining for the preparation of a permanent slide. What would be the colour of the stained xylem and phloem?

(a) Red and green (b) Green and red

(c) Orange and yellow (d) Purple and orange

Thinking Process Different kinds of stains are used to colour the plant tissues to facilitate the histological studies. Safranin and fast green are few of them.

Ans. ***(a)*** The xylem is coloured red from safranin and phloem coloureed green from fast green stain.

Q. 2 Match the following columns.

	Column I		Column II
A.	Meristem	1.	Photosynthesis, storage
B.	Parenchyma	2.	Mechanical support
C.	Collenchyma	3.	Actively dividing cells
D.	Sclerenchyma	4.	Stomata
E.	Epidermal tissue	5.	Sclereids

Codes

	A	B	C	D	E		A	B	C	D	E
(a)	1	3	5	2	4	(b)	3	1	2	5	4
(c)	2	4	5	1	3	(d)	5	4	3	2	1

Thinking Process The cells get specialised to perform special functions in different plant organs.

Ans. ***(b)*** **Meristem** It is a group of actively dividing cells which is responsible for the life long growth occurring in the plants.

Parenchyma It is a permanent tissue and widely distributed in plant body. It is mainly involved in photosynthesis in chlorophyll containing cells and also store food materials.

Collenchyma The cells of collenchyma tissue have thickening at corners of cells and this provide mechanical strength to herbaceous green stems.

Sclerenchyma This tissue is dead at maturity, have thickening along all sides of walls. Sclereids and fibres are this types of tissue.

Epidermal tissue The epidermal tissue system forms the outer most covering of the whole plant body and comprises epidermal cells, stomata and the epidermal appendages, the trichomes and hair.

Q. 3 Match the following columns.

	Column I		Column II
A.	Cuticle	1.	Guard cells
B.	Bulliform cells	2.	Single layer
C.	Stomata	3.	Waxy layer
D.	Epidermis	4.	Empty colourless cell

Codes

	A	B	C	D		A	B	C	D
(a)	3	4	1	2	(b)	1	2	3	4
(c)	3	2	4	1	(d)	3	2	1	4

Ans. *(a)* **Cuticle** It is a waxy layer present all over the plant body except root.

Bulliform Cells These are empty colourless cells when the bulliform cells in the leaves absorb water and become turgid the leaf surface is exposed. When they are flaccid due to water stress, they make the leaves, curl inwards to minimise water loss.

Stomata These are minute apertures in the epidermis, meant for gas exchange. Each aperture is bounded by two kidney shaped cells called guard calls. Guard cells control closing and opening of stomata.

Epidermis It is generally uniseriate, *i.e.*, composed of single layer of epidermal cells. In some cases epidermis may be multilayered, *e.g.*, *Ficus*, *Nerium*.

Q. 4 Identify the simple tissue system from among the following.

(a) Parenchyma (b) Xylem (c) Epidermis (d) Phloem

Ans. *(a)* **Parenchyma** is a kind of simple tissue system present in all organs of the plant, *e.g.*, roots, stems, leaves, flowers, fruits and seeds.

Xylem and **phloem** are the complex tissues found in all vascular plants.

Epidermis is usually a single layered structure, present on the entire body surface of the plant and this makes epidermal tissue system. It consists of epidermis, cuticle, stomata unicellular hairs and multicellular trichomes.

Q. 5 Cells of this tissue are living and show angular wall thickning. They also provide mechanical support. The tissue is

(a) xylem (b) sclerenchyma (c) collenchyma (d) epidermis

Thinking Process Cell walls of the plant tissue sometimes get deposited with chemicals like lignin, suberin and harden to give mechanical strength to tissues and plant parts.

Ans. *(c)* **Collenchyma** This tissue provide mechanical support mainly to herbaceous young growing stem. The cells have angular thickening at the corners. Whereas, **xylem** is conductive complex tissue, transports water and mineral.

While **Sclerenchyma** is dead at maturity, it provides mechanical support the plant. **Epidermis** is usually a single layered structure present on the entire body surface of the plant.

Q. 6 Epiblema of roots is equivalent to

(a) pericycle (b) endodermis (c) epidermis (d) stele

Ans. *(c)* **Epidermis** It is usually a single layered structure, present all over the body surface of the plant. In case of root, it is called epiblema instead of epidermis.

Whereas **stele** is collective term for vascular tissues in case of vascular plants (pteridophytes, gymnosperms and angiosperms).

Endodermis and **Pericycle** are the parts of root or stem encircling vascular strands.

Q. 7 A conjoint and open vascular bundle will be observed in the transverse section of

(a) monocot root (b) monocot stem (c) dicot root (d) dicot stem

Ans. *(d)* **Dicot Stem** Vascular bundles are said to be open when cambium is present in between the xylem and phloem. Conjoint means the xylem and phloem are united on the same radius.

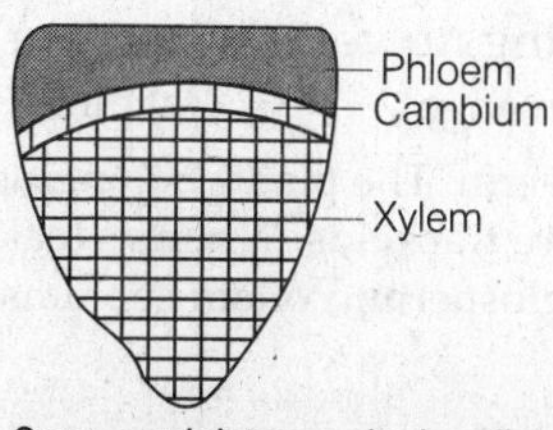

Open, conjoint vascular bundle

Q. 8 Interfascicular cambium and cork cambium are formed due to

(a) cell division (b) cell differentiation
(c) cell dedifferentiation (d) redifferentiation

Ans. *(c)* Interfascicular cambium and cork cambium are formed due to cell dedifferentiation.

Dedifferentiation A differentiated cell can regain its capacity for cell division under certain conditions. Formation of interfascicular cambium and cork cambium from fully differentiated parenchyma cells is an example of dedifferentiation.

Redifferentiation A dedifferentiated plant cell once again loses its capacity to divide and becomes mature.

Differentiation The process which leads to maturation of cells is called differentiation. During differentiation, a few or major changes happen in protoplasm and cell walls of the cells.

Q. 9 Phellogen and phellem respectively denote

(a) cork and cork cambium (b) cork cambium and cork
(c) secondary cortex and cork (d) cork and secondary cortex

Ans. *(b)* **Cortical Cells** In the dicot stem the cortical cells gets differentiated to give rise to another meristematic tissue which is called cork cambium or phellogen. On the outer side it forms phellem (cork) and in the inner region it forms secondary cortical cells (phelloderm).

Q. 10 In which of the following pairs of parts of a flowering plant is epidermis absent?

(a) Root tip and shoot tip
(b) Shoot bud and floral bud
(c) Ovule and seed
(d) Petiole and pedicel

Ans. *(a)* Root and shoot tip of an actively growing plant has high meristematic activity. The cells in this region are highly active and keep dividing. So, the cells do not differentiate into epidermal tissue, so epidermis is absent in root and shoot tips.

Q. 11 How many shoot apical meristems are likely to be present in a twig of a plant possessing, 4 branches and 26 leaves?

(a) 26 (b) 1 (c) 5 (d) 30 (e) 4

Ans. *(c)* **Apical Meristem** It is always present at the growing apices. Plants with 4 branches and 26 leaves will have 5 growing shoot apical meristems (4 growing apex of the branches + one growing apex of the main plant axis).

Q. 12 A piece of wood having no vessels (trachea) must be belong to

(a) teak (b) mango (c) pine (d) palm

Ans. *(c)* **Pine** It is a gymnosperm. The plants belonging to this group do not have vessels instead, they have tracheids. Whereas teak, mango and palm are angiospermic trees. Angiospermic xylem contains vessels, tracheids, parenchyma and fibres.

Q. 13 A plant tissue, when stained, showed the presence of hemicellulose and pectin in cell wall of its cells. The tissue represents

(a) collenchyma (b) sclerenchyma (c) xylem (d) meristem

Ans. *(a)* **Collenchyma** It is a group of specialised cells meant for mechanical support. It has thickening at the corners of the cells, mainly because of the deposition of pectin and hemicellulose.

Q. 14 In conifers fibres are likely to be absent in

(a) secondary phloem
(b) secondary xylem
(c) primary phloem
(d) leaves

Thinking Process Leaves have mainly photosynthetic tissues so, the cells are adapted to carry out photosynthesis.

Ans. *(d)* **Leaves** The leaves of the plants are mainly the organ of photosynthesis. It has specialised parenchymatous cells having chlorophyll. It does not have any fibrous cells.

Q. 15 When we peel the skin of a potato tuber, we remove

(a) periderm
(b) epidermis
(c) cuticle
(d) sapwood

Ans. *(a)* **Periderm** Potato is a underground stem. The outer epidermal layer of the stem is known as periderm. So, when we remove the skin of potato, we are actually removing the periderm.

Q. 16 A vesselless piece of stem possessing prominent sieve tubes would belong to

(a) *Pinus* (b) *Eucalyptus*
(c) Grass (d) *Trochodendron*

Ans. ***(d) Trochodendron*** The species of this genus have a unique feature of the angiosperms, *i.e.*, it lacks vessel elements in its wood, but has prominent sieve tube cells.

Q. 17 Which one of the following cell types always divide by anticlinal cell division?

(a) Fusiform initial cells (b) Root cap
(c) Protoderm (d) Phellogen

Ans. ***(c)*** **Protoderm** This is a part of the apical meristem that gives rise to the epidermis, which is the outer layer of the plant. It divides by anticlinal division.

Q. 18 What is the fate of primary xylem in a dicot root showing extensive secondary growth?

(a) It is retained in the centre of the axis
(b) It gets crushed
(c) May or may not get crushed
(d) It gets surrounded by primary phloem

Ans. ***(a)*** **Primary xylem** is present in the centre of the root. As secondary growth occurs in the root, the primary phloem is pushed outside whereas, primary xylem remains inside of the root.

Very Short Answer Type Questions

Q. 1 Product of photosynthesis is transported from the leaves to various parts of the plants and stored in some cell before being utilised. What are the cells/tissues that store them?

Thinking Process Glucose is the first product of photosynthesis. It is a highly reactive molecule. It gets converted into a disaccharide-sucrose which has 2 glucose molecule. This is a ready form of sugar for transportation.

Ans. The food gets stored in specialised parenchymatous cells present either in roots and stems or in their modifications in the form of a polysaccharide called starch.

Q. 2 Protoxylem is the first formed xylem. If the protoxylem lies next to phloem what kind of arrangement of xylem would you call it?

Thinking Process Xylem is a complex permanent tissue which develops from primary meristematic tissue. It functions for the transportation of water and minerals in the plant.

Ans. If protoxylem lies next to phloem, the arrangement of the xylem is called as exarch. It is found in roots.

Q. 3 What is the function of phloem parenchyma?

Thinking Process Phloem is complex conductive tissue responsible for conduction of food material to all parts of the plant. It has four kinds of cells-sieve tube/cell, phloem parenchyma, phloem fibre and companion cells.

Ans. The main function of phloem parenchyma is to store food and other substances like resins, latex and mucilage. They also help in transport of food.

Q. 4 What is present on the surface of the leaves which helps the plant prevent loss of water but is absent in roots?

Thinking Process Plants continuously lose water from their body surface, specially leaves through the process of transpiration. To prevent this loss, different plants have devised different mechanisms to prevent this loss of water.

Ans. **Cuticle** It is a waxy coating covering the entire plant body surface. It is absent in roots, it prevents the loss of water through the surface of the plant body.

Q. 5 What is the epidermal cell modification in monocot plants which prevents water loss?

Ans. **Bulliform cells** prevent water loss. Bulliform or motor cells are modified epidermal cells present in monocots or grasses. Under stressed conditions, they help in shutting down stomata and thus, reduce water loss through transpiration.

Q. 6 What part of the plant would show the following?
(a) Radial vascular bundle
(b) Polyarch xylem
(c) Well developed pith

Thinking Process Plant tissues exhibit special characteristics in root, stem and leaves. Just by looking at them, it can be confirmed which tissue is from which part of the plant.

Ans. (a) **Radial Vascular Bundle** The xylem and phloem are present on the separate radii of the root. This arrangement of vascular bundle is known as radial vascular bundle.

(b) **Polyarch Xylem** When many strands of xylem are present, it is referred to as polyarch condition. This is a characteristic feature of monocot root.

(c) **Well Developed Pith** Dicot stem and monocot roots have well developed pith formed of parenchymatous cell with intercellular spaces.

Q. 7 What are the cells that make the leaves curl in plants during water stress?

Thinking Process Plant loses water continuously by the process of transpiration. It is called the 'necessary Evil'. The plants have developed certain structures and mechanism to combat this problem.

Ans. **Bulliform cells** are bubble shaped cells present in grasses. Loss of turgor pressure in these cells causes leaf to curl during water stress, thus reduce transpiration.

Q. 8 What constitutes the cambial ring?

Thinking Process Cambium is a lateral meristematic tissue. It is found in dicot plants and is responsible for secondary growth of stem and roots.

Ans. **Interfascicular** and **Intrafascicular** cambia together form a ring of cambium called **cambial ring**. It is formed due to the meristematic activity of cambium. The cambium which is found between the xylem and phloem is called **fascicular** or **Intrafascicular cambium** and the newly formed cambium between the two vascular bundle is known as **Interfascicular cambium**.

Q. 9 Give one basic functional difference between phellogen and phelloderm.

Ans. The paric functional difference between Phellogen and phelloderm is that Phellogen is a meristematic tissue that divides to produce new cells, while phelloderm is a permanent tissue that does not divide and serves to support and protect the plant.

Q.10 Arrange the following in the sequence you would find them in a plant starting from the periphery-phellem, phellogen, phelloderm.

Ans. Phellem or cork is the outer most layer, followed by phellogen (cork cambium) which in turn is followed by phelloderm (secondary cortex).

Q. 11 If one debarks a tree, what parts of the plant is being removed?

Thinking Process Bark is a dead tissue of the plant stem, usually present on dicotyledonous trees.

Ans. Debark means the removal of bark, *i.e.*, all tissue exterior to the vascular cambium, including secondary phloem.

Bark refers to a number of tissue types, *viz.*, periderm (phellogen, phellem and phelloderm) and secondary phloem.

Q. 12 The cross-section of a plant material showed the following features when viewed under the microscope.

(a) The vascular bundles were radially arranged.

(b) Four xylem strands with exarch condition of protoxylem.

To which organ should it be assigned?

Ans. Root is the organ which exhibits features given in the question. Vascular bundles are present on separate radii thus called **radial arrangement.** Protoxylem is towards periphery of root thus making exarch condition. Four xylem strands (tetrarch) condition is found in dicot roots.

Q. 13 What do hardwood and softwood stand for?

Thinking Process Wood is secondary xylem. It is formed as a result of secondary growth in gymnosperms and dicotyledonous angiosperms.

Ans. Hardwood refers to the wood from angiosperms which is typically denser and stronger due to presence of vessels in the xylem and lignin.

While **softwood** refers to the wood from gymnosperms which is typically lighter and less dense than hardwood with a simpler xylem structure lacking vessels primarily Contains tracheids.

Short Answer Type Questions

Q. 1 While eating peach or pear it is usually seen that some stone like structures get entangled in the teeth, what are these stone like structures called?

Thinking Process The peach or pear is a pome fruit. The fleshy thalamus is the edible part of the fruit.

Ans. The pulpy part of the peach and pear fruit contain the stone cell or scbrieids. which are an sclerenchymatous cells that are dead in nature.

Their function is to give mechanical support to the soft tissue.

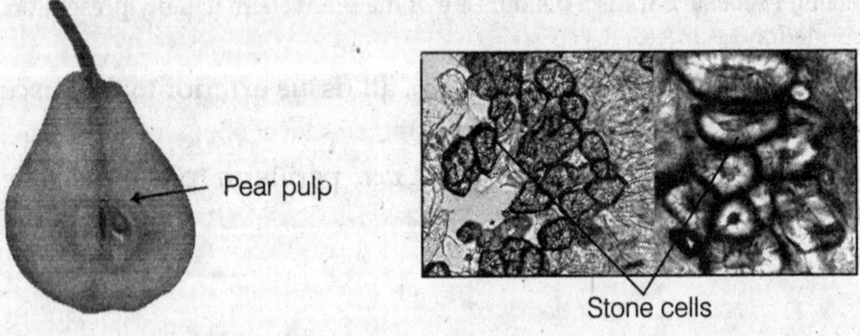

Q. 2 What is the commercial source of cork? How is it formed in the plant?

Ans. The commerical cork is obtained from the cork tissue of *Quercus suber,* which yields bottle cork. Cork is formed by cork cambium or phellogen cell. Cork cambium cells divide periclinally, producing cells towards the inside and outside. The cells produced towards the outside become suberised and dead. These are compactly packed in radial rows without intercellullar spaces and form cork of phellem. Cork is impervious to water due to suberin deposition and provides protection to the underlying tissues.

Q. 3 Below is a list of plant fibres. From which part of the plant these are obtained

(a) coir (b) hemp (c) cotton (d) jute

Ans. (a) **Coir** It is a natural fibre obtained from husk of coconut. It is the fibrous mesoderm of the coconut fruit *Cocos nucifera*.

(b) **Hemp** The fibre is obtained from the stems of *Cannabis sativa*. It is the bast fibre (soft or stem fibre) obtained from secondary phloem.

(c) **Cotton** The fibre is the epidermal growth of cotton (*Gossypium hirsutum*) seed. It is elongated structure made up of cellulose.

(d) **Jute** It is a natural bast fibre obtained from *Corchorus capsularis* and made up of cellulose and lignin.

Q. 4 What are the characteristic differences found in the vascular tissue of gymnosperms and angiosperms?

Thinking Process Vascular tissue is a complex tissue made up of more than one type of cell. In gymnosperms, it is in primitive form and advanced in angiosperms.

Ans. Difference between gymnosperm and angiosperm is as follows

Gymnosperm	Angiosperm
Gymnosperms lacks vessels in their xylem.	Vessels are present in the xylem.
Phloem lacks companion cells.	Phloem possesses companion cells.
Vascular tissue is less advanced.	Vascular tissue is more advanced and efficient.

Q. 5 Epidermal cells are often modified to perform specialised functions in plants. Name some of them and function they perform.

Thinking Process The epidermal tissue system forms the outer most covering of the whole plant body and comprises of one cell thick layer of epidermal tissue.

Ans. **Modification of Epidermal Cells**

The epidermal tissue has the following modifications

(i) **Root hair**

Structure	Function
Unicellular hairs are the extensions of epidermal cell in the root hair zone	It increases the surface area for absorption of water and minerals.

(ii) **Epidermal Appendages**

Structure	Function
These are called trichomes and are epidermal cell modifications. that can be unicellular or multicellular.	They help in preventing water loss due to transpiration.

Q. 6 The lawn grass (*Cyandon dactylon*) needs to be mowed frequently to prevent its overgrowth. Which tissue is responsible for its rapid growth?

Thinking Process Lawn grass is a runner stem modification of the family–Poaceae. It grows beautifully on the surface of the soil, thus covering entire soil surface, so, it is grown for landscaping in gardens.

Ans. The meristematic tissue is responsible for the rapid growth of the lawn grass. When the apex of grass is cut frequently, it leads to the growth of the lateral branches, that makes it more bushy.

Q. 7 Plants require water for their survival. But when watered excessively, plants die. Discuss.

Thinking Process Water is a need of every living being (all unicellular or multicellular organisms). So water is called 'Elixir of life'.

Ans. Plants use water for several metabolic process such as photosynthesis, transpiration and respiration. Plants die when watered in excess, because excess water removes the air trapped between the soil particles. So, plant roots do not get O_2 for respiration. Once root cells die, water and mineral absorption is stopped and this leads to gradual death of a plant.

Q. 8 A transverse section of the trunk of a tree shows concentric rings which are known as growth rings. How are these rings formed? What is the significance of these rings?

Thinking Process A tree grows in the height as well as width. The growth of width of a tree is a characteristic growth pattern resulted due to the activity of lateral meristematic tissues in dicot plants.

Ans. The concentric growth rings are called annual rings. These rings are formed due to the secondary growth. This occurs in dicot trees due to the activity of cambium which is a meristematic tissue.

The rate of activity of cambium is more in spring so the wood formed has larger and wider xylem cells, whereas wood formed in winter has narrower and smaller xylem elements. This results in the formation of rings called growth rings.

By counting these rings, age of the tree can be determined. This branch of science is known as **dendrochronology** or **growth ring analysis**.

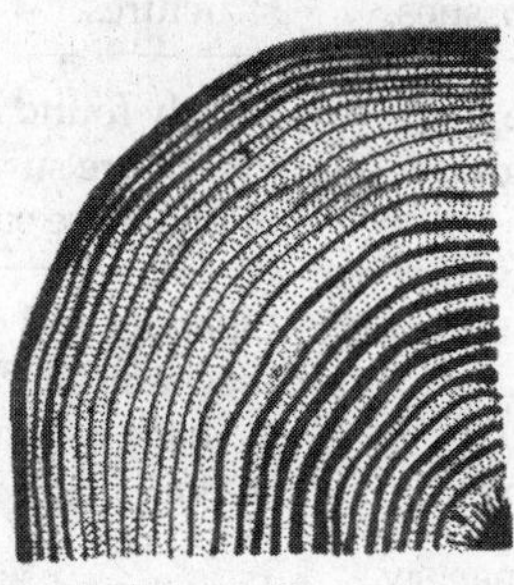

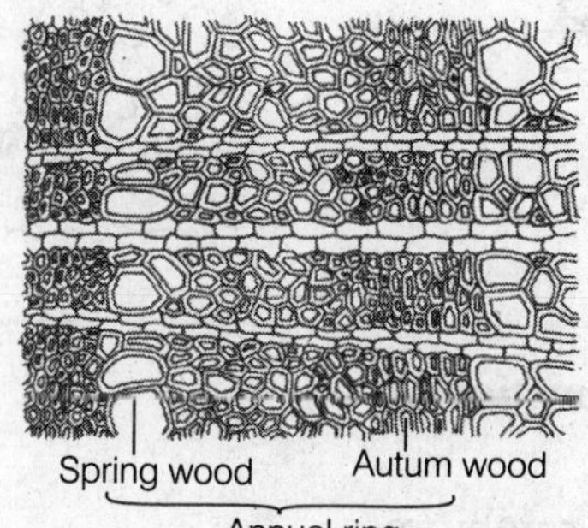

Diagram representing annual rings in an old stem

Q. 9 Trunks of some of the aged tree species appear to be composed of several fused trunks. Is it a physiological or anatomical abnormality? Explain in detail.

Ans. It is anatomical abnormality. It is an abnormal type of secondary growth, where a regular vascular cambium or cork cambium is not formed in its normal position. In case of old tree trunks, anomalous secondary growth produces cortical and medullary vascular bundles.

Thus, the additional or accessory vascular bundles give appearance of several fused trunks.

Q. 10 What is the difference between lenticels and stomata?

Thinking Process The gaseous exchange of mainly O_2 and CO_2 is the need of all plants. This occurs by means of several openings present in the plant body.

Ans. Difference between lenticels and stomata is as follows

Lenticels	Stomata
Lenticels are formed due to loosening of the epidermal and cortical tissues.	Stomata are specialised epidermal structures.
These are mostly found on the stem region. Lenticels do not have guard cells.	Mostly found on lower surface of leaves. Which are surrounded by guard cells. Stomata are surrounder by guard cells.
These openings are not regulated. They are used for removal of waste.	Opening and closing is a regulated mechanism. They are involved in gaseous exchange, removal of extra water and waste.

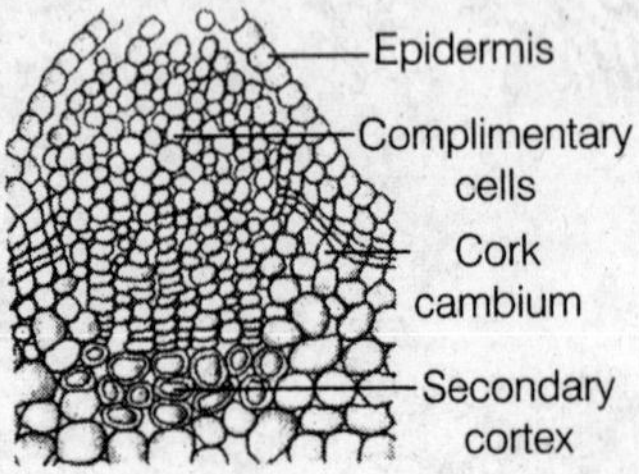

Lenticels

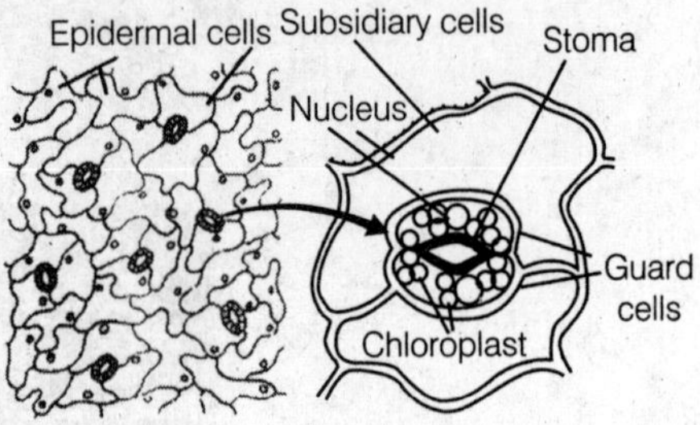

Stomata

Q. 11 Write the precise function of

(a) Sieve tube

(b) Interfascicular cambium

(c) Collenchyma

(d) Aerenchyma

Ans. (a) **Sieve tube**

It is present in the phloem tissue. Its function is the transportation of synthesised food throughout the plant.

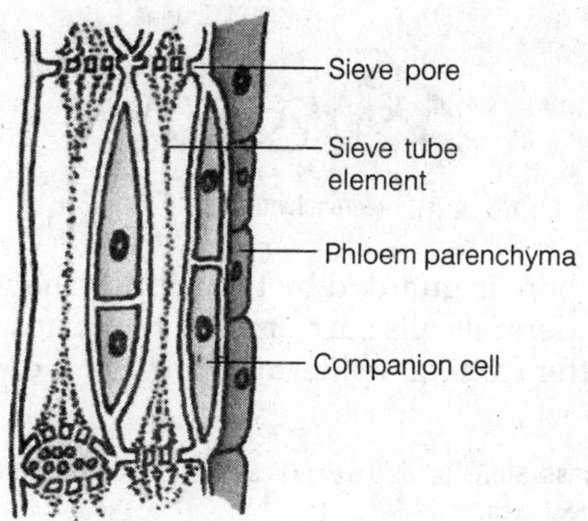

Structure of phleom tissue

(b) **Interfascicular Cambium**

Its function is to bring about secondary growth in the dicot stem and root. It is a kind of secondary meristematic tissue present in between two vascular bundles.

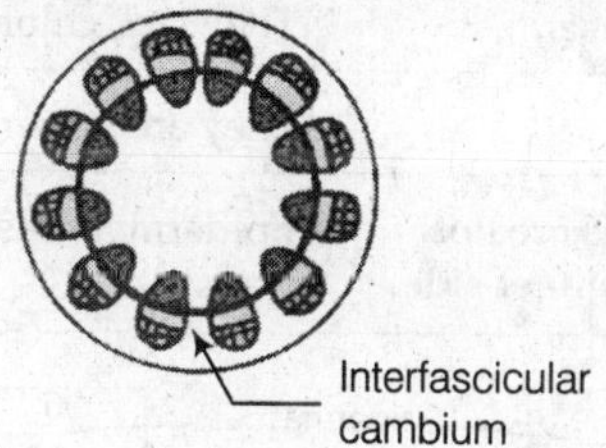

TS of stem of dicot plant

(c) **Collenchyma**

Its function is to provide mechanical support to young growing herbaceous stem. Its cells have **angular thickening** at corners.

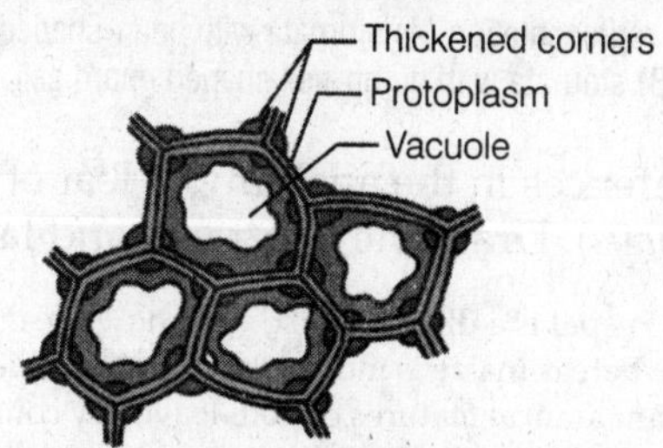

Collenchyma cells

(d) **Aerenchyma**

It provides buyoncy to the hydrophytic plants. It is a specialised parenchyma which have large air space.

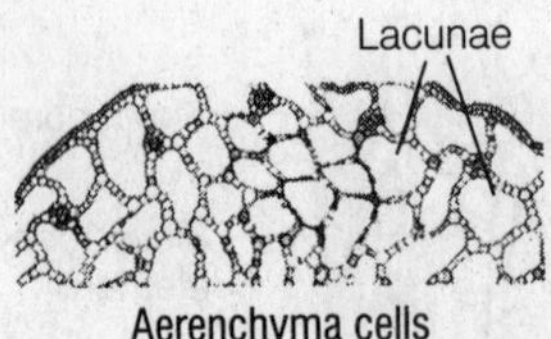

Aerenchyma cells

Q. 12 The stomatal pore is guarded by two kidney shaped guard cells. Name the epidermal cells surrounding the guard cells. How does a guard cell differ from an epidermal cell? Use a diagram to illustrate your answer.

Thinking Process Stomatal apparatus is a special modification of epidermal tissue present over leaf area.

Ans. The epidermal cells surrounding the guard cells of stomata are called **subsidiary cells.** Differences between guard cells and epidermal calls are as follows:

Guard cells	Epidermal cells
They are bean or kidney shaped.	They are barrel shaped.
They possess chloroplasts.	They lack chloroplasts.
They are smaller.	They are larger.
Cell walls of guard cells are not uniform and thicker at inner side	Epidermal cells have uniformly thin walls.

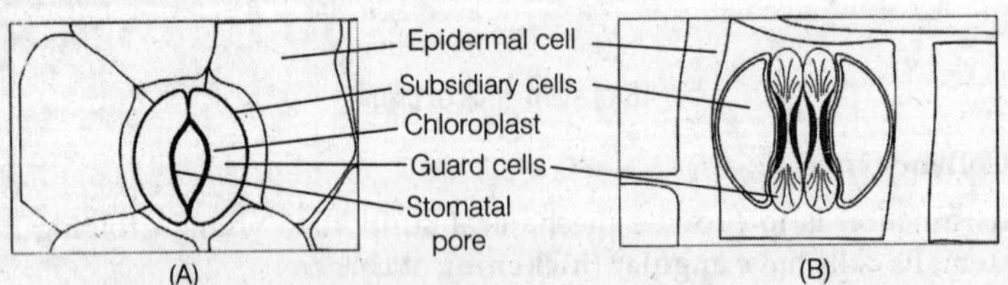

Diagrammatic representation (A) stomata with bean-shaped guard cells (B) stomata with dumb-bell shaped guard cell

Q. 13 Point out the differences in the anatomy of leaf of peepal (*Ficus religiosa*) and maize (*Zea mays*). Draw the diagrams and label the differences.

Thinking Process Peepal is a dicot plant so will show the characteristic feature of dorsiventral leaf whereas maize is monocotyledonous, so leaf will be of isobilateral type. Discuss the anatomical features of both leaves by comparing different tissues like epidermis, stomata, vascular bundles, etc.

Ans. Difference between *Ficus* leaf and maize leaf are as follows

Character	***Ficus* leaf** (Dicot Leaf)	**Maize leaf** (Monocot Leaf)
Type of leaf	Dorsiventral.	Isobilateral.
Stomata	Usually more on lower epidermis	Equal on both, lower and upper epidermis.
Mesophyll	Made up of two types of tissues (a) Lower spongy parenchyma with large intercellular spaces. (b) Upper palisade parenchyma.	Only spongy parenchyma is present which has very small intercellular spaces.
Bundle sheath	Made up of parenchyma just above and below the vascular bundle some parenchymatous cells or collenchymatous cells are present (up to epidermis).	Made of parenchyma, but just above and below, the vascular bundles are found made up of sclerenchymatous cells (up to epidermis).
Bulliform cells	Absent in dicot leaves.	Present, particularly in grasses (monocot leaves).

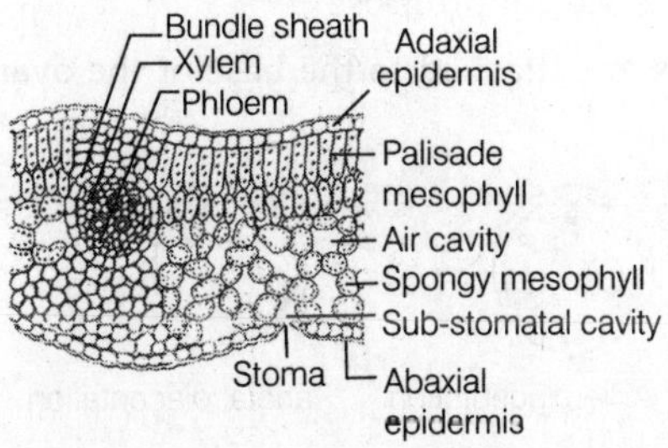

Dicot leaf

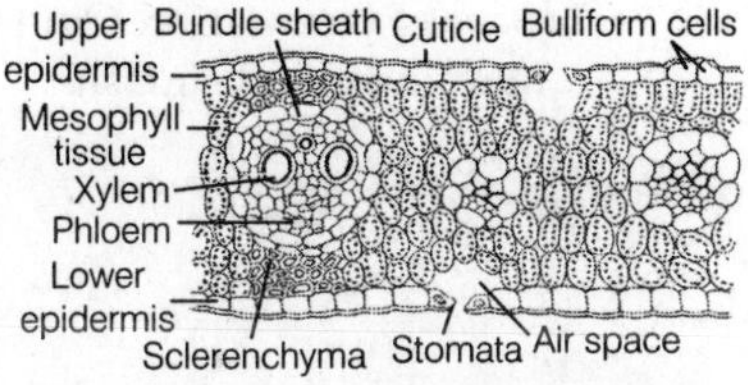

Monocot leaf

Q. 14 Palm is a monocotyledonous plant, yet it increases in girth. Why and how?

Ans. Palms, despite being monocotylednous plant shows secondary growth, *i.e.*, increase in girth. This is due to the division and enlargement of parenchymatous cells in the ground tissue. Thus, repeated divisions cause increase in girth of stem and this type of growth is referred to as **diffused secondary growth**.

Long Answer Type Questions

Q. 1 The arrangement of ovules within the ovary is known as placentation. What does the term placenta refer to? Draw various types of placentations in the flower as seen in T.S. aned V.S.

Ans. **Placenta** refers to the tissue within the **ovary** of a flower where the **ovules** are attached. It is composed of **vascular tissues** that supply nutrients to the developing ovules. The arrangement of the ovules on the placenta is known as **placentation**. It determines how the ovules are arranged within the ovary and varies across different plant species.

There are several types of placentation based on how the ovules are arranged in relation to the placenta. The common types of placentation seen in plants are

1. **Marginal Placentation** Ovules are arranged along the margin of a single locule (chamber) in the ovary. This is seen in legumes (*e.g.*, pea)
2. **Axile Placentation** Ovules are attached to the central axis of a compound ovary (with more than one locule).It is seen in tomato, lemon and lilies.
3. **Parietal Placentation** Ovules are attached to the inner walls of the ovary or to the partition of the ovary. It are seen in mustard, raspberry etc.
4. **Free Central Placentation** Ovules are attached to a central column within a single locule (chamber). It is seen in primrose.
5. **Basal Placentation** Ovules are attached to the base of the ovary. It is seen in sunflower and squash.

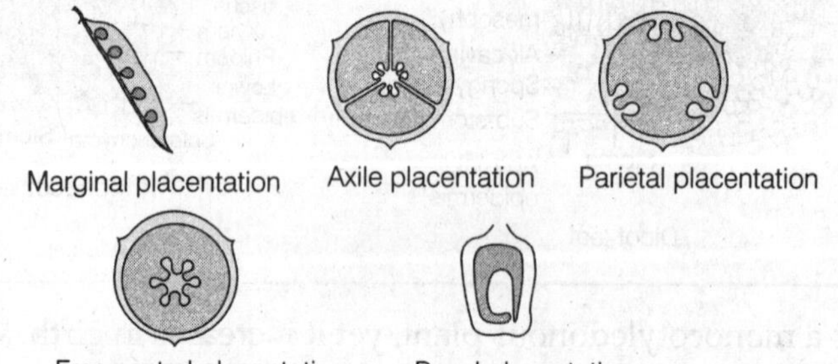

Q. 2 Deciduous plants shed their leaves during hot summer or in autumn. This process of shedding of leaves is called abscission. Apart from physiological changes what anatomical mechanism is involved in the abscission of leaves.

Thinking Process Deciduous means 'tending to fall off'. Leaves take up energy to maintain essential process for any plant. During peak hot summer/winter (adverse conditions) plants have to save energy to survive. So, they shed their leaves to conserve energy.

Ans. The process of shedding of leaves during hot summer or in autumn by deciduous plants is known as **abscission**. Anatomically, the cells of abscission zone are thin-walled and without deposition of lignin or suberin. At the time of abscission, the middle lamella may dissolve between the cells of two middle layers but the primary wall remains intact.

The middle lamella as well as the primary walls of the adjacent cells is dissolved. This is due to presence of enzymes like pectin and cellulose. Ultimately all the cells of middle layer found in the abscission layer gets dissolves completely. Thus, there is separation of plant organ, *i.e.*, leaf from the plant, wherever there is rainfall or wind.

Q. 3 Is *Pinus* an evergreen tree? Comment.

Ans. Evergreen plant are those which have leaves persistent in all the four seasons. In contrast to deciduous plants which completely loose their foliage during winter or dry season. *Pinus* belonging to gymnosperms is an evergeen tree. The flowering plants under conditions of extreme cold shed their leaves and become dormant. But *Pinus* due to the presence of thick, needle-like leaves having sunken stomata, reduce surface area and minimize the rate of transpiration.

The cold areas are both physiologically and physically dry due to scanty rainfall, precipitation as snow, decreased root absorption at low temperature and exposed habitats.

But, *Pinus* is well adapted to such conditions. It continues to manufacture food during this period and grown to dominate other plants. This shows that *Pinus* is an evergreen tree. It do not shed its leaves, *i.e.*, needless under any condition.

Q. 4 Assume that a pencil box held in your hand, represents a plant cell. In how many possible planes can it be cut? Indicate these cuts with the help of line drawings.

Ans. A plant cell can be cut in different planes. i.e. vertically horizontally and diagonally.

A. If a plant cell is cut in different planes it results in radial symmetry if each part is same.

B. If a plant cell is cut in two equal halves it result in bilateral symmetry.

Q.5 Each of the following terms has some anatomical significance. What do these terms mean? Explain with the help of line diagrams.

(a) Plasmodesmata

(b) Middle lamella

(c) Secondary wall

Ans. a. **Plasmodesmata** are **microscopic channels**which act as bridges between plant cells. They pass through the **cell wall** and connect the **cytoplasm** of adjacent plant cells.

Anatomical Significance Plasmodesmata play a crucial role in the movement of water, nutrients and signaling molecules between plant cells. They allow for cell-to-cell communication, making them important for maintaining the coordination of plant processes.

Structure: These are fine cytoplasmic threads that extend through the **primary cell wall** and are lined with the plasma membrane. They enable the exchange of materials between plant cells.

b. **Middle Lamella** It is the **layer** that **cements** adjacent plant cells together. It is primarily composed of **peçtin**, a polysaccharide.

Anatomical Significance The middle lamella plays a crucial role in maintaining the structural integrity of plant tissues by holding the cell walls of neighboring cells together.

Structure It is located between the **primary cell walls** of two adjacent plant cells, and its main component is **pectin**. It is the first layer formed during cell division.

c. **Secondary Wall** The **secondary wall** is a thickened layer of the **cell wall** found in certain plant cells, formed after the cell has stopped growing. It is usually deposited inside the **primary cell wall**.

Anatomical Significance The secondary wall provides **rigidity** and **strength** to plant cells. It is particularly important in cells that serve structural functions, such as **xylem vessels** and **sclerenchyma fibers**.

Structure: The secondary wall consists of multiple layers of cellulose, hemicellulose, and lignin, making it more **rigid** and **impermeable** than the primary wall. It is typically found in **mature cells** like those of **wood** (xylem) and **fibers**.

The line diagram is shown below.

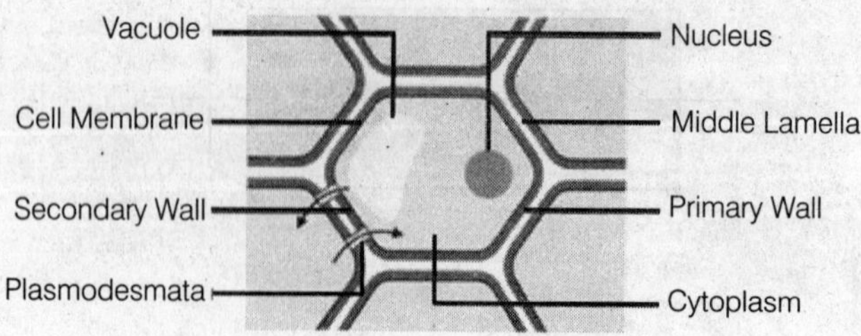

Q. 6 Distinguish between the following.

(a) Exarch and endarch
(b) Stele and vascular bundle
(c) Protoxylem and Metaxylem
(d) Interfascicular cambium and Intrafascicular cambium
(e) Open and closed vascular bundles
(f) Stem hair and root hair

Ans. Differences between the following

	Exarch Protoxylem	Endarch Protoxylem
(a)	In exarch condition, the protoxylem is present towards the periphery and metaxylem towards centre in vascular bundle, as it is found in roots.	In endarch condition, the protoxylem is present towards the centre and metaxylem towards periphery in the vascular bundle, as it is found in stem.

	Stele	Vascular Bundle
(b)	Stele refers to conducting tissue or the central part of root or stem in plants. It comprises of vascular tissue, ground tisssue, pith and limiting boundaries, *i.e.*, endodermis and pericycle.	Vascular bundle comprises of vascular tissues xylem and phloem. Some times cambium is also included as in dicots.

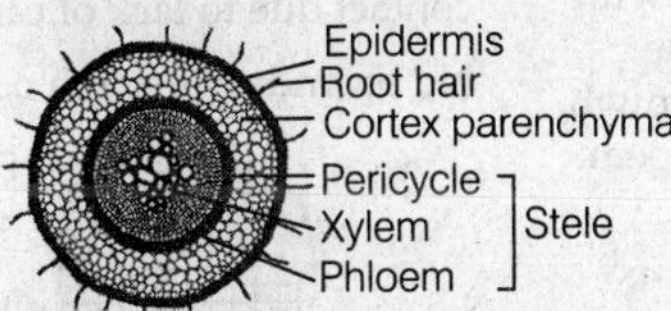

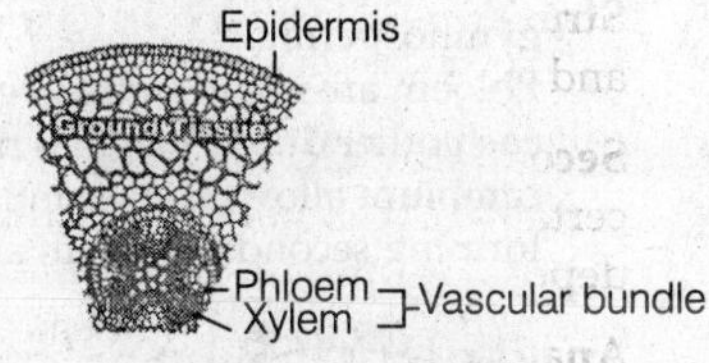

	Protoxylem	Metaxylem
(c)	It is the first or earlier formed xylem which matures before the growth and differentiation of plant organs. Protoxylem elements are smaller in diameter.	It is the later formed xylem which matures after the growth and differentiation of plant organs. Metaxylem delements are broader and greater in diameter.
	Fibres are also absent.	Fibres may be present.

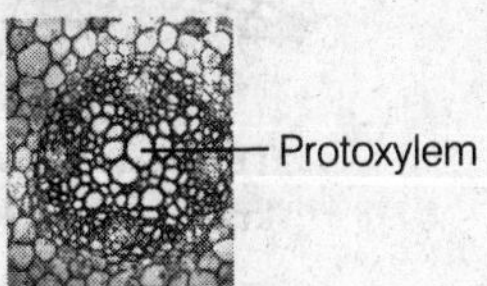

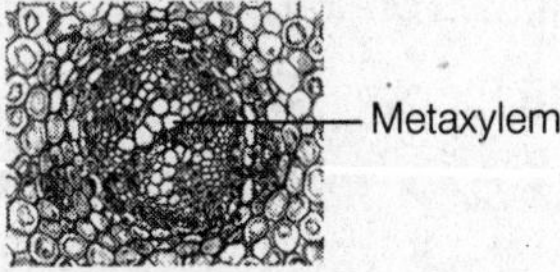

	Intrafascicular Cambium	Inter fascicular Cambium
(d)	Cambium present in between the primary xylem and primary phloem is called. Intra fascicular cambium, as in dicot stems.	The cambium present in between the two vascular bundles making the cambium continuous and forming a complete ring of cambium is called interfascicular cambium.

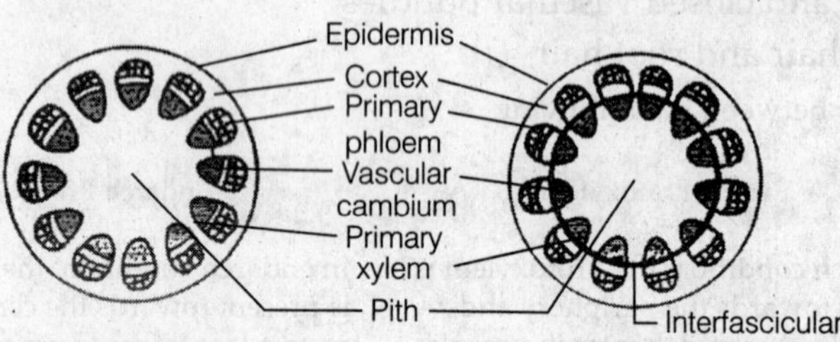

	Open Vascular Bundle	Closed Vascular Bundle
(e)	Cambium is present between xylem and phloem Intrafascicular cambium between the phloem and xylem is present. It occurs in the stems of dicot and gymnosperm Phloem are not in indirect contact with each other due to cambial ring. The cambium allows for secondary, growth, forming secondary xylem and phloem.	Combium is not present in between the xylem and phloem Intrafascicular cambium is absent. It occurs in leaves and monocot stems. Xylem and phloem are in direct contact due to lack of cambium ring No secondary growth occurs

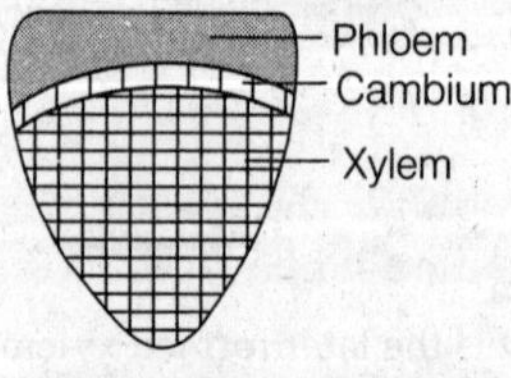

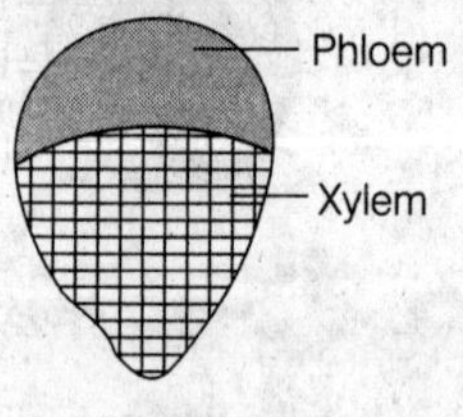

	Root Hair	Stem Hair
(f)	Root hairs are unicellular	Stem hairs are multicellular

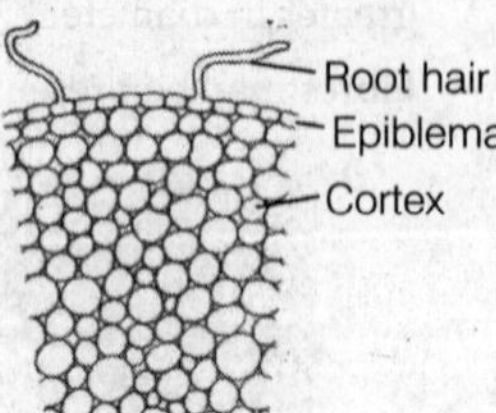

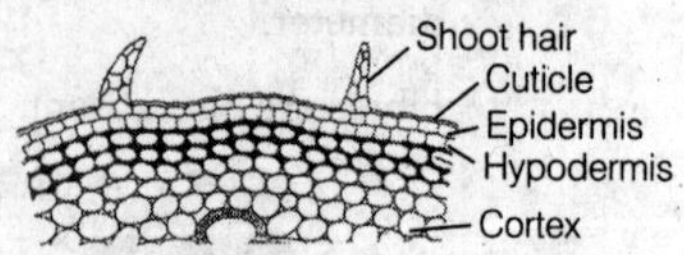

	Root Hair	Stem Hair
	They are the extensions of the epidermal cells in root. It increase the surface area of root for absorption of water and minerals.	They are epidermal outgrowths known as trichomes. They help in preventing water loss due to transpiration.

Chapter

07

Structural Organisation in Animals

Multiple Choice Questions (MCQs)

Choose the correct answer from the given four options in the following questions.

Q. 1 Which one of the following types of cell is involved in making of the inner walls of large blood vessels?

(a) Cuboidal epithelium
(b) Columnar epithelium
(c) Squamous epithelium
(d) Stratified epithelium

Thinking Process Epithelium is the tissue covering the external and internal exposed lining of the body cavity. Blood vessels lymph vessels, glands and their ducts are derived from epithelium. Epithelium originates from three germ layers, *i.e.,* ectoderm (e.g., skin, epidermis) mesoderm (e.g., peritoneum) and endoderm (e.g., gut epithelium).

Ans. *(c)* **Squamous epithelium** is involved in the making of the inner walls of large blood vessels, where it is known as endothelium.

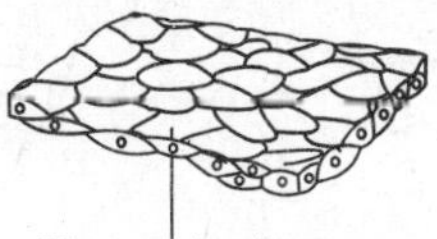

Squamous epithelium

Q. 2 To which one of the following categories does adipose tissue belong?

(a) Epithelial
(b) Connective
(c) Muscular
(d) Neural

Ans. *(b)* **Adipose tissue** is a type of connective tissue, located mainly beneath the skin. The cells of adipose tissue are specialised in storing fats in the form of fat globules.

Epithelial tissue formed of a single layer of cells, resting on the basement membrane. These can be many layers without basement membrane.

Muscular tissue has contractibility, it can be shorten forcefully and relaxed state is regained. These are also called **muscle fibres** as they are long and elongated.

Neural tissue is made up of **neurons** and **neuroglial cells,** essential in transmitting electrical signals *via* neurotransmitter from one part of body to the another. *e.g.,* CNS (Central Nervous System) and PNS (Peripheral Nervous System), are the chief components involved in nervous system.

Q. 3 Which one of the following is not a connective tissue?

(a) Bone
(b) Cartilage
(c) Blood
(d) Muscles

Ans. ***(d)*** Muscle is not a connective tissue. It is composed of long, cylindrical, numerous fine fibrils called myofibrils.

Bone is a solid, rigid, connective tissue.

Blood is a fluid connective tissue.

Cartilage is a solid but semi-rigid and flexible connective, tissue.

Q. 4 Setae help in locomotion in earthworm but are not uniformly, present in all the segments. They are present in

(a) 1st segment (b) last segment

(c) clitellar segment (d) 20th - 22nd segment

Thinking Process Setae or chaetae are the locomotary structures in earthworm. They hold the substratum firmly, helps earthworm to move through, burrows.

Ans. ***(d)*** In earthworm, except for the 1st, last and clitellar segment, each segment bears a ring of tiny, curved, chitinous structures called **setae**.

Q. 5 Which one of the following statements is true for cockroach?

(a) The number of ovarioles in each ovary are ten

(b) The larval stage is called caterpillar

(c) Anal styles are absent in females

(d) They are ureotelic

Thinking Process Anal styles are a pair of short thread like structures found in male cockroach. These act as a sense organ and allows the cockroach to run in opposite direction.

Ans. ***(c)*** Anal styles in male cockroach are present in the 9th segment. These are absent in females.

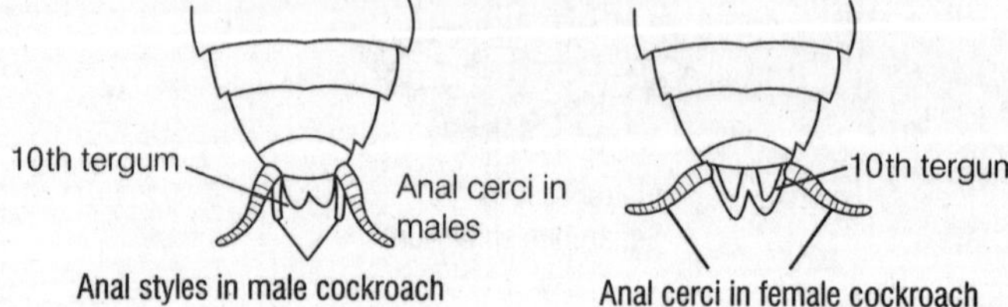

Anal styles in male cockroach   Anal cerci in female cockroach

Other statement are incorrect because

The female cockroach has paired ovaries, each consisting of 8 ovarioles

Cockroaches possess **nymphal stage** instead of larval stage.

Excretory organ of cockroach is **Malpighian tubules,** they remove the nitrogenous waste in the form of uric acid. *i.e.,* they are uricotelic.

Q. 6 Match the following.

	Column I		Column II
A.	Adipose tissue	1.	Nose
B.	Stratified epithelium	2.	Blood
C.	Hyaline cartilage	3.	Skin
D.	Fluid connective tissue	4.	Fat storage

Codes

	A	B	C	D		A	B	C	D
(a)	1	2	3	4	(b)	4	3	1	2
(c)	3	1	4	2	(d)	2	1	4	3

Thinking Process Connective tissues are the most diverse tissues, with variety of functions. They range in consistency from gel-like softness of areolar connective tissue to the hardness of the bone.
This tissue connects body with the vital organs and plays an important role in variety of functions like protection, secretion and absorption.

Ans. *(b)* **Adipose Tissue** are specialised tissue associated with storing fats in the form of oil droplets.

Stratified Epithelium occurs in the epidermis of the skin of terrestrial vertebrates.

Hyaline Cartilage is a semi-transparent cartilage and is extremely strong but very flexible and elastic. It consists of living cells, chondrocytes, which are situated far apart in fluid filled spaces, the lacunae. Nose is composed of hayline cartilage.

Fluid Connective Tissue is a type of connective tissue in which the matrix is in the liquid form. It is known as plasma. Types of fluid connective tissue are blood and lymph.

Q. 7 Match the following.

	Column I		Column II
A.	Hermaphrodite	1.	Produces blood cells and haemoglobin
B.	Direct development	2.	Testis and ovary in the same animal
C.	Chemoreceptor	3.	Larval form absent
D.	Blood gland in earthworm	4.	Sense of chemical substances

Codes

	A	B	C	D		A	B	C	D
(a)	2	3	4	1	(b)	3	2	4	1
(c)	1	3	2	4	(d)	2	4	3	1

Ans. *(a)* **Hermaphrodites** bear testis and ovary within the same organism, (*e.g.*, earthworm or *Pheretima*).

Direct development occurs in organisms in which there is no larval stage in the life-cycle and therefore no metamorphosis takes place, (*e.g.*, *Pheretima* and *Lumbricus*).

Chemoreceptors or **chemosensors** are the sensory receptors used in sensing chemical substances,(*e.g.*, olfactory receptor and taste buds in mammals).

Blood gland in earthworm are specialised glands that are associated with the generation of blood cells and haemoglobin in *Pheretima*.

Q. 8 Match the following with reference to cockroach and choose the correct option.

	Column I		Column II
A.	Phallomere	1.	Chain of developing ova
B.	Gonopore	2.	Bundles of sperm
C.	Spermatophore	3.	Opening of the ejaculatory duct
D.	Ovarioles	4.	The external genitalia

Codes

	A	B	C	D		A	B	C	D
(a)	3	4	2	1	(b)	4	3	2	1
(c)	4	2	3	1	(d)	2	4	3	1

Ans. ***(b)***

A. → (4) B. → (3) C. → (2) D. → (1)

Phallomere (also called as pseudopenis), is the external genitalia in cockroach.

Gonopore is a specific reproductive pore or aperture which acts as an opening of ejaculatory duct.

Spermatophore is a capsule or bundle of sperms formed by male cockroach containing spermatozoa during copulation. It is transferred as a whole in to the female.

Ovarioles are group of ovarian tubules contain chains of developing ova.

Q. 10 Match the following.

	Column I		Column II
A.	Touch	1.	Nasal epithelium
B.	Smell	2.	Foramen magnum
C.	Cranial nerves	3.	Sensory papillae
D.	Medulla oblongata	4.	Peripheral nervous system

Codes

	A	B	C	D		A	B	C	D
(a)	3	1	2	4	(b)	2	1	4	3
(c)	3	4	2	1	(d)	3	1	4	2

Ans. ***(d)*** A. → (3) B. → (1) C. → (4) D. → (2)

Sensory papillae are sensitive to touch.

Nasal epithelium is specialised epithelial tissue inside the nasal cavity that is involved in smell.

Crainal nerves are a part of peripheral nervous system. These nerves emerge from brain and the brain stem.

Foramen magnum is a large opening in the occipital bone of the cranium, through which spiral cord (extension of medulla oblongata) enters and exits the skull vault.

Very Short Answer Type Questions

Q. 1 State the number of segments in earthworm which are covered by a prominent dark band or clitellum.

Thinking Process Clitellum is a saddle shaped region made of glandular tissue in the body of earthworm, after copulation secretes a cocoon in which the eggs and sperms are deposited for fertilisation.

Ans. **Segments 14-16** are covered by a prominent dark band of glandular tissue called clitellum in a mature earthworm, which secretes mucus and albumen that helps in the formation of cocoon and is used for fertilisation of eggs and sperms.

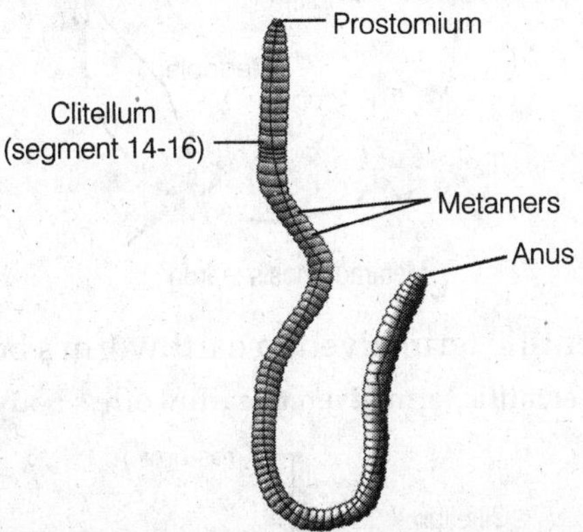

Dorsal view of earthworm showing clitellum and metamer

Q. 2 Where are sclerites present in cockroach?

Thinking Process Sclerites are hardened plates present in the exoskeleton of cockroach.

Ans. Sclerites are present in all the body segments of cockroach. *These are of two types*

Dorsal sclerites often known as **tergites**, and

Ventral sclerites which are referred to as **sternites.**

Q. 3 How many times do nymphs moult to reach the adult form of cockroach?

Ans. The nymph grows by moulting a about 13 times to reach the adult form. In cockroach, the development is indirect and paurometabolous. It means, it has three stages. *i.e.*, egg, nymph and adult. The nymph resembles adult except for undeveloped wings and genitalia.

Q. 4 Identify the sex of a frog in which sound producing vocal sacs are present.

Ans. In amphibians, sex of frogs can be distinguished with the presence of sound producing vocal sacs. These organs are present in males which make them croak louder, than females, so as to attract females for mating.

Q. 5 Name the process by which a tadpole develops into an adult frog.

Thinking Process Metamorphosis is an essential feature in growth for lower animals including both invertebrates and vertebrates. In this phenomenon, organism shows change in physical form and structure especially during the growth process.

Ans. Metamorphosis is the process by which a tadpole develops into an adult frog.

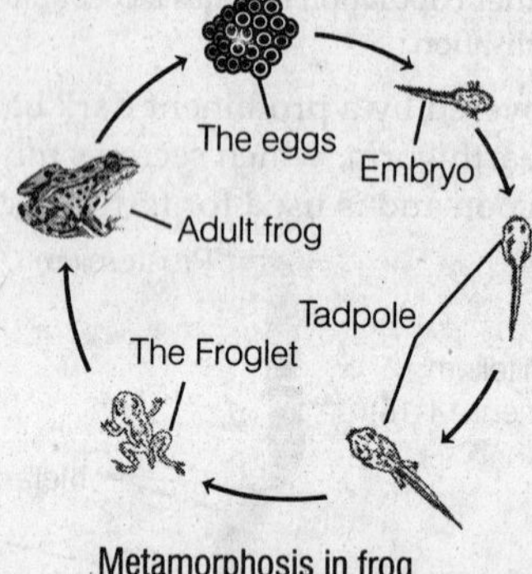

Metamorphosis in frog

Q. 6 What is the scientific term given to earthworm's body segments?

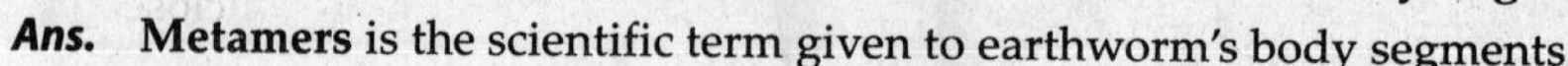

Ans. **Metamers** is the scientific term given to earthworm's body segments.

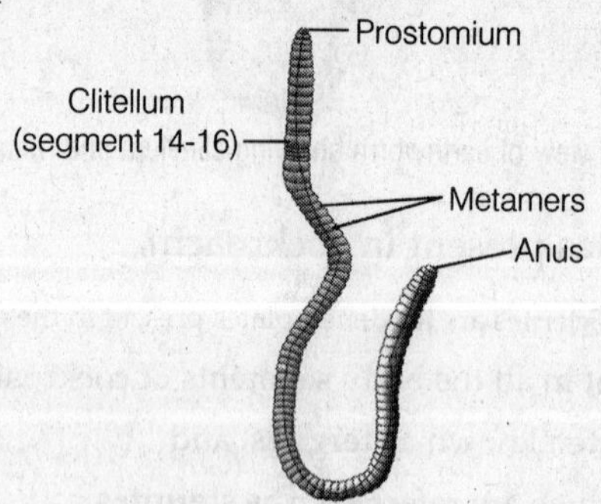

Dorsal view of earthworm showing clitellum and metamers

Q. 7 A muscle fibre tapers at both ends and does not show striations. Name the muscle fibre.

Ans. Smooth muscle fibres tapers at both the ends (fusiform) and do not show striations. They are also called involuntary muscles.

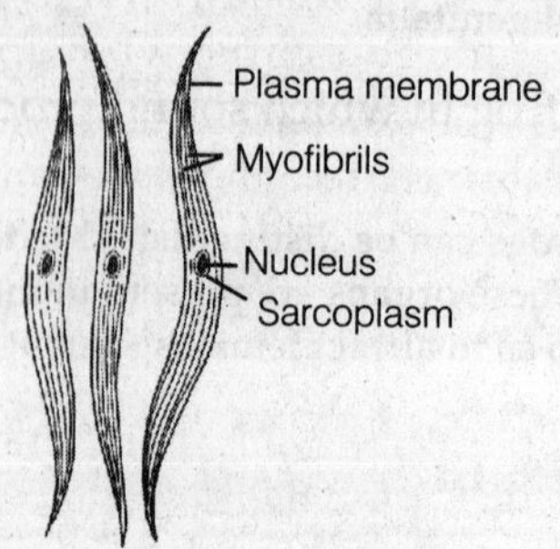

Muscle Non-striated smooth muscles

Q. 8 Name the different cell junctions found in tissues

Ans. The different cell junctions found in tissues are

(i) **Tight junctions** are regions where plasma membrane of adjacent epithelial cells are held close together. They check the movement of material between them.

(ii) **Gap junctions** are meant for chemical exchange between adjacent cells.

(iii) **Adhering junctions** perform connecting function to keep neighbouring cells together.

Q. 9 Give two identifying features of an adult male frog.

Ans. The two identifying features of an adult male frog are as follows

(a) **Vocal Sacs** These are loose skin folds on throat of male frogs for producing louder croak.

(b) **Nuptial Pad** This copulatory pad present on the first digit of the forelimb of male frog and helps in clasping (holding) female during amplexus (means mating position).

Q. 10 Which mouth part of cockroach is comparable to our tongue?

Ans. **Hypopharynx** acts as a tongue in cockroach and lies within a cavity enclosed by the mouth parts.

Q. 11 The digestive system of frog is made of the following parts. Arrange them in an order beginning from mouth.
Mouth, oesophagus, buccal cavity, stomach, intestine, cloaca, rectum, cloacal aperture.

Ans. The correct arrangement of the parts of digestive system in frog is as follows

Mouth → Buccal cavity → Oesophagus → Stomach → Intestine → Rectum → Cloaca → Cloacal aperture.

Q. 12 What is the difference between cutaneous and pulmonary respiration?

Ans. In frog respiration takes place *via* two means, *i.e.*, skin (cutaneous) and lungs (pulmonary).

Cutaneous respiration occurs through highly vascular moist skin. It takes place in water as well as land.

Pulmonary respiration occurs through lungs. It takes place outside the water.

Q. 13 Special venous connection between liver and intestine and between kidney and intestine is found in frog, what are they called?

Ans. Special venous connection between liver and intestine is called hepatic portal system and venus connection between the kidney and the lower parts of the frog is called **renal portal system.**

Short Answer Type Questions

Q. 1 Give the location of hepatic caeca in a cockroach. What is their function?

Ans. Hepatic or gastric caecae are 6-8 narrow and hollow blind tubules which are present at the junction of foregut and midgut. The hepatic caecae are similar to vertebrate liver, secretes digestive juices and help in the digestion.

Q. 2 Frogs are beneficial for mankind, justify the statement.

Ans. Frogs are beneficial for mankind because they eat insects and thus, protect our crops. They serve as an important link of food chains and hence food web in the ecosystem, thus maintaining the ecological balance. Some countries use the muscular legs of frog as a food source.

Q. 3 The body of sponges does not possess tissue level of organisation though it is made of thousands of cells. Comment.

Ans. The body of sponges is made up of thousands of cells, but it does not possess the tissue level of organisation because their cells are **loosely organised** and **do not form true tissues**. In sponges, cells are specialised for specific functions, such as digestion, support, and reproduction, but they **do not work together in a coordinated manner** to form distinct tissue layers. Instead, the cells are arranged in a **mesohyl**, a gelatinous matrix, and can function somewhat independently. This lack of true tissue organisation is a characteristic feature of the **cellular level of organisation** in sponges.

Q. 4 Structural organisation in animals attains different levels as cell-organ-organ system. What is missing in this chain? Mention the significance of such an organisation.

Ans. **Tissue** is missing in the chain. Structural organisation can be shown as cell → tissue → organ → organ → system.

Number of cells together form tissue, number of tissue together form organ and multiple organ together form an organ-system.

In organisms like *Hydra,* the body is comprised of thousands of cells in which each cell works independently whereas in a complex body system as that in humans, billions of cells perform various functions together by connecting each other through connective tissue.

Q. 5 Stratified epithelial cells have limited role in secretion. Justify their role in our skin.

Ans. **Stratified epithelium** Stratified epithelial cells is composed of keratin protein, which forms the keratinised stratified squamous epithelium in the skin. These cells primarily act as a protective barrier, shielding against mechanical injury, microbial invasian, and dehydration.

Q. 6 How does a gap junctions facilitate intercellular communication?

Ans. Gap junctions facilitate intercellular communication by allowing the direct transfer of small signaling molecules from cell to cell. These are fine hydrophilic channels between adjacent animal cells that are formed from protein called **connexin.**

Each connexon consists of six proteins subunits that form a hydrophilic channel. pH and Ca^{2+} ion concentration controls, opening or closing of channels.

Q. 7 Why are blood, bone and cartilage called connective tissue?

Ans. Connective tissue provides the structural framework and support to different organ forming tissue. Blood is a fluid or vascular connective tissue, which connects various organs and transports substances from one place to another.

Bone is a solid, rigid and strong skeletal connective tissue, which support the body and help in locomotion. Cartilage is also a skeletal connective tissue, not as rigid bone but pliable and resist compression. It plays a role in support and protection, it present in tip of nose, outer ear, joints etc.

Q. 8 Why are neurons called excitable cells? Mention special features of the membrane of the neuron.

Ans. **Neurons** are called excitable cells because these membranes are in a polarised state. Different types of ion channels are present in the neural membrane, *i.e.*, are selectively permeable to different ions. When a neuron is suitably stimulated, an electric disturbance is generated, which swiftly travels along its plasma membrane. Arrival of the disturbance at the neuron's ending or output zone, triggers events that may cause stimulation of adjacent neuron. These are excitable cells due to differential concentration gradient of ions (specially N^+ and K^+) across the membrane.

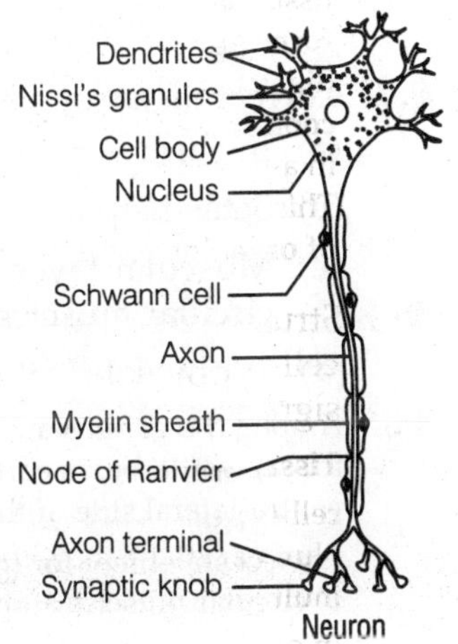

Neuron

The special features of membrane of neuron are

(i) **Excitability** The ability to percieve stimulus and enter a state activity caused by change in electrial potential difference across its covering membrane.

(ii) **Conductivity** Change in potential difference, spreads through the membrane to the whole neuron.

(iii) **Connectivity** Neurons are connected to other, neurons receiving and transmitting impulses to various directions.

(iv) **Response** The processed message may elicit a response in the form of a sensation.

Q. 9 Why earthworm is called the friend of farmer?

Ans. Earthworms are called 'friends of farmer' because they make burrows in the soil and make it porous which helps plants in respiration and penetration within the soil.

The worm casting is rich in urea and ammonia which improves fertility of soil. Thus, they are of much importance to mankind and used in vermicomposting

Q. 10 How do you distinguish between dorsal and ventral surface of the body of earthworm?

Ans. The body of earthworm can be distinguished into dorsal and ventral sides due to the presence of certain peculiar feature that are given below:

(i) The dorsal surface is darker than the ventral surface because it is marked by a **dark median mid dorsal** line along the longitudinal axis of body. This is due to dorsal blood vessel, seen through integument.

(ii) On the ventral surface **genital openings** (pores), both male and female are present

(iii) Genital papilla is located on ventral surface and help in copulation.

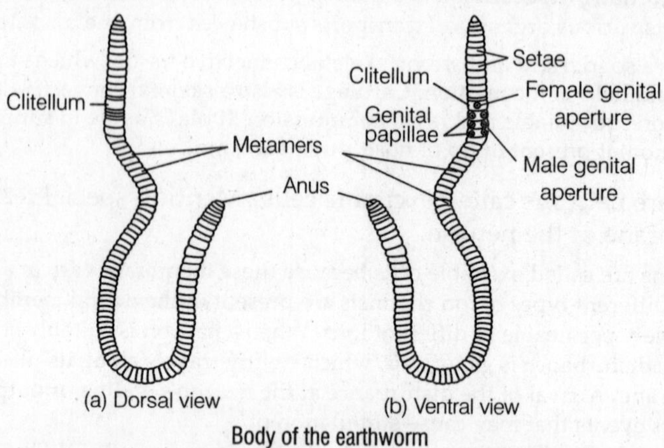

Body of the earthworm

Q. 11 Correct the wrong statements among the following.

(a) In earthworm, a single male genital pore is present.

(b) Setae help in locomotion of earthworm.

(c) Muscular layer in the body wall of earthworm is made up of only circular muscles.

(d) Typhlosole is the part of intestine of earthworm.

Ans. Among the given statements (b) and (d) are correct statement. Correct statement for (a) would be, in earthworm there are a pair of male genital pore lying on the ventro-lateral side of the **18th segment**.

Correct statement for (c) Muscular layer in earthworm consists of an outer layer of circular muscles and the inner layer of longitudinal muscles.

Q. 12 Why nephridia in earthworm that are basically similar in structure classified into three types? Mention the names of each.

Ans. Nephridia are the excretory organs in earthworms. They are associated with excretory and osmoregulatory functions.

The nephridia occur in all segments of earthworm except the first two segments. Nephridia in earthworms are classified into three types based on their location and structure which are as follows :

1. **Protonephridia** Found in the anterior segments (1–3) these nephridia are involved in excretion and osmoregulation. They consist of a flame cell that helps in filtering waste products.

2. **Metanephridia** Found in the posterior segments, metanephridia are the primary excretory organs in earthworms. Each segment has a pair of these, and they filter waste from the coelomic fluid and excrete it through the nephridiopore.

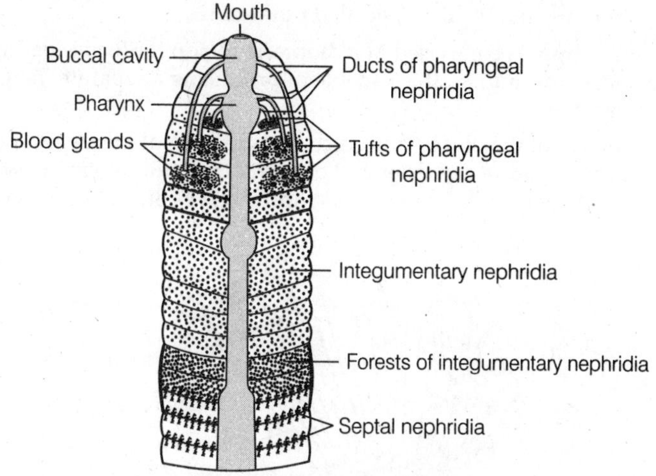

Nephridia in earthworm

3. **Septal Nephridia** These are present on both sides of inter segmental septa of the segment starting from 15th to the last that open into intestine. They are enteronephric.

Q. 13 Common name of some animals are given in Column A, write their scientific name in Column B.

Column A	Column B
A. Tiger	....
B. Peacock	....
C. Housefly	....

Ans. Here are the scientific names for the animals listed:

(a) Tiger: *Panthera tigris* (b) Peacock: *Pavo cristatus*

(c) Housefly: *Musca domestica*

Q. 14 Complete the following statement.

(a) In cockroach grinding of food particle is performed by ....

(b) Malpighian tubules help in removal of ....

(c) Hind gut of cockroach is differentiated into ....

(d) In cockroach blood vessels open into spaces called ....

Ans. (a) **Gizzard** It is a muscular and greatly folded structure which marks the end of foregut and bears six plates with teeth for crushing and grinding the food.

(b) **Malpighian tubules** They help in the removal of nitrogenous wastes in arthropods, hence are excretory in function.

(c) **Ileum, colon and rectum** and rectum opens through the anus.

(d) **Haemocoel** It is the body cavity of cockroach divided into sinuses and contains visceral organs of cockroach floating in haemolymph.

Q. 15 Mention special features of eye in cockroach.

Ans. The eyes of cockroach are large, sessile, paired, bean-shaped and present on either side of head. These are compound in nature. Each compound eye consists of a large number of visual units called **ommatidia.**

Each ommatidium is composed of a diopteric region for focussing light and reticular (receptor) region. It is capable of producing a separate image of a small part of object seen.

Thus, the image of the object viewed consists of several pieces and hence known as **mosaic image**. From the inner end of each ommatidium, fine nerve fibres arise, all of which combine to form one **optic nerve** connected to the brain.

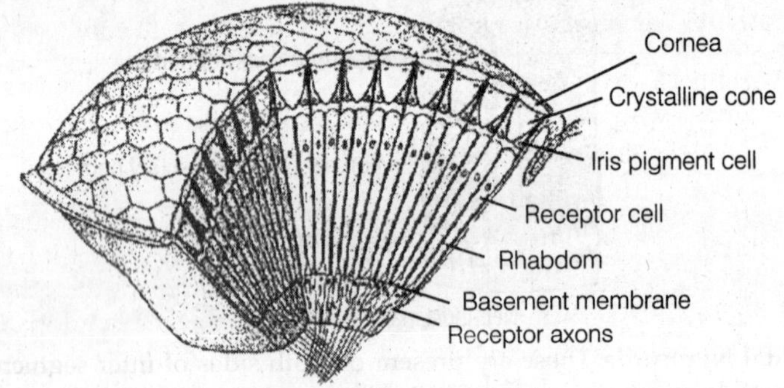

Compound eyes in arthropods

Q. 16 Frog is a poikilotherm, exhibits camouflage and undergoes aestivation and hibernation, how are all these beneficial to it?

Thinking Process An adaptation, also called as adaptive tract in biology, is a trait with a current functional role in the life history of an organism that is maintained and evolved by means of natural selection and evolution and help organism in its survival.

Ans. Frog is a poikilotherm (cold blooded animal), *i.e.*, it can not regulate its body temperature according to its environment.

For withstanding very cold temperatures, it undergoes winter sleep (hibernation) and summer sleep in hot temperatures (aestivation). During this period, it lives in a dormant stage with very minimal vital body activities.

Also, frog is capable of changing its body colour, with the change in its surrounding and climatic conditions. This capability in frog is called as **camouflage** it helps to escape from the predators, an essential survival parameter for living.

Q. 17 Write the functions in brief in column II, appropriate to the structures given in column I.

Column I	Column II
A. Nictitating membrane	1. ....
B. Tympanum	2. ....
C. Copulatory pad	3. ....

Ans. (a) **Nictitating Membrane** It protects the eye from water and any other damaging matter by covering the eye ball of forg.

(b) **Tympanum** It is present on each side of frog's head and is involved in the hearing process.

(c) **Copulatory Pad** These pads are present in the limbs of the male frog and help in copulation by holding the female during mating.

Q. 18 Write the appropriate type of tissues in column II according to the functions mentioned in column I.

	Column I	Column II
A.	Secretion and absorption	1. ....
B.	Protective covering	2. ....
C.	Linking and supporting framework	3. ....

Ans. (a) **Simple Columnar Epithelium** This epithelium lines the stomach, intestine, gall bladder etc. It forms gastric and intestinal glands, where it has a secretory role and is called as glandular epithelium. In intestinal mucosa, this epithelium has microvilli which increase the absorptive surface area and is called brush bordered columnar epithelium.

(b) **Stratified Epithelium** These are made up of more than one layer of epithelial cells (also called compound epithelium). They are the only cells of the deepest layer and rest on the basement membrane they cover the surface where constant wear and tear take place. They mainly function as a protective epithelium.

(c) **Connective Tissue** It is the tissue which connects different tissues or organs and provides support to various structures of animal body. These tissues are mesodermal in origin and consist of living cells and extra cellular matrix, *e.g.*, blood is a fluid or vascular connective tissue.

Q. 19 Using appropriate examples, differentiate between false and true body segmentation.

Ans. **Segmentation** is the serial repetition of similar body parts along with the length of an animal. The body of animals can be truely segmented or pseudo/false segmented.

True segmentation is found in annelids, arthropods and chordates. In this, there is a linear repetition of body parts and each repeated unit is called somite (metamere).

In earthworms, the successive somites are essentially similar but they are dissimilar in different body regions of a crayfish or insect. Metamerism is conspicuous both externally and internally in annelids.

Pseudosegmentation is seen when body is divided into number of **pseudosegments** which are independent of each other. Each segment is able to perform all the vital function of body. Body grows by the addition of new segments from the anterior end, *e.g.*, tapeworm's, proglottids.

Q. 20 What is special about tissue present in the heart?

Ans. Special tissue present in heart is **cardiac muscle,** these have the following features

(i) Cardiac muscle fibres are supplied with both central and autonomic nervous system and are not under the control of animal will (involuntary).

(ii) These muscles are immune to fatigue and show rhythmicity.

(iii) They have rich blood supply.

(iv) They possess the property of contraction even if isolated from the body completely, *i.e.,* they are myogenic

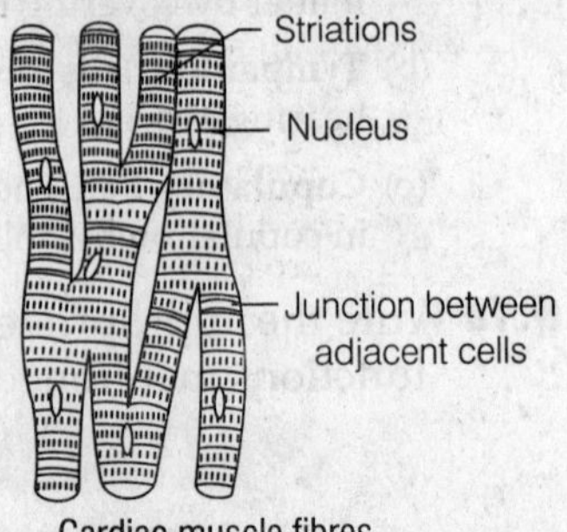

Cardiac muscle fibres

Long Answer Type Questions

Q. 1 Classify and describe epithelial tissue on the basis of structural modifications of cells.

Ans. The table given below summarises the structure, location and function of the epithelial tissue

Structure	Location	Functions
Simple squamous epithelium (pavement epithelium) Its composed of single layer of flat cells. Nucleus Basement membrane	This epithelium is present in the terminal bronchioles and alveoli of the lungs, walls of Bowman's capsules and descending limb of loop of Henle. In the blood vessels and heart it is called **endothelium.** In coelom, it is called as **mesothelium.**	Protection, excretion gaseous exchange and secretion of coelomic fluid.
Simple cuboidal epithelium It is composed of short cube-shaped cells with round nuclei located in centre of the cells. The cells of cuboidal epithelium often form microvilli on their free surface. Basement membrane Nucleus Cytoplam	This epithelium is present in the small ducts of salivary glands and pancreas, thyroid vesicles, part of membranous labyrinth, proximal and distal convoluted tubules of the nephrons of kidneys, ovaries, seminiferous tubules and ciliary bodies.	Protection, secretion absorption and excretion.

Structure	Location	Functions
Simple columnar epithelium In this, the cells are elongated and placed side by side like column. The outer free surface of each cell is slightly broader. This epithelium contains goblet (or mucous) cells. Columnar cell Goblet cell Nucleus Basement membrane	It lines the stomach, intestine, gall bladder and bile duct. It also forms the gastric glands, intestinal glands and pancreatic lobules.	Protection,secreti on and absorption.
Simple ciliated epithelium This is made of cell bearing numerous delicate hair like outgrowth, arising from basal granules. Mucous secreting goblet cells are also present in them Cilia Basal granule Mucus Ciliated cell Nucleus Cytoplasm Goblet cell Replacement cell Basement membrane	These are present in the respiratry tract and Fallopian tubes (oviducts), in certain parts of nephrons in the kidney.	Protection as well as movement of mucus, urine, eggs and cerebrospinal fluid in particular direction with the help of cilia.
Compound stratified epithelium It has many layers of epithelial cells, the deepest layer made of cuboidal cells. It is of four types (i) Stratified squamous epithelium. (ii) Stratified cuboidal epithelium. (iii) Stratified columnar epithelium. (iv) Stratified ciliated columnar epithelium.	Occurs in the epidermis of skin of land vertebrates. Oral cavity, tongue, pharynx, eye lids and cornea of eyes. Covers the epiglottis, lines the larynx and upper part of palate.	It is found on dry surfaces and are subjected to wear and tear *i.e.*, skin, nails. Protects, underlying structures of body.

Structure	Location	Functions
Compound transitional epithelium It consists of 4 to 6 layers of cells. There is no germinative layer or basement membrane but shows mitosis. The inner most cells rest on under lying connective tissue.	It lines the larynx and upper part of the soft palate.	It forms epidermis of fishes and many urodeles.
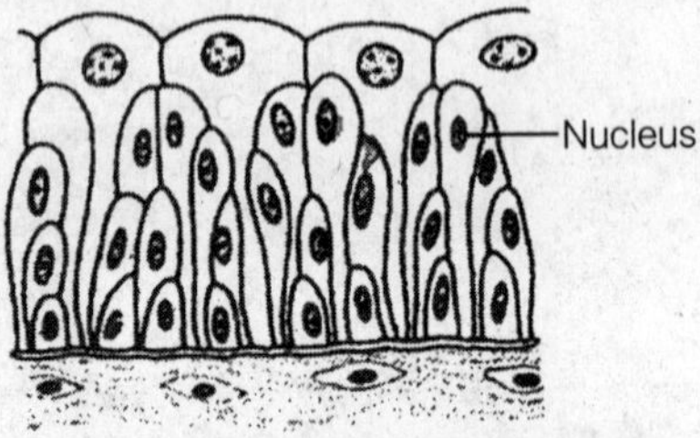 Nucleus	It is present in renal pelvis, ureters, urinary bladder and part of the urethra.	It permits distention thus, urinary bladder can be stretched considerably without being damaged.

Q. 2 Write down the common features of the connective tissue. On the basis of structure and function. Differentiate between bones and cartilages.

Ans. Common features of connective tissue are as follows

(i) Connective tissue is the most abundant and widely distributed tissue of the body. It connect with tissue with organs and also provides support to various body structures in animals.

(ii) Connective tissue is developed from the embroyonic mesoderm.

(iii) Three components are majorly present in the connective tissue these are matrix, cells and fibres.

(iv) The extracellular matrix has nearly amorphous ground substance made of glycoproteins with associated monopolysaccharides. This ground substance may be liquid, gel or solid.

(v) The tissue has good amount of regenerative ability.

(vi) Functions of connective tissue include storage of energy, protection of organs and body's structural integrity.

Differences between Bone and Cartilage

	Bone	Cartilage
Type	Bones are either compact or spongy. Bones are classified into long, short, flat, irregular, sesamoid and structural bones.	Cartilage is flexible and classified as Hyaline cartilage, fibro cartilage and elastic cartilage
Function	Protect the body against the mechanical damage, assist in the movement of the body, provide a framework and shape for the body, store minerals and produce red blood and white blood cells.	Reduces friction at joints, supports the respiratory tract, acting as shock absorbers between weight bearing bones and maintaining the shape and flexibility of fleshy appendages.

	Bone	Cartilage
Structure	Bones are made up of mostly osteoblasts (progenitor cells), osteocyte (mature bone cell) and osteoclasts (large cells, that breakdown bone tissue for growth and repair). A bone is highly vascularised.	Cartilages comprise chondroblasts (precursor cells), chondrocytes and dense matrix of collagen and elastin fibres, which provide strength and flexibility. Mature chordrocytes are embedded in spaces called lacunae with in the matrix unlike bone cartilage is avascular.
Location	Bones make up the majority of the axial and appendicular skeleton.	Cartilage is much softer, more pliable component that is mostly found in between joints of bones (articular cartilage).
Fibrous covering	Periosteum is rich in sensory nerve endings.	Perichondrium (but does not surround articular cartilage).

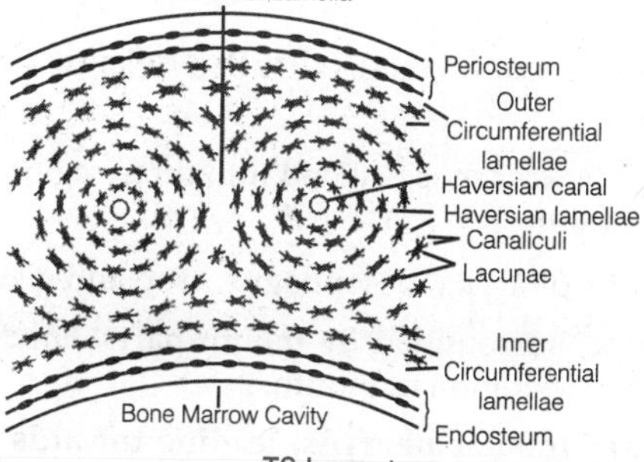

TS bone

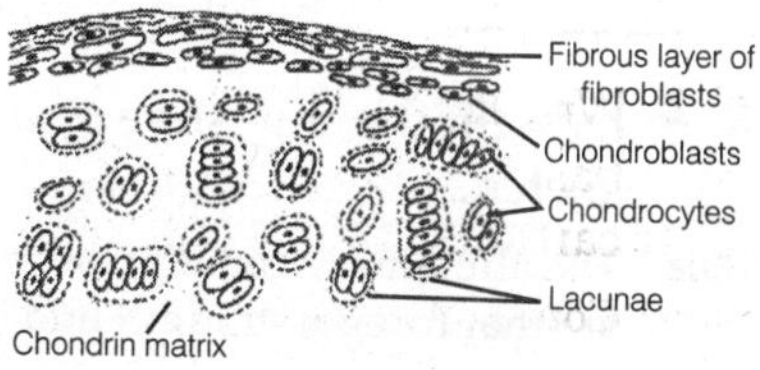

TS cartilage

Q. 3 Comment upon the gametic exchange in earthworm during mating. Discuss the physiology in reproduction of earthworm.

Ans. Mating in earthworm is a unique process, earthworm is a hermaphrodite organism. Breeding in earthworm takes place during rainy season and begins with copulation soon after maturation of the sperms.

The gametic exchange and the physiology reproduction during mating can described as below

(i) Earthworms are **protandrous animal** (*i.e.*, maturation of sperm takes place much earlier then that of ova).

(ii) Mating process in earthworm occurs through cross-fertilisation.

(iii) The mating process involves exchange of sperms between the two worms.

(iv) Two individuals from adjacent burrows half emerge out and lie in contact with each other, and opposite gonadal opening exchange the packets of sperms called **spermatophores**.

(v) During this process, the skin encircling male pore, elevates a little to form a temporary papilla that fits like a penis into the opposite spermathecal pore to keep it open.

(vi) After filling of spermathecal pore, the copulating worm moves a bit to adjust another pair of spermathecae to face the male pores of the other. This is accomplished in about an hour's copulation.

(vii) Within the spermathecae, the sperms mostly remain in their diverticula and the ampulla is associated with the secretion of nutritive substances for the sperms.

(viii) The sperm and egg are passed into cocoon which is secreted by clitellar gland.

(ix) Fertilisation is external and it involves cross fertilisation.

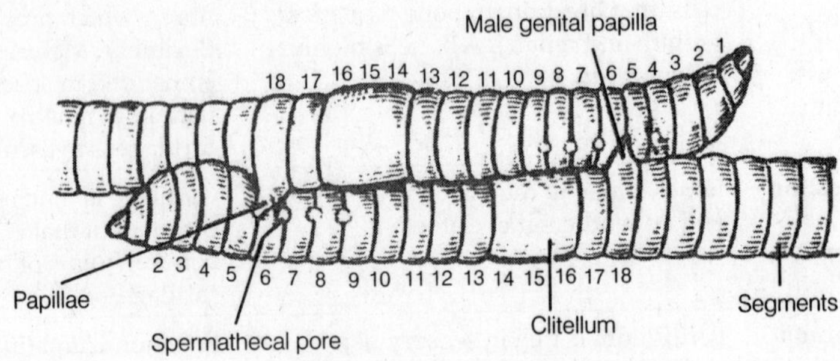

Anterior parts of two earthworms copulating

Q. 4 Explain the digestive system of cockroach with the help of a labelled sketch.

Ans. The alimentary canal present in cockroach is divided into three regions which are that foregut, midgut and hindgut.

(i) **Foregut** includes mouth cavity, pharynx, oesophagus, crop and gizzard.

(ii) Mouth cavity is a small space, surrounded by mouth parts. Food is crushed and acted upon by the salivary secretion in mouth.

(iii) The mouth opens into a short tubular **pharynx**, leading towards the narrow tubular passage called **oesophagus** into a sac-like structure called crop which acts as a storage organ.

(iv) **The crop** is followed by gizzard (proventriculus). **Gizzard** is the structure composed of thick circular muscles and thick inner cuticle forming six highly chitinous plates. It is associated with the grinding and crushing of food particles after it is softened in the crop . Entire forgut is lined by a thick cuticle.

(v) **Midgut or mesentron** is about one-third of the middle part of alimentry canal. The internal lining of midgut is an endodermal epithelium of columnar cells raised into several small villi like folds.

(vi) Anterior part of midgut surrounding the **stomodaeal valve** is called the **cardia** and finger like blind processess are called as enteric or **hepatic caeca**, present at the junction of foregut and midgut.

(vii) A ring of yellow filamentous structures formed between the midgut and hindgut are called **Malpighian tubules**. They help in the removal of excretory products from hemolymph.

(viii) **Hindgut** is the remaining one-third posterior part of alimentary canal. It is relatively thicker than the midgut and is lined by cuticle and ectodermal epithelium.

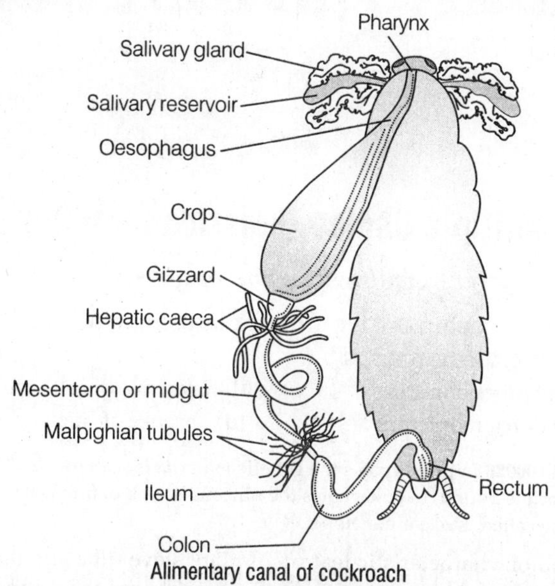

Alimentary canal of cockroach

(ix) Hindgut is differentiated into three parts, *i.e.,* anterior ileum, middle colon and posterior rectum. **Ileum** is short and relatively narrower and its cuticle bears minute spines. **Colon** is the longest, relatively thicker and a coiled part of hindgut. **Rectum** is a small and oval chamber that opens out through **anus**.

Q. 5 Draw a neat and well labelled diagram of male reproductive system of a frog.

Ans. A well labelled diagram of male reproductive system is shown below

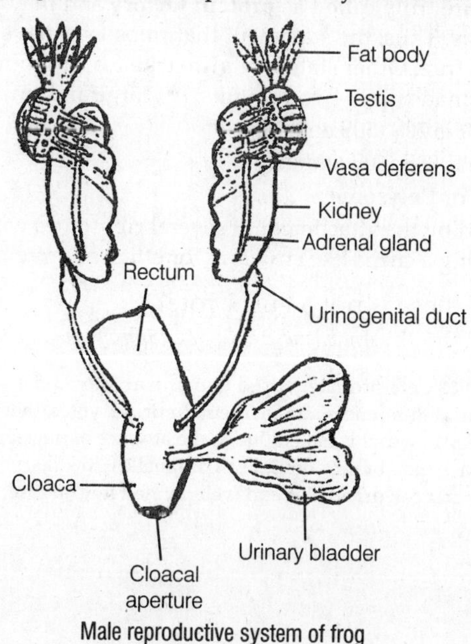

Male reproductive system of frog

Chapter

08

Cell : The Unit of Life

Multiple Choice Questions (MCQs)

Choose the correct answer from the given four options in the following questions.

Q. 1 A common characteristic feature of plant sieve tube cells and most of mammalian erythrocytes is

(a) absence of mitochondria (b) presence of cell wall

(c) presence of haemoglobin (d) absence of nucleus

Thinking Process In prokaryotes the genetic material is scattered and irregular and is not membrane bound. In eukaryotes the nucleus is well defined and enclosed in a membrane called, nuclear envelope.

Ans. *(d)* The common characteristic feature of plant sieve tube and mammalian erythrocyte is the absence of nucleus. Sieve tubes are the component of phloem and do not contain nucleus. Similarly, erythrocytes are mammalian cell that also do not posses nucleus. Erythrocytes are the RBCs which helps in gaseous exchange.

Q. 2 Select one which is not true for ribosome?

(a) Made up of two sub-units (b) Form polysome

(c) May attach to *m*RNA (d) Have no role in protein synthesis

Ans. *(d)* **Ribosomes** are truly called as **protein factory** and they play a vital role in protein synthesis. Thus, the statement that ribosomes have no role in protein synthesis is not true. Other statements are true for ribosome

Ribosomes are made up of two subunits, *i.e.,* large and small.

In prokaryotes it is 70S (50S and 30S).

In eukaryotes it is 80S (60S and 40S).

Polyribosomes or **Polysome**

They are formed by the attachment of several ribosomes with a single *m*RNA moelcule, creating a chain-like structure for efficient protein synthesis.

Q. 3 Which one of these is not a eukaryote?

(a) *Euglena* (b) *Anabaena* (c) *Spirogyra* (d) *Agaricus*

Thinking Process Cells are categorised into prokaryotes and eukaryotes on the basis of certain structural differences among them. In prokaryotes, there is no well defined nucleus, genetic material is naked due to the absence of nuclear membrane and the cells do not have membrane bound cell organelles. In eukaryotes, the presence of membrane bound cell organelles and well defined nucleus are the determining features.

Ans. ***(b)*** *Anabaena* is the only organism that is not an eukaryote and only possess prokaryotic characteristic features. *i.e.*, absence of membrane bound organelles and undefined nucleus.

Whereas, *Euglena, Spirogyra* and *Agaricus* are eukaryotes, possessing membrane bound organelles as mitochondria and well a defined nucleus.

Q. 4 Which of the following stain is not used for staining chromosomes?

(a) Basic Fuchsin
(b) Safranin
(c) Methylene green
(d) Carmine

Thinking Process Staining is an auxillary technique that is used in microscopy to enhance contrast of the microscopic images. Stains and dyes are frequently used in biology and medical science for observing structural differentiation of biological tissue, microbes, blood cells and other different organelles within the cells.

Ans. ***(b)*** **Safranin** It is used as a counterstain in gram staining and endospore staining. It can also be used for detection of cartilage, mucin and mast cell granule.

Carmine The basic dye, is used to stain nucleic acid and chromosomes. It gives chromosomes a pink colour thus, differentiating from other cellular organelles.

Basic Fuchsin It involves in staining of human chromosomes elastic fibres, cardiac or skeletal muscle tissue.

Methylene blue It is used to stain nuclei, Golgi bodies and pectic substances.

Q. 5 Different cells have different sizes. Arrange the following cells in an ascending order of their size. Choose the correct option among the followings.

I. *Mycoplasma*
II. Ostrich eggs
III. Human RBC
IV. Bacteria

(a) I, IV, III, II
(b) I, III, IV and II
(c) II, I, III, IV
(d) III, II, I, IV

Ans. ***(a)*** Represents the correct ascending order of cell's size.

Cells in organism vary greatly in their size, shapes and activities.

I. Mycoplasmas are the smallest cell with size only 0.3 μm.
II. Bacterial cell are of size 2 – 5 μm. (10^{-6} meter)
III. In human red blood cells are of about 7.0 μm in diameter.
IV. Ostrich eggs are among the largest cells with size (15 × 13) cm.

Mycoplasma Like Organisms (MLOs) or mycoplasma are the smallest cell followed by the size of bacterial cell, then RBCs and ostrich egg cell is the largest known cell.

Q. 6 Which of the following features is common to prokaryotes and many eukaryotes?

(a) Chromatin material present
(b) Cell wall present
(c) Nuclear membrane present
(d) Membrane bound sub-cellular organelles present

Ans. ***(b)*** Presence of cell wall is the common feature that is observed in both prokaryotic and many eukaryotic cells.

Cell wall is present in bacteria (prokaryotes) and in plants (eukaryotes) however cell wall is absent in animal cells. Cell wall acts as protection unit for cell and also provides shape to the cell. Cell wall is made up of cellulose, hemicellulose or pectins.

The genetic material in prokaryotes is naked and not enveloped by nuclear membrane. Chromatin material is present in eukaryotes only.

Sub-cellular organelles in prokaryotes are not well defined and are not membrane bound while eukaryotes have membranous organelles which are complex structures with multifunctions.

Q. 7 Who proposed the fluid mosaic model of plasma membrane?

(a) Camillo Golgi
(b) Schleiden and Schwann
(c) Singer and Nicolson
(d) Robert Brown

Ans. *(c)* **Singer** and **Nicolson** (1972) proposed the structure of cell membrane that was widely accepted and called as fluid mosaic model, which states that lipids form a fluid bilayer and proteins are embedded or loosely associated within the membrane, allowing for movement.

Schleiden and **Schwann** (1839) Observed thin outer layer in cells called plasma membrane and proposed cell theory.

Camillo Golgi (1898) discovered the Golgi apparatus.

Robert Brown (1831) discovered the nucleus in the cell which was later termed as chromatin by Flemming.

Q. 8 Which of the following statement is true for a secretory cell?

(a) Golgi apparatus is absent
(b) Rough Endoplasmic Reticulum (RER) is easily observed in the cell.
(c) Only Smooth Endoplasmic Reticulum (SER) is present.
(d) Secretory granules are formed in nucleus.

Ans. *(b)* Rough Endoplasmic Reticulum (RER) is observed in the cells that are actively involved in the protein synthesis and secretion.

Other options are incorrect as

Golgi apparatus is present in secretory cells.

Secretary cell has both SER and RER. SER in the major site for the synthesis of lipids. Secretory granules are not formed in nucleus but in the Golgi apparatus.

Q. 9 What is a tonoplast?

(a) Outer membrane of mitochondria
(b) Inner membrane of chloroplast
(c) Membrane boundary of the vacuole of plant cells
(d) Cell membrane of a plant cell

Ans. *(c)* **Tonoplast** In plant cell the vacuole in bound by a single membrane called tonoplast. The tonoplast facilitates the transport of ions and other material into the vacuole. Hence, their concentration is higher inside the vacuole than in the cytoplasm. The outer membrane of mitochondria is formed of porin proteins and inner membrane of chloroplast encloses the stroma.

The cell membrane of the plant cell is not a tonoplast. It is simple biological membrane present in every cellular organism.

Q. 10 Which of the following is not true for a eukaryotic cell?

(a) Cell wall is made up of peptidoglycans

(b) It has 80S type of ribosome present in the cytoplasm

(c) Mitochondria contain circular DNA

(d) Membrane bound organelles are present

Ans. *(a)* A cell wall made up of peptidoglycan is found in bacteria and not in eukaryotes. Eukaryotic cell wall is made up of cellulose, hemicellulose, pectin, chitin etc. Thus, is not true for eukaryotic cell.

In eukaryotes ribosomes present in cytoplasm is of 80S type but the ribosome in mitochondria is of 70S type, which represents the type present in prokaryotic cell.

In eukaryotes cell organelles are highly complex and membrane bound and the mitochondria in eukaryotes bear a separate circular DNA.

Q. 11 Which of the following statement is not true for plasma membrane?

(a) It is present in both plant and animal cell

(b) Lipid is present as a bilayer in it

(c) Proteins are present integrated as well as loosely associated with the lipid bilayer

(d) Carbohydrate is never found in it

Ans. *(d)* Statement is false.

Carbohydrates are never found in plasma membrane is not true. The biochemical investigation done on cell membrane clearly demonstrate that the cell membrane possess protein and carbohydrates as biochemical components.

The other options stand true for plasma membrane

Plasma membrane is present in both plant and animal cells. Lipid is present as a bilayer and lipid component is made of phosphoglycerides (fluid mosaic model by Singer and Nicolson). Proteins are present integrated as well as loosely associated with the lipid bilayer. The ratio of protein and lipid varies considerably in different cell types.

Q. 12 Plastid differs from mitochondria on the basis of one of the following features. Mark the right answer.

(a) Presence of two layers of membrane (b) Presence of ribosome

(c) Presence of thylakoids (d) Presence of DNA

Ans. *(c)* Presence of thylakoids (the structural elements of chloroplast) is the key difference between plastids and mitochondria. Thylakoids are flattened sacs stacked one above the other to form grana. They help in photosynthesis

Rest of the features- presence of two layers of membrane, ribosome and presence of DNA are common to both plastids and mitochondria.

Q. 13 Which of the following is not a function of cytoskeleton in a cell?

(a) Intracellular transport (b) Maintenance of cell shape and structure

(c) Support of the organelle (d) Cell motility

Thinking Process An elaborate network of filamentous proteinaceous structure present in cytoplasm is referred to as cytoskeleton.

Ans. *(a)* Cytoskeleton is not associated with the intracellular transport. The microtubules and microfilaments, are the components of cytoskeleton and are responsible for cellular and intercellular movements. Rest of the options are functions of cytoskeleton is a cell.

Cytoskeleton provides mechanical support to the cell that helps in maintaining cell shape and structure.

The cytoskeleton also keeps other organelles separated from mitochandria and ribosomes avoid interference in their activities. It also helps in supporting the cell organelles.

Q. 14 The stain used to visualise mitochondria is

(a) fast green (b) safranin

(c) acetocarmine (d) janus green

Ans. *(d)* **Janus green** is used to stain mitochondria. Janus green act as an indicator and changes colour according to the amount of oxygen present. It oxidizes to blue colour in presence of oxygen and in its absence changes its colour to pink.

The other options are incorrect because

Safranin is used to stain nuclei and lignified walls of cell.

Acetocarmine is used for staining nucleic acid and chromosomes.

Fast green It is used for staining histones at alkaline pH after acid extraction from DNA.

Very Short Answer Type Questions

Q. 1 What is the significance of vacuole in a plant cell?

Ans. The vacuole is a membrane bound space found in the cytoplasm. It contains water, sap, excretory product and other materials that are not useful for the cell. In plants cell, vacuoles occupy 90% of the volume of the cell. They help in maintaining cell fluid balance, and shape of the cell by maintaining turgor pressure against the cell well.

Q. 2 What does 'S' refer in a 70S and an 80S ribosome?

Ans. 'S' refers to Svedbergs unit which measures the sedimentation coefficient. Sedimentation coefficient depicts that how fast a cell organelle sediments during the ultracentrifugation.

The heavier the structure, higher is the sedimentation coefficient.

The value of S is equal to 10^{-13} seconds $(1\ s = 1 \times 1 = ^{-13}$ seconds). The value of 'S' represents the rate at which particles sediment, and is not directly related to time in seconds. It is a dimensionless unit based on the shape and size of the particle in a centrifugal field.

Q. 3 Mention a single membrane bound organelle which is rich in hydrolytic enzymes.

Thinking Process The different parts of the cell preforming different functions are known as the organelles. Some of these organelles are nucleus, Golgi apparatus, endoplasmic reticulum and mitochondria.

Ans. Lysosomes are the membrane bound vesicular structures formed by Golgi apparatus. These vesicles are rich in various hydrolytic enzymes *i.e.,* hydrolases, lipases, proteases and carbohydrases which digest carbohydrates, proteins, lipids and nucleic acid at an acidic pH.

Q. 4 What are gas vacuoles? State their functions.

Ans. Gas vacuoles are also known as pseudovacuoles or air vacuoles. Gas vacuoles are the characteristic feature of prokaryotes (reported only in prokaryotes). Each gas vacuole are made of sub-microscopic hexagonal vesicles and are surrounded by a thin protein membrane. Gas vacuoles store metabolic gases and take part in buoyancy regulation, enabling the organism to float or sink in its environment.

Q. 5 What is the function of a polysome?

Ans. A polysome consist of a cluster of ribosomes that are held, simultaneously to a strand of messenger RNA (*m*RNA) in rosette or helical arrangement.They contain a portion of the *m*RNA that each ribosome is translating and are used in formation of multiple copies of same polypeptide. They are found in the cytoplasm during the process of active protein synthesis.

Q. 6 What is the feature of a metacentric chromosome?

Thinking Process During cell division, a short thick rod-like organelle is formed, known as chromosomes. These are formed by the condensing and tight coiling of the chromatin fibres. The chromosomes are divided into following types on the basis of their arms and location of centromere.

(i) Telocentric
(ii) Acrocentric
(iii) Submetacentric
(iv) Metacentric

Ans. In a metacentric chromosome, the centromere is median, *i.e.*, centromere lie in the middle of the chromosome. Thus, forming two equal arms of chromosome.

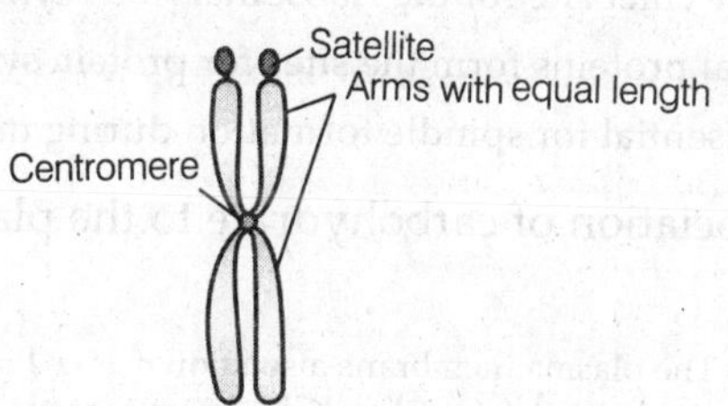

Metacentric chromosome

Q. 7 What is referred to as satellite chromosome?

Ans. The chromosomes may have additional constriction or secondary constriction at distal part of the arm, formed by chromatin thread, that are known satellite chromosome. These constrictions give appearance of an out growth or small fragment, referred to as "satellite".

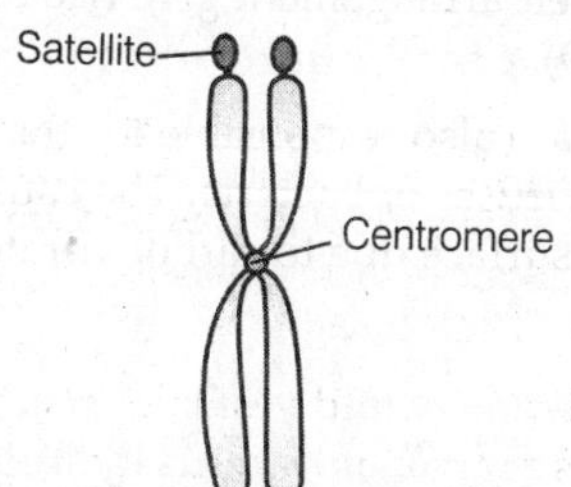

Diagram representing satellite chromosomes

Short Answer Type Questions

Q. 1 Discuss briefly the role of nucleolus in the cells actively involved in protein synthesis.

Ans. **Nucleolus** is the round, naked and a slightly irregular structure, which is attached to the chromatin at a specific region called as **Nucleolar Organizer Region** (NOR). Nucleolus was first discovered by Fontana (1774).

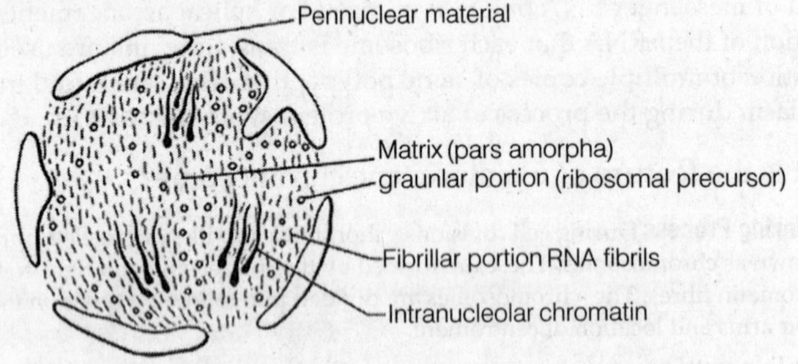

Ultrastructure of nucleous

(i) It is the centre for the transcription of *r* RNA genes

(ii) Nucleolus is the chief site for the ribosomal RNA synthesis.

(iii) These ribosomal proteins form the sites for protein synthesis in the cell.

(iv) Nucleolus is essential for spindle formation during nuclear division.

Q. 2 Explain the association of carbohydrate to the plasma membrane and its significance.

Thinking Process The plasma membrane also known as cell membrane, surrounds the cell. It consists of lipids, proteins and carbohydrates that are imperative in both structure and function of the cell.

Ans. Sugar residues or carbohydrates attached either to proteins or lipids usually making up less han 10% of the membrane weight. They can give rise to a wide variety of structures in relatively short chains. These carbohydrate individual cell types a distinguishing features. Therefore, they may be involved in:

Cell Recognition *e.g.*, surface of RBC have carbohydrates arranged in branched chains. Differences in their arrangement give rise to different blood group antigens (*i.e.*, A, B and O).

Cell surface differences are also responsible for the specificity of action of cells with hormones, drugs, viruses or bacteria. The cause of cell surface differences is related to characteristic surface due to carbohydrate component.

Q. 3 Comment on the cartwheel structure of centriole.

Ans. Centrosome is an organelle usually containing two cylindrical structures called centrioles. These are surrounded by amorphous pericentriolar materials. Both the centriole in centrosome lie perpendicular to each other and each has an organisation resembling a 'cartwheel'.

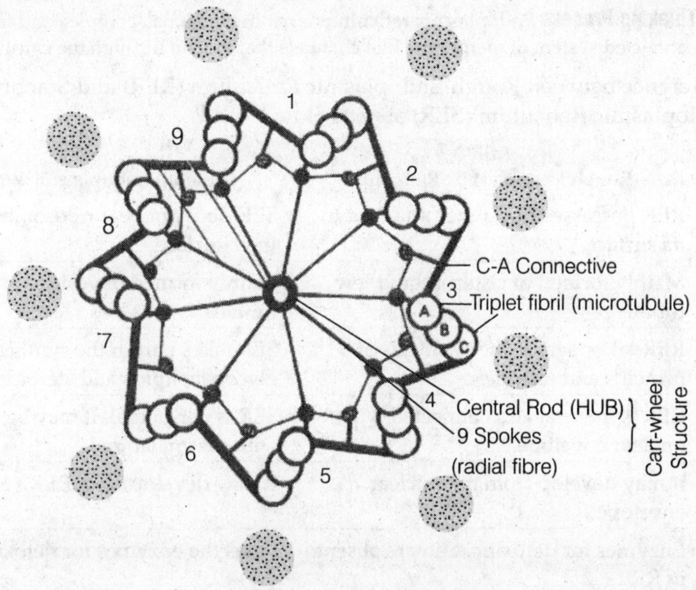

Cartwheel structure of centriole

A centriole possess a whorl of 9 peripheral fibrils. There fibrils are absent in the centre, hence the arrangement is called 9 + 0. Each fibrils is made of 3 sub-fibres. Therefore, called triplet fibril. The centrioles form the basal body of cilia and flagella. It also forms spindle fibres that gives rise to spindle apparatus during cell division in animals.

Q. 4 Briefly describe the cell theory.

Ans. Schleiden and Schwann in 1838-39, formulated the cell theory, which originally contained following two statements

(i) All living beings are made up of cells and products formed by the cells.

(ii) Cells are the structural and functional units of life.

The cell theory stated by **Schleiden** and **Schwann** did not address the origin of cells. A major expansion of the cell theory was expressed by **Virchow** in 1855, in his statement '*Omnis cellula e cellula*' (all cells arise from pre-existing cells).This concept, was originally proposed by Nagelli (1846), which later on was elaborated by Virchow, along with considerable evidences in its support. The work of Nagelli and Virchow established cell division as the central phenomenon in the continuity of life.

Thus, the modern cell theory is based on the following facts

(i) All living organisms are composed of cells and products of cell.

(ii) Cells are the basic structural and functional unit of life.

(iii) All cells arise from pre-existing cells.

Viruses are exception to cell theory as they are not composed of cell. They consist of a nucleic acid (DNA or RNA) surrounded by a protein sheath and are incapable of independent existence, self regulation and self reproduction.

Q. 5 Differentiate between Rough Endoplasmic Reticulum (RER) and Smooth Endoplasmic Reticulum (SER).

Thinking Process Endoplasmic reticulum is a 3-dimensional, complex and inter connected system of membrane like channels that extend through the cytoplasm.

Ans. Difference between Rough Endoplasmic Reticulum (RER) and Smooth Endoplasmic Reticulum (SER) are as below

	RER (Rough Endoplasmic Reticulum)	SER (Smooth Endoplasmic Reticulum)
1.	RER possesses ribosomes attached to its surface.	SER does not bear ribosomes attach to their surface.
2.	Mainly formed of cisternae and few tubules.	Mainly formed of vesicles and the tubules.
3.	RER takes part in the synthesis of proteins and enzymes.	SER takes part in the synthesis of glycogen, lipids and steroids.
4.	RER is internal and connected with nuclear envelope.	SER is peripheral. It may be connected with plasmalemma.
5.	It may develop from the nuclear envelope.	It may develop from RER.
6.	Enzymes for detoxification are absent in RER	It has the enzymes for detoxification.
7.	It forms lysosomes through the agency of Golgi apparatus.	SER gives rise to sphaerosomes.

Q. 6 Give the biochemical composition of plasma membrane. How are lipid molecules arranged in the membrane?

Thinking Process To stay alive all living things need membranes. Membranes are the barrier which give cells their outer boundaries (plasma membrane) and their inner compartments (organelles).
Being selectively permeable, plasma membranes control the movement of substances into and out of the cell, regulating fluid composition, control flow of information and finally involve in capture and release of energy.

Ans. Chemical composition of plasma membrane is as follows:

Component	Composition
Lipids	(20-79%)
Proteins	(20-70%)
Carbohydrates	(1-5%)
Water	20%

Lipids are the major components of the cell membrane as they form the continuous structural framework. Lipids such as phospholipids, glycolipids, and steroids are found in membranes.

The lipid molecule possess both polar hydrophilic (water loving) and non-polar hydrophobic (water repelling) ends. The hydrophilic region is in the form of a head, while the hydrophobic part contains two tails of fatty acid. Hydrophobic tail is present towards the centre of the membrane. This structure results is the formation of lipid bilayer known as unit membrane, biological membrane or cell membrane.

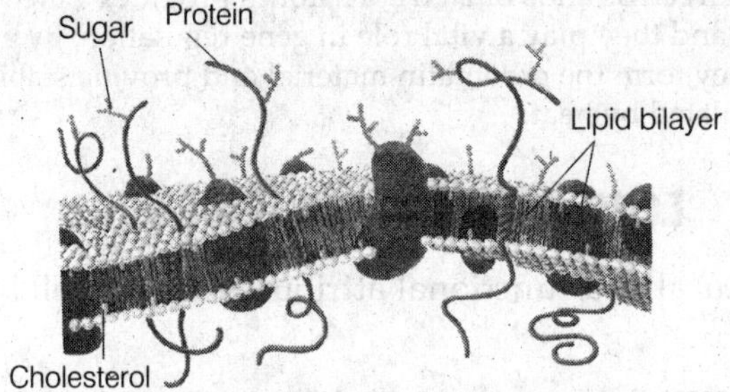

Fluid mosaic model of plasma membrane

Q. 7 What are plasmids? Describe their role in bacteria.

Ans. A plasmid is usually a circular (sometime linear), double strandad DNA, that can replicate itself autonomously. These are found in the cytoplasm of the bacterial cell and generally separated from the chromosome, but sometimes may integrate into it temporarily and replicate with it incidentally.

Role of Plasmids in Bacteria Plasmids are the extrachromosomal circular, independently replicating unit located besides nucleoid in the bacterial cell. Plasmids are used to transfer the information from one cell to another, *i.e.*, transfer of important genes, they may confer resistance of particular, antibiotics to their bacterial cells, enable to metabolise a nutrient, which normally a bacteria is unable to. It also helps in conjugation of bacteria. Today, plasmids are used in a variety of recombination experiments, as cloning vectors.

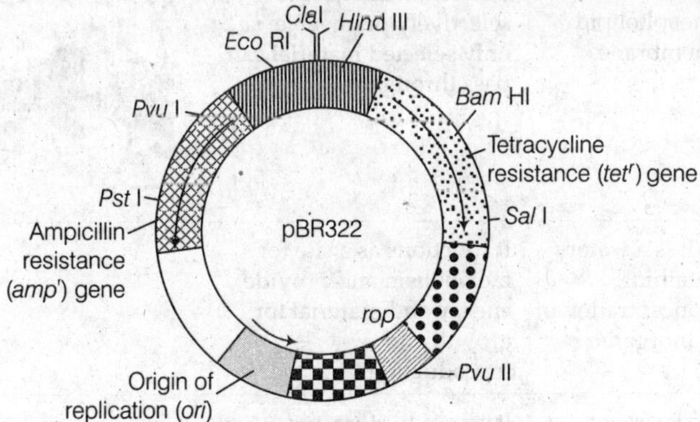

Structure of plasmid showing antibiotic resistant genes

Q. 8 What are histones? What are their functions?

Thinking Process Due to DNA's large size that has to be packed within tiny nucleus, it require certain proteins, that helps in DNA packaging.

Ans. **Histones** are the basic group of globular proteins that have a high content of basic amino acis, *i.e.*, arginine and lysine. Histones forms the part of the chromosomal material in eukaryotic cells.

There are five types of histone proteins H_1, H_2A, H_2B, H_3 and H_4. Four of these (H_2A, H_2B, H_3 and H_4) occur in pairs to produce histone octamer, around which DNA wrappes to form nucleosome. Histone H_1 helps to stabilise the nucleosome structure.

Functions of Histones Histones bear positively charged ends, that attaract negetively charged strands of DNA. Histones provides a medium around which DNA winds, and they play a vital role in gene regulation, by acting as gene repressor. They form the chromatin material and provide stability to the DNA as are not coagulated by heat.

Long Answer Type Questions

Q. 1 What structural and functional attributes must a cell have to be called a living cell?

Thinking Process Cell is the structural and functional unit of all living organism. A single cell is capable of independent existence and also performs the essential functions of life. All cells have certain functions in common so as to carry out basic life processes, but the differential distribution of organelles gives cell a distinct characteristic.

Ans. All organisms are made up of cells, which further organises into tissues, organs and organ systems. Thus, forming the building blocks of organisms, cells also have the property of totipotency, which allow them to develop into a new organism. Besides, forming the structural unit they perform different specialised functions in the same way as each organ or system carries out in an organism. Thus, exhibiting division of labour is evident in how cell organelles are specific in their functions. A living cell must have certain structural and functional attributes, which are as follows.

	Structure	Function	Diagram
1.	**Cell membrane** All cell possess a phospholipid based cell membrane.	The cell membrane is selectively permeable, *i.e.*, only selected material can pass through it.	
2.	**Cytoplasm** It is a watery solution containing controlled concentration of organic and inorganic compounds.	It functions as a site for metabolism and provide energy and material for growth and reproduction.	
3.	**Nucleus** It consists of DNA, the nuclear matrix or the nucleoplasm containing nucleolus and chromatin.	It serves to store and transmit information to direct the synthetic activities of the entire cell. It also transfers the genetic information required for growth and reproduction.	Inner nuclear membrane; Nucleolus; Nucleoplasm; Outer nuclear membrane; Chromatin strands; Nuclear pores; Ribosomes

Structure	Function	Diagram
4. **Golgi apparatus** (Golgi complex) They consist of many flat disc shaped sacs or cistermae of 0.5 μm – 1.0 μm diameter. These stacks are arranged parallel to each other.	These are mainly involved in packaging the materials to be delivered either to intracellular targets or secreted outside the cells.	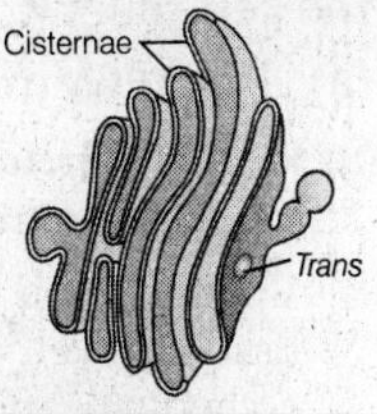
5. **The Endoplasmic Reticulum** (ER) It is an extensive 3– dimensional network of intracellular membranes formed by three elements– cisternae, tubules and vesicles	The ER bearing ribosomes on it surface is called rough endoplasmic reticulum (RER). These are involved in protein synthesis and secretion. The ER without ribosomes are called smooth endoplasmic reticulum involved in synthesis of lipids like steroidal hormones.	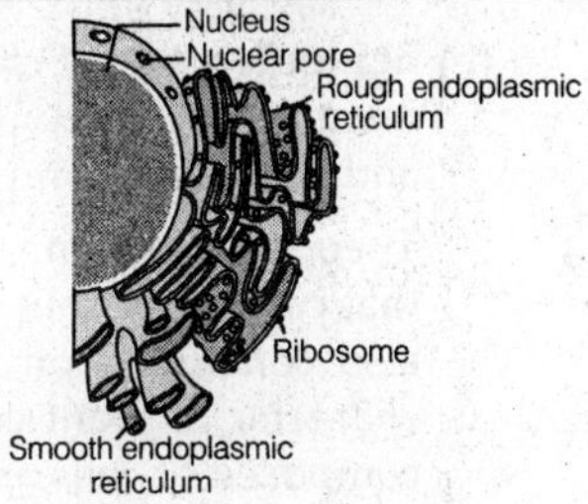
6. **Mitochondria** It is a double membrane bound structure with outer and inner membrane dividing its lumen into two compartments. The inner membrane forming number of infoldings called the cristae.	Mitochondria are the sites for aerobic respiration. It is known as power house of the cell since producing cellular energy in the form of ATP.	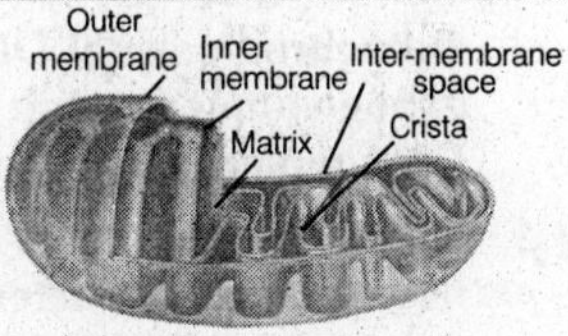
7. **Lysosomes** These are membrane bound vesicular structures, formed by the process of packaging in the Golgi apparatus.	These are rich in many types of hydrolytic enzymes (hydrolases lipases, proteases, carbohydrates).	
8. **Vacuoles** The vacuole is the membrane bound space found in the cytoplasm, it contain water, sap, excretory product and other material not useful for the cell. The vacuole is bound by single membrane called tonoplast.	In plants the tonoplast facilitate the transport of ions and other materials against concentration gradients into the vacuole.	

All these factors, *i.e.*, structural and functional attributes it to be called a living cell.

Q. 2 Briefly give the contributions of the following scientists in formulating the cell theory

(a) Rudolf Virchow (b) Schleiden and Schwann

Ans. (a) **Rudolf Virchow** (1855) proposed that the cells divide and new cells are formed from the pre-existing cells (*omnis cellula e cellula*).

Virchow was the first to demonstrate that the cell theory applies to diseased tissue as well as to healthy tissue. He also engaged his research in the fields of archeology and anthropology.

(b) **Schleiden** and **Schwann** were among the first to observe cells and their membranes. They proposed the **cell theroy** which explains that the animals and plants are composed of cells and their product.

Theodore Schwann (1839) studied different types of animal cells and reported that cells had a thin outer layer which is called as plasma membrane. Schleiden also concluded on plant studies, *i.e.*, the presence of cell wall is a unique character of plant cells. Together, they proposed that plants and animals are composed of cells and that these cells are the fundamental units of life.

Q. 3 Is extragenomic DNA present in prokaryotes and eukaryotes? If yes, indicate their location in both the types of organisms.

Ans. *Yes*, extragenomic DNA is present in both prokaryotes and eukaryotes.

Extrachromosomal DNA in Prokaryotes In case of prokaryotic cells, the extragenomic DNA is present in the form of plasmids. Plasmids are circular DNA molecules that confer unique phenotypic traits to the bacteria.

One such character is antibiotic resistance to bacteria. The plasmid DNA is also used to monitor bacterial transformation with foreign DNA. Transformation is the method of sexual reproduction in bacteria.

Extrachromosomal DNA in Eukaryotes

Extragenomic DNA is present in two organelles, *e.g.*, plastids and mitochondria. Mitochondrial DNA (*mt*DNA) is usually circular. Mitochondrial DNA spans about 16,500 DNA building blocks (base pairs) representing a small fraction of the total DNA in cells.

***mt*DNA** contains 37 genes, all of which are essential for normal mitochondrial functions. Thirteen of these genes provides instruction for making enzymes involved in oxidative phosporylation.

Mitochondrial DNA is distinct from nuclear DNA and the 37 mitochondrial genes are part of the mitochondrial genome. In contrast, the human nuclear genome contains an estimated 20,000 to 25,000 protein-coding genes.

Plastids These are small bodies found free in most plant cells and are of three types leucoplast, chromoplast and chloroplast. These are double membrane bound structures for trapping radiation and storage purpose. It contains small, double stranded circular DNA molecules and ribosomes essential in synthesising certain proteins. As they both can synthesise proteins and replicate on their own they are known as semi-autonomous organelles.

Q. 4 Structure and function are correlatable in living organisms. Can you justify this by taking plasma membrane as an example?

Ans. Yes, In animals and plants, plasma membrane structure and function are correlated. The membrane consists of protein, lipid and carbohydrates :

The **protein component** present in membrane acts as a solute channels allowing the flow of minerals, hormones and cellular matter from cell to extra-cellular space and vice-versa. In plants minerals are actively absorbed from the soil. The plasma membrane possess proteinaceous carrier.

The **oligosaccharides** attached to the membrane serve as recognition centres and help in recognising foreign entities before allowing them entry into the cell.

The **lipid** content of plasma membrane is bilayered in plant and animal cells are arranged with their hydrophilic polar head directed outwards and non-polar hydrophobic tails directed inwards providing fluidity to the membrane. **Glycocalyx** a carbohydrate-rich layer present on cell membrane also helps in cellular attachment.

Q. 5 Eukaryotic cells have organelles which may

(a) not be bound by a membrane

(b) bound by a single membrane

(c) bound by a double membrane

Group the various sub-cellular organelles into these three categories.

Thinking Process In eukaryotic cells, there is an extensive compartmentalisation of cytoplasm through the presence of membrane bound organelles serving for specific functions.

Ans. (a) **Cell organelles with no membrane** In eukaryotic cells, ribosomes occur freely in the cytoplasmic matrix and are attached to the outer cytoplasmic surface of the rough endoplasmic reticulum and nuclear envelope. The ribosomes are also found in the matrix of mitochondria and stroma of plastids called as mitoribosomes and plastidoribosomes, respectively.

(b) **Cell organelles with single membrane** A lysosome is a tiny sac, bounded by a single unit membrane of lipoprotein. The lysosomes occurs in all animal cells and protozoans. Prokaryotic cell lack lysosomes. Number of lysosomes varies with the cell type. Lysosome contain a dense, finely granular fluid consisting of glycoproteinaceous hydrolytic (digestive) enzymes called acid hydrolases. Cell organelles like sphaerosomes and microbodies also possess single membranes.

(c) **Cell organelles with double membrane** Mitochondria are double membrane bound structures with the outer membrane and inner membrane dividing its lumen distinctly into two aqueous compartments. The inner compartment is called the matrix whereas the outer membrane forms the continuous limiting boundary of the organelle. Chloroplast and nucleus are also double membrane bound organelles.

Q. 6 The genomic content of the nucleus is constant for a given species where as the extrachromosomal DNA is found to be variable among the members of a population. Explain.

Ans. In bacteria, in addition to the genomic DNA, small circular DNA molecules are present in cytoplasm. These small molecules are called plasmids. These plasmids carry genes that confer unique phenotypic character *i.e.*, resistance to antibiotics and vary among individual bacteria within a population. It is also used to monitor bacterial transformation with foreign DNA.

In eukaryotes, the extrachromosomal DNA molecules are present in chloroplast (stroma) and mitochondria (matrix). Because of the presence of this DNA molecule, they are treated as semi autonomous organelles. In case of highly active organism, the extrachromosomal DNA is found to be more as compared to the less active ones.

The genomic control of the nucleus is constant for a given species because DNA is the carrier of inheritable traits, and each species has its own unique set of characteristics. In contrast, extrachromosomal DNA can vary among members of a population because it is found organelles like mitocondria and chloroplasts as well as plasmids.

Q. 7 Justify the statement, 'Mitochondria are power houses of the cell'.

Ans. Mitochondria are sausage shaped or cylindrical structure having a diameter of 0.2 to 1.0 μm and length 1.0 - 4.1 μm. Each mitochondria is a double membrane bound structure with an outer membrane and inner membrane, dividing its lumen distinctly into two aqueous compartments. The inner compartment is called matrix and outer one form number of infoldings called cristae towards the matrix. These cristae are associated with an increase in surface area for ATP production as there are ATPase enzyme present attached on cristae.

The mitochondria are the sites of aerobic respiration. They produce cellular energy in the form of ATP, hence are called as **power house of the cell**.

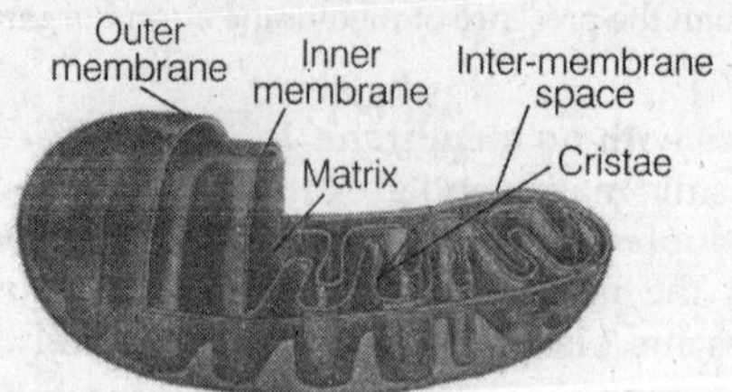

Structure of mitochondira

This generated ATP is used in performing vital functions by the organism. The matrix of mitochondria also possess a single circular DNA molecule of itself and a few RNA molecules, ribosomes (70S) and the other materials required for the protein synthesis. These proteins are nothing but the enzymes (ATPase) required for ATP generation.

Q. 8 Is there a species specific or region specific type of plastids? How does one distinguish from the other?

Ans. Yes, Plastids are species specific and are found in all plant cells and in euglenoids. They bear some specific pigments thus, imparting specific colours to the part of the plant which possess them. Based on the type of pigments plastids are classified into three main types, *i.e.*, leucoplasts, chromoplasts and chloroplasts.

Leucoplasts They are colourless plastids which store food material based on there storage products, they are of three types

(a) **Amyloplasts** Stores starch, *e.g.*, tuber of potato, grain of rice, grain of wheat.

(b) **Elaioplasts** These store oils and fats, *e.g.*, Tuberose

(c) **Aleuroplasts** They are protein storing plastids, *e.g.*, castor endosperm

Chromoplast These are non photosynthetic coloured plastids which synthesise and store carotenoid pigments. They appear orange, red or yellow. These mostly occur in ripe fruits (tomato and chilles), carrot roots, etc.

Chloroplasts These are green colour plastids which help in synthesising food material by photosynthesis. They contain chorophyll and carotenoid pigments which trap light energy. Each chloroplast is oval or spherical, double membrane bound cell organelle. The space present inside inner membrane is called stroma. A number of organised flattened membranous sacs called thylakoids are present in the stroma.

Thylakoids are arranged in stacks called grana. The thylakoids of different grana are connected by membranous tubules called the stroma lamellae. The stroma of the chloroplast contain the enzymes that are required for the synthesis of carbohydrates and proteins.

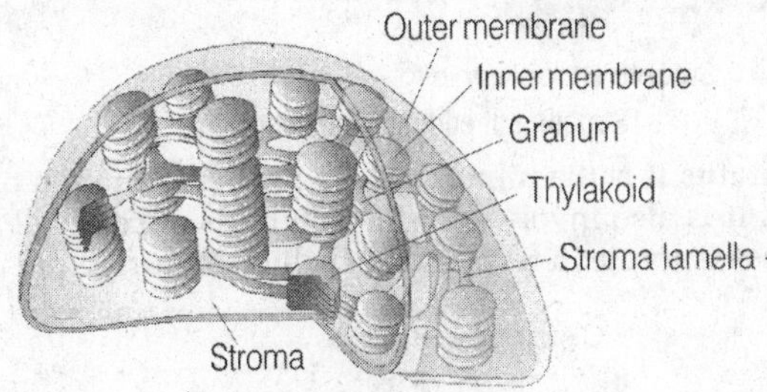

Structure of chloroplast

Q. 9 Write the functions of the following

(a) Centromere (b) Cell wall

(c) Smooth ER (d) Golgi apparatus

(e) Centrioles

Ans. (a) **Centromere** : It is required for proper chromosome segregation. The centromere is the constrited point at which the two chromatids forming the chromosomes are joined together. The centromere consists of two kinetochores. It is the region of the chromosome to which the spindle fibre attaches during cell division (in both mitosis and meiosis).

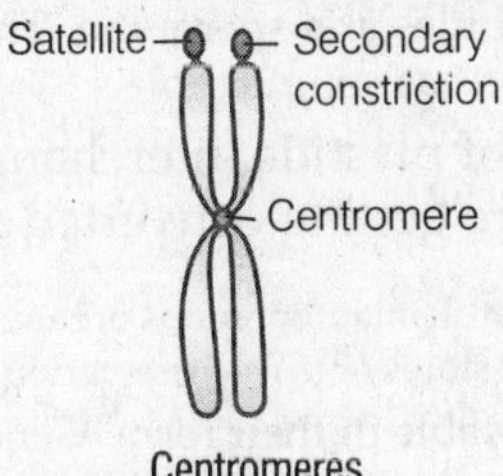

Centromeres

(b) **Cell wall** It gives a definite shape to the cell and protects the cell from mechanical injury and infections. It also helps in cell to cell interaction and act as a barrier for undesirable macromolecules.

(c) **Smooth ER** It helps in synthesis of lipids, metabolism of carbohydrates, regulation of calcium concentration, drug detoxification and attachment of receptor on cell membrane proteins.

It also playes a role in the synthesis of steroid hormones.

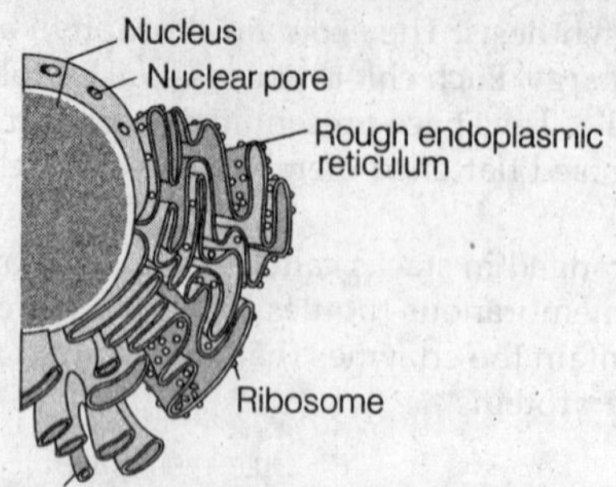

Structure of endoplasmic reticulum

(d) **Golgi apparatus** It is the important site for the formation of glycoprotein and glycolipids. It is also involved in the synthesis of cell wall materials and also play an important role in formation of cell plate during cell division.

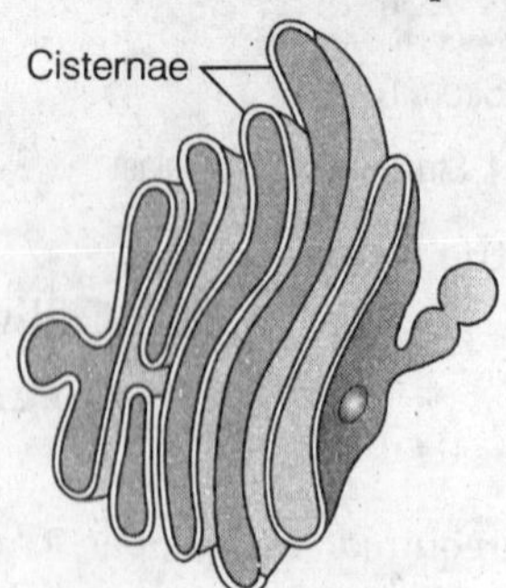

Structure of Golgi body

(e) **Centrioles** They form the base body of cilia and flagella and spindle fibres that gives rise to spindle apparatus during cell division in animal cells. They help in formation of microtubules and sperm tail. They also help in cell division by forming asters, which acts as spindle pole.

Q. 10 Are the different types of plastids interchangeable? If yes, give examples where they are getting converted from one type to another.

Thinking Process Plastids are semiautonomous organelles having DNA and double membrane envelope which stores or synthesise various types of organic compounds.

Ans. *Yes,* plastids are interchangeable in their form. Generally, three types of plastids are present in plant cells, *i.e.,* leucoplasts (storage), chromoplast (coloured) and chloroplasts (synthesis of food). Depending upon the circumstances, one type of plasmid may be converted into another type. *e.g.,*

(i) In *Capsicum,* the cells of ovary consist of leucoplasts. When ovary changes into fruit, leucoplasts are transformed into chloroplasts. When the fruit ripens chloroplast are converted into chromoplast.

(ii) The leucoplast in stem tubers of potato, on exposure to sunlight transform to chloroplasts.

In some cases the chloroplasts get converted during ripening of fruits, *e.g.,* tomato and chilli when they change colour from green to red. It occurs because of chlorophyll changes into carotenoid (red coloured pigment) and degeneration of lamella.

Chapter

09 Biomolecules

Multiple Choice Questions (MCQs)

Choose the correct answer from the given four options in the following questions.

Q. 1 It is said that elemental composition of living organisms and that of inanimate objects (like earth's crust) are similar in the sense that all the major elements are present in both. Then what would be the difference between these two groups? Choose a correct answer from among the following.

(a) Living organisms have more gold in them than inanimate objects
(b) Living organisms have more water in their body than inanimate objects
(c) Living organisms have more carbon, oxygen and hydrogen per unit mass than inanimate objects
(d) Living organisms have more calcium in them than inanimate objects

Ans. *(c)* All living organisms and non-living matter in our biosphere are made of similar elements and compounds. Several researches performed on plants, animals and microbes confirmed that a relative abundance of organic compound *i,e.,* carbon, hydrogen and oxygen is more in living organisms than in the earth's crust (non-living matter).

Whereas, the percent composition of other inorganic molecules like calcium and silicon is more in earth's crust as compared to living matter.

A Comparison of Elements Present in Non-Living and Living Matter

Element	% Weight in	
	Earth's Crust	Human Body
Hydrogen (H)	0.14	0.5
Carbon (C)	0.03	18.5
Oxygen (O)	46.6	65.0
Calcium (Ca)	3.6	1.5
Silicon (Si)	27.7	Negligible

Q. 2 Many elements are found in living organisms either free or in the form of compounds. One of the following is not found in living organisms.

(a) Silicon (b) Magnesium (c) Iron (d) Sodium

Ans. *(a)* **Silicon** is not found freely in nature, but it does occur as oxides and silicates, whereas magnesium, iron and sodium are present in living organisms as ions. Silicon is essential to plant life but is often found in minute quantities in human body and its function is still unknown.

Magnesium is an abundant element. It is essential for a number of enzymes and their action, particularly those utilising ATP.

Iron is an important constituent of haemoglobin and plays a vital role by taking part in O_2 transport, and electron transport chain.

Sodium plays a vital role in animals by regulating nerve impulse transmission and altering the membrane permeability. It also has indispensable role in osmoregulation.

Q. 3 Amino acids have both an amino group and a carboxyl group in their structure. Which amongst the following is an amino acid?

(a) Formic acid (b) Glycerol
(c) Glyolic acid (d) Glycine

Ans. *(d)* **Glycine** is the **simplest amino acid** containing both an amino group and a carboxyl group. Whereas formic acid is the simplest carboxylic acid, glycerol is in alcohol and glycolic acid is carboxylic acid substituted with hydroxyl group.

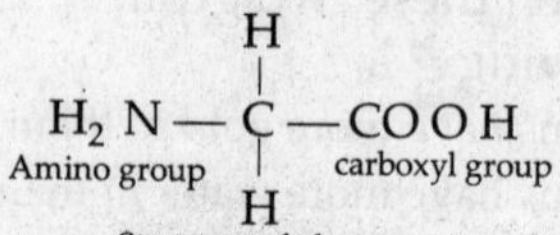

$$H_2N - \underset{H}{\overset{H}{\overset{|}{\underset{|}{C}}}} - COOH$$

Amino group — carboxyl group

Structure of glycine

Q. 4 An amino acid under certain conditions have both positive and negative charges simultaneously in the same molecule. Such a form of amino acid is called

(a) acidic form
(b) basic form
(c) aromatic form
(d) zwitterionic form

Ans. *(d)* A zwitterion is a neutral molecule having both the cation and anion charges on the same molecule. Amino acids are the well known examples of zwitterion. In acidic solution' amino group accepts a hydrogen ion to become positively charged. Whereas, in alkaline solution the carboxyl group donates a hydrogen ion to become negatively charged. The pH at which the amino acid is electrically neutral is called isoelectric pH.

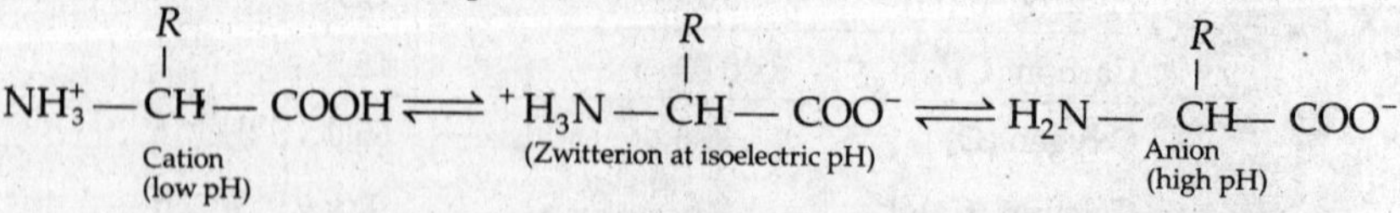

$$\underset{\text{Cation (low pH)}}{NH_3^+ - \overset{R}{\overset{|}{CH}} - COOH} \rightleftharpoons \underset{\text{(Zwitterion at isoelectric pH)}}{{}^+H_3N - \overset{R}{\overset{|}{CH}} - COO^-} \rightleftharpoons \underset{\text{Anion (high pH)}}{H_2N - \overset{R}{\overset{|}{CH}} - COO^-}$$

Q. 5 Sugar are technically called carbohydrates, refering to the fact that their formulae are only multiple of $C(H_2O)$. Hexoses therefore have six carbons, twelve hydrogens and six oxygen atoms. Glucose is a hexose. Choose from among the following another hexose.

(a) Fructose (b) Erythrose
(c) Ribulose (d) Ribose

Thinking Process Glucose is an aldohexose. Its first carbon atom is attached to a hydrogen atom by a single bond and another to an oxygen atom by a double bond.

Ans. ***(a)*** **Fructose** is a ketohexose. Its carbon atom is attached to an oxygen atom by a double bond.

CH_2OH
C=O
HO—H
H—OH
H—OH
CH_2OH

Structure of D-fructose

Erythrose is a **tetrose** carbohydrate ($C_4H_8O_4$). It is a part of tetrose family and possesses one aldehyde group.

O=—H
H—OH
H—OH
CH_2OH

Structure of D-erythrose

Ribulose is a **ketopentose**, containing five carbon atoms and includes 'ketone' as a functional group.

CH_2OH
=O
H—OH
H—OH
CH_2OH

Structure of D-ribulose

Ribose is a **pentose** which is a major component of RNA.

O=—H
H—OH
H—OH
H—OH
CH_2OH

Structure of D-ribose

Q. 6 When you take cells or tissue pieces and grind them with an acid in a mortar and pestle, all the small biomolecules dissolve in the acid. Proteins, polysaccharides and nucleic acids are insoluble in mineral acid and get precipitated. The acid soluble compounds include aminoacids , nucleosides, small sugars etc. When one adds a phosphate group to a nucleoside, one gets another acid soluble biomolecule called.

(a) Nitrogen base (b) Adenine

(c) Sugar phosphate (d) Nucleotide

Ans. *(d)* Each nucleoside is made up of cyclic nitrogenous base, (purine or pyrimidine) and a pentose sugar.

On phosphorylation, it forms a nucleotide which consists of a nitrogenous base pentose sugar and phosphate groups.

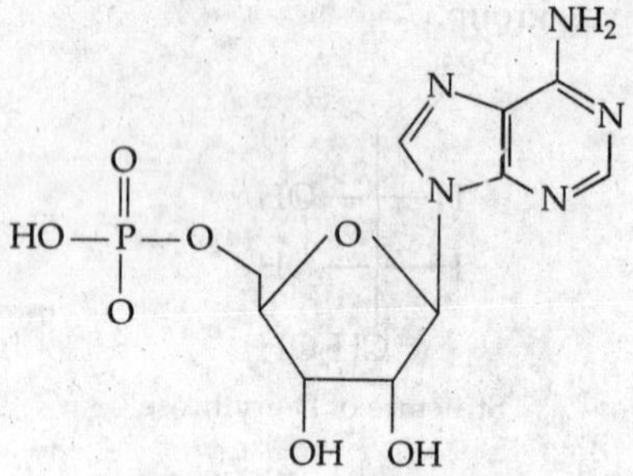

NH_2 N N N N HO—P—O O O O OH OH

Structure of a nucleotide

Q. 7 When we homogenise any tissue in an acid, the acid soluble pool represents

(a) Cytoplasm (b) Cell membrane

(c) Nucleus (d) Mitochondria

Thinking Process Homogenisation is achieved by a mechanical device called homogeniser. The plant/animal tissues are homogenised for cytological and biochemical studies.

Ans. *(a)* On homogenising any tissue in an acid, the acid soluble pool represents cytoplasm. Homogenisation is a process whereby a biological sample is brought to a state such that all fractions of the sample are equal in composition.

Q. 8 The most abundant chemical in living organisms is

(a) protein (b) water (c) sugar (d) nucleic acid

Ans. *(b)* There is abundance of water in living matter. It is the only polar molecule in living organisms, that can diffuse through a cell membrane without active transport. It is vital for a number of metabolic reactions and one of the raw materials for photosynthesis.

Q. 9 A homopolymer has only one type of building block called monomer repeated '*n*' number of times. A heteropolymer has more than one type of monomer. Proteins are heteropolymers usually made of

(a) 20 types of monomers (b) 40 types of monomers

(c) 30 types of monomers (d) only one type of monomer

Ans. *(a)* Proteins are heteropolymers made of about **20 different kinds of monomer,** *i.e.*, **amino acids**. Each of these amino acids is made up of carbon, amino group, carboxyl group, hydrogen and a *R*—group. This variable *R*—group makes each monomer different from one another.

Q. 10 Proteins perform many physiological functions. For example, some functions as enzymes. One of the following represents an additional function that some proteins discharge?
(a) Antibiotics
(b) Pigment conferring colour to skin
(c) Pigments making colours of flowers
(d) Hormones

Ans. *(d)* Proteins can sometimes function as hormones, *i.e.*, peptide hormones such as insulin, growth hormone etc. Other compounds such as antibiotics, florigen and melanin are non-proteineceous in nature.

Q. 11 Glycogen is a homopolymer made of
(a) glucose units
(b) galactose units
(c) ribose units
(d) amino acids

Thinking Process In humans, glycogen is made and stored primarily in the cells of liver and the muscle, and it functions as the secondary long term **energy storage.** Glycogen is converted into glucose by muscle cells and liver also glycogen is converted to glucose for entire body use including CNS, PNS and other body parts.

Ans. *(a)* **Glycogen** is the storage polysaccharide present in animals. Glycogen consist of glucose molecule linked together with α (1→ 4) linkages with α (1→ 6) branch points occurring every 8-12 residues.

Galactose, on the other hand is a monosaccharide, and combines with glucose through condensation reaction, resulting in the formation of disaccharide, **lactose.**

Ribose is a **pentose monosaccharide** which has all hydroxyl group on the same side in fisher projection. It forms a part of backbone in RNA. Amino acids are the monomers of proteins.

Q. 12 The number of 'ends' in a glycogen molecule would be
(a) Equal to the number of branches plus one
(b) Equal to the number of branch points
(c) One
(d) Two, one on the left side and another on the right side

Ans. *(a)* **Glycogen** is the highly branched polysaccharide of glucose units popularly known as **animal starch,** as it is chemically similar to starch. It has 30,000 glucose residues and a molecular weight of about 4.8 million. Glucose residues in glycogen are arranged in a highly branched chains that resemble a bush.

There are two main linkage patterns, observed in glycogen, *i.e.*, α(1→4) linkage in the straight part and α(1→6) linkage in the area of branching. The distance between two branching points is 10-14 glucose residues. Glycogen has as many non-reducing ends as branches plus one.

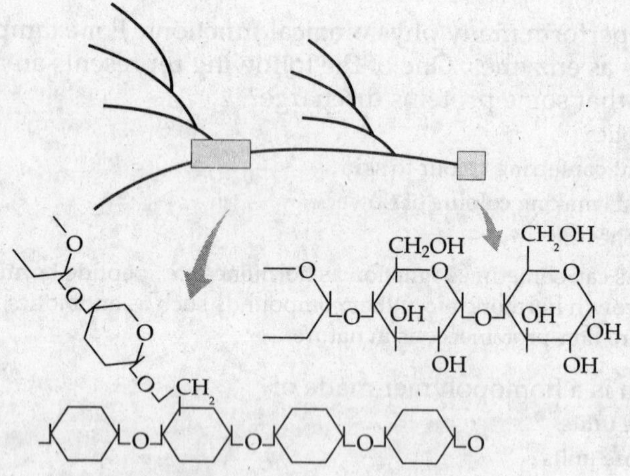

Diagrammatic representation of a portion of glycogen

Q. 13 The primary structure of a protein molecule has

(a) two ends (b) one end (c) three ends (d) no ends

Ans. ***(a)*** The primary structure of a protein refers to a linear sequence of amino acids in polypeptide chain, held together by peptide bonds. A polypeptide chain has two ends carboxyl terminus (C-terminus) and the amino terminus (N-terminus) based on the nature of the free group on each extremity.

Q. 14 Enzymes are biocatalysts. They catalyse biochemical reactions. In general they reduce activation energy of reactions. Many physico-chemical processes are enzyme mediated. Which of the following reactions is not enzyme mediated in biological system?

(a) Dissolving CO_2 in water (b) Unwinding the two strands of DNA

(c) Hydrolysis of sucrose (d) Formation of peptide bond

Ans. ***(a)*** Dissolving CO_2 in water, is a non-enzyme catalysed reaction.

Unwinding of the two strands of DNA is catalysed by the enzymes helicase, gyrase **topoisomerase. Hydrolysis** of sucrose is catalysed by **sucrase. Peptide bonds** are formed by the action of enzyme **peptidyl transferase.**

Very Short Answer Type Questions

Q. 1 Medicines are either man made (*i.e.*, synthetic) or obtained from living organisms like plants, bacteria, animals, etc., and hence, the latter are called natural products. Sometimes, natural products are chemically altered by man to reduce toxicity or side effects. Write against each of the following whether they were initially obtained as a natural product or as a synthetic chemical.

(a) Penicillin (b) Sulfonamide (c) Vitamin-C (d) Growth hormone

Ans. (a) **Penicillin** is a group of **antibiotics** derived from fungi *Penicillium* and is obtained a natural product.

(b) **Sulphonamide** is a synthetic chemical. It is an antimicrobial agent and is the basis of several groups of drugs.

(c) **Vitamin-C** or L-ascorbic acid or ascorbate is a natural product and an essential nutrient for humans. It is present in citrus fruits.

(d) **Growth hormone** (GH or HGH) also known as somatotropin is a peptide hormone occuring naturally in the body. It stimulates growth.

Q. 2 Select an appropriate chemical bond among ester bond, glycosidic bond, peptide bond and hydrogen bond and write against each of the following.

(a) Polysaccharide (b) Protein (c) Fat (d) Water

Ans. (a) **Polysaccharide** is linked by glycosidic bond. Glycosidic bond is a type of covalent bond joining simple units carbohydrate molecules together to form a long chain polysaccharide.

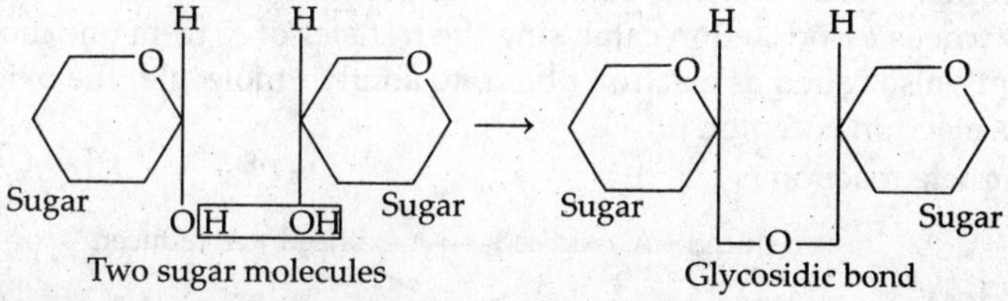

Sugar — O[H OH] — Sugar → Sugar — O — Sugar

Two sugar molecules Glycosidic bond

(b) **Protein** are linked by peptide bonds. Peptide bond is a covalent chemical bond formed between two amino acids when the carboxyl group of one reacts with the amino group of other causing release of water molecule. Hence, called as dehydration synthesis reaction (condensation reaction).

Peptide bonds between a chain of amino acids results in the formation of protein.

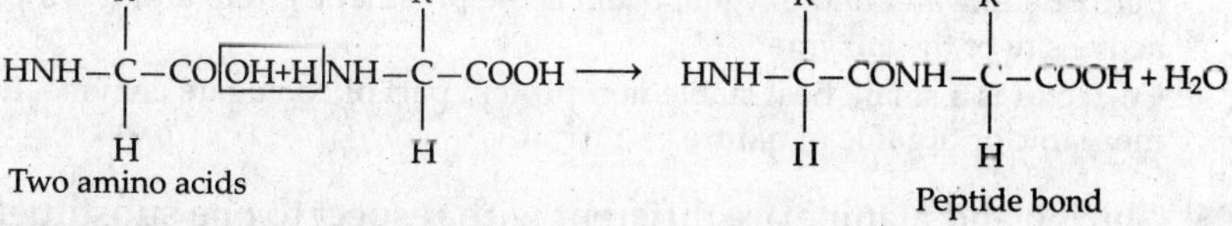

$$\text{HNH}-\underset{\text{H}}{\overset{R}{\text{C}}}-\text{CO}\boxed{\text{OH+H}}\text{NH}-\underset{\text{H}}{\overset{R}{\text{C}}}-\text{COOH} \longrightarrow \text{HNH}-\underset{\text{H}}{\overset{R}{\text{C}}}-\text{CONH}-\underset{\text{H}}{\overset{R}{\text{C}}}-\text{COOH} + H_2O$$

Two amino acids Peptide bond

(c) **Ester bonds** are formed by the reaction between carboxyl group of fatty acid and hydroxyl group of triglycerols to form fat. This reaction occurs when the hydroxyl group (—OH) of glycerol reacts with the carboxyl group (—COOH) of fatty acids, releasing water.

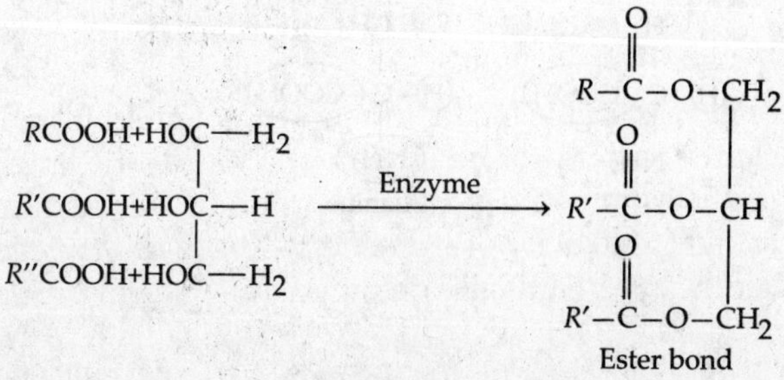

$$\begin{array}{l} R\text{COOH+HOC}-H_2 \\ R'\text{COOH+HOC}-\text{H} \\ R''\text{COOH+HOC}-H_2 \end{array} \xrightarrow{\text{Enzyme}} \begin{array}{l} R-\overset{\text{O}}{\overset{\|}{\text{C}}}-\text{O}-\text{CH}_2 \\ R'-\overset{\text{O}}{\overset{\|}{\text{C}}}-\text{O}-\text{CH} \\ R'-\overset{\text{O}}{\overset{\|}{\text{C}}}-\text{O}-\text{CH}_2 \end{array}$$

Ester bond

(d) **Hydrogen bond** is electrovalent interaction between polar molecules in which hydrogen is bound to a highly electronegative atom, such as N, O, F, etc. Water is the best known example

Hydrogen bond

$O \cdots H^+ \quad H^+ \quad H^+ \quad O^- \quad O^-$

Q. 3 Write the name of any one amino acid, sugar, nucleotide and fatty acid.

Ans. (a) Amino acid – Leucine (b) Sugar – Glucose

(c) Nucleotide – Adenosine triphosphate (d) Fatty acid – Palmitic acid

Q. 4 Reaction given below is catalysed by oxidoreductase between two substrates A and A′, complete the reaction.

A reduced + A′ oxidised ⟶

Ans. Oxidoreductase is an enzyme that catalyses oxidation and reductions reactions. This enzyme is associated in catalysing the transfer of e^- from one molecule (the reductant), also called as electron donor, to another molecule (the oxidant), also called as electron acceptor.

The complete reaction is

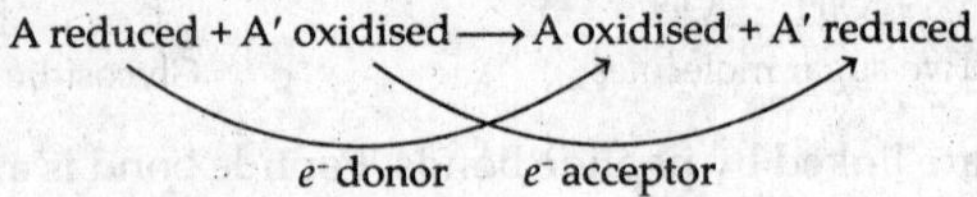

Q. 5 How are prosthetic groups different from co-factors?

Ans. **Prosthetic groups** are organic compounds that are tightly bound to the apoenzyme, (an enzyme without cofaetor) by covalent or non-covalent forces, *e.g.*, in peroxidase and catalase, which catalyse the breakdown of hydrogen peroxide to water and oxygen, haem is the prosthetic group and it is a part of the active site of the enzyme.

Co-factor is a small, heat stable non-protein part of conjugate enzyme. It may be inorganic or organic in nature.

Q. 6 Glycine and alanine are different with respect to one substituent on the α-carbon. What are the other common substituent groups?

Ans. In both the amino acids the common substituent groups are NH_2, COOH and H. However the key difference is in their side chains (R groups): Glycine has hydrogen (H) whereas alanine has methyl group as its side chain.

H | (H)–C–(COOH) | NH_2

Glycine

CH_3 | (H)–C–(COOH) | (NH_2)

Alanine

Q. 7 Starch, cellulose, glycogen, chitin are polysaccharides found among the following. Choose the one appropriate and write against each.

Cotton fibre ....
Exoskeleton of cockroach ....
Liver ....
Peeled potato ....

Ans. (a) Cotton fibre — **Cellulose** (b) Exoskeleton of cockroach — **Chitin**

(c) Liver — **Glycogen** (d) Peeled potato — **Starch**

Cellulose is a long chain of linked glucose molecules and is the main component of plant cell walls. **Cotton** is the purest natural form of **cellulose**. The cellulose content of cotton fibre is 90%.

Chitin is a long chain polymer that forms the hard part of the outer integument or exoskeleton of crustaceans and insects such as cockroach. It is also the main component of the cell walls of fungi.

Glycogen is a multibranched polysaccharide of glucose acting as a form of stored energy in the liver of animals. It is also found in some fungi as stored food material.

Starch is a carbohydrate consisting of along chain of glucose units joined by glycosidic bonds. This polysaccharide is produced mostly by green plants for energy storage, *e.g.*, peeled potato.

Short Answer Type Questions

Q. 1 Enzymes are proteins. Proteins are long chains of amino acids linked to each other by peptide bonds. Amino acids have many functional groups in their structure. These functional groups are many of them at least, ionisable. As they are weak acids and bases in the chemical nature, this ionisation is influenced by pH of the solution. For many enzymes, activity is influenced by surrounding pH. This is depicted in the curve below, explain briefly.

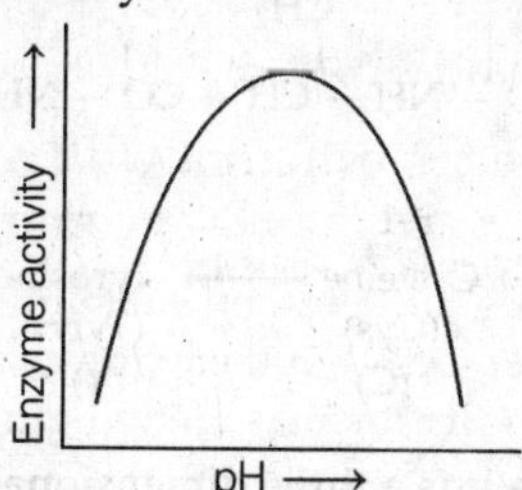

Ans. Enzymes, generally function within a narrow range of pH. Most of the enzyme shows their highest activity at a particular pH called **optimum pH**, and their activity **declines** below and above from this value.

Extremely high or low pH values generally results in complete loss of activity for most enzyms. The graph above represents the maximum enzyme activity at the optimum pH.

Q. 2 Is rubber a primary metabolite or a secondary metabolite? Write four sentences about rubber.

Ans. Rubber (*cis* 1, 4-polyisopyrene) is a secondary metabolite. Secondary metabolites are chemicals produced by plants for which no role has been found yet in growth, photosynthesis, reproduction or other primary functions.

(i) Rubber is extracted from *Havea brasiliensis* (rubber tree).

(ii) It is a byproduct of the lactiferous tissue of the vessels that are in the form of latex.

(iii) It is a polymer of isoprene (*cis*-1, 4-polyisoprene) and is one of the largest natural polymers.

(iv) It is elastic, water proof and a good electrical conductor.

Q. 3 Schematically represent primary, secondary and tertiary structures of a hypothetical polymer say for example a protein.

Ans. Proteins are the large-sized, heteropolymeric macromolecules having one or more polypeptides (chains of amino acid).

Primary Structure The primary structure of a protein is the linear sequence of amino acid residues, which forms the basic sequence of the protein. The amino acids are linked together in a sequence by peptide bonds.

The primary structure of protein extends from an amino-terminal (N) to the carboxyl terminal (C) end

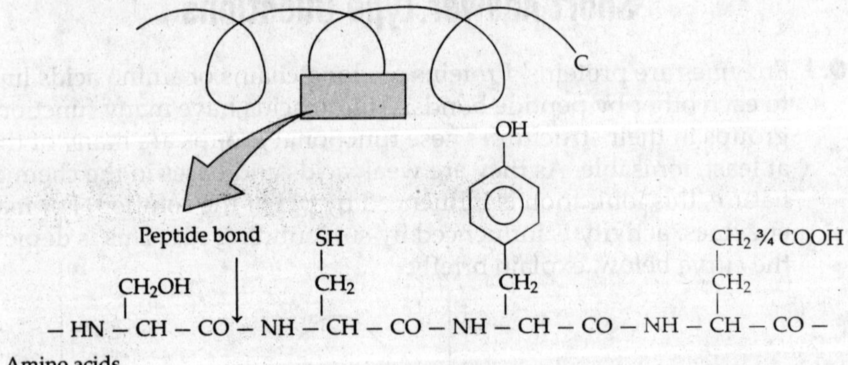

	n-2	*n*-1	*n*	*n*+1	
First amino acidrepresents left end of chain	Serine → (Ser) (S)	Cysteine → (Cys) (C)	Tyrosine → (Tyr) (Y)	Glutamic acid (Glu) (E)	Last amino acid represents right end of polypeplide chain

Secondary Structure It is a three dimensional form of local segments of bipolymers such as proteins. Secondary structure of proteins is defined by hydrogen bonds between backbone amino and carboxyl groups. Mainly secondary structure in proteins possess two forms, *i.e.*, α-helix and β-pleated sheet.

α-helix is a polypeptide chain spirally coiled to form a right handed helix. This helix may be coiled regularly in some places and randomly in others. The helix is stabilised by hydrogen bonds which are formed between the carbonyl group (CO) of one amino acid and the amide group (NH) group of fourth amino acid.

β-pleated sheets two or more polypeptide chains are joined together by intermolecular hydrogen bonds to produce a sheet like structure instead of fibre as in α-helix. The polypeptide strands in a sheet may run parallel in same direction, (*e.g.*, keratin) or in opposite direction called antiparallel β-sheet, (*e.g.*, fibroin).

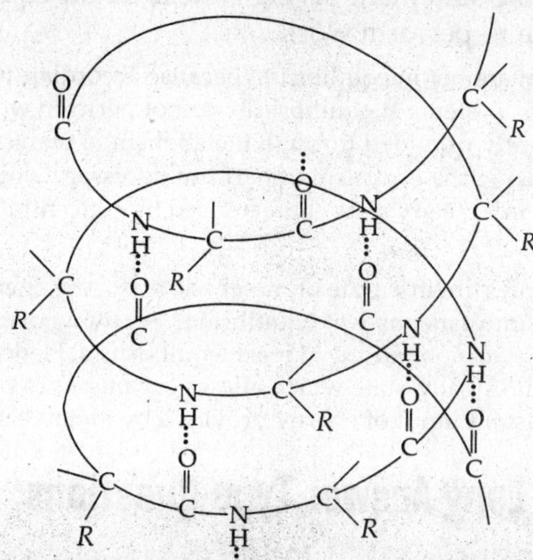

α-helix (secondary structure of protein)

Tertiary structure involves the overall three-dimensional folding of the polypeptide chain into its final shape. This folding is driven by interactions such as H-bonds, ionic bonds, covalent bonds, van der Waat's interactions hydrophobic interactions and disulphide linkages. It gives the protein a three dimensional conformation.

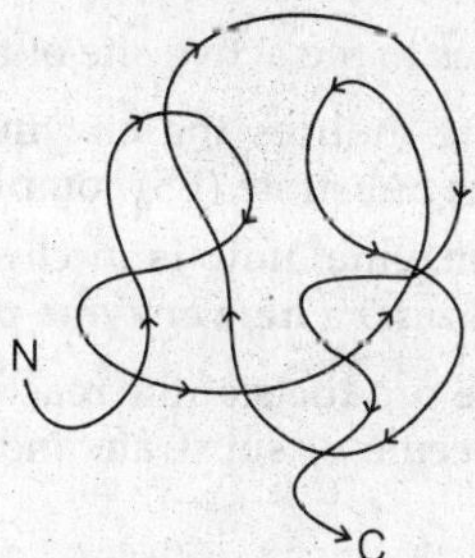

A tertiary structure of Protein

Q. 4 Nucleic acids exhibit secondary structure, justify with example.

Ans. Nucleic acids are polymeric macromolecules or large biological molecules, essential for all known forms of life. The secondary structrure of a nucleic acid molecule refers to the base pairing interactions within a single strands or between two interacting strands.

DNA and RNA represent two main nucleic acids, and their secondary structures differ *e.g.*, the secondary structure of DNA comprises of two complementary strands of polydeoxyribonucleotide, spirally coiled on a common axis forming a helical structure.

This double helical structure of DNA is stabilised by phosphodiester bonds (between 5' of sugar of one nucleotide and 3' of sugar of another nucleotide), hydrogen bonds (between complementary bases, such as between adenine and thymine, and between guanine and cytosine) and ionic interactioins.

Q. 5 Comment on the statement 'living state is a non-equilibrium steady state to be able to perform work'.

Ans. **Living organism** are not in equilibrium because according to the laws of thermodynamics, systems at equilibrium cannot perform work. In a steady state energy is constantly provided through metabolism to maintain non-equilibrium conditions, allowing the organism to perform necessary work. The living organisms exist in a steady state characterised by concentration of each of the biomolecules.

These biomolecules are in a state of metabolic flux. Any chemical or physical process moves simultaneously to equilibrium. As living organisms work continuously, they cannot afford to reach equilibrium. Hence, the living state is a non-equilibrium steady-state which allows organisms to perform work. This is achieved by constant input of energy provided by metabolism.

Long Answer Type Questions

Q. 1 Formation of Enzyme substrate complex (ES) is the first step in the catalysed reactions. Describe the other steps till the formation of product.

Ans. Each enzyme molecule has an active site for specific binding of substrate molecules . The enzyme work by altering the activation energy of the reaction.

The catalytic process of an enzyme can be described as follows

(i) The substrate approaches to the active site of the enzyme, fitting into it.

(ii) Binding of the substrate induces the enzymes to alter its shape leading to formation of the Enzyme Substrate (ES) complex.

(iii) The active site of the enzyme, now is in close proximity with the substrate, break its chemical bonds and a **new enzyme product complex is formed**.

(iv) The enzyme releases the products of the reaction and the free enzyme is ready to bind to another molecule of substrate and run through the catalytic cycle once again.

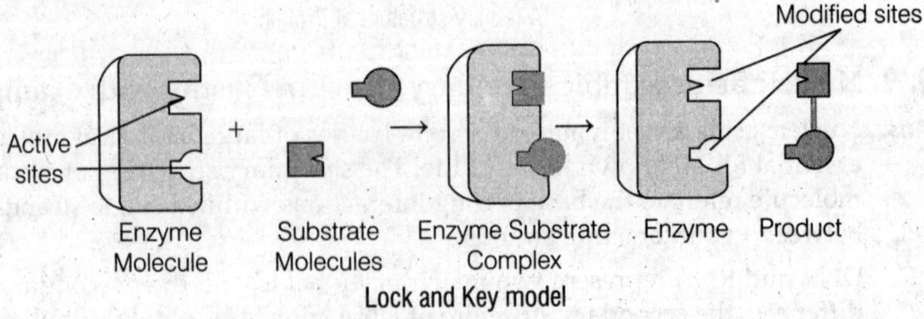

Lock and Key model

Q. 2 What are different classes of enzymes? Explain any two with the type of reactions they catalyse.

Ans. Enzymes are divided into six classes each with 4-13 sub classes and named accordingly by a four-digit number.

(i) **Oxidoreductases/dehydrogenases** These enzymes take part in oxidation and reduction or transfer of e^-.

$$\text{S (reduced)} + \text{S}' \text{ (oxidised)} \longrightarrow \text{S (oxidised)} + \text{S}' \text{ (reduced)}$$

(ii) **Transferases** These enzymes transfer a functional group from one molecule to another (other than hydrogen).

$$\text{S-G} + \text{S}' \xrightarrow{\text{Transferase}} \text{S} + \text{S}'\text{-G}$$

(iii) **Hydrolases** These enzymes catalyse the hydrolysis of bonds like ester, ether, peptide, glycosidic C-C, C-halide, P-N etc.

$$\underset{\text{Maltose}}{C_{12}H_{22}O_{11}} + H_2O \xrightarrow{\text{Maltase}} \underset{\text{Glucose}}{2C_6H_{12}O_6}$$

(iv) **Lyases** These enzymes causes cleavage, removal of groups without hydrolysis they catalyse removal of groups producing double bond.

$$\begin{matrix} X & Y \\ | & \| \\ C & - C \end{matrix} \xrightarrow{\text{lyase}} X-Y+C=C$$

(v) **Isomerases** These enzymes cause rearrangement of molecular structure to effect isomeric changes. They are of three types, *i.e.*, isomerases, epimerases and mutases.

$$\text{Glucose - 6 - phosphate} \xrightarrow{\text{Isomerase}} \text{Fructose 6 - phosphate}$$

(Aldose to ketose group or *vice-versa*)

$$\text{Glucose - 6 - phosphate} \xrightarrow{\text{Mutase}} \text{Glucose-1-phosphate}$$

(Shifting the position of side group)

$$\text{Xylulose 5-phosphate} \xrightarrow{\text{Epimerase}} \text{Ribulose-5-phosphate}$$

(Change in position of one constituent or carbon group)

(vi) **Ligases** are enzymes catalysing bonding of two chemicals with the help of energy obtained from ATP resulting formation of bonds such as C — O, C — S, C — N and P — O *e.g.*, pyruvate carboxyl use

$$Ab + C \longrightarrow A - C + b$$

$$\text{Pyruvric acid} + CO_2 + \text{ATP} + H_2O \xrightleftharpoons{\text{pyruvate carboxylase}} \text{Oxaloacetate} + \text{ADP} + \text{Pi} -$$

Q. 3 Nucleic acids exhibit secondary structure. Describe through Watson-Crick model.

Ans. Nucleic acids are long chain macromolecules which are formed by end to end polymerisation of large number of repeated units called **nucleotides**. Nucleic acids show a wide range of secondary structures.

A secondary structure is formed by the interactions between bases and sugar phosphate backbone and is responsible for the shape of that nucleic acid.

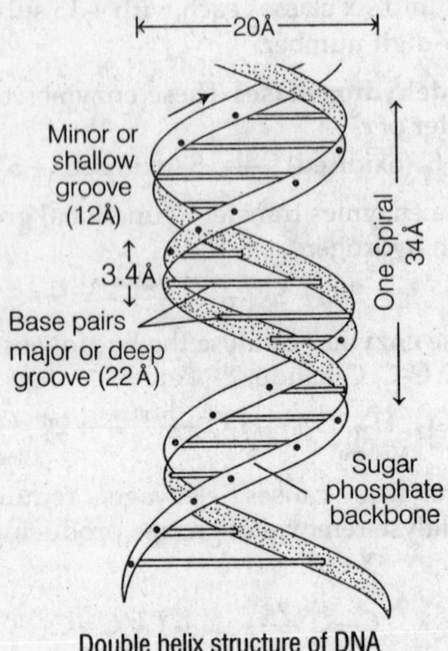

Double helix structure of DNA

James Watson and Francis Crick proposed a secondary structure of DNA molecules based on the crystallographic studies.

(i) **DNA or deoxyribonucleic acid** is a helically twisted double-chain polydeoxyribo- nucleotide macromolecule.

(ii) The two strands of DNA run anti-parallel to each other called as DNA duplex.

(iii) The spiral twisting of DNA has two types of alternate grooves, *i.e.,* major and minor.

(iv) One turn of 360° of the spiral has about 10 nucleotides on each strand of DNA, occupying a distance of about 3.4 nm.

(v) The nucleotides within each strand are held together by the **phosphodiester bonds** between the 5' carbon of one nucleotide and the 3' carbon of the adjacent nucleotide. These strong covalent bonds holds the sugar-phosphate backbone together.

(vi) The two strands of DNA are held together by weak **hydrogen bonds** between the nitrogenous bases. These hydrogen bonds are base specific. That is adenine forms 2 hydrogen bonds with thymine (A=T) and cytosine forms 3 hydrogen bonds with guanine (C≡G)).

(vii) In a double stranded chain of DNA the purine lies opposite to pyrimidine. This purine-pyrimidine pairing also contributes to the thickness of strand, *i.e.*, 2nm, and makes the two chains complementary.

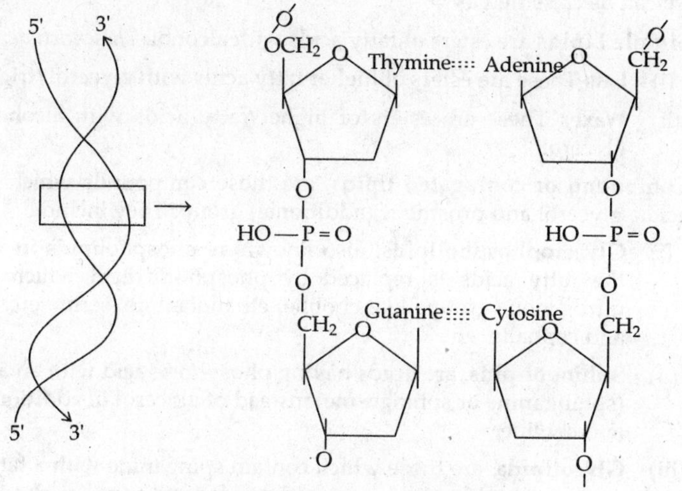

5' 3' OCH$_2$ Thymine:::: Adenine CH$_2$ O HO—P=O O HO—P=O O CH$_2$ Guanine:::: Cytosine CH$_2$ O O 5' 3'

Formation of bonds in double helix of DNA

Q. 4 What is the difference between a nucleotide and nucleoside? Give two examples of each with their structure.

Ans. Difference between a nucleotide and nucleoside are as follows

Nucleoside	Nucleotide
Nucleoside is a compound formed by the union of the nitrogenous base with a pentose sugar	Nucleotide is compound formed by union of nitrogen base, a pentose sugar and phosphate.
It is slightly basic in nature	A nucleotide is acidic in nature
It is a component of nucleotide and forms with both ribose and deoxyribose sugars.	Nucleotide is formed through phosphorylation of nucleoside
e.g., cytidine, uridine, adenosine, guanosine, thymidine and inosine.	*e.g.*, AMP, GMP, CMP, UMP dTMP

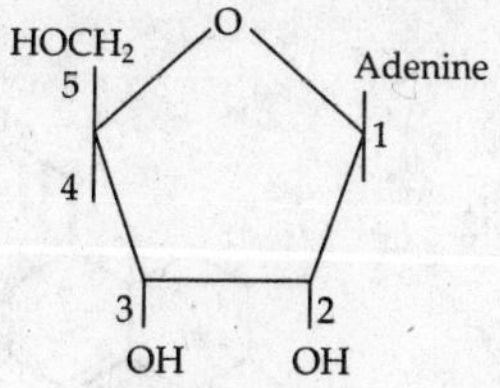

HOCH$_2$ 5 O Adenine 1 4 3 2 OH OH

Adenosine

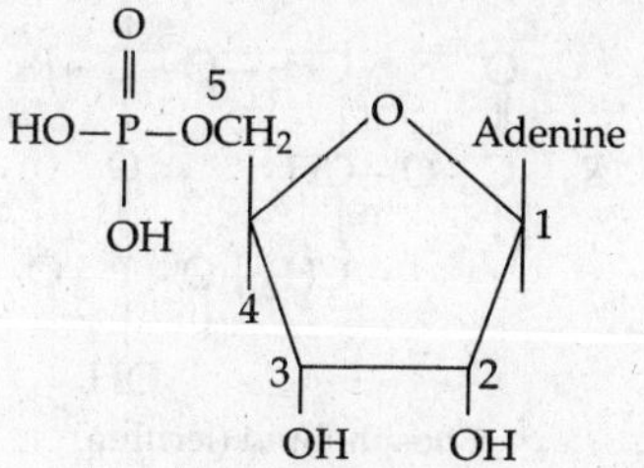

O ‖ 5 HO—P—OCH$_2$ O Adenine | OH 1 4 3 2 OH OH

AMP (Adenosine monophosphate)

Q. 5 Describe various forms of lipid with a few examples.

Ans. Lipids are the esters of higher fatty acid with alcohol, such as glycerol, etc.

These can be classified as

1. **Simple Lipids** are esters of fatty acids with alcohol. *These include:*
   - (i) **Fats** These are esters of higher fatty acids with glycerol (triglycerides).
   - (ii) **Waxes** These are esters of higher fatty acids with alcohol other than glycerol.
2. **Compound or conjugated lipids**, are those compounds which contain fatty acids, glycerol and prosthetic (additional) group. They include
   - (i) **Glycerophospholipids**, also known as phospholipids in which one of the fatty acids is replaced by phosphoric acid which is linked to nitrogenous groups like choline, ethanolamine, serine etc, *e.g.*, Lecithin and cephalin, etc.
   - (ii) **Sphingolipids**, are lipids having phosphoric acid with an amine alcohol (sphinganine or sphingosine) instead of glycerol in addition to fatty acid and choline.
   - (iii) **Glycolipids**, are those which contain spinganine with a fatty acid and a monosaccharide sugar, *e.g.*, cerebrosides and gangliosides.
3. **Steroids** are compounds with different chemical structure but similar physical properties. Their structure is based upon a 4 ring cyclopentano-perhydro phenanthrene, *e.g.*, cholesterol.
4. **Prostoglandins** are derivatives of arachidonic acid and contain 20 C-atoms. These are biologically active lipids.

$CH_3-(CH_2)_{14}-COOH$

Fatty acid (palmitic acid)

CH_2-OH / $CH-OH$ / CH_2-OH

Glycerol

$CH_2-O-C(=O)-R_1$ / $R_2-C(=O)-O-CH$ / $CH_2-O-C(=O)-R_3$

Triglyceride (R_1, R_2 and R_3 are fatty acids)

$CH_2-O-C(=O)-R_1$ / $R_2-C(=O)-O-CH$ / $CH_2-O-P(=O)(OH)-O-CH_2-CH_2-N(CH_3)_3$

Phospholipid (lecithin)

HO

Cholesterol

Fats and oils (lipids)

Chapter

10

Cell Cycle and Cell Division

Multiple Choice Questions (MCQs)

Choose the correct answer from the given four options in the following questions.

Q. 1 Meiosis in diploid organisms results in

(a) production of gametes
(b) reduction in the number of chromosomes
(c) introduction of variation
(d) All of the above

Thinking Process Sexual reproduction involves the union of male and female gametes. Fusion of gametes is accomplished by the plasmogamy (union of protoplasm) followed by karyogamy (union of nucleus). This results in doubling of chromosome numbers in the resultant cell.

Ans. *(d)* Meiosis is a reductional division which reduces the chromosomes number by half in gametes. Since, it is a special kind of cell division in which exchange of genetic material occurs, it brings about variation in next generations. So all options are characteristic features of meiotic cell division.

Q. 2 At which stage of meiosis does the genetic constitution of gametes is finally decided

(a) Metaphase-I (b) Anaphase-II (c) Metaphase-II (d) Anaphase-I

Ans. *(d)* The genetic constitution of gametes is finally decided when the sister chromatids of each chromosome separate and move toward opposite poles. It connot be metaphase-I or metaphase-II because during these stages, the chromosomes or chromatids, merely arrange themselves at the metaphase plate. During anaphase-I the separation of homologous chromosomes takes place.

Q. 3 Meiosis occurs in organisms during

(a) sexual reproduction
(b) vegetative reproduction
(c) Both (a) and (b)
(d) None of the above

Ans. *(a)* Meiosis occurs in sexually reproducing organisms to reduce the chromosome number by half before their gametes unite, to maintain the constant chromosome number ($2n$) in the progery.

Vegetative reproduction is a kind of asexual reproduction occurring in plants that does not involve the formation or fusion of gametes.

Q. 4 During Anaphase-I of meiosis

(a) homologous chromosomes separate
(b) non-homologous autosomes separate
(c) sister chromatids separate
(d) non-sister chromatids separate

Ans. *(a)* **During Anaphase-I** homologous chromosomes separate, while sister chromatids remain associated at their centromeres.

Rest of the options do not take place during anaphase-I of meiosis, hence they are incorrect.

Q. 5 Mitosis is characterised by

(a) Reduction division
(b) Equal division
(c) Both (a) and (b)
(d) Pairing of homologous chromosomes

Thinking Process Growth and multiplication is the characteristic feature of all living organisms. It is accomplished by mitotic cell division by which there is an increase in the number of cells. This is also involved in asexual reproduction in lower organisms and plants.

Ans. *(b)* Mitosis is characterised by equal division where the chromosome numbers in the daughter cells remain same as in the parent cell. While reduction division is the characteristic feature of meiosis.

Q. 6 A bivalent of meiosis-I consists of

(a) Two chromatids and one centromere
(b) Two chromatids and two centromeres
(c) Four chromatids and two centromeres
(d) Four chromatids and four centromeres

Ans. *(c)* The complex formed by a pair of synapsed homologous chromosome is called bivalent or a tetrad. It has two centromeres and four chromatids.
Rest of the options are incorrect.

Q. 7 Cells which are not dividing are likely to be at

(a) G_1
(b) G_2
(c) G_0
(d) S-phase

Thinking Process Cell division is a very important process in all living organisms. The cell prepares itself, by DNA duplication and cell growth takes place prior to cell division.

Ans. *(c)* G_0, (G signifies growth and zero means no growth takes place at this stage). It is also called as **quiescent stage (G_0)**. Some cells of the body like heart cells, neuron which do not divide, exit at G_1 stage and enter G_0 of the cell cycle which is an inactive stage.
The cells in this stage remain metabolically active but no longer proliferate unless required.
G_1 phase is the first growth phase that lasts between the end of mitotic cycle and initiation of DNA replication.

G_2 phase is the second growth phase in which cell prepares itself to initiate cell division, *i.e.*, mitosis.
S-phase is the synthetic phase in which chromosomes replicate, *i.e.*, DNA replication, formation of new chromatin fibres, etc.

Q. 8 Which of the events listed below is not observed during mitosis?

(a) Chromatin condensation

(b) Movement of centrioles to opposite poles

(c) Appearance of chromosomes with two chromosome joined together at the centromere

(d) Crossing over

Ans. *(d)* **Crossing over** is the exchange of genetic material between homologous chromosomes and is a characteristic feature of meiotic cell division. It does not occur in mitosis. Rest of the options represent stages in mitosis.

Q. 9 Identify the wrong statement about meiosis

(a) Pairing of homologous chromosomes

(b) Four haploid cells are formed

(c) At the end of meiosis the number of chromosomes are reduced to half

(d) Two cycle of DNA replication occurs

Ans. *(d)* Two cycles of DNA replication does not occur in meiosis. DNA replication occurs only once that to before meiosis-I.

Other options (a), (b) and (c) define the meiotic cell division.

Q. 10 Select the correct statement about G_1 phase

(a) Cell is metabolically inactive

(b) DNA in the cell does not replicate

(c) It is not a phase of synthesis of macromolecules

(d) Cell stops growing

Ans. *(b)* G_1 phase means gap 1 phase. It is the interval between mitosis and initiation of DNA replication. The cell is metabolically active and continuously grows but does not replicate its DNA. The cell also synthesizes proteins that are required for DNA replication.

Rest of the options are not characteristics of G_1 phase.

Very Short Answer Type Questions

Q. 1 Between a prokaryote and an eukaryote, which cell has a shorter cell division time?

Thinking Process Prokaryotic cell has simple cell structure and cellular organisation. Its nucleus does not contain nuclear membrane.

Ans. Prokaryotic cell has shorter cell cycle time than the eukaryotic cell.

Q. 2 Which of the phases of cell cycle is of longest duration?

Ans. Interphase is of the longest duration. It consists of the following events

(a) **G_1 phase** (Gap 1) Corresponds to the interval between mitosis and initiation of DNA replication. Cell is metabolically active and continuously grows but does not replicate its DNA.

(b) **S-phase** (Synthesis phase) Marks the period during which DNA synthesis or replication takes place.

(i) Amount of DNA per cell doubles.

(ii) No increase in chromosome number.

(c) **G_2 Phase** (Gap 2) Proteins are synthesised in the preparation for cell division, while cell growth continues.

Q. 3 Name a stain commonly used to colour chromosomes.

Thinking Process The chromosomes are the thickest and the shortest at metaphase. They are stained for karyotyping for further study of chromosomes.

Ans. **Acetocarmine** and **Giemsa** stain can be used to stain the chromosomes.

Q. 4 Which tissue of animals and plants exhibits meiosis?

Ans. Meiosis is a special kind of cell division, also called as reductional division, which occurs in germ cells or sex cells of male and female reproductive organs in both plants and animals. These cell include male (sperm) and female (egg) gametes that take part in sexual reproduction.

Q. 5 Given that the average duplication time of *E. coli* is 20 minutes, how much time will two *E. coli* cells take to become 32 cells?

Ans. 1 hour -20 minutes

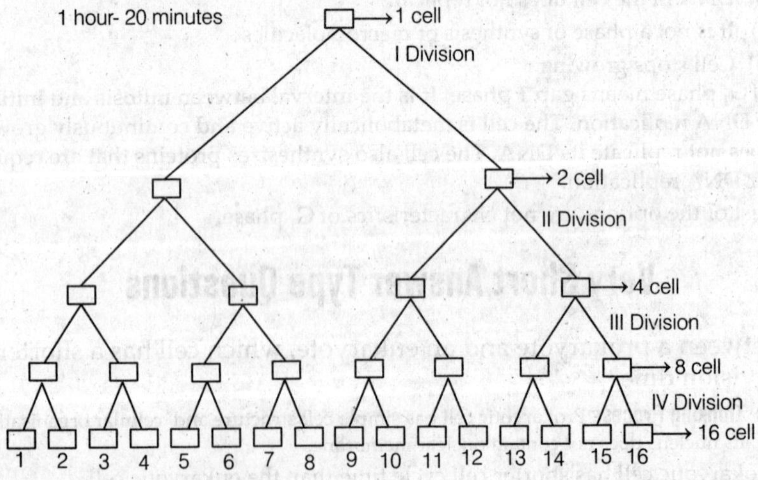

These are the 4 subsequent cell divisions to produce 16 cells and each division takes =20 min

Total time = $20 \times 4 = 80$ minutes or 1 hr 20 minutes

If 1 cell produces 16 cells in 1 hour 20 minutes.

So, two cells will also take the same time to become 32 cells (16×2). Therefore, it will take 1 hour and 20 minutes for 2 *E. coli* cells to become 32 cells.

Q. 6 **Which part of the human body should one use to demonstrate stages in mitosis?**

Ans. All the cells in the human body are somatic cells except germ cells in the male and female reproductive organs. The somatic cells divide by mitotic cell division for growth and regeneration.These can be used to demonstrate mitosis.

Q. 7 **What attributes does a chromatid require to be classified as a chromosome?**

Ans. Chromatid is one copy of a duplicated chromosome, which is joined to its identical copy by centromere. The duplication of chromosome material takes place during synthetic phase of cell cycle.

During mitosis, at late **metaphase** and early anaphase, there is longitudinal splitting of chromosomes, with each chromatid becoming a chromosome that is separated into daughter cells.

Q. 8 **The diagram shows a bivalent at prophase-I of meiosis. Which of the four chromatids can cross over?**

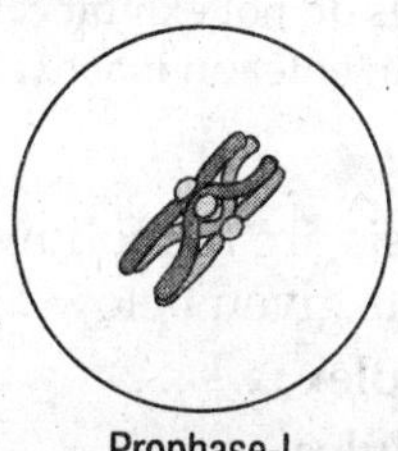

Prophase-I

Ans. The homologous chromosomes lie parallel to each other in **leptotene stage**. Each chromosome has four chromatids and are **bivalent**. The non-sister chromatids of homologous chromosomes cross over in pachytene stage of prophase- I.

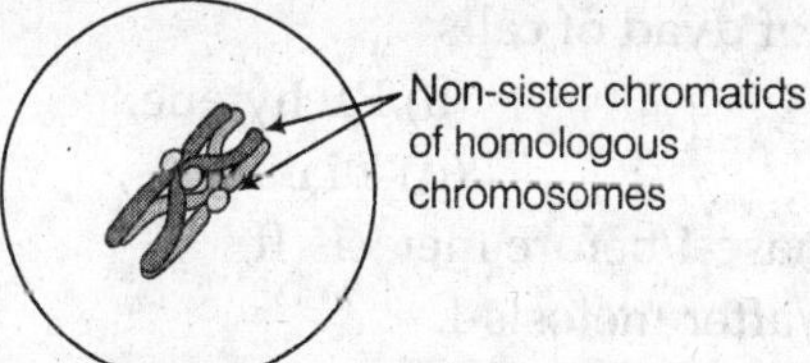

Pachytene of prophase-I of meiosis

Q. 9 **If a tissue has at a given time 1024 cells, how many cycles of mitosis had the original parental single cell undergone?**

Ans. The parental cell undergoes 10 divisions of mitotic cycle to give 1024 cells.

Q. 10 **An anther has 1200 pollen grains. How many pollen mother cells must have been there to produce them?**

Thinking Process The pollen mother cell (2n) undergoes meiotic cell divisions, each such cell produces four daughter cells with haploid (n) number of chromosomes.

Ans. Three hundred pollen mother cells have to be there to produce 1200 pollen grains. because one pollen mother cell will produce four pollen grains.

Q. 11 At what stage of cell cycle does DNA synthesis take place?

Ans. Synthetic phase or S-phase is the stage of cell cycle where DNA synthesis or replication takes place.

Q. 12 It is said that the one cycle of cell division in human cells (eukaryotic cells) takes 24 hours. Which phase of the cycle, do you think occupies the maximum part of cell cycle?

Thinking Process Cell cycle is a sequential event and is under genetic control. Every cell prepares itself before it starts dividing. This preparation takes place in interphase stage of the cell cycle.

Ans. If a cell takes 24 hours to divide, it will have 18- 20 hours spend on interphase, which is the longest phase to prepare itself to undergo cell division.

Q. 13 It is observed that heart cells do not exhibit cell division. Such cells do not divide further and exit ___ phase to enter an inactive stage called___ of cell cycle. Fill in the blanks.

Ans. It is observed that heart cells do not exhibit cell division. Such cells do not divide further and exit **G_1-phase** to enter an inactive stage called **quiescent stage** (G_0) of cell cycle.

Q. 14 In which phase of meiosis are the following formed? Choose the answers from hint points given below.

(a) Synaptonemal complex ....
(b) Recombination nodules ....
(c) Appearance/activation of enzyme recombinase ....
(d) Termination of chiasmata ....
(e) Interkinesis ....
(f) Formation of dyad of cells

(a) Zygotene, (b) Pachytene,
(c) Pachytene, (d) Diakinesis,
(e) After Telophase-I/before meiosis-II,
(f) Telophase-I/after meiosis-I.

Ans. (a) Synaptonemal complex = **Zygotene.**
(b) Recombination nodules = **Pachytene.**
(c) Appearance/activation of enzyme recombinase = **Pachytene.**
(d) Termination of chiasmata = **Diakinesis.**
(e) Interkinesis = **After telophase-I/Before meiosis-II.**
(f) Formation of dyad of cells = **Telophase-I** or **After meiosis-I.**

Short Answer Type Questions

Q. 1 State the role of centrioles other than spindle formation.

Thinking Process The animal cell has few membrane less cell organelles. Centrosome is one of them. Two cylindrical structures are the part of centrosome, these are called centrioles.

Ans. The two centrioles in the centrosome lie **perpendicular** to each other. Each has organisation like a **cart wheel**. These form the basal body of cilia and flagella of plant/animal cells besides forming spindle fibre during cell division. Centrioles also helps in the formation of microtubuless and sperm tail.

Q. 2 Mitochondria and plastids have their own DNA (genetic material). What is known about their fate during nuclear division like mitosis?

Ans. The DNA present in mitochondria and plastids is **extrachromosomal DNA**. It does not participate in nuclear divisions. In mitosis, only nuclear DNA undergoes division, while the mitochondria and plastids replicate independently and then segregate into daughter cells.

Q. 3 Label the diagram and also determine the stage at which this structure is visible.

Thinking Process Cell division is an important event in the cell cycle. The cell passes through various phases in which number of changes are seen in its nuclear content.

Ans. The diagram shows the **transition** stage between **prophase** and **metaphase** stage of mitotic cell division.

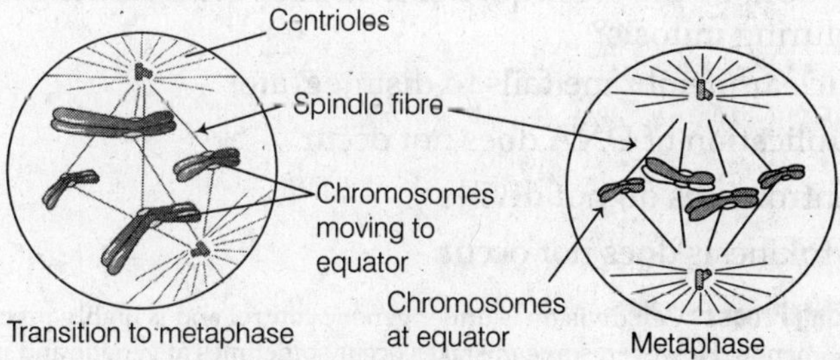

Q. 4 A cell has 32 chromosomes. It undergoes mitotic division. What will be the chromosome number (n) during metaphase? What would be the DNA content (C) during anaphase?

Thinking Process Mitotic cell division helps in the growth of organism and its development. It also plays a vital role in asexually reproducing organisms.

Ans. The mitotic cell division occurs in somatic cells of an organism. The chromosome number in the daughter cells remains same as that of the parent (dividing) cell, so even at metaphase or anaphase, the chromosome number does not change.

The DNA content gets doubled at the **synthetic phase** of interphase and gets halved after anaphase but the chromosome number remains same.

Q. 5 While examining the mitotic stage in a tissue, one finds some cells with 16 chromosomes and some with 32 chromosomes. What possible reasons could you assign to this difference in chromosome number. Do you think cells with 16 chromosomes could have arisen from cells with 32 chromosomes or *vice-versa*?

Ans. Such a condition may arise in case of mosaicism, which denotes preservation of two or more populations of cells with different genotypes in one individual.

It can result from various mechanisms including **non-disjunction, anaphase lagging** and **endoreduplication.** It may also result from a mutation during development which is propagated to only a subset of the adult cells.

In this case, cells with 16 chromosomes could have arisen from cells with 32 chromosomes.

Q. 6 The following events occur during the various phases of the cell cycle. Name the phase against each of the events.

(a) Disintegration of nuclear membrane ....

(b) Appearance of nucleolus ....

(c) Division of centromere ....

(d) Replication of DNA ....

Ans. (a) Prophase (b) Telophase

(c) Anaphase (d) S-phase

Q. 7 Mitosis results in producing two cells which are similar to each other. What would be the consequence if each of the following irregularities occur during mitosis?

(a) Nuclear membrane fails to disintegrate

(b) Duplication of DNA does not occur

(c) Centromeres do not divide

(d) Cytokinesis does not occur

Thinking Process Cell division is under genetic control and is highly precised phenomenon. However, some mistakes occur sometimes at genetic and molecular level in cell cycle which may lead to certain abnormalities.

Ans. (a) If nuclear membrane fails to disintegrate, the spindle fibres would not be able to reach chromosomes and they would not move towards opposite poles of the cell. In certain protozoans, such as *Amoeba,* the spindle is formed within the nucleus and this is called intranuclear mitosis or pre-mitosis.

(b) If DNA duplication does not occur than cell might not be able to surpass S-phase of cell-cycle as no chromosome duplication take place and will not be able to enter M-(mitotic phase) and the cycle will cease.

(c) If the centromeres do not divide one of the daughter cell will receive a complete pair of chromosomes and other cell would not get any of them. This may result in chromosome imbalances such as trisomy or monosomy.

(d) If cytokinesis does not occur, then multinucleate condition called **coenocyte** or **syncytium** is produced, as in *Rhizopus* and *Vaucheria*, etc.

Q. 8 Both unicellular and multicellular organisms undergo mitosis. What are the differences, if any, observed in the process between the two?

Ans. In unicellular organisms, the type of cell division is known as **amitosis** in which a somatic cell is divided into two parts directly. In multicellular organisms mitosis (equational division) occurs, which is an indirect process.

Both cell division in unicellular and multicellular organisms undergo mitosis have differences as given below

Cell Division in Unicellular Organism (Amitosis)	**Cell Division in Multicellular Organism** (Mitosis)
It is direct division of cellular and nuclear content. Without the duplication of chromosomes.	Nucleus and cellular content do not divide directly and involves duplication of chromosomes.
Different phases of cell divisions are not seen. Parent cell Stage 1 Nucleus divides. Stage 2 Cytoplasm divides having each of the two nuclei Division of unicellular organism *e.g., Amoeba* by amitosis	It involves different phases of cell division. Parent cell Prophase Metaphase Two daughter cells Anaphase Division of cell in multicellular organism by mitosis

Q. 9 Name the pathological condition when uncontrolled cell division occurs.

Ans. **Cancer** is the pathological condition in which the cells loose control over cell division and this results in abnormal growth and the formation of tumors.

Cancer tissue

Q. 10 Two key events take place, during S-phase in animal cells, DNA replication and duplication of centriole. In which parts of the cell these events occur?

Ans. DNA replication takes place in nucleus and duplication of centriole occurs in the cytoplasm. Centriole forms spindle fibres during cell division in animal cells which direct the movement of chromosomes within the cell. The position of centriole determines the position of the nucleus and plays a crucial role in the spatial arrangement of the cell.

Q. 11 Comment on the statement-meiosis enables the conservation of specific chromosome number of each species even through the process results in reduction of chromosome number.

Ans. Meiosis is the mechanism by which the specific chromosome number of each species is conserved across generations in sexually reproducing organisms. Even though meiosis results in reduction of chromosome number by half, it is gradually conserved by union of male gamete (n) and female gamete (n) in next generation. Meiosis also increases the genetic variability in the population contributing to diversity from one generation to the next.

Q. 12 Name a cell that is found arrested in diplotene stage for months and years. Comment in 2-3 lines how it completes cell cycle?

Ans. **Meiotic arrest** at diplotene stage commonly occurs in **mammalian occytes**. In females, meiosis starts in the embryo and proceeds upto diplotene. At diplotene the chromosomes become diffused and oocyte enter a prolonged resting phase. This arrest is under hormonal control. In many amphibians, birds and mammals the oocyte may be arrested in the diplotene stage for many years until hormonal signals trigger the resumption of meiosis.

This stage is characterised by formation of **lampbrush chromosomes** and intense RNA synthesis occurs with most of the genes in the DNA loops are actively transcribed and expressed.

Q. 13 How does cytokinesis in plant cells differ from that in animal cells?

Ans. Difference between cytokinesis in plant cell and animal cell are as follows

Cytokinesis in Plant Cell	Cytokinesis in Animal Cell
The division of cytoplasm takes place by cell plate formation.	The division of cytoplasm takes place by furrow formation.
The cell plate formation starts at the centre of the cell and grows outward, toward the lateral walls.	Cleavage starts at the periphery and then moves inward, dividing the cell into two parts.

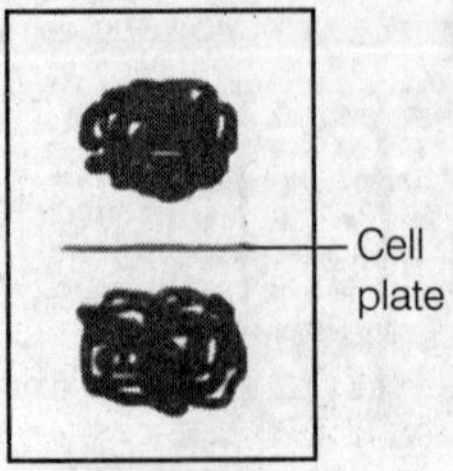

Cell plate

Plants cell

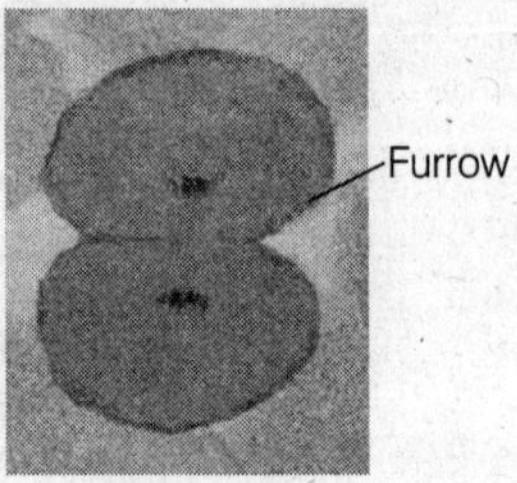

Furrow

Animals cell

Long Answer Type Questions

Q. 1 Comment on the statement- Telophase is reverse of prophase.

Ans. The following contrasting differences reveals that telophase is reverse of prophase, in cell division

Prophase	Telophase
First stage of karyokinesis in cell division,	Last stage of karyokinesis in cell division.
The chromatin disappears and chromosome fibres get shortened and thickened.	Chromosomes elongate and overlap each other to form chromatin.
Spindle fibres appears (towards the poles from the centriole connected in animals with astral rays and in plants without asters).	Spindle fibres disappear around the poles. Astral rays also disappear in plants.
Nucleolus degenerates completely.	Nuclear envelope reappears and two daughter nuclei are formed at the poles.
Cell organelles such as ER, Golgi complex disorganise, and difference between cytoplasm and nucleoplasm disappears.	Cell organelles, *i.e.*, ER and Golgi complex are reformed in the cell. Nucleoplasm also appears in the chromatin area. Making it distinct from rest of cytoplasmic area.

Nuclear envelope disintegrating

Chromatin fibre arranged as chromosomes

Late prophase

Nuclear envelope reforming

Cleavage furrow

Telophase

Q. 2 What are the various stages of meiotic prophase-I? Enumerate the chromosomal events during each stage?

Ans. **Prophase-I** occurs over a long duration and involves several complicated changes in meiotic cell division. It is important for genetic recombination and variation in sexually reproducing organism. The stages are

I. **Leptotene**

(i) The chromatin network opens out and threads become clear.

(ii) The chromosomes are thin, slender and long.

(iii) Chromosome number is diploid.

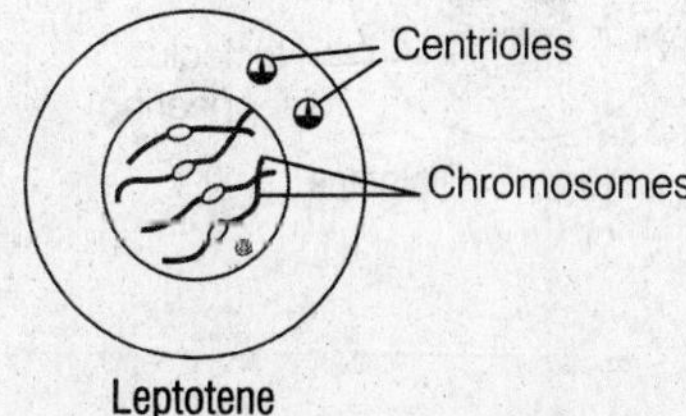

Leptotene

II. **Zygotene**

(i) Corresponding chromosomes become intimately associated, called homologous chromosomes.

(ii) The process of **pairing** is known as **synapse**. It is so exact that pairing is not merely between corresponding chromosomes but between corresponding individual units. Synapsis then accompanied by formation of synaptonemmal complex.

(iii) Pair of homologous chromosomes is called a **bivalent** or a **tetrad**.

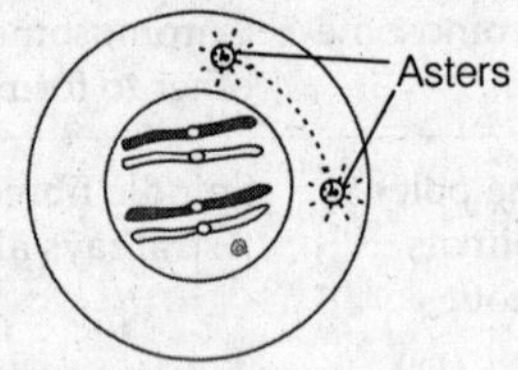

III. **Pachytene**

(i) The four chromatids of each bivalent chromosome become distinct and clearly visible as tetrad.

(ii) Crossing over between non-sister chromatids occurs at this stage.

(iii) This stage is characterised by recombination nodules formation at the site of crossing over between non-sister chromatieds of homologous chromosomes.

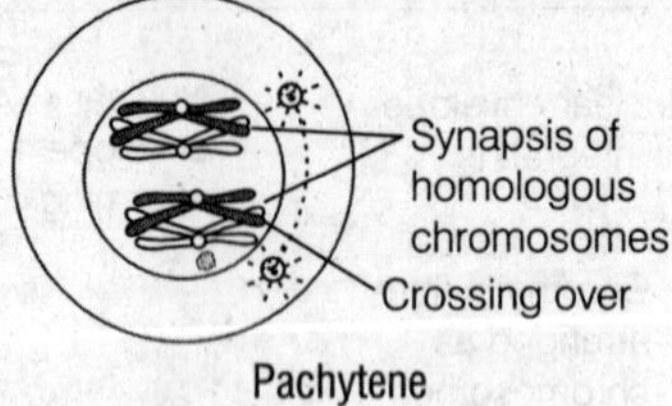

Pachytene

IV. **Diplotene**

(i) Homologous chromosomes start separating from one another, *i.e.*, dissolution of synaptonemal complex.

(ii) Recombined homologous chromosomes of the bivalents, start separating from each other except at the sites of cross over forming X-shaped structures.

(iii) These X-shaped structure are called **chiasmata**.

(iv) Nuclear membrane and nucleolus start disappearing.

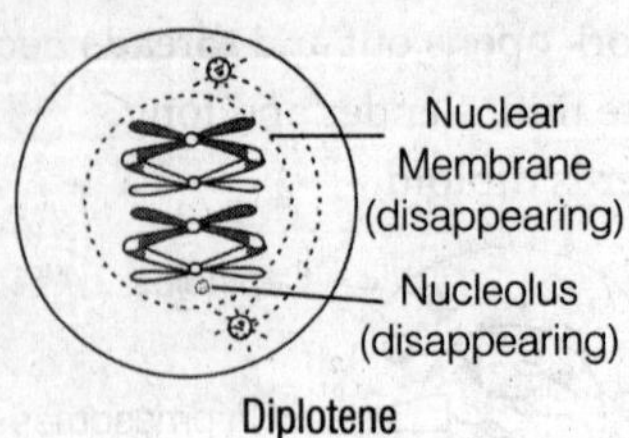

Diplotene

V. **Diakinesis**

(i) The bivalents condense further and get randomly distributed.

(ii) Meiotic spindle is assembled to prepare the homologous chromosomes for separation.

(iii) **Terminalisation** of chiasmata is almost complete.

(iv) Nuclear membrane and nucleolus disappear.

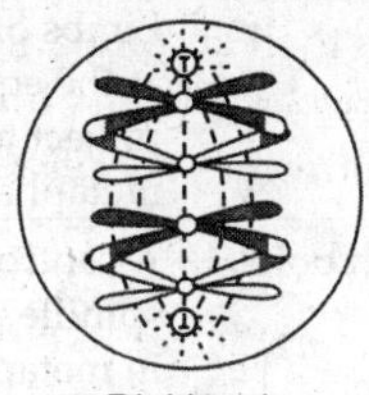

Diakinesis

Q. 3 Differentiate between the events of mitosis and meiosis.

Ans. Mitotic cell division results into the increase in the number of cells that have same genetic composition, whereas meiosis has its importance in the life cycle of sexually reproducing organisms.

Mitosis	Meiosis
Event	
Prophase	
Chromomeres are not conspicuous.	Chromomeres are quite conspicuous.
Prophase is of shorter duration.	Prophase-I is of longer duration while prophase-II is very brief.
Prophase is simpler and is hardly distinguishable into substages.	Prophase-I is complicated and is divisible into five substages. Prophase-II is, however very simple.
Each chromosome has two distinct chromatids.	Chromosomes of prophase-I do not show distinct chromatids.
No bouquet stage is recorded.	Chromosomes of animals and some plants show convergence towards one side during early prophase-I. It is known as **bouquet stage.**
Chiasmata are absent.	Chiasmata or visible connections between homologous chromosomes of bivalents are observed during diplotene, diakinesis (prophase- I) and metaphase- I.
Metaphase	
Centromeres produce a single metaphasic plate.	A double metaphasic plate is formed by centromeres in metaphase-I but only one in metaphase-II.

Mitosis	Meiosis
Chromosomes are independent and do not show connections.	Homologous chromosomes are interconnected. Hence, the chromosomes occur in pairs or bivalents in metaphase-I. They are however, free in metaphase-II.
Only the centromeres lie at the equator. The limbs of chromosomes are oriented in opposite direction.	Limbs of the chromosomes mostly lie at the equator while the centromeres project towards the poles in metaphase-I.
A centromere is connected with both the spindle poles.	A centromere is connected to one spindle pole in metaphase-I but both in metaphase-II.
Two chromatids of a chromosome are genetically similar.	The two chromatids of a chromosome are often genetically different due to crossing over.
Anaphase	
A centromere splits length-wise to form two centromeres in the beginning of anaphase.	Centromeres do not split during anaphase-I but do so in anaphase-II.
Anaphasic chromosomes are single stranded.	Chromosomes are double-stranded in anaphase-I, but single stranded in anaphase-II.
Similar chromosomes move towards the opposite poles in anaphase.	Dissimilar chromosomes move toward the opposite poles both in anaphase-I and anaphase-II.
Telophase	
It is followed by cytokinesis	Telo phase-I is followed by prophase-II and Telophase-II is followed by cytokinesis.
Cytokinesis	
2 New cells with same chromosomes number are formed	Four new cells with half number of chromosomes are formed.

Q. 4 Write brief note on the following

(a) Synaptonemal complex (b) Metaphase plate

Ans. (a) **Synaptonemal complexes** are zipper-like structures that forms between homologous chromosomes during the prophase of the first meiosis. Their asssembly and disassembly correlate with the successive chromatin rearrangements of meiotic prophase namely the condensation, pairing, recombination and dysfunction of homologous chromosomes.

They are considered to be the structures that control the number and distribution of reciprocal exchanges between homolgous chromosomes. They are also known to convert cross over into functional chiasmata.

(b) In metaphase, the centromeres of the chromosomes assemble themselves on the metaphasic plate (equatorial plate), an imaginary line that is equidistant from two centrosome poles. This even alignment is due to the opposing **kinetochore** microtubules. At this plate, chromosomes, especially sister chromatids are attached to the bundle of four to eight spindle fibres.

Q. 5 Write briefly the significance of mitosis and meiosis in multicellular organism.

Ans. Multicellular organisms grow and develop with the involvement of mitotic cell division. Meiosis occurs in them to form gametes in their reproductive phase of life cycle.

Significance of Mitosis

(i) Multicellular plants and animals start life as single cells. The process of mitosis gives rise to many cells which differentiate to form tissues, organs and organ-systems of the organism.

(ii) It results in increase in size and growth of an organ.

(iii) Cell reproduction is used to form new cells to renew certain tissues and to replace worn out cells.

(iv) Mitosis is also involved in asexual reproduction in some organisms like in unicellular–*Amoeba* and multicellular-*Hydra* as well as in vegetative reproduction in plants.

Significance of Meiosis

(i) Meiosis is the mechanism by which conservation of specific chromosome number of each species is achieved across generations in sexually reproducing organisms.

(ii) Meiosis also increases the genetic variability in the population of organisms from one generation to the next. Variations are very important for the process of evolution.

Q. 6 An organism has two pair of chromosomes (*i.e.*, chromosome number= 4). Diagrammatically represent the chromosomal arrangement during different phases of meiosis-II.

Thinking Process Meiosis is a reductional division, in which, chromosome number reduces to half in daughter cells. The number reduces as half set of chromosomes move to 2 daughter cells of the meiosis-I. Thus, two cells with half set of chromosomes again re-enter meiosis-II which is a similar to mitotic cell division.

Ans. The stages of meiosis-II is shown below

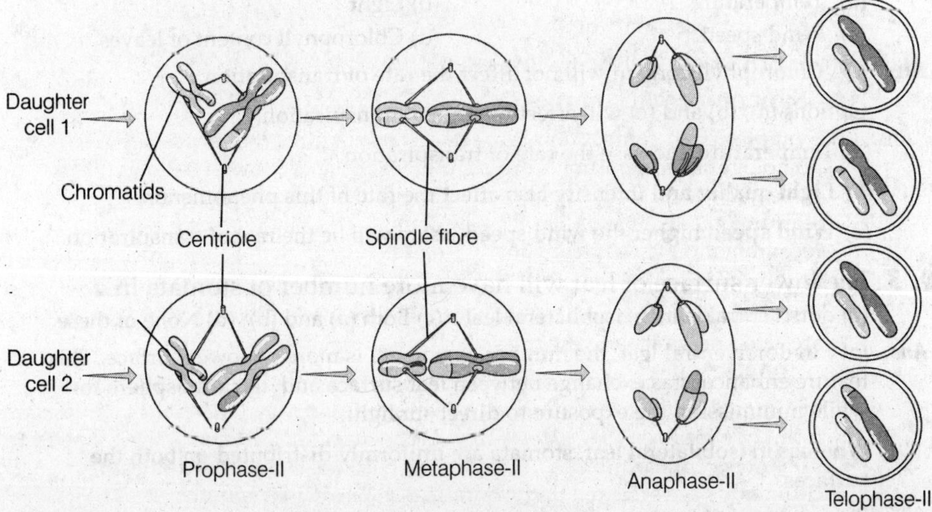

Stages of meiosis II

Chapter 11

Transport in Plants*

Multiple Choice Questions (MCQs)

Choose the correct answer from the given four options in the following questions.

Q. 1 Which of the following statements does not apply to reverse osmosis?

(a) It is used for water purification

(b) In this technique, pressure greater than osmotic pressure is applied to the system

(c) It is a passive process

(d) It is an active process

Thinking Process Osmosis is special type of diffusion of water molecules across a semipermeable membrane from a region of higher concentration to that of a lower concentration . The net direction and rate of osmosis depends on pressure and concentration gradient.

Ans. *(c)* Reverse osmosis is not a passive process as the movement of water molecules against concentration gradient require energy (or pressure from outside). Other statements are correct.

Q. 2 Which one of the following will not directly affect transpiration?

(a) Temperature (b) Light

(c) Wind speed (d) Chlorophyll content of leaves

Ans. *(d)* Chlorophyll content will not affect the rate of transpiration.

Options (a), (b) and (c) will affect the rate of transpiration.

(a) **Temperature** increase the rate of transpiration.

(b) **Light** quality and intensity also affect the rate of this phenomenon.

(c) **Wind speed** higher the wind speed, more will be the rate of transpiration.

Q. 3 The lower surface of leaf will have more number of stomata in a

(a) dorsiventral leaf (b) isobilateral leaf (c) Both (a) and (b) (d) None of these

Ans. *(a)* In dorsiventral leaf, the number of stomata is more on lower surface. This feature enhances gas exchange between leaf surface and the atmosphere for while minimissing the exposure to direct sunlight.

Whereas in isobilateral leaf, stomata are uniformly distributed on both the surfaces.

Note (*) *This chapter has been deleted from latest NCERT.*

Q. 4 The form of sugar transported through phloem is

(a) glucose (b) fructose
(c) sucrose (d) ribose

Thinking Process Glucose is the first product of photosynthesis in plant and also is the source of energy for every cell. Plants cannot transport it to the other cell as such because it is an reactive molecule.

Ans. *(c)* Sucrose a disaccharide sugar is transported through phloem. It comprises of glucose and fructose joined by α-1-2 linkage. It is the inactive (non-reducing) form of sugar so used in the transport of food.

Q. 5 The process of guttation takes place

(a) when the root pressure is high and the rate of transpiration is low.
(b) when the root pressure is low and the rate of transpiration is high.
(c) when the root pressure equals the rate of transpiration.
(d) when the root pressure as well as rate of transpiration are high.

Ans. *(a)* Guttation occurs when root pressure is high and rate of transpiration is low and there is high humidity in the air.

The other given conditions do not favor guttation.

Q. 6 Which of the following is an example of imbibition?

(a) Uptake of water by root hair
(b) Exchange of gases in stomata
(c) Swelling of seed when put in soil
(d) Opening of stomata

Thinking Process Imbibition is a physical phenomenon. Water is absorbed by the surface of seed and other biological materials.

Ans. *(c)* Swelling of seed in soil is an example of imbibition. Imbibition is a type of diffusion process along the concentration gradient enabling the solid to absorb water and increase in volume. When seed is put in the soil it absorbs water which activate enzymes present in seed and this induces the seed germination.

The other options, *i.e.*, uptake of water by root hair is an example of absorption, exchange in of gases stomata is an example of diffusion and opening of stomata is an example of turgor pressure or turgidity.

Q. 7 When a plant undergoes senescence, the nutrients may be

(a) accumulated (b) withdrawn
(c) translocated (d) None of these

Ans. *(c)* Senescence is the programmed death of a plant. During senescence, nutrients are translocated (moved) from aging parts to the other parts of the plants to be reused.

Q. 8 Water potential of pure water at standard temperature is equal to

(a) 10 (b) 20
(c) zero (d) None of these

Ans. *(c)* Water potential of pure water at standard temperature is zero. It is the highest value of water potential.

Q. 9 Mycorrhiza is a symbiotic association of fungus with root system which helps in

A. absorption of water B. mineral nutrition
C. translocation D. gaseous exchange

(a) Only A (b) Only B (c) Both A and B (d) Both B and C

Thinking Process **Symbiosis** is a phenomenon in which two organisms are associated with each other in such a way that both of them derive benefit from each other.

Ans. *(c)* Mycorrhiza associated with roots of plants helps in both absorption of water and minerals from the soil. The other options are incorrect.

Q. 10 Based on the figure given below which of the following statements is not correct?

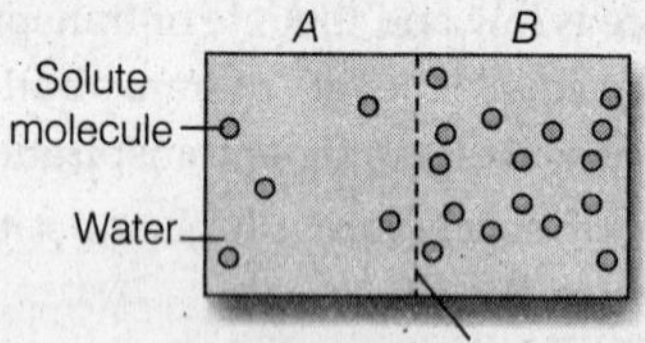

(a) Movement of solvent molecules will take place from chamber *A* to *B*.
(b) Movement of solute will take place from *A* to *B*.
(c) Presence of a semipermeable is a pre-requisite for this process to occur.
(d) The direction and rate of osmosis depends on both the pressure gradient and concentration gradient.

Ans. *(b)* Movement of water will take place from chamber A to B. It is not the solute which will move from chamber A to B. The is because osmosis is a process in which solvent molecules move from a region of higher concentration to a region of lower concentration through a semi-permeable membrane.

Q. 11 Match the followings and choose the correct option.

Column I	Column II
A. Leaves	(1) Anti-transpirant
B. Seed	(2) Transpiration
C. Roots	(3) Negative osmotic potential
D. Aspirin	(4) Imbibition
E. Plasmolysed cell	(5) Absorption

Codes

	A	B	C	D	E		A	B	C	D	E
(a)	2	4	5	1	3	(b)	3	2	4	1	5
(c)	1	2	3	4	5	(d)	5	4	3	2	1

Ans. *(a)* The correct matched sequence of the two columns is as follows.

Leaves – Transpiration
Seed – Imbibition
Roots – Absorption
Aspirin – Anti-transpirant
Plasmolysed cell – Negative osmotic potential

Q. 12 Mark the mismatched pair.

a.	Amyloplast	(i)	Store protein granule
b.	Elaioplast	(ii)	Store oils or fats
c.	Chloroplasts	(iii)	Contain chlorophyll pigments
d.	Chromoplasts	(iv)	Contain coloured pigments other than chlorophyll

Thinking Process Plants have plastids as an cell organelles. They are of three types i.e., chromoplasts, chloroplasts and leucoplasts (amyloplast) .

Ans. *(a)* Amyloplasts are the colourless plastids which store starch but not the protein granules. Other pairs are correctly matched.

Very Short Answer Type Questions

Q. 1 Smaller, lipid soluble molecules diffuse faster through cell membrane, but the movement of hydrophilic substances are facilitated by certain transporters which are chemically ....

Thinking Process The movement of substances across the limiting membrane in a living cell is a highly specific and regulated phenomenon. This regulation is done mainly by membrane proteins.

Ans. The movement of hydrophilic substances are facilitated by transporters which are chemically proteins. These proteins form porins, which are huge pores in the outer membranes of the plastids, mitochondria and some bacteria. These porins allow the small molecules to pass through the membrane.

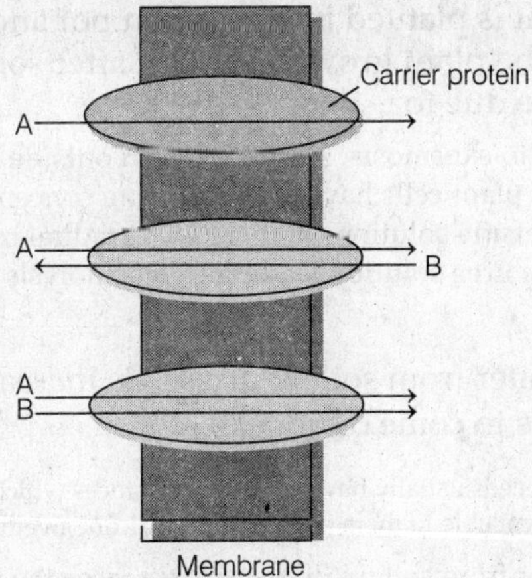

Q. 2 In a passive transport across a membrane. When two protein molecules move in opposite direction and independent of each other, it is called as ....

Ans. **Antiport** This process facilitates transport of molecules in opposite directions across the membrane through same protein carrier.

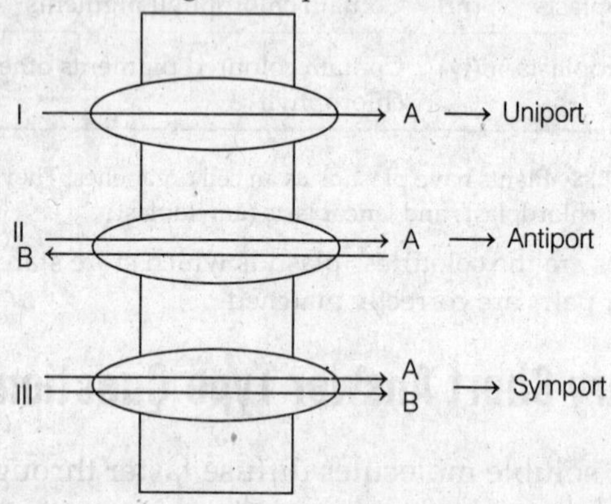

Q. 3 Osmosis is a special kind of diffusion, in which water diffuses across the cell membrane. The rate and direction of osmosis depends upon both ....

Thinking Process Osmosis is an important biological phenomenon in the living world. It is governed by number of factors.

Ans. The rate and direction of osmosis depends upon both the **pressure gradient** and **concentration gradient**.

Q. 4 A flowering plant is planted in an earthen pot and irrigated. Urea is added to make the plant grow faster, but after sometime the plant dies. This may be due to ....

Ans. The plant dies due to exosmosis. As the solution outside the plant is an hypertonic and the plant cells have a lower solute concentration are hypotonic compared to the outside solution, so there will gradual movement of water from plant cell to outside urea solution leading to plasmolysis of root cells and plant dies gradually.

Q. 5 Absorption of water from soil by dry seeds increases the .... , thus helping seedlings to come out of soil.

Thinking Process Seeds usually have colloid substances which absorb and adsorb lot of water when it is available to them and show significant swelling and increase in size.

Ans. Absorption of water from soil by dry seeds increases the **imbition pressure,** thus helping seedings to come out of soil.

Q. 6 Water moves up against gravity and even for a tree of 20 m height, the tip receives water within two hours. The most important physiological phenomenon which is responsible for the upward movement of water is ....

Ans. **Transpiration pull** is the physiological phenomenon which is responsible for the upward movement of water in trees of height up to 20m.

The transpiration from leaf creates a pressure gradient between the atmosphere and sub-stomatal cavity and intercellular spaces of leaf. This gradient is transferred to photosynthetic cells and then on to xylem of leaf vein.

It results in a force called "transpirational pull" that can lift water upto 130m high, through a xylem column.

Q. 7 The plant cell cytoplasm is surrounded by both cell wall and cell membrane. The specificity of transport of substances are mostly across the cell membrane, because ....

Ans. The transport takes place through the cell membrane because **cell membrane** is **selectively-permeable** and composed of lipids that are arranged in bilayer structure along with proteins and carbohydrates.

The lipid soluble molecules pass readily across lipid bilayer of cell membrane whereas movement of other molecules of small size is facilitated by porins, pores made up of proteins. While cell wall does not helps in transport of substances.

Cell wall is basically a non-living rigid structure forming outer covering over plasma membrane and provides shape, mechanical strength and protection to the plant cell from damages and infection.

Q. 8 The C_4 plants are twice as efficient as C_3 plants in terms of fixing CO_2 but lose only ...... as much water C_3 plants for the same amount of CO_2 fixed.

Ans. The evolution of the C_4 or plants photosynthetic system is probably one of the strategies for maximising the ability of CO_2 while minimising water loss. C_4 plants are twice as efficient as C_3 plants in terms of fixing carbon in the form of glucose, but lose only half as much water as a C_3 plant for the same amount of C_2 fixed.

Q. 9 In plants, translocation in xylem is unidirectional while in phloem it is bidirectional. Explain

Thinking Process Xylem and phloem are complex permanent tissues found in vascular plants (gymnosperms and angiosperms).

Ans. **Xylem** is involved in the one way transport of water and minerals from soil$\rightarrow$ root $\rightarrow$ stem $\rightarrow$ leaves. Several forces act in this mechanism like imbibition, root pressure and finally transpiration pull. Thus, it is a unidirectional process.

Phloem's main function is to transport food from source to sink where source implies with the part of plant responsible for synthesising food and sink to those parts and organs that needs or consumes food for their growth and development. These source and sink parts of a plants may vary in different phases of its growth, thus the food need to travel in both upwards and downward direction. So, phloem shows bidirectional movement of substances.

Q. 10 Identify the process occurring in I, II and III

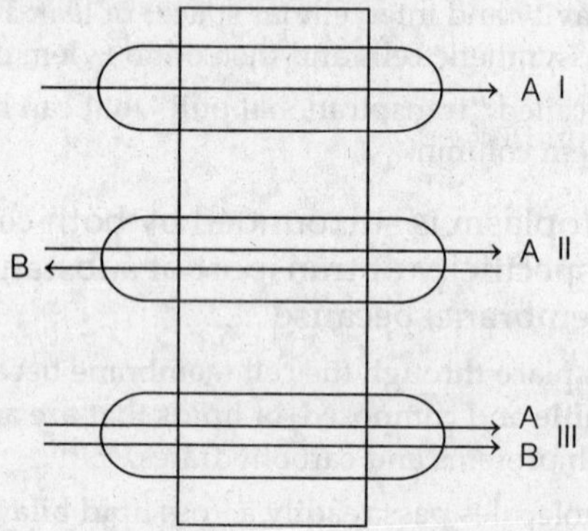

Thinking Process Facilitated diffusion involves special proteins that help in moving substances across membranes without the expenditure of energy, i.e., ATP.

Ans. I. **Uniport** In this process, there is movement of a single molecule across a membrane.

II. **Antiport** In this process, there is a movement of two types of molecules in opposite direction.

III. **Symport** In this process, there is a movement of more than one molecule across the membrane in the same direction, at one time.

Q. 11 Given below is a table. Fill in the gaps.

Property	Simple Diffusion	Facilitated Transport	Active Transport
Highly selective	No	Yes	—
Uphill transport	—	—	Yes
Requires ATP	—	—	—

Ans.

Property	Simple Diffusion	Facilitated Transport	Active Transport
Highly selective	No	Yes	Yes
Uphill transport	No	No	Yes
Requires ATP	No	No	Yes

Active Transport It uses energy to pump molecules against a concentration gradient. Hence, different proteins in the membrane play a major role in active transport.

Carrier protein involved in active transport is very specific in what it carries across the membrane.

Facilitated Transport In facilitated transport special proteins help in movement of substances across the membrane without the expenditure of ATP. Facilitated transport is very specific as it allows cell to select substances for uptake.

Simple Diffusion It is a physical phenomenon which involves the movement of water from higher concentration to lower concentration. It is not a selective process and do not require energy.

Q. 12 Define water potential and solute potential.

Ans. **Water potential** is a measure of free energy associated with water per unit volume (JM^{-3}). The water potential of pure water (ψ_w) at atmospheric pressure is zero. The unit of water potential is bars or Pascal (1 mPa = 10 bars).

Solute Potential The addition of solutes reduce water potential (to a negative value). This occurs because solute lower the concentration of free water moleules. Hence, solution have a lower water potential than pure water, the magnitude of this lowering due to dissolution of a solute is called **solute potential** or ψ_s.

Q. 13 Why is solute potential always negative? Explain $\psi_w = \psi_s + \psi_p$.

Ans. If some solute is dissolved in pure water, solution has fewer free water molecules and the concentration of water decreases, reducing its water potential.

Hence, all the solutions have a lower water potential than pure water. The magnitude of this lowering is due to dissolution of solute is called solute potential or ψ_s. ψ_s is always negative. The more the solute molecules, the lower (more negative) is the solute potential (ψ_s). Water potential of a cell is affected by both solute and pressure potential. The relationship can be illustrated as

$$\psi_w = \psi_s + \psi_p$$

Where, ψ_w = water potential,

ψ_s = solute potential,

ψ_p = pressure potential.

Q. 14 Tradescantia leaf epidermal peel was taken and

(a) placed in salt solution for five minutes.

(b) after that it was placed in distilled water.

When seen under the microscope what would be observed in (a) and (b)?

Ans. **(a)** Trades cantia when placed in salt solution, shrinks as water from cells cytoplasm moves out of the cell.

(b) When it is placed again back in distilled water, cell regains it's shape and absorbs water and become turgid (full of water).

Q. 15 Differentiate between apoplast and symplast pathways of water movement. Which of these would need active transport?

Ans. Difference between apoplast pathway and symplast pathway is as follows

Apoplast Pathway	Symplast Pathway
It consists of the non-living parts of plant body, *i.e.*, cell walls and inter cellular spaces.	It consist of living parts of plant body, *i.e.*, protoplast connected by the plasmodesmata.
There is a little resistance in the movement of water in apoplastic pathway.	Some resistance occurs in the movement of water through symplast.
It is a faster process.	It is a slightly slower process.

Q. 16 How does most of the water moves within the root?

Thinking Process The responsibility of absorption of water and minerals is more specifically is the function of the root hairs that are present in millions in the root hair zone.

Ans. Most of the water flow in the root occur *via* the apoplast pathway since, the cortical cells are loosly packed and hence offer no resistance to water movement, which is through mass flow. This mass flow of water occurs due to adhesive and cohesive properties of water.

However, symplast pathway is also involved in the movement of water molecules within the root (*i.e.*, *via* endodermis to xylem through protoplasm).

Q. 17 Give the location of casparian strip and explain its role in the water movement.

Ans. Casparian strip is found in the **endodermis**. The walls of this layer are impervious to water because of the presence of suberin. So, it does not allow movement of water across the epidermis via endodermis to xylem. Rather is forced to enter the symplast pathway through cell membranes and reach the xylem through protoplasm.

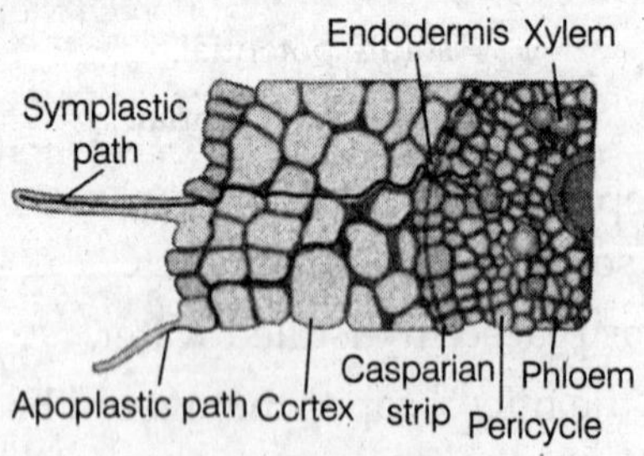

Symplastic and apoplastic pathways of water and ion absorption and movement in roots

Q. 18 Differentiate between guttation and transpiration.

Ans. Difference between guttation and transpiration is as follows

Guttation	Transpiration
It is the loss of liquid droplets from the plants.	It is the loss of water by a plant in the form of vapours.
Guttated water is a dilute solution of both inorganic and organic substances.	Transpired water is a pure water.
Guttation occurs at the margins and the tips of the leaves.	Transpiration occurs through the general surface of the leaves and the young stem.
Excessive guttation does not cause loss of turgidity.	Excessive transpiration results in wilting and in severe cases, could be lethal to plant.

Q. 19 Transpiration is a necessary evil in plants. Explain

Thinking Process Loss of water in the form of water vapours from the surface of leaves of plant is called transpiration.

Ans. Transpiration is called a necessary evil because, despite causing water loss, it is essential for the plant's survival. Transpiration creates a transpiration pull to absorb more and more water from soil through roots.

Q. 20 Describe briefly the three physical properties of water which helps in ascent of water in xylem.

Thinking Process Water is a chemical substance which has chemical formula H_2O. Two hydrogen atoms attach to oxygen (O) with covalent bonds

Ans. The three physical properties of water that helps in ascent of xylem are as given

Cohesive properties	Mutal attraction between molecules allowing them to stick together and move as continuous column.
Adhesive properties	Attraction of water molecules to walls of xylem vessels, helping water climb up against gravity.
Surface tension	Water molecules are more strongly attracted to each other in liquid phase than in gas phase.

Q. 21 A gardener forgot to water a potted plant for a day during summer, what will happen to the plant? Do you think it is reversible? If yes, how?

Thinking Process No living being (plant or animal) can survive without water.

Ans. If gardener forgets to water the plants, it will start it wilting (a physiological state of plant in which plant leaves droop down). If watered in time, the plant may recover and become normal.

But if watering is delayed, the plant will not recover and it reaches at physiological wilting stage, and will dies.

Q.22 Identify a type of molecular movement which is highly selective and requires special membrane proteins, but does not require energy.

Ans. Facilitated diffusion's is the mechanism which is highly selective passive process. In facilitated diffusion special proteins help in movement of substances across the membrane without expenditure of ATP energy because facilitated diffusion cause net transport of molecules from a high to low concentration and this would not require input of energy.

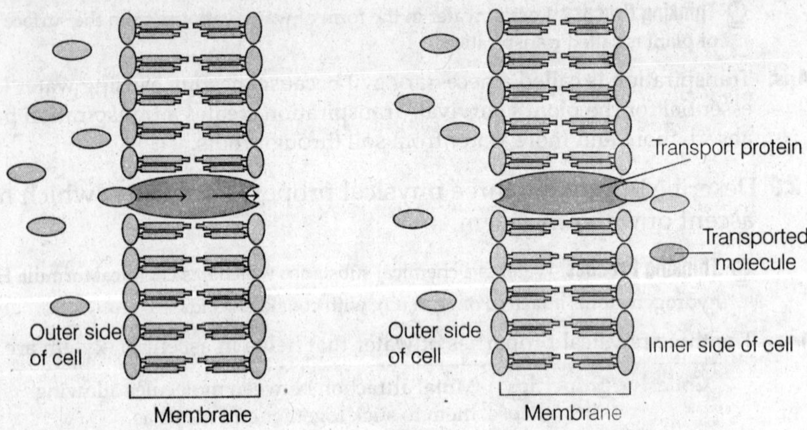

Q. 23 Correct the statements.

(a) Cells shrink in hypotonic solutions and swell in hypertonic solutions.

(b) Imbibition is a special type of diffusion when water is absorbed by living cells.

(c) Most of the water flow in the roots occurs *via* the symplast.

Ans. (a) The cell **swell** in hypotonic solution and **shrink** in hypertonic solution.

(b) Imbibition is a special type of diffusion when water is **absorbed** by solid-colloids.

(c) Most of the water flow in roots occurs *via* the **apoplast** pathway.

Short Answer Type Questions

Q. 1 Minerals absorbed by the roots travel up the xylem. How do they reach the parts where they are needed most? Do all the parts of the plant get the same amount of the minerals?

Ans. The minerals absorbed are transported up the stem, to all parts of plant through the **transpiration stream**. The chief **sinks** for the mineral elements are the growing region of the plant, such as the apical and lateral meristems, young leaves, developing flowers, fruits, seeds and the storage organs.

Unloading of the mineral ions occurs *via* fine vein endings through diffusion and active uptake by the cells. In plants, xylem are involved in transport of inorganic nutrients where as phloem transport only organic materials.

Mineral ions are frequently remobilised from older parts of plant like leaves to the younger regions. Elements most readily mobilised are **phosphorus, sulphur, nitrogen, potassium**, and **some elements** that forms the structural component are not remobilised *e.g.*, calcium.

Q. 2 If one wants to find minerals and their form in which they are mobilised in the plant, how will an analysis of the exudate help?

Ans. The plant exudate (plant sap) is a mixture of the organic/inorganic compounds and ions, minerals, sugars and amino acids. If we chemically analyse these we can get to know which mineral nutrient is transported in which form in the plants. *e.g.*, nitrogen is absorbed and transported as NO_2 and NO_3^- and sulphur as sulphate ion forms etc.

Q. 3 From your knowledge of physiology can you think of some method of increasing the life of cut plants in a vase?

Ans. The life of cut plant in a vase can be increased by placing them in water immediately as air will rapidly move into the water conducting tissue and plug the cell. Also, provide nutrients and elements in a varied concentration can increase the life span of plants. A phytohormone called cytokinin can also be sprayed or plants can be dipped in its the solution, as it delays the senescence of plant.

Q. 4 Do different species of plant growing in the same area show the same rate of transpiration at a particular time? Justify your answer.

Ans. No, different species of plants, growing in the same area do not show same rate of transpiration. The rate of transpiration varies between species due to several factors which include leaf structure, stomatal density and side etc. But if the two species are related and have similar morphology then only external factors will determine the rate of transpiration like wind velocity, humidity temperature, light intensity etc.

Q. 5 Water is indispensable for life. What properties of water make it useful for all biological processes on the earth?

Thinking Process Water is indispensable for life. No life on earth is possible without water. It is required by all organisms in performing vital functions, in plants water is required for the various vital activities.

Ans. Properties of water that make it useful for all biological processes on the earth are

(i) Water is the major solvent through which mineral nutrients enter a plant from the soil solution.

(ii) It is an ideal solvent with neutral pH.

(iii) Water is the major constituent of protoplasm. It constitute approximately 90% of the protoplasm.

(iv) Water acts as a medium for translocation of nutritive substances. Mineral nutrients are absorbed by the roots. Carbohydrates that are formed during photosynthesis are transported by water from cell to cell, tissue to tissue and organ to organ.

(v) In plants, water plays a crucial role in photosynthesis by providing hydrogen atom that are used in synthesis of carbohydrate. During this process the oxygen atoms are further released as O_2 as by product.

(vi) Water act as agent for temperature control. The specific heat of water helps plant in maintaining a relative stable internal temperature.

(vii) In some plants water is necessary for pollination. Like in bryophytes and pteridophytes, they essentially require water for the fertilisation process.

Q. 6 How is it that the intracellular levels of K^+ maintained higher than extracellular levels in animal cells?

Thinking Process The excitability of sensory cells, neurons and muscles depends on ion channels, signal **transducers** that provide a regulated path for the movement of inorganic ions such as Na^+, K^+, Ca^{2+}, and Cl^- across the plasma membrane in response to various stimuli.

Ans. Ion channels are 'gated', *i.e.*, they may be open or closed. The Na^+, K^+, ATPase create a charge imbalance across the plasma membrane by carrying $3Na^+$ out of the cell for every $2K^+$ ion carried inside making the inside negative relative to outside. The membrane is said to be polarised. That is the reason the intracellular levels of K^+ are higher than extracellular levels in animals cells.

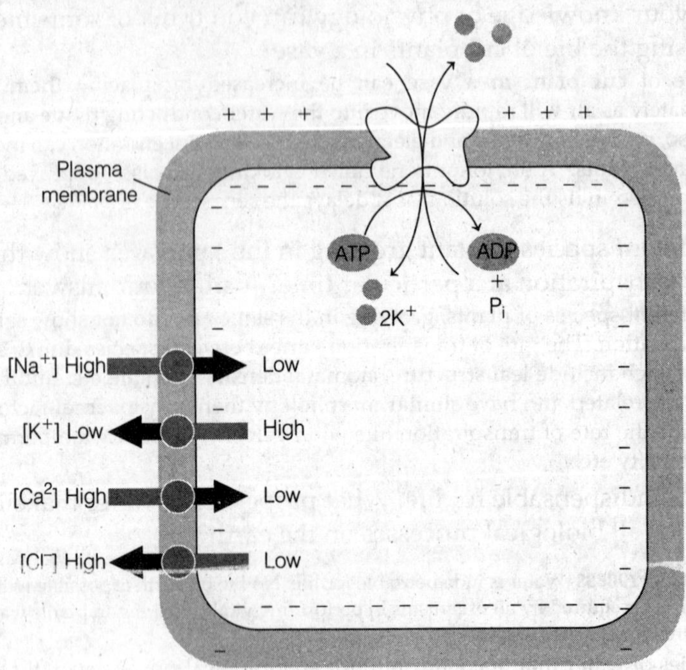

Showing ion balance in animal cell

Q. 7 Cut pieces of beetroot do not leave the colour in cold water but do so in hot water. Explain.

Ans. Cut pieces of beetroot do not leave colour in cold water but do so in hot water because pigment of beetroot dissolve and diffuse readily in hot water as hot temperature help in leaking out of the plasma membrane and release of beetroot pigment.

Q. 8 In a girdled plant, when water is supplied to the leaves above the girdle, leaves may remain green for sometime then wilt and ultimately die. What does it indicate?

Ans. In a girdled plant, when water is supplied to the leaves above the girdle, leaves may remain green for sometime because leaves can synthesise their own carbohydrate food through photosynthesis, However, they will eventually wilt due to non-availability of water.

The system of xylem vessels from root to the leaf vein can supply the needed water, during girdling there is a possible loss of xylem vessels and the water supply cuts off, resulting in death of plant.

Q. 9 Various types of transport mechanisms are needed to fulfil the mineral requirements of a plant. Why are they not fulfilled by diffusion alone?

Ans. Various types of ions, minerals and organic compound are transported in plants in various modes, *e.g.*,

(i) Food substances synthesised in leaves are translocated downward towards root and stem.

(ii) Similarly food is translocated upwards to the developing leaves, buds and fruits.

(iii) Radial transport of food occurs across the stem from the cells of pith, from cortex *etc*, towards epidermis.

(iv) Ions and minerals are transported upwards through xylem.

Since, diffusion is a slow process and allows movement of molecules for short distances only, it cannot carry out the above mentioned movements of organic and inorganic substances alone. Therefore, a need arises for special long distance transport systems that permits and move substances at a much faster rate, *i.e.*, mass or bulk flow system through conducting tissues (translocation).

Q. 10 How can plants be grown under limited water supply without compromising on metabolic activities?

Ans. Under limited water supply, plants can reduce the loss of water through transpiration by closing or partially closing stomata. But, they can still carry out the important life processes like photosynthesis, respiration and transport of food, etc.

Q. 11 Will the ascent of sap be possible without the cohesion and adhesion of the water molecules? Explain.

Ans. No, the ascent of sap is not possible without the cohesive and adhesive properties of water as they play an important role in transport of water because of the following reasons

(i) Cohesion forces hold together the water molecule in the conducting channels, preventing breakage or formation of air bubbles in the xylem.

(ii) Adhesive forces between the water molecule and cellulose of cell wall make a thin film of water along the channels so, this film can be pulled up by transpiration pull drawing more and more water upwards in the conducting channels from the root.

Q. 12 Keep some freshly cut flowers in a solution of food colour. Wait for sometime for the days to rise in the flower, when the stem, of the flower is held up in light, coloured strands can be seen inside. Can this experiment demonstrate which tissue is conducting water up the stem?

Ans. *Yes*, this experiment shows that xylem tissue conducts water, as the coloured dye rises through the xylem vessels.

Q. 13 When a freshly collected *Spirogyra* filament is kept in a 10% potassium nitrate solution, it is observed that the protoplasm shrinks in size

(a) What is this phenomenon called?

(b) What will happen if the filament is replaced in distilled water?

Ans. (a) Plasmolysis is the name of the phenomenon, occurring in *Spirogyra* filament when placed in 10% potassium nitrate solution (hypertonic solution). It occurs as water from the cell is move out to extracellular fluid causing the protoplast to shrink away from cell wall.

(b) When filament is placed back in distilled water, the *Spirogyra* will reabsorb water and protoplast will swell back to its original shape. This phenomenon is known as **deplasmolysis.**

Q. 14 Sugar crystals do not dissolve easily in ice cold water. Explain.

Ans. Pure water has tremendous free energy at normal room temperature. That is called **water potential**. When the water temperature drops down, the free energy is reduced so, sugar does not get dissolved easily in, *i.e.*, cold water.

Q. 15 Salt is applied to tennis lawns to kill weeds. How does salting tennis lawns help in killing of weeds without affecting the grass?

Ans. Salt solution being hypertonic, causes exoosmosis in plants. Excessive loss of water from plants, kills the plant.1 cup salt in 2 cup of water, fairly well dissolved when sprayed on weed plants, start killing them. This salt concentration is then increased in subsequent sprays, if the weeds are still thriving in the field. However this is a misconception that applying salt will only kill weeds and will not affect the grass. To limit the damage to useful plants, a care is taken to directly sprinkle the weeds only with this solution.

Q. 16 What is the chemical composition of xylem and phloem sap?

Ans. **Xylem sap** consists of mainly water and some solutes or mineral nutrients.

Phloem sap mainly consists of the sucrose, a kind of transport sugar which is a diasaccharide, hormones and amino acids are also found in phloem sap of the plants.

Q. 17 Observe the figure and answer the questions provided below the figure.

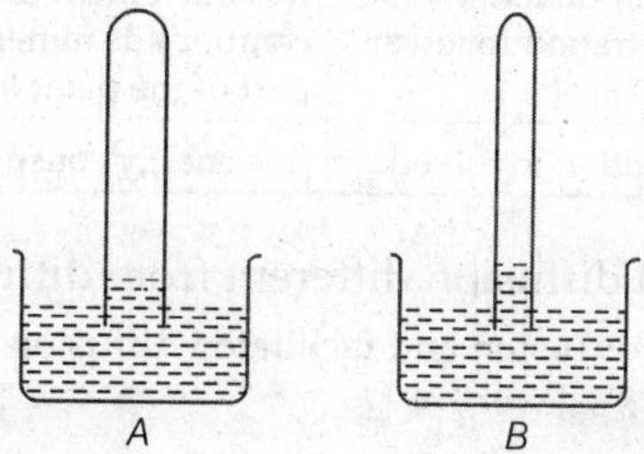

Why does tube *B* show higher water rise than *A*?

Ans. The tube *B* will show higher level than tube *A* because of the capillary action.

The lumen of tube *B* is smaller than that of *A*. Tube *B* creates more capillary effect, being narrow than tube *A*. Due to this, the water rises higher in tube *B* than in tube *B*.

Q. 18 What are 'aquaporins'? How does presence of aquaporins affect osmosis?

Thinking Process Peter Agre was awarded Nobel Prize in chemistry (2003) for discovering Aquaporins.

Ans. **Aquaporins** are integral membrane proteins. These form pores or channels in the membrane. The water can flow more rapidly through these pores to inside of the cell, as compared to the process of diffusion.

These are plumbing systems of the cells. These selectively conduct water in and out of the cells, while preventing the passage of ions and other solutes.

Q. 19 ABA (Abscisic Acid) is called a stress hormone.

A. How does this hormone overcome stress conditions?

B. From where does this hormone get released in leaves?

Ans. A. ABA (Abscisic Acid) gives signals to stomata to get closed, whenever there is scarcity of water to the plant. This prevents the loss of water through transpiration by leaves. It also increases the tolerance of plants to various kinds of stresses.

B. ABA is released or transported from the stem apices to the leaves.

Q. 20 We know that plants are harmed by excess water. But plants survive under flooded condition. How are they able to manage excess water?

Ans. Plants can get rid of excess water by increasing the transpiration rate but upto a certain limit. Prolong water logged conditions for roots may lead to the death of the plant (as they can not respire efficiently).

Q. 21 Differentiate between diffusion and translocation in plants.

Ans. Difference between diffusion and translocation in plants is as follows

Diffusion	Translocation
It is the movement of materials from higher concentration to lower concentration.	It is movement of organic compounds mineral salts from one part of the plant to another.
No energy consumption involved.	It is energy consuming process.

Q. 22 How is facilitated diffusion different from diffusion?

Ans. Difference between diffusion and facilitated diffusion is as follows

Diffusion	Facilitated Diffusion
In **diffusion**, molecules move in a random fashion, the net result being substances moving from regions of higher concentration to regions of lower concentration.	The diffusion of substance along a concentration gradient, which is facilitated by the proteins is known as **facilitated diffusion** without expenditure of ATP energy.
Diffusion is a slow process and is not dependent on a 'living system'. No expenditure of energy takes place.	Facilitated diffusion is faster than simple diffusion because protein like channels or carriers assist in the process. No energy (ATP) is required but it requires the help of specific membrane proteins.

Q. 23 Explain the mass flow hypothesis of transport in phloem.

Ans. Mass flow hypothesis was first proposed by Ernst Munch (1930). It explains the transport of solute or sugars, *i.e.*, sucrose in the phloem tissue.

It involves the following three steps

(a) Phloem loading

(b) Translocation of solutes

(c) Phloem unloading

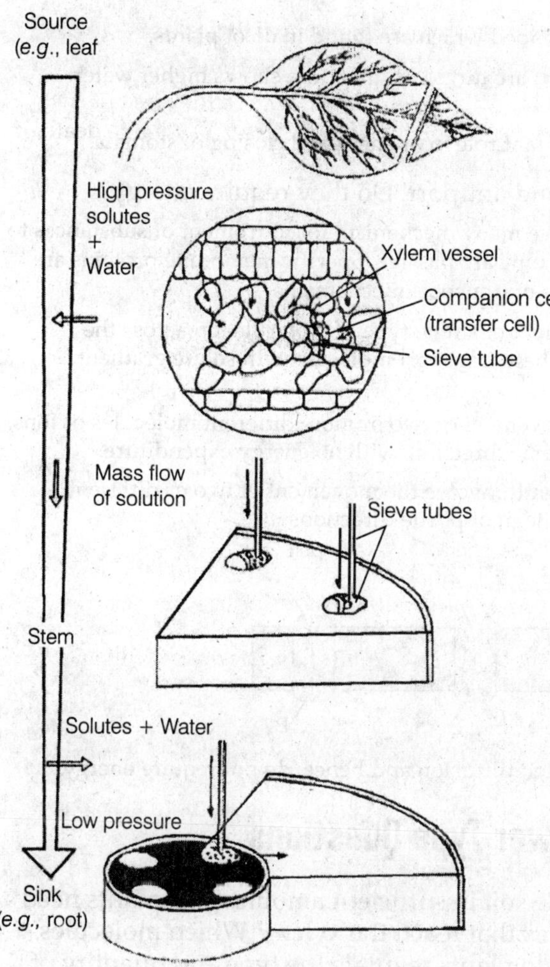

Movement of solutes such as sucrose through the phloem of a plant

Loading of sieve tubes takes place in leaves. Photosynthetic cells make sugars, particularly sucrose, and other organic solutes.

Companion cells use energy to collect solutes by active transport. As solute concentration increases in the companion cells, water enters by osmosis.

A pressure is created, which pushes the solutes through plasmodesmata into the sieve tubes. It is an active process.

Translocation of sucrose takes place through phloem column. Increase in hydrostatic pressure inside sieve tubes is greatest at the source and lowest at the sink. It pushes sucrose etc., from source to sink.

Unloading of the sieve tubes takes place at the sink sites.

It results in active transport of sugars out of the pholem converting them into complex sugars. Loss of solutes from the phloem create a high water potential, and water moves out of phloem, returning back to xylem.

Sinks are the regions where solutes *i.e.*, sugars or food are being used, *e.g.*, roots, fruits, storage organs and regions of growth.

Q.24 Observe the diagram and answer the following.

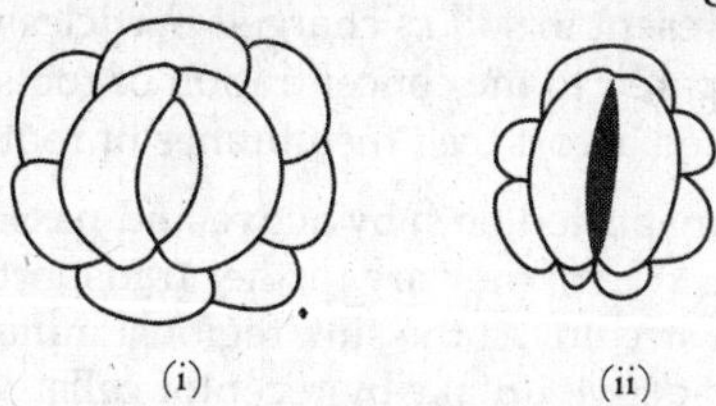

(a) Are these types of guard cells found in monocots or dicots?

(b) Which of these shows a higher water content (i) or (ii)?

(c) Which element plays an important role in the opening and closing of stomata?

Ans. (a) The guard cells are bean-shaped which are found in dicot plants.

(b) The guards cells in figure (i) are turgid as, therefore shows higher water content.

(c) The K^+ ions plays an important role in opening and closing of stomata.

Q. 25 Define uniport, symport and antiport. Do they require energy?

Ans. The biological membranes have many mechanism for movement of substances to and fro. Some are active and some are passive. Specific membrane proteins are also involved for special types of transport mechanisms.

Uniport It involve the movement of single type of molecule ion across the membrane in one direction. These transport molecule with solute gradient without energy expenditure.

Symport This involves the movement of two or more different molecules or ions, across the membrane in the same direction, with no energy expenditure.

Antiport also called exchanger. It involve the movement of two or different molecules across the membrane in opposite directions.

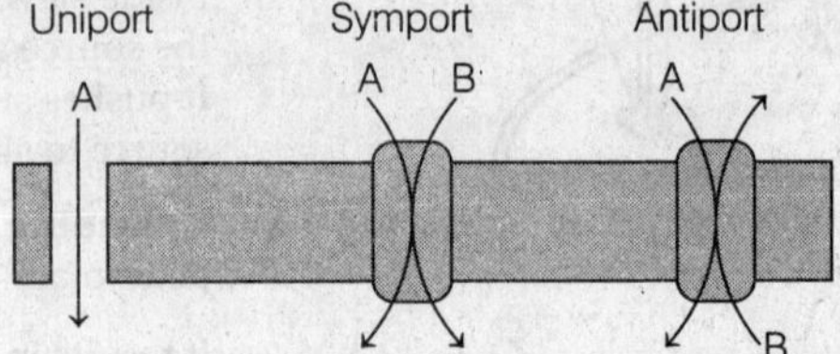

No, these are types of facilitated diffusion and hence, do not require energy.

Long Answer Type Questions

Q. 1 Minerals are present in the soil in sufficient amounts. Do plants need to adjust the type of solutes that reach the xylem? Which molecules help to adjust this? How do plants regulate the type and quantity of solutes that reach xylem?

Ans. *Yes*, plants need to adjust the type and quantity of solutes that reach the xylem. The transport proteins in the endodermal cell help in regulating solute movement.

As the minerals are present in soil as charged particles with a very low concentration as compared to the concentration of roots. Not all of these ions can be passively transported across cell membranes of root hairs.

Thus, minerals are transported both by active and passive processes, to the xylem. Upon reaching xylem, they are further transported, *i.e.*, upwards to sink through transpiration stream. At the sink regionsi mineral ions are unloaded through diffusion and active uptake by receptor cells.

Some of the mineral ions moving frequently through xylem are

(i) **Nitrogen** travels in plants as inorganic ions NO_2 and NO_3 but much of the nitrogen moves in the form of amino acids and related organic compounds.

(ii) **Sulphur and Phosphorus** small amount of these two nutrients are carried in organic forms.

(iii) Mineral ions are frequently remobilised particularly from older senescing parts. Older dying leaves export much of their mineral content to younger leaves. Similarly, before leaf fall in decidous plants, minerals are removed to other parts.

Elements most readily mobilised are phosphorus, sulphur, nitrogen and potassium. Some elements that are structural components like calcium are not remobilised.

Q. 2 Plants show temporary and permanent wilting. Differentiate between the two. Do any of them indicate the water status of the soil?

Ans. Wilting refers to the loss of turgidity in the leaves and other soft aerial parts of a plant causing drooping, folding and rolling of non-woody plants. It occurs when rate of loss of water is higher than the rate of absorption.

Temporary Wilting	Permanent Wilting
Temporary drooping of young leaves and shoots due to loss of turgidity especially during noon.	State of permanent loss of turgidity in leaves and other parts of plant.
Occurs when rate of transpiration is more than water absorption due to shrinkage of roots.	Rate of transpiration is more than rate of absorption but difference is below critical level.
Wilting recovers as soon as water is replenished in the soil around root hairs.	Wilting is not recovered as cells do not regain their turgidity even in presence of plentiful water.
Plant regains its normal growth.	Plant eventually dies.

Temporary wilting indicates short term water shortage while permanent wilting indicates the soil does not have water for plant's uptake.

Q. 3 Why are natural membranes selectively permeable. Give examples.

Ans. Natural membranes are selectively permeable due to their structural characteristics and the presence of specific proteins that regulate the movement of substances in and out of the cell. Selective permeability is crucial for maintaining homeostasis within the cell or organism by controlling which molecules and ions can enter or leave, depending on the needs of the cell.

Reasons for selective permeability

(i) **Lipid Bilayer Structure**

- The core of the membrane consists of a **phospholipid bilayer**, with hydrophobic (water-repelling) tails facing inward and hydrophilic (water-attracting) heads facing outward.
- This structure allows small, non-polar molecules (*e.g.*, oxygen, carbon dioxide) to pass through easily, while large or polar molecules (*e.g.*, ions, glucose) are blocked unless facilitated by proteins.

(ii) **Presence of Transport Proteins** Membranes contain specialized transport proteins such as channel proteins, carrier proteins, and active transport pumps. These proteins help move specific molecules (*e.g.*, ions, glucose) across the membrane, either passively or by using energy (ATP).

(iii) **Size and Charge of Molecules** Small, non-polar molecules can diffuse directly through the lipid bilayer, while larger or charged molecules require specific transport mechanisms to cross.

(iv) **Membrane Carbohydrates** The membrane may contain glycoproteins and glycolipids that assist in signaling and recognition, affecting how the membrane interacts with other molecules and contributing to selective permeability.

Examples of selectively permeable membrane are plasma membrane of cells, endoplasmic recticulum membrane, vacoule membrane in plants, mitochondrial membrane etc.

Q. 4 Halophytes may show cell pressure very much higher than atmospheric pressure. Explain how this can happen?

Thinking Process Halophytes have been defined as salt tolerant plants having cellular, biochemical, physiological and anatomical mechanisms allowing them to survive in high salinity conditions.

Ans. The halophytes have salt secreting glands in their epidermal tissue. They help in removal of excess salts from their internal tissue to maintain their osmolarity and the atmospheric pressure on them. This mechanism contributes to the regulation of turgor pressure which may exceed atmospheric pressure as the plants actively manages the accumulation and secretion of salts.

Q. 5 The radio labelled carbon in carbon dioxide supplied to potato plants in an experiment was seen in the tuber eventually. Trace the movement of the labelled carbon dioxide.

Ans. If a radio labelled carbon C^{14} is supplied to potato plants while it's carrying out photosynthesis in the presence of light, the CO_2 will be fixed and form radioactive products of photosynthesis, *i.e.*, radioactive glucose.

This radioacative glucose is converted to sucrose which would again be radioactive due to transfer of C^{14} from previous sugar molecule. These sucrose molecules then move into pholem and transported to other parts of plant.

Autoradiography technique detects the radioactive carbon (present in sugars) and traces its the components and movement in the plant, *i.e.*, through sieve tube channels of phloem from leaves (sources) to different parts (sink).

Q. 6 Water molecule is very polar. Polar end of molecule attracts opposite charges on another water molecule (acts like magnet). How will you explain this property of water with reference to upward movement of water? Comment on the upward movement of water given the intermolecular hydrogen bonding in water.

Ans. Attraction of water molecules to polar surfaces describes the adhesive properties of water. Besides, the cohesive properties include the attraction between water molecules. These two cohesive and adhesive properties contributes and help in the upward movement of water by providing

(i)	High tensile strength	Capability to resist a pulling force, *i.e.*, gravitational force.
(ii)	High capillarity	Ability to rise in thin tubes or columns, *i.e.*, of tracheids and vessels.

The intermolecular hydrogen bonding in water ensures that more water molecules are attracted to each other in liquid state than in the gaseous state. This contributes to surface tension which in turn accounts for high capillarity in the xylem column.

Q. 7 Comment on the experimental setup.

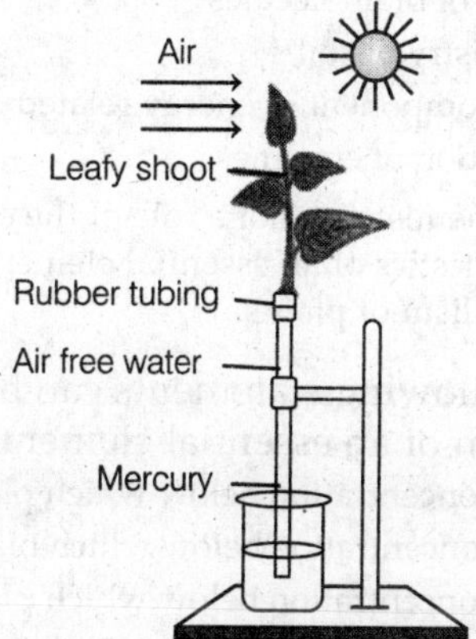

(a) What does the setup demonstrate?

(b) What will happen to the level of water if a blower is placed close to setup?

(c) Will the mercury level fluctuate (go up/down) if phenyl mercuric acetate is sprayed on leaves?

Thinking Process There is continuous loss of water from plant's body surface in the form of water. Maximum amount of water plants absorb gets lost to environment in this form. This process transpiration. This is a necessary evil in the plants.

Ans. (a) The process of transpiration is demonstrated by this set up.

(b) Constant air blowing will increase the rate of transpiration so, level of water will go down.

(c) The mercury level will go down, if phenyl mercuric acetate is sprayed on leaves. This is because phenyl mercuric acetate is an antitranspirant that reduces the rate of transpiration by covering stomata with a film.

Chapter 12

Mineral Nutrition*

Multiple Choice Questions (MCQs)

Choose the correct answer from the given four options in the following questions.

Q. 1 Which one of the following roles is not characteristic of an essential element?

(a) being a component of biomolecules
(b) changing the chemistry of soil
(c) being a structural component of energy related chemical compound
(d) activation or inhibition of enzymes

Ans. ***(b)*** Changing the soil chemistry is not a role of the essential element. Whereas rest all are the characteristics of an essential element. These elements are directly involved in the metabolism of plants.

Q. 2 Which one of the following statements can best explain the term critical concentration of an essential element?

(a) Essential element concentration below which plant growth is retarded.
(b) Essential element concentration below which plant growth becomes enhanced.
(c) Essential element concentration below which plant remains in the vegetative phase.
(d) None of the above

Ans. ***(a)*** The concentration of the essential element below which the plant growth is retarded is termed as critical concentration. Plants start showing deficiency symptoms if a particular element is present below the critical concentration.

Q. 3 Deficiency symptoms of an element tend to appear first in young leaves. It indicates that the element is relatively immobile. Which one of the following elemental deficiency would show such symptoms?

(a) Sulphur (b) Magnesium (c) Nitrogen (d) Potassium

Thinking Process Plants show deficiency symptoms of the elements when that particular nutrient is not available to the plants or if it is available, the plant is not able to use it.

Ans. ***(a)*** The sulphur is needed by young leaves, stem and root tips. If it is not available, these parts will show the deficiency symptoms which include

(i) reduced growth (ii) extensive root growth
(iii) hard and woody stem (iv) chlorosis of young leaves.

Relatively immobile elements are transported in plant only upto the tip level, so their deficiency appears first at the tips of growing apices of roots and shoot.

Note (*) *This chapter has been deleted from latest NCERT*

Q. 4 Which one of the following symptoms is not due to manganese toxicity in plants?

(a) Calcium translocation in shoot opex is inhibited

(b) Deficiency in both iron and Nitrogen induced

(c) Appearance of brown spot surrounded by chlorotic veins

(d) None of the above

Ans. ***(b)*** Manganese is an essential micronutrient which is mainly required by the leaves and seeds of plants. Manganese becomes toxic when absorded by plants in higher amounts. Its toxicity result into inhibition of Ca^{2+} translocation in shoot apex, appearance of brown spots surrounded by chlorotic veins etc. Its toxicity also induces deficiencies of iron, magnesium and calcium. Nitrogen deficiency is not typically induced by manganese toxicity. Hence, option (b) is correct.

Q. 5 Reaction carried out by N_2 fixing microbes included

(a) $2NH_3 + 3O_2 \longrightarrow 2NO_2^- + 2H^+ + 2H_2O$ ...(i)

(b) $2NO_2 + O_2 \longrightarrow 2NO_3^-$ ...(ii)

Which of the following statements about these equations is not true?

(a) Step (i) is carried out by *Nitrosomonas* or *Nitrococcus*

(b) Step (ii) is carried out by *Nitrobacter*

(c) Both steps (i) and (ii) can be called nitrification

(d) Bacteria carrying out these steps are usually photoautotrophs

Ans. ***(d)*** Option (d) is not true because the bacteria involved in the process are not photoautotrophs but chemoautotrophs. These bacteria oxidise inorganic substances like NH_3 and NO_2 and use the released energy hence are called **chemoautotrophs.**

Simultaneously, they help in the conversion of ammonia (NH_3) to absorbable form (NO_2^- and NO_3^-) of nitrogen.

Q. 6 With regard to the biological nitrogen fixation by *Rhizobium* in association with soyabean, which one of the following statement/ statements does not hold true.

(a) Nitrogenase may require oxygen for its functioning.

(b) Nitrogenase is Mo-Fe protein

(c) Leg-haemoglobin is a pink coloured pigment.

(d) Nitrogenase helps to convert N_2 gas into two molecules of ammonia.

Ans. ***(a)*** The enzyme, nitrogenase which is capable of nitrogen reduction is present exclusively in prokaryotes (*e.g., Rhizobium*). It is highly sensitive to O_2 and gets inactivated when exposed to it, Thus does not require oxygen for its functioning. Other statements (b), (c) and (d) are true.

Q. 7 Match the element with its associated functions/roles and choose the correct option among given below

A.	Boron	1.	Splitting of H_2O to liberate O_2 during photosynthesis
B.	Manganese	2.	Needed for synthesis of auxins
C.	Molybdenum	3.	Component of nitrogenase
D.	Zinc	4.	Pollen germination
E.	Iron	5.	Component of ferredoxin

Codes

(a) 1, 2, 3, 4, 5 (b) 4, 1, 3, 2, 5
(c) 3, 2, 4, 5, 1 (d) 2, 3, 5, 1, 4

Thinking Process The plants require few minerals in large quantities and few in small quantities. Thus, they are called macro and microelements respectively. The B, Mn, Zn and Fe are the elements required by the plants in smaller quantities but are very much essential for normal growth, development and reproduction of the plants.

Ans. ***(b)*** Correct match is as follows

A.	Boron	4. Pollen germination
B.	Manganese	1. Splitting of H_2O to liberate O_2 during photosynthesis
C.	Molydenum	3. Component of nitrogenase
D.	Zine	2. Needed for synthesis of auxins
E.	Iron	5. Component of ferredoxin.

Q. 8 Plants can be grown in (Tick the incorrect option)

(a) soil with essential nutrients.
(b) water with essential nutrients.
(c) either water or soil with essential nutrients.
(d) water or soil without essential nutrients.

Ans. ***(c)*** The plants can be grown in any medium either water or soil if it is supported with all essential elements. Medium does not affect the plant growth but availability of essential elements does affect the growth of the plants.

Very Short Answer Type Questions

Q. 1 Name a plant, which accumulate silicon.

Thinking Process There are few macro elements and micro elements needed by all plants for the completion of their life cycle in a normal way. But few plants have some specific requirements for some elements like Na, Si, Cl and Ni.

Ans. *Oryza sativa* and *Triticum aestivum* are silicon accumulators. These plants actively absorb silicon and accumulate it in their biomass.

Q. 2 Mycorrhiza is a mutualistic association. How do the organisms involved in this association benefit from each other?

Ans. A mycorrhiza is a symbiotic association between a fungus and the roots of vascular plants (mainly gymnosperms). This mutualistic association provides the fungus with a constant and direct supply of carbohydrates (glucose and sucrose).

In return, plant gains the benefit of the mycelium of fungus which enhances its absorptive capacity for water and minerals due to the large surface area of mycelium.

Q. 3 Nitrogen fixation is shown by prokaryotes and not eukaryotes. Comment.

Ans. Some prokaryotes like *Rhizobium*, *Anabaena* and *Nostoc* contains the enzyme nitrogenase, needed for the biological nitrogen-fixation. Eukaryotes do not possess this enzyme, therefore are unable to fix nitrogen.

Q. 4 Carnivorous plants like *Nepenthes* and venus fly trap have nutritional adaptations. Which nutrient do they especially obtain and from where?

Ans. *Nepenthes* and venus fly trap grow in nitrogen-deficient soil. So, they make up their nitrogen deficiency by trapping insects for which they have developed special adaptations.

Q. 5 Name a plant which lacks chlorophyll. How will it obtain nutrition?

Ans. An angiospermic plant called *Monotropa* do not contain chlorophyll. It grows on other plant as a parasite and derive nutrition from the host plant. This plant is commonly known as ghost plant.

Q. 6 Name an insectivorous angiosperm.

Ans. (i) *Nepenthes (Pitcher plant)*

(ii) *Utricularia (bladder wort)*

Q. 7 A farmer adds *Azotobacter* culture to soil before sowing maize. Which mineral element is being replenished?

Ans. *Azotobacter* is a free living bacteria in the soil. It helps cereal crops like maize (*Zea mays*) in nitrogen fixation. The farmer adds *Azotobacter* culture to the maize field for enhancing the nitrogen content in the soil by the process of biological nitrogen-fixation.

Q. 8 What type of conditions are created by leghaemoglobin in the root nodule of a legume?

Ans. Leghaemoglobin is responsible for creating anaerobic conditions in the root nodules of the legume plant. It acts as an oxygen scavenger, protecting enzyme nitrogenase to come in contact with oxygen and help in the proper functioning of enzyme, *i.e.*, conversion of atmospheric nitrogen to ammonia (NH_3).

Q. 9 What is common to *Nepenthes, Utricularia* and *Drosera* with regard to mode of nutrition?

Ans. All the above mentioned plants are carnivorous (insectivorous) plants. These trap insects and digest them by proteolytic enzymes and thus, make up their nitrogen deficiency.

Q. 10 Plants with zinc deficiency show reduced biosynthesis of ____ .

Ans. Plant with zinc deficiency shows, reduced biosynthesis of auxin (growth hormone). Zinc is the micronutrient that is absorbed by almost all parts of the plant in the form of Zn^{2+} ion.

It functions as a constituent of carbonic anhydrase and auxin. It also activates various enzymes especially carboxylases and dehydrogenases.

Q. 11 Yellowish edges appear in leaves deficient in mineral?

Ans. Yellowish edges or chlorosis appears in the leaves, deficient in potassium. Potassium deficiency also causes interference in protein synthesis, opening and closing stomata and delayed metabolic activities.

Q. 12 Name the macronutrient which is a component of all organic compounds but its not obtained from soil.

Ans. Carbon is an essential element. Plant take it from atmosphere in the form of CO_2. Its concentration in atmosphere is about 0.03%. Plants use CO_2 for photosynthesis (as a source of carbon) to synthesise glucose.

Q. 13 Name one non-symbiotic nitrogen fixing prokaryote.

Ans. *Azotobacter* is a non-symbotic nitrogen fixing prokaryote. It flourishes in the rice fields.

Q. 14 Rice fields produce an important green house gas. Name it.

Ans. Rice fields remain logged with excess water which harbour the great microbial activity. Many anaerobic bacteria also grow in these areas and release methane which is a green house gas.

Q. 15 Complete the equation for reductive amination ....

$$+ NH_4^+ + NADPH \xrightarrow{?} \text{glutamate} + H_2O + NADP$$

Ans. **Reductive Amination** Ammonia combines with a keto acid (like α-ketoglutaric acid or oxaloacetic acid) to form amino acid in presence of a reduced coenzyme (NADH, NADPH) and enzyme dehydrogenase (*e.g.*, glutamate dehydrogenase, aspartate dehydrogenase).

$$\alpha\text{-ketoglutaric acid} + NH_4^+ + NAD\,(P)\,H \xrightarrow[\text{dehydrogenase}]{\text{Glutamate}} \text{Glutamate} + H_2O + NAD\,(P)$$

Q. 16 Excess of Mn in soil leads to deficiency of Ca, Mg and Fe. Justify.

Ans. Manganese (Mn^{2+}) becomes toxic when absorbed by plants in higher amounts. The toxicity expressed in form of brown spots surrounded by chlorotic vein. This is due to the following reasons

(i) Reduction in uptake of Fe^{3+} and Mn^{2+}.

(ii) Inhibition of binding of Mn^{2+} to specific enzymes.

(iii) Inhibition of Ca^{2+} translocation in shoot apex.

Thus, excess of Mn^{2+} causes deficiency of iron, magnesium and calcium.

Short Answer Type Questions

Q. 1 How is sulphur important for plants? Name the amino acids in which it is present.

Thinking Process Sulphur is a macronutrient and is important for normal plant growth and development. It is an integral part of some amino acids and proteins and helps in deciding the secondary structure of proteins as it forms disulphide bonds.

Ans. Sulphur (S) is an important macronutrient in plants that is absorbed by the plants as SO_4^{2-} ion. It mainly functions as a component of vitamins (biotin, thiamine), proteins, coenzyme-A, and amino acid (cystein and methionine) etc. It is also an essential component of allyl sulphide food vegetable (onion, garlic) and sinigrin (mustard).

Deficiency of sulphur can cause symptoms such as chlorosis in young leaves, extensive root growth, formation of hard and woody stem. It also causes the reduction in juice content of citrus fruit and yellow disease of tea.

Sulphur is found in amino acids cysteine and methionione, which are crucial for photosynthesis.

Q. 2 How are organisms like *Pseudomonas* and *Thiobacillus* of great significance in nitrogen cycle?

Thinking Process Biological nitrogen fixation is a process is which gaseous nitrogen is converted to nitrogen which can be used by the plants as a nutrient.

Ans. *Pseudomonas* and *Thiobacillus* are significant in the nitrogen cycle through the process of denitrification. In biological nitrogen fixation, the atmospheric N_2 gets reduced to NH_3 by nitrogenase reductase present in some prokaryotes. NH_3 then oxidises to NO_2^- and NO_3^- by some other bacteria (*Nitrosomonas* and *Nitrobacter*). *Various steps involved in nitrogen fixation are as follows*

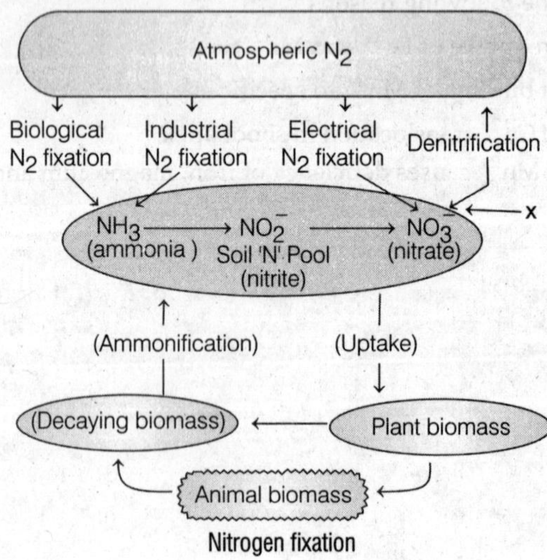

Nitrogen fixation

However, Pseudomonas and *Thiobacillus* play a role in denitrification. Where they convert nitrate (NO_3^-) and nitrite (NO_2^-) into free nitrogen (N_2), which is released into the atmosphere. This process is crucial for maintaining nitrogen balance in the soil.

Q. 3 Carefully observe the following figure

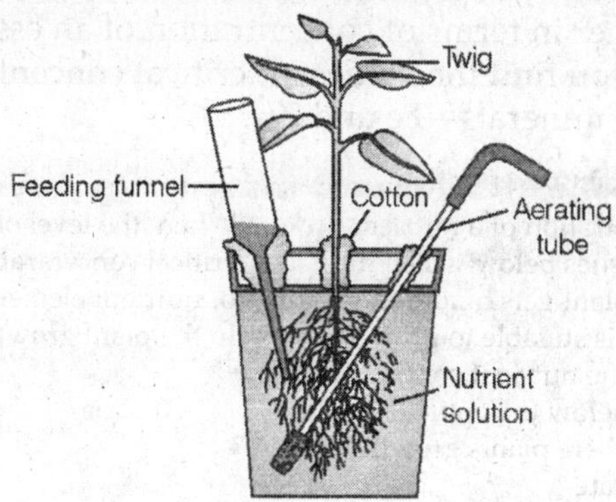

(a) Name the technique shown in the figure and the scientist who demonstrated this technique for the first time.

(b) Name atleast three plants for which this technique can be employed for their commercial production.

(c) What is the significance of aerating tube and feeding funnel in this setup?

Ans. (a) The technique shown is Hydroponics, and the scientist who discovered this technique was Julius Von Sachs (1860)

(b) (i) *Solanum lycopersicum* (tomato)
(ii) *Hibiscus asculentus* (okra)
(iii) *Solanum melongena* (brinjal)

(c) **Aerating tube** Provides oxygen for the normal growth and development of the roots growing in the liquid solution. Feeding funnel is used to add water and nutrients in the hydroponic system when required, ensuring that the plant receives all the necessary elements for optimal growth.

Q. 4 Name the most crucial enzyme found in root nodules for N_2-fixation? Does it require a special pink coloured pigment for its functioning? Elaborate.

Ans. Nitrogenase is the most crucial enzyme found in the root nodules for N_2-fixation. It is a Mo – Fe protein complex. This enzyme catalyses the conversion of atomospheric nitrogen to ammonia. Pink coloured pigment called **leghaemoglobin** creates anaerobic conditions for the functioning of nitrogenase enzyme by binding with oxygen which is essential because nitrogenase is sensitive to oxygen. This allows nitrogenase to effectively convert nitrogen into a usable form for the plant.

Q. 5 How are the terms 'critical concentration' and 'deficient' different from each other in terms of concentration of an essential element in plants? Can you find the values of 'critical concentration' and 'deficient' for minerals—Fe and Zn?

Ans.

Critical Concentration	Deficient
It is the concentration of a nutrient measures in tissues below which the growth of the plant gets hindered. At this level, the plant is stiuable to grow, but at reduced rate. The nutrient concentration is present just below the optimal level of concentration where plants growth in at the maximum rate. *e.g.*, N, P and K are known as critical elements.	When the level of a nutrient is below the critical concentration and the deficiency of nutrient element leads to a gradual fall in the plant growth is called deficient.

	Critical concentration	Deficient
Zn	0.5 - 1%	less than 0.5%
Fe	3.5 - 5%	less than 3.5%

Q. 6 Carnivorous plants exhibit nutritional adaptation. Citing an example explain this fact.

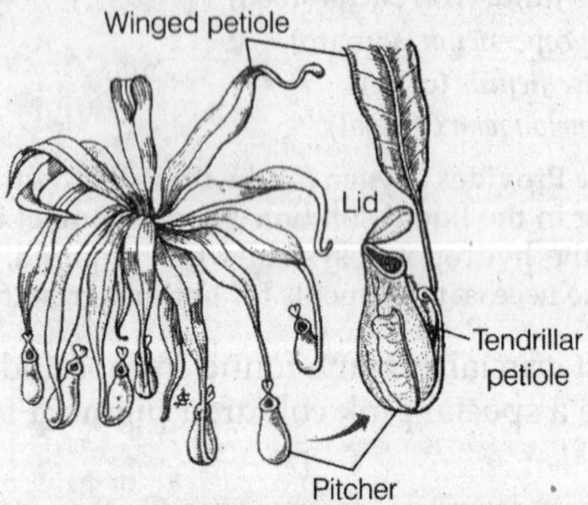

Nepenthes showing Pictcher shaped leaft

Ans. Carnivorous (insectivorous) plants are mainly found in nitrogen deficient soil. To overcome the nitrogen deficiency, they have developed insect trapping mechanism in which leaves have taken the shape of a pitcher containing insect digesting proteolytic enzymes. They trap insect and absorb the nitrogen derived from them. An example is the pitcher plant (*Nepethes*), which has pitcher-shaped leaves filled with digestive enzymes to break down trapped insects and absorb nitrogen from them.

Q. 7 A farmer adds/supplies Na, Ca, Mg and Fe regularly to his field and yet he observes that the plants show deficiency of Ca, Mg and Fe. Give a valid reason and suggest a way to help the farmer improve the growth of plants.

Ans. The farmer may observe deficiencies of Ca, Mg, and Fe despite supplying them due to ion **antagonism** or **toxicity**. Excessive levels of one element can inhibit the absorption of others. For example high sodium (Na) levels can reduce the uptake of calcium (Ca), magnesium (Mg), and iron (Fe) by the plants.

Additionally, micronutrient toxicity can lead to the reduced absorption of other essential nutrients. The **toxic concentration** of a nutrient refers to the level at which it reduces plant growth or cause harm. For example, $\mathbf{Mn^{2+}}$ can be toxic to soyabeans at concentration above 600 μ/g and to sunflowers at concentration above 5300 μg/g. To help the farmer, the following steps can be taken

- Regularly **monitor soil nutrient levels** through soil testing.
- Use **balanced fertilisers** with proper nutrient ratios to avoid excess of one element.
- **Ensure proper irrigation practices** to prevent ion buildup in the soil.
- **Use chelated forms of micronutrients,** which are more readily available to plants and less likely to cause antagonistic effects.

Long Answer Type Questions

Q. 1 It is observed that deficiency of a particular element showed its symptoms initially in older leaves and then in younger leaves.

(a) Does it indicate that the element is actively mobilised or relatively immobile?

(b) Name two elements which are highly mobile and two which are relatively immobile.

(c) How is the aspect of mobility of elements important to horticulture and agriculture?

Ans. (a) The plants try to supply more nutrients to its younger leaves than the older leaves. When nutrients are mobile, the deficiency symptoms shows up first in the older leaves because the nutrient is mobilised from the older tissues to the younger ones, and older leaves become deficient first.

(b) Highly mobile elements are P, K and N and relatively immobile elements are Ca, Fe, B.

(c) The aspect of mobility of essential elements is important in horticulture and agriculture in the following ways

(i) A crop in which older leaves are harvested if show deficiency symptoms, will decrease its economic value.

(ii) The crops in which flowers, fruits and inflorescence are harvested, if the immobile nutrients will not reach to the apex/tip because of immobility, so this will reduce the yield.

Q. 2 We find that *Rhizobium* forms nodules on the roots of leguminous plants. Also *Frankia* another microbe forms nitrogen fixing nodules on the roots of non-leguminous plant *Alnus.*

(a) Can we artificially induce the property of nitrogen-fixation in a plant, leguminous or non-leguminous?

(b) What kind of relationship is observed between mycorrhiza and pine trees?

(c) Is it necessary for a microbe to be in close association with a plant to provide mineral nutrition? Explain with the help of one example.

Ans. (a) Artificial induction of nitrogen fixation in leguminous and non-leguminous plants has been attempted by scientists. However, the success rate is very low because gene expression is highly specific phenomenon.
Even if desired gene is introduced, it may not work because conditions for its expressions are very specific.

(b) A mutualistic symbiotic relationship (mutualism) is found between the pine roots and mycorrhiza as both are benefitted mutually.

(c) *Yes,* microbe must be in close association, with plants to provide mineral nutrition for example *Rhizobium* bacteria enters the root from nodules, where they helps in nitrogen-fixation.

Q. 3 What are essential elements for plants? Give the criteria of essentiality? How are minerals classifieds depending upon the amount in which they are needed by the plants?

Ans. Essential elements are those chemical elements required by plants to complete their life cycle. Including growth, reproduction and metabolism. These play critical roles in various physiological and biochmical processes in plants.

Criteria for Essentiality

An element can not be considered as essential merely on the basis of its presence in the plant. It is considered essential on the basis of the following criteria

(i) The plant is unable to grow normally and complete its life cycle in the absence of the element.
(ii) The element is specific and can not be replaced by another element.
(iii) The element plays a direct role in the metabolism of the plants.

The essential elements are further classified into two categories

(a) **Macroelements** These are the elements required by plants in larger quantities. These are C, H, O, N, P, K, Mg, Ca and S.

(b) **Microelements** (Trace elements) These are required by plants in low quantities (often less than 1 ppm). These include B, Zn, Mn, Cu, Mo, Cl, Fe and Ni.

Q. 4 With the help of examples describe the classification of essential elements based on the function they perform.

Ans. Essential elements are involved in performing various vital functions in plants. Some of the major functions are enlisted below

(i) **Frame work elements** Essential elements as components of biomolecules and hence are structural elements of the cell. Carbon, hydrogen and oxygen are considered as framework elements because they constitute carbohydrates which form cell wall.

(ii) **Protoplasmic elements** N, P and S are considered as protoplasmic elements as they form protoplasm which are essential for cellular functions and metabolism.

(iii) **Catalytic elements** these elements activates or inhibit enzymes, Without the presence of these elements some enzymes can not function *e.g.*, Mg^{2+} acts as an activator for both ribulose bisphosphate carboxylase oxygenase (Rubisco) and phosphoenolpyruvate carboxylase (PEP carboxylase).

Both are the critical enzymes involved in photosynthetic carbon fixation in plants.

(iv) **Balancing elements** Elements counteract the toxic effect of other minerals by causing ionic balance (*e.g.*, calcium, magnesium and potassium).

(v) **Element Influencing osmotic pressure** Some essential elements alters the osmotic potential of plant cell influencing processes like water uptake and stomatal regulation. *e.g.*, K is involved in opening and closing of stomata.

Q. 5 We know that plants require nutrients. If we supply these in excess, will it be beneficial to the plants? If yes, how/ if no, why?

Ans. No, excess nutrients are harmful for plants because of the followign reasons:

(i) Excess nutrients can interfere with the uptake of other essential elements (*e.g.*, high manganese reduces iron uptake).

(ii) Toxicity symptoms can be difficult to identify because they often result from nutrient imbalances, not just the excess of one element.

Plants can tolerate a specific amount of micronutrient. A slight lesser amount of it can cause deficiency symptom and a slight higher amount can cause toxicity. The mineral ion concentration which reduces the dry weight of a tissue by 10% is called toxic concentration.

This concentration is different for different micronutrients as well as for different plant, *e.g.*, Mn^{2+} is toxic beyond 600 μgg^{-1} for soyabean and beyond 5300 μgg^{-1} for sunflower.

It is very difficult to identify the toxicity symptoms of mineral ion. It is because excess uptake of one element can reduces the uptake of other element at a time.

For example manganese (Mn^{2+}) becomes toxic when absorbed by plants in higher amounts. The toxicity is expressed in form of brown spots surrounded by chlorotic vein.

It is duc to thc following

(i) Reduction in uptake of Fe^{3+} and Mg^{2+}.

(ii) Inhibition of binding of Mg^{2+} to specific enzymes.

(iii) Inhibition of Ca^{2+} translocation in shoot apex.

Thus, excess of Mn^{2+} causes deficiency of iron, magnesium and calcium.

Q. 6 Trace the events starting from the coming in contact of *Rhizobium* to a leguminous root till nodule formation. Add a note on importance of leg haemoglobin.

Ans. **Formation of Root Nodule** The coordinated activities of the legume and the *Rhizobium* bacteria depend on the chemical interaction between the symbiotic partners.

The principle stages in the nodule formation are summerised in the following diagram

Importance of Leghemoglobin are as follows

Leghaemoglobin is an oxygen binding protein found in the root nodules of legumes. It serves to protect the nitrogenase enzyme from oxygen, which would otherwise inhibit nitrogen fixation. By maintaining an anaerobic environment in the nodule, leghemoglobin ensures efficient nitrogen fixation by *Rhizobium*.

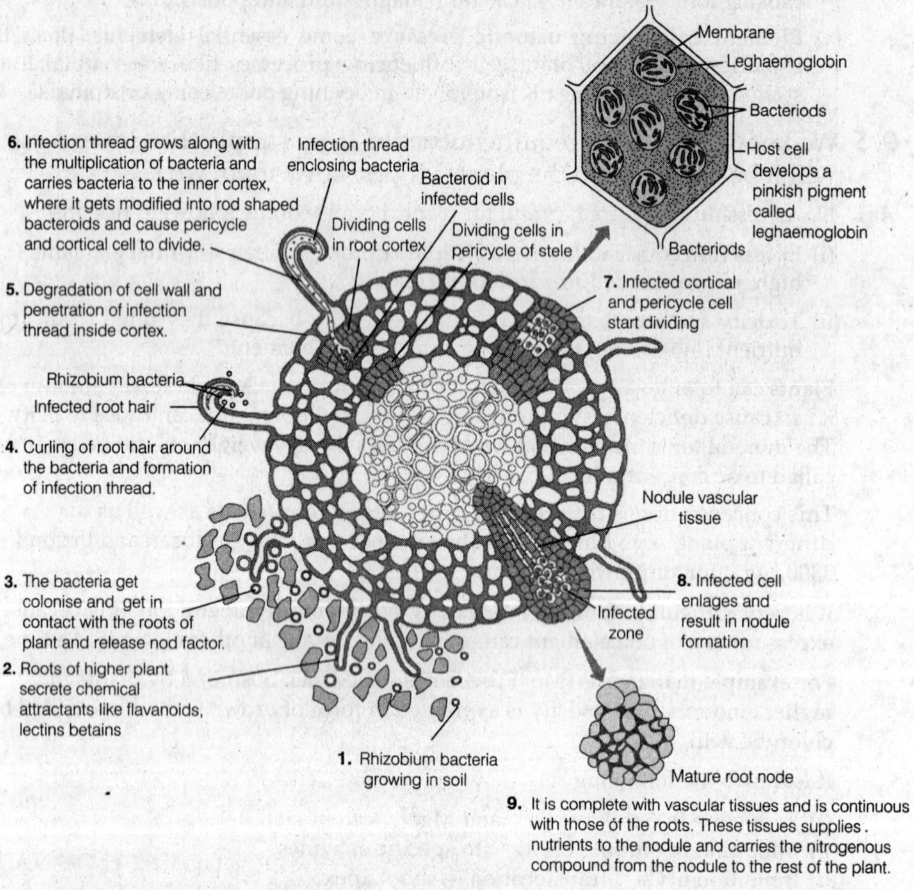

Membrane
Leghaemoglobin
Bacteriods
Host cell develops a pinkish pigment called leghaemoglobin
Bacteriods
6. Infection thread grows along with the multiplication of bacteria and carries bacteria to the inner cortex, where it gets modified into rod shaped bacteroids and cause pericycle and cortical cell to divide.
Infection thread enclosing bacteria
Bacteroid in infected cells
Dividing cells in root cortex
Dividing cells in pericycle of stele
7. Infected cortical and pericycle cell start dividing
5. Degradation of cell wall and penetration of infection thread inside cortex.
Rhizobium bacteria
Infected root hair
4. Curling of root hair around the bacteria and formation of infection thread.
Nodule vascular tissue
3. The bacteria get colonise and get in contact with the roots of plant and release nod factor.
8. Infected cell enlages and result in nodule formation
Infected zone
2. Roots of higher plant secrete chemical attractants like flavanoids, lectins betains
1. Rhizobium bacteria growing in soil
Mature root node
9. It is complete with vascular tissues and is continuous with those of the roots. These tissues supplies nutrients to the nodule and carries the nitrogenous compound from the nodule to the rest of the plant.

Q. 7 Give the biochemical events occurring in the root nodule of a pulse plant. What is the end product? What is its fate?

Ans. Formation of root nodule in pulse plant is the result of infection of roots by *Rhizobium*.

The following figure shows the process of nodule formation

Infection thread containing bacteria
Inner cortex and pericycle cells under division

(a) *Rhizobiun* divide near the root hair

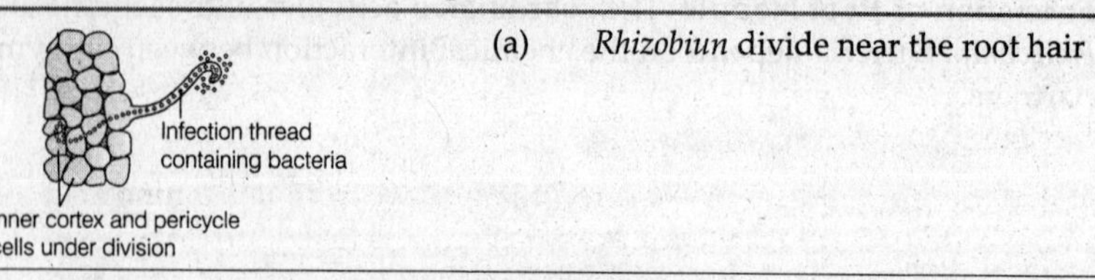

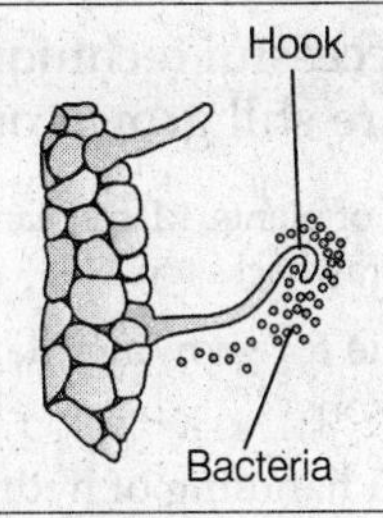

(b) Successful infection of the root hair causes it to curl

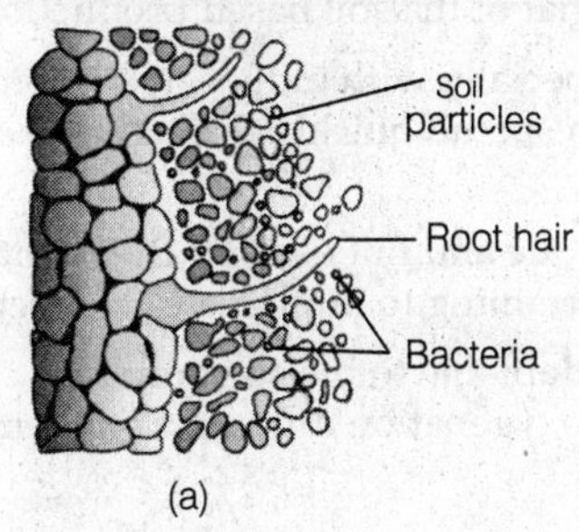

(a)

(c) Infection thread carries the bacteria to the inner cortex. Bacteria get modified into rod-shaped bacteroids and cause inner cortical and pericycle cells to divide. Division and growth of cortical and pericycle cells lead to nodule formation.

(d) Mature nodule with vascular tissues continuous with those of the roots.

The chemical reaction is as follows

$$N_2 + 8e^- + 8H^+ + 16\ ATP \longrightarrow 2NH_3 + H_2 + 16\ ADP + P_i$$

The reaction takes place in presence of enzyme nitrogenase which acts in anaerobic conditions created by leghaemoglobin. The end product of nitrogen fixation is ammonia (NH_3).

Fate of Ammonia

There are two ways by which ammonia is further used

(a) **Reductive Amination**

$$\alpha\text{-ketoglutaric acid} + NH_4^+ + NADPH \xrightarrow[\text{Dehydrogenase}]{\text{Glutamate}} \text{glutamate} + H_2O + NADP$$

Ammonia reacts with α-ketoglutaric acid to form glutamate.

(b) **Transamination**

$$\underset{\text{Amino-donor}}{R_1-\overset{\overset{\large H}{|}}{\underset{\underset{\large NH_3^+}{|}}{C}}-COO^-} + \underset{\text{Amino-acceptor}}{R_2-\underset{\underset{\large O}{\|}}{C}-COO^-} \rightleftharpoons R_1-\underset{\underset{\large O}{\|}}{C}-COO^- + R_2-\overset{\overset{\large H}{|}}{\underset{\underset{\large NH_3^+}{|}}{C}}-COO^-$$

In this process, transfer of NH_2 group take place from one amino acid to other amino acid; enzyme transaminase catalyses this reaction.

Q. 8 Hydroponics have been shown to be a successful technique for growing of plants. Yet most of the crops are still grown on land. Why?

Thinking Process Hydroponics is a soil less culture of plants. Many plants have been grown in nutrient rich solutions but it has certain drawbacks too.

Ans. Although, hydrophonics is a successful technique for growing plants, many crops are still grown on land due to several reasons:

(i) The cost is the major concern. The setting and handling of hydrophonics requires much more investment than that of the soil based production.

(ii) Sanitization is extremely important especially with indoor hydroponic environments. Water borne disease can spread quickly through some methods of hydroponic production.

(iii) Hydroponics is relatively a new technique and not used by the traditional farmers due to lack of knowledge and training to implement in effectively.

(iv) Plants in hydroponic system are less adaptable to the surrounding atmosphere. Hot weather and narrow oxygenation can effect on their yield and quality.

Chapter 13

Photosynthesis in Higher Plants

Multiple Choice Questions (MCQs)

Choose the correct answer from the given four options in the following questions.

Q. 1 Which metal ion is a constituent of chlorophyll?

(a) Iron
(b) Copper
(c) Magnesium
(d) Zinc

Thinking Process Chloroplast is a type of plastid (a cell organelle) which is green in colour. It absorbs light energy and convert it to chemical energy with the help of the chlorophyll pigments.

Ans. *(c)* Magnesium (Mg) is present in the centre of porphyrin ring of the chlorophyll molecule. Other ions, *i.e.*, iron, copper and zinc participate in other metabolic processes which are

Fe is an important part of **cytochrome** and **ferridoxin**.

Cu plays an important role in enzyme catalysing redox reactions.

Zn is associated with auxin (a phytohormone) synthesis.

Q. 2 Which pigment acts directly to convert light energy to chemical energy?

(a) Chlorophyll-*a*
(b) Chlorophyll-*b*
(c) Xanthophyll
(d) Carotenoid

Ans. *(a)* **Chlorophyll-*a*** acts directly to convert light energy to chemical energy.

The other pigments chlorophyll-*b*, xanthophyll and carotenoids are accessory pigments associated with the main pigment, *i.e.*, chlorophyll-*a* to harvest the light energy.

Q. 3 Which range of wavelength (in nm) is called Photosynthetically Active Radiation (PAR)?

(a) 100-390
(b) 390-430
(c) 400-700
(d) 760-100,00

Ans. *(c)* **Photosynthetically Active Radiation** (PAR) ranges from 400-700 nm. This is the visible range of light energy.

The range of other wavelength are associated with

100-400 nm : Ultraviolet (UV) range

390-430 nm : Infrared (NIR) range

760-100,00 nm : Infrared (IR) range

Q. 4 Which light range is most effective in photosynthesis?
(a) Blue (b) Green (c) Red (d) Violet

Thinking Process The visible spectrum wavelength ranges from 400 - 700 nm of which red light has 700 nm.

Ans. *(c)* **Red** light is most effective in photosynthesis.

In other lights namely blue and violet the photosynthesis takes place but the rate is slow, whereas in green light the photosynthesis is least because plants do not absorb this range of light they reflect back green light thus, they appear green.

Q. 5 Chemosynthetic bacteria obtain energy from
(a) sun (b) infrared rays
(c) organic substances (d) inorganic chemicals

Ans. *(d)* Chemosynthetic bacteria were the first organism on earth synthesise their own food by obtaining energy from chemicals like H_2S, NO_2, etc. Photosynthetic bacteria evolved later.

Sun, infrared rays and organic substances are not used as the sources of energy for chemosynthetic bacteria. Hence, these options are incorrect.

Q. 6 Energy required for ATP synthesis in PS II comes from
(a) proton gradient (b) electron gradient
(c) reduction of glucose (d) oxidation of glucose

Ans. *(a)* The synthesis of ATP is driven by the proton gradient across the thylakoid membranes of a chloroplast. It results when the water molecule splits inside the inner membrane and form H^+ and OH^- ions.

The energy for ATP synthesis comes from proton gradient which develops along the inner membrane, *e.g.*, in case of mitochondria in electron transport chain and in chloroplast in the PS II.

The other options (b), (c) and (d) are not involved in the synthesis of ATP molecule.

Q. 7 During light reaction in photosynthesis the following are formed
(a) ATP and sugar (b) hydrogen, O_2 and sugar
(c) ATP, hydrogen donor and O_2 (d) ATP, hydrogen and O_2 donor

Ans. *(c)* Light dependent reaction uses solar power to generate ATP and $NADPH_2$ which provide chemical and reducing power respectively to sugar synthesising reaction of the Calvin cycle, while the O_2 in released as a by product of light dependent reaction.

Other options are incorrect because

(a) ATP is produced in light reaction but sugar is produced in dark reaction.

(b) H^+ is produced by splitting of water $\left(H_2O \rightarrow 2H^+ + \frac{1}{2}O_2\right)$ H^+ are released. The $2H^+$ is accepted by $NADP^+$ to form NADPH and oxygen (O_2) is of course produced but sugar is not.

(d) O_2 donor and ATP is produced in light reaction but not the hydrogen.

Q. 8 Dark reaction in photosynthesis is called so because
(a) it can occur in dark also
(b) it does not depend on light energy
(c) it cannot occur during day light
(d) it occurs more rapidly at night

Ans. *(b)* Dark reaction in photosynthesis is called so because it does not depend on light. It is also called as light independent reaction.

Q. 9 PEP is primary CO_2 acceptor in
(a) C_4 plants
(b) C_3 plants
(c) C_2 plants
(d) both C_3 and C_4 plants

Ans. *(a)* C_4 plants have evolved PEP as primary acceptor of CO_2 to avoid the sensitivity of RuBP carboxylase-oxygenase in high concentration of oxygen, so that they can avoid photorespiratory loss of CO_2 occuring in them.

Other options (b), (c) and (*d*) are incorrect as PEP is not primary acceptor in them.

Q. 10 Splitting of water is associated with
(a) photosystem I
(b) lumen of thylakoid
(c) both photosystem I and II
(d) inner surface of thylakoid membrane

Ans. *(d)* The thylakoid is a photosynthetic unit in the chloroplast. It is a membrane bound structure. The membrane has photosystems I and II embedded in it, in the form of chemicals and molecules. Splitting of water is associated with PS-II, which occurs in presence of Mn^{2+} and Cl^- ions on the inner surface of thylakoid membrane.

$$2H_2O \xrightarrow[Cl^-]{Mn^+} 4H^+ + O_2 + 4\,e^-$$

Photosystem I and II are associated with light reactions.

Q. 11 The correct sequence of flow of electrons in the light reaction is
(a) PS II, plastoquinone, cytochromes, PS I, ferredoxin
(b) PS I, plastoquinone, cytochromes, PS II, ferredoxin
(c) PS I, ferredoxin, PS II
(d) PS I, plastoquinone, cytochromes, PS II, ferredoxin

Thinking Process The light reaction of photosynthesis is mainly involved in trapping of solar radiation and converting it to ATP and produce $NADPH_2$ also. The excited electron move through chains of pigments and their energy is used in ATP formation.

Ans. *(a)* Option (a) is the correct sequence of movement of electrons.

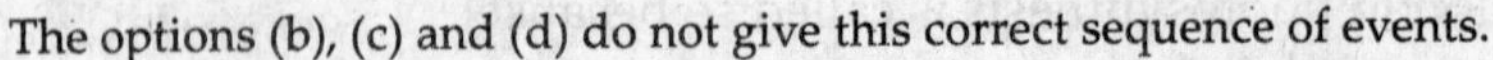

The options (b), (c) and (d) do not give this correct sequence of events.

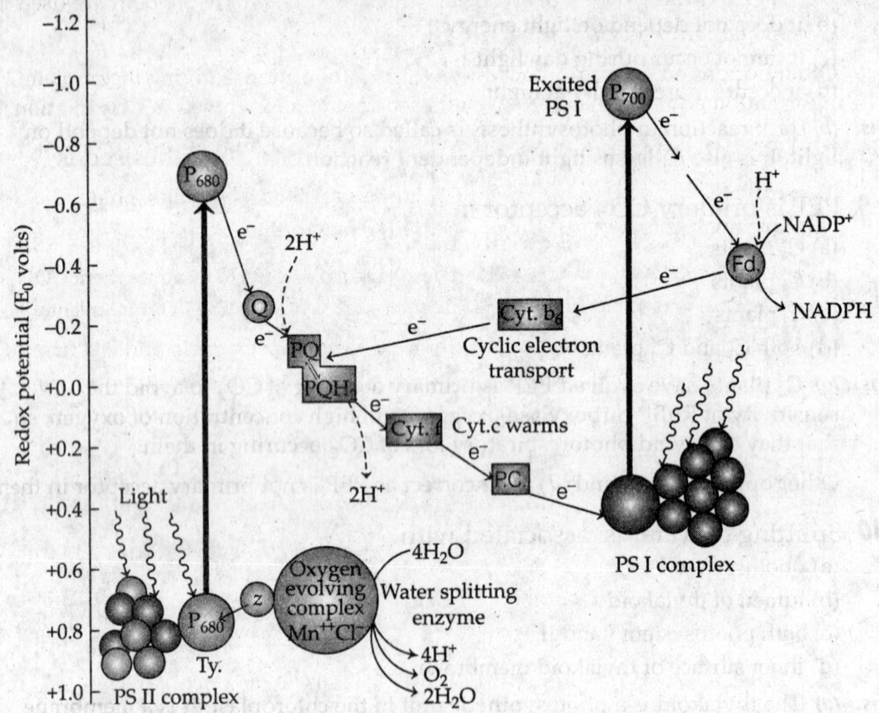

Q. 12 The enzyme that is not found in a C_3 plant is

(a) RuBP carboxylase (b) PEP carboxylase
(c) NADP reductase (d) ATP synthase

Thinking Process C_3 plants are those plants which have calvin cycle to produce glucose molecules in dark reaction. C_3 cycle is found in all photosynthesising plants.

Ans. ***(b)*** PEP carboxylase enzyme is found in C_4 plants to carry out initial fixation of CO_2 and is not found in C_3 plants.

The functions of other enzymes in options (a), (c) and (d) are as follows

(a) RuBP carboxylase operates in C_3 plants as well as C_4 plants.

(c) NADP reductase is involved in electron transport chain.

(d) ATP synthase is used in ATP synthesis.

Q. 13 The reaction that is responsible for the primary fixation of CO_2 is catalysed by

(a) RuBP carboxylase
(b) PEP carboxylase
(c) RuBP carboxylase and PEP carboxylase
(d) PGA synthase

Ans. *(c)* In C_3 cycle **RuBP carboxylase** is used to fix atmospheric CO_2 whereas, in C_4 plants **PEP carboxylase** is involved in primary CO_2 fixation. So, both are used in CO_2 fixation but in different cycles.

Other options are incorrect because in (a) and (b) option is giving incomplete information and option (d) PGA synthase is not at all involved in CO_2 fixation.

Q. 14 When CO_2 is added to PEP, the first stable product synthesised is

(a) pyruvate (b) glyceraldehyde-3-phosphate
(c) phosphoglycerate (d) oxaloacetate

Thinking Process C_4 plants use PEP (phosphoenol pyruvate) to fix atmospheric CO_2. In a normal photosynthetic cycle RuBP carboxylase is used to trap CO_2 in C_3 plants.

Ans. *(d)* **Oxaloacetate** is a four carbon compound formed in C_4 cycle and is a first stable product, that is why such plants are called C_4 plants.

Rest of the options are incorrect as because

(a) Pyruvate is formed in glycolysis.

(b) Glyceraldehyde-3-phosphate is also an intermediate compound of glycolysis.

(c) Phosphoglycerate is also an intermediate compound of glycolysis.

Very Short Answer Type Questions

Q. 1 Examine the figure

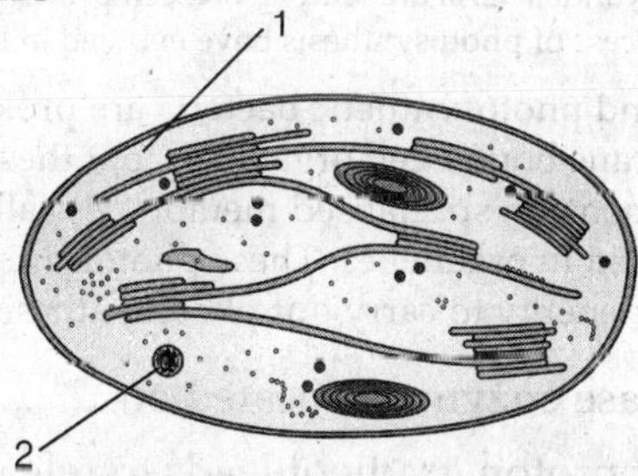

(a) Is this struture present in animal cell or plant cell?
(b) Can these be passed on to the progeny? How?
(c) Name the metabolic processes taking place in the places marked 1 and 2.

Ans. (a) The above figure show the **chloroplast** which is green in colour and performs photosynthesis in plants thus, the structure is present in plant cell.

(b) *Yes,* Chloroplasts can be passed to the progeny as chloroplast has the power of self replication because of presence of extranuclear DNA.

(c) The metabolic processes that occurs in the marked places are as follows.

1–It is the stroma of chloroplast, here dark reaction of photosynthesis takes place.

2–It is the structure of extra nuclear DNA and is responsible for replication of chloroplast, when it is required in the photosynthesising cells.

Q. 2 $2H_2O \rightarrow 4H^+ + O_2 + 4e^-$

Based on the above equation, answer the following questions

(a) Where does this reaction take place in plants?

(b) What is the significance of this reaction?

Thinking Process Water is a universal solvent, every living cell contains 70% water with in the protoplasm. It plays an important role in the process of photosynthesis.

Ans. (a) The reaction takes place in reaction centre PS II, located on the inner surface of thylakoid membrane. It is known as water splitting centre where electrons are extracted from water. The Mn^+ and Cl^- ions catalyse this reaction.

(b) Splitting of water is an important event in photosynthesis as

(i) It releases molecular oxygen as byproduct of photosynthesis which is the significant source of oxygen in atmosphere and is essential for all living beings on earth.

(ii) Hydrogen ions produced, are utilised in reducing NADP to NADPH, a strong reducing agent.

(iii) The electrons released are transferred from PS II to PS I through a series of electron carriers thus, creating a proton gradient for the synthesis of ATP.

Q. 3 Cyanobacteria and some other photosynthetic bacteria don't have chloroplasts. How do they conduct photosynthesis?

Thinking Process Cyanobacteria are simple, one cell prokaryotic organisms belonging to Monera. The process of photosynthesis have evolved in the organisms of this group.

Ans. The cyanobacteria and photosynthetic bacteria are prokaryotes. They do not have well-defined membrane bound cell organelles, but these organisms have photosynthesis pigments in specialised membranes called thylakoid membranes, which are not enclosed in organelles. These photosynthetic pigments allow them to trap and use solar energy to carry out photosynthesis.

Q. 4 (a) NADP reductase enzyme is located on ....

(b) Breakdown of proton gradient leads to release of ....

Ans. (a) NADP reductase enzyme is located on the outer side of **thylakoid membrane.** It is bounded to the thylakoid membrance in light dependent reactions and becomes free in stroma during dark reactions.

(b) Breakdown of proton gradient leads to release of **ATP molecules**. These ATP molecules are produced as the movement of H^+ ions across the membrane is coupled with the formation of ATP synthesis in presence of enzyme ATP synthase.

Q. 5 Can girdling experiments be done in monocots? If yes, How? If no, why not?

Thinking Process Xylem and phloem are conducting tissues in angiosperms. Xylem transports water and minerals and phloem transports food. It has been proved by many experiments.

Ans. The girdling experiment cannot be done in monocots because monocot stem has vascular bundles scattered throughout the stem, unlike dicots, where the phloem is arranged in a continuous ring.

Q. 6 $3CO_2 + 9ATP + 6NADPH + \text{water} \longrightarrow \text{Glyceraldehyde 3–phosphate} + 9ADP + 6NADP^+ + 8Pi.$

Analyse the above reaction and answer the following questions

(a) How many molecules of ATP and NADPH are required to fix one molecule of CO_2?

(b) Where in the chloroplast does this process occur?

Ans. (a) Three molecules of ATP for phosphorylation and two molecules of NADPH for reduction are required per CO_2 molecule fixed.

(b) The calvin cycle occurs in the stroma of the chloroplast.

Q. 7 Does moonlight support photosynthesis? Find out.

Thinking Process Solar radiation is the main source of energy for the survival of plant and animal life on the planet earth.

Ans. Plants cannot carry out photosynthesis in moonlight because moonlight does not carry enough energy to excite chlorophyll molecule, in the reaction centres PS I and PS II. So light dependent reactions does not get initiated thus, no photosynthesis occurs in presence of moonlight.

Q. 8 Some of these terms/chemicals are associated with the C_4 cycle. Explain.

(a) Hatch Slack pathway
(b) Calvin cycle
(c) PEP carboxylase
(d) Bundle sheath cells

Ans. The terms associated with C_4 cycle are

(a) **Hatch Slack Pathway** It is the CO_2 fixation pathway in C_4 plants, where CO_2 is first fixed into C_4 carbon compound in mesophyes cell before being transferred to bundle sheeth cell for calvin cycle.

(b) **Calvin Cycle** This cycle operates in bundle sheath cells in C_4 plants and fixes CO_2 to form glucose molecules.

(c) **PEP Carboxylase** It is an enzyme present in mesophyll cells of C_4 plants. It fixes CO_2 to form 4-carbon compound, *i.e.*, oxaloacetate (OAA).

(d) **Bundle Sheath Cells** These are specialised sclerenchymatous cells present around the vascular bundle, in the veins of monocot leaves. These have agranal chloroplast. Calvin cycle occurs in these cells to manufacture glucose in C_4 plants.

Q. 9 Where is NADP reductase enzyme located in the chloroplast? What is the role of this enzyme in proton gradient development?

Ans. NADP reductase enzyme is located on the stroma side of the thylakoid membrane of the chloroplast. This enzyme is responsible for transferring electrons to $NADP^+$ to form NADPH.

Q. 10 ATPase enzyme consists of two parts. What are those parts? How are they arranged in the thylakoid membrane? Conformational change occur in which part of the enzyme?

Thinking Process Thylakoid is a photosynthetic unit present in the grana of chloroplast, the cell organelle. It is the site for many important photosynthetic reactions.

Ans. ATP synthase enzyme has two parts

(a) F_1-is a peripheral portion of enzyme and contain the catalytic site for synthesis of ATP from ADP +pi (inorganic phosphate).

(b) F_0-integral membrane bound portion of enzyme that forms the channel through which proton across the inner membrane.

The arrangment of F_1 and F_0 in thylakoid membrane is as follows

F_0-portion is present within the thylakoid membrane.

F_1-portion of ATP synthase enzyme is present in the stroma of chloroplast.

The conformational change occurs in F_1 portion of ATP synthase thus, facilitaling the ATP synthesis.

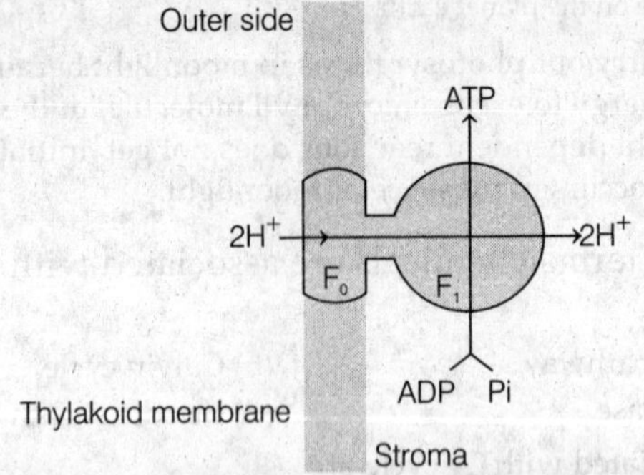

Diagramatic presentation of ATP synthesis in chloroplast

Q. 11 Which products formed during the light reaction of photosynthesis are used to drive the dark reaction?

Ans. ATP and NADPH formed during light reaction of photosynthesis are used in dark reaction, for fixing CO_2 and to form glucose molecule.

Q. 12 What is the basis for designating C_3 and C_4 pathways of photosynthesis?

Ans. The basis for designating C_3 and C_4 pathways of photosynthesis is as follows

C_3 Pathway	C_4 Pathway
In Calvin cycle or C_3 cycle (dark reaction), carbon dioxide is fixed into first stable compound called **3-PGA**, (3-phorphoglyceric acid) which is a 3 carbon compund. This pathway is typical in most plants (*e.g.*, wheat, rice). The fixation of CO_2 into 3 PGA occurs in the stroma of the chloroplasts.	In C_4 plants, CO_2 is initially fixed into oxaloacetate (OAA), a 4-carbon compound, by PEP carboxylase in mesophyll cells. The CO_2 is then transferred to the bundle sheath cells where the calvin cycle occurs. This pathway is characteristic of plants like maize and sugarcane.

Short Answer Type Questions

Q. 1 Succulents are known to keep their stomata closed during the day to check transpiration. How do they meet their photosynthetic CO_2 requirements?

Thinking Process Succulents plants have water conserving tissue and adaptations to conserve water because they grow in xeric conditions. They have other mechanisms to prevent loss of water.

Ans. Succulent plants grow in dry and xeric conditions so, they closed their stomata during day time, to prevent water loss through transpiration. As a result the gaseous exchange does not take place during day.

To meet their CO_2 requirements, these plants have developed the mechanism to fix CO_2 during night in the form of malic acid, which is a 4 carbon compound and store in the vacoule. During the day, stomata close to conserve water and the stored CO_2 is released from malic acid and used in the calvin cycle for photosynthesis.

Q. 2 Chlorophyll-'*a*' is the primary pigment for the light reaction. What are accessory pigments? What is their role in photosynthesis?

Ans. Accessory pigments are also photosynthetic pigments which include chlorophyll-*b*, xanthophyll and carotenoids. These are not directly involved in emission of excited electrons, but they help in harvesting solar radiation and pass it on to chlorophyll-*a*. They also protect chlorophyll-*a* from photo-oxidation.

Chlorophyll-*a* itself absorbs maximum radiation at blue and red region. So, chlorophyll-a is the chief pigment of photosynthesis and others (*i.e.*, chlorophyll-*b*, xanthophyll and caroteinoids) are accessory pegment.

Q. 3 Do reactions of photosynthesis called, as 'Dark Reaction' need light? Explain

Ans. Dark reactions are actually light independent reactions. In these reactions, CO_2 is reduced through various biochemical reactions to produce $C_6H_{12}O_6$ (glucose) and they does not need light. But they depend on the products formed during light reactions, *i.e.*, $NADPH_2$ and ATP which are needed to drive the dark reactions.

Q. 4 How are photosynthesis and respiration related to each other?

Thinking Process Photosynthesis and respiration both are important in plant metabolism. One is anabolic process (synthesising) other is catabolic (breakdown) process.

Ans. **Photosynthesis and respiration** are interconnected processes in plants, as in both mechanisms, the plant is involved in energy transformation.

In photosynthesis, plants use energy from solar radiations to synthesize glucose whereas, in respiration, they break down glucose molecule to get energy in the form of ATP molecules.

They are related because they are dependent on each other. The product of photosynthesis *i.e.*, glucose (food) is utilised in respiration to yield energy (ATP). While doing so, it releases many other simple molecules (CO_2 + H_2O) which are utilised in photosynthesis to produce more sugars.

Q. 5 If a green plant is kept in dark with proper ventilation, can this plant carry out photosynthesis? Can anything be given as supplement to maintain its growth or survival?

Ans. The plant under given conditions cannot carry out photosynthesis. Light is must for any green plant to make its own food.

The plant should be watered properly for its survival. However, it cannot produce its own food in the dark and will eventually need light to thrive.

Q. 6 Photosynthetic organisms occur at different depths in the ocean. Do they receive qualitatively and quantitatively the same light? How do they adapt to carry out photosynthesis under these conditions.

Thinking Process The major part of photosynthesis occuring on earth is performed under water by plants specially algae present in ocean.

Ans. Plant present at various depth in ocean are mostly algae. These exhibit great variations in its photosynthetic pigments. These can absorb different wave lengths of light and performs photosynthesis.

Green algae–chlorophyll-*a*, (absorbs red light) and b(absorbs blue violet light).
Brown algae–chlorophyll-*a*, *c* and fucoxanthin (absorbrs yellow light).
Rhodophyceae–chlorophyll-*a*, *d* and phycoerythrin (absorbs blue and green light). These adaptations enable the algae to efficiently capture light at various depths, ensuring that they can perform photosythesis despite receiving different amount and types of light.

Q. 7 In tropical rain forests, the canopy is thick and shorter plants growing below it, receive filtered light. How are they able to carry out photosynthesis?

Ans. Plants in the understory of tropical rainforests can still carry out photosynthesis, even with filtered light. The rate of photosynthesis is influenced by the internsity and quality of light, but photosynthesis can still occur at lower rates under such conditions. These plants are adapted to low-light environments, often possessing larger leaves or specialised pigment to capture as much light as possible.While photosynthesis is slower under low light, these plants can still make their own food.

Q. 8 What conditions enable RuBisCO to function as an oxygenase? Explain the ensuing process.

Thinking Process RuBisCo is the largest occurring enzyme which is involved in photosynthesis.

Ans. RuBisCo is an enzyme which has dual nature. It acts as carboxylase, when CO_2 concentration is good enough in atmosphere. But if O_2 concentration increases, its nature changes and it binds with O_2 and acts as oxygenase enzyme, which forces CO_2 to enter C_2 cycle thus leading to photorespiration and loss of CO_2.

Q. 9 Why does the rate of photosynthesis decrease at higher temperatures?

Ans. Photosynthesis is an enzyme driven process. All enzymes act at an optimum temperature (*i.e.*, 25-35°C). If temperature increases beyond this range, enzymes get denatured, thus leading to fall in the rate of photosynthesis.

Q. 10 Explain how during light reaction of photosynthesis, ATP synthesis is a chemiosmotic phenomenon.

Thinking Process Chemiosmosis refers to the movement of protons (H^+) from the region of higher concentration to lower concentration. Their movement is coupled with ATP synthesis in thylakoid membrane.

Ans. In light reaction plants trap solar radiation by photosynthetic pigments which convert light energy into chemical energy. Main event of light reaction is photophosphorylation, *i.e.*, formation of ATP from ADP and inorganic phosphate Pi by using energy released by excited electron movement through electron transport chain, present in thylakoid membrane.

Chemiosmosis is the movement of hydrogen ions across a selectively permeable membrane, down the electrochemical/ proton gradient.

Chemiosmosis hypothesis of ATP formation was first proposed by Mitchell (1961) according to which the enzyme ATP synthase generates ATP *via* a membrane, proton pump and the resulting proton gradient. ATP synthase allows hydrogen ions protons to pass through the thylakoid membrane via protein pump. This movement creates a high cocentration of protons (H^+) in the lumen of the thylakoid and then diffuses across the membrane to activate ATPase, releasing ATP molecules. One molecule of ATP is released for every two (H^+) ions passing Through ATPase.

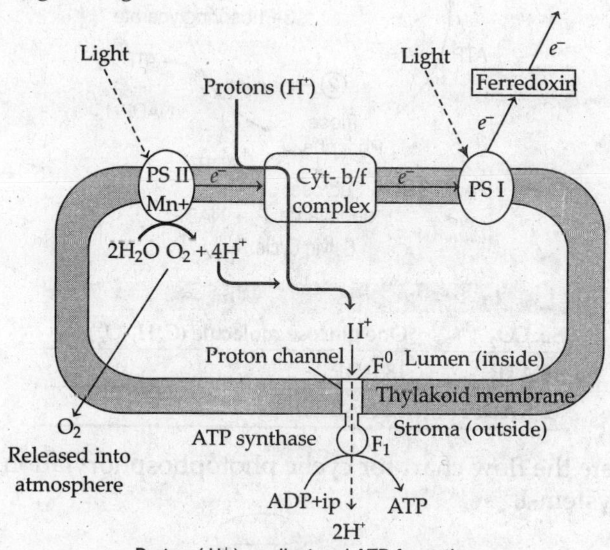

Proton (H^+) gradient and ATP formation

Q. 11 Find out how Melvin Calvin worked out the complete biosynthetic pathway for synthesis of sugar.

Thinking Process Melvin Calvin was awarded Nobel Prize in 1961 for developing the technique to trace the path of carbon in glucose synthesis in dark reaction of photosynthesis.

Ans. Melvin Calvin used *Chlorella* algae as an experimental material and discovered the first stable compound of photosynthesis, *i.e.*, 3 phosphoglyceric acid (PGA) He trace the path of carbon in calvin cycle by using a radioactive isotope of carbon (C^{14}) and autoradiography technique.

He then, compared the radioactive compounds on the chromatogram as a result of which he found and concluded that the PGA (phosphoglyceric acid), as the first stable product of photosynthesis and gradually the other sugars including hexoses, tetroses and pentoses etc. By anlyzing the radioactive compounds on chromatograms, Calvin was able to determine the sequence of reactions that lead to formation of sugars. His work helped elucidate the entire Calvin cycle pathway, from the fixation of CO_2 to the production of glucose.

Q. 12 Six turns of Calvin cycle are required to generate one mole of glucose. Explain.

Ans. Ribulose 5 phosphate is a five carbon compound which accepts atmospheric CO_2 in presence of RuBisCo and form 2 molecules of 3PGA, a three-carbon carbon compound. It uses 3 ATP and 2 NADPH to fix one molecule of CO_2 per cycle of Calvin.

So, to fix 6 CO_2 molecules six turns of cycles are required as mentioned below.

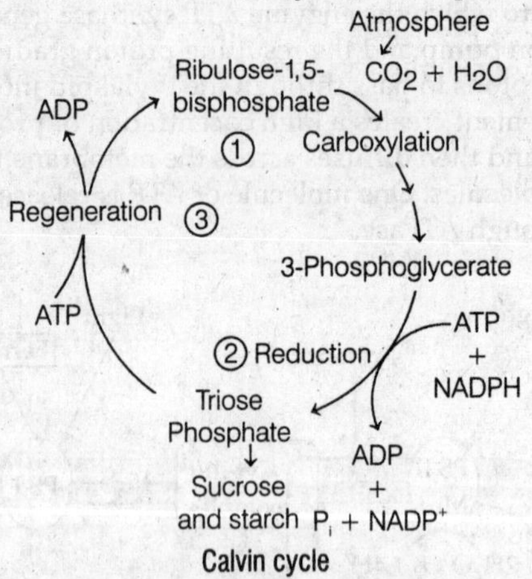

Calvin cycle

In	Out
Six CO_2	One glucose molecule ($C_6H_{12}O_6$)
18 ATP	18 ADP
12 NADPH	12 NADP

Q. 13 Complete the flow chart for cyclic photophosphorylation of the photosystem-I.

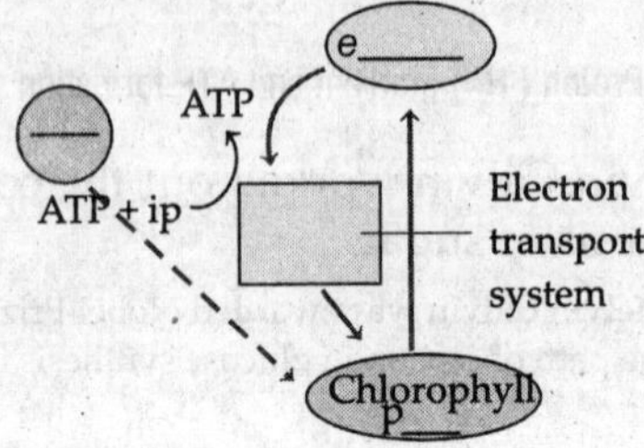

Ans. The flow chart showing cyclic photophosphorylation of photosystem-I is given below :

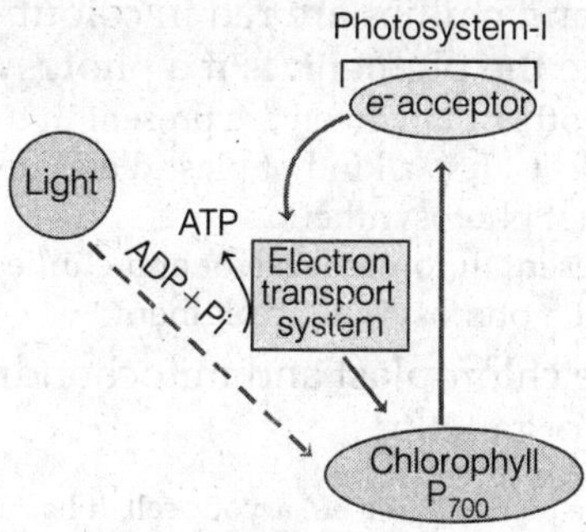

Cyclic photophosphorylation

Q. 14 In what kind of plants do you come across 'Kranz anatomy'? To which conditions are those plants better adapted? How are these plants better adapted than the plants, which lack this anatomy?

Ans. Kranz anatomy refers to the specialised leaf structure found in C_4 plants. These plants, such as maize and sugarcane, have two types of chloroplasts in their leaves *i.e.*,

Granal Chloroplast It is found in the mesophyll cells of leaves. Chloroplast have well developed grana in them. These chloroplast effectively fix CO_2 even if it is present in lower concentrations. PEP carboxylase is present which fix CO_2 and to form oxaloacetic acid (4 carbon compound).

Agranal Chloroplast Present in bundle sheath cells of the leaves. C_3 cycle occurs in these cells with the presence of RuBisCo enzyme.

The O_4 plants are well adapted to high O_2 concentrations and high temperature. C_4 plants can absorb CO_2 even when CO_2 concentration in much low thus O_4 plants can perform high rate of photosynthesis even the stomata are closed or there is the shortage of water thus, they can conserve water. Since, PEP-carboxylase is insensitive to O_2 thus excess O_2 has no inhibitory effect in C_4 pathway and there is no photorespiration in C_4 plant. Thus, C_4 plants are better adapted to tropical and desert (hot acid habitats) areas than the plants, that lack this anatomy.

Q. 15 A process is occurring throughout the day, in 'X' organism. Cells are participating in this process. During this process ATP, CO_2 and water are evolved. It is not a light dependent process.

(a) Name the process.

(b) Is it a catabolic or an anabolic process?

(c) What could be the raw material of this process?

Ans. (a) The process is cellular respiration.

(b) It is a catabolic process because it involves break down of glucose molecule.

$$\underset{\text{Carbohydrate + oxygen}}{C_6H_{12}O_6 + 6O_2} \longrightarrow \underset{\text{carbon dioxide + water + (ATP)}}{6CO_2 + 6H_2O + \text{Energy}}$$

(c) Raw material for this process is glucose and oxygen, which are products of photosynthesis, occurring in plants.

Q. 16 Tomatoes, carrots and chillies are red in colour due to the presence of one pigment. Name the pigment. Is it a photosynthetic pigment?

Ans. The different colours other than green are present in the plant because of presence of chromoplasts. It is a kind of plastid and develops different coloured pigments which are not photosynthetic.
Pigment lycopene present in tomato, carrot and chillies, imparts red colour to them. Lycopene is not a photosynthetic pigment.

Q. 17 Why do we believe chloroplast and mitochondria to be semi-autonomous organelle?

Thinking Process The plant cell is a eukaryotic cell. It has number of well developed cell organelles. Few are single membrane bound, few are double membrane bound (chloroplast and mitochondria) structures.

Ans. Both the cell organelles, chloroplast and mitochondria have extra chromosomal DNA and 70S type of ribosomes. The presence of DNA enables them to duplicate, when cell need more mitochondria and the chloroplasts. So due to their ability to divide independently within the cell and their evolutionary history as free organisms they are semi-autonomous cell organelles.

Q. 18 Observe the diagram and answer the following.

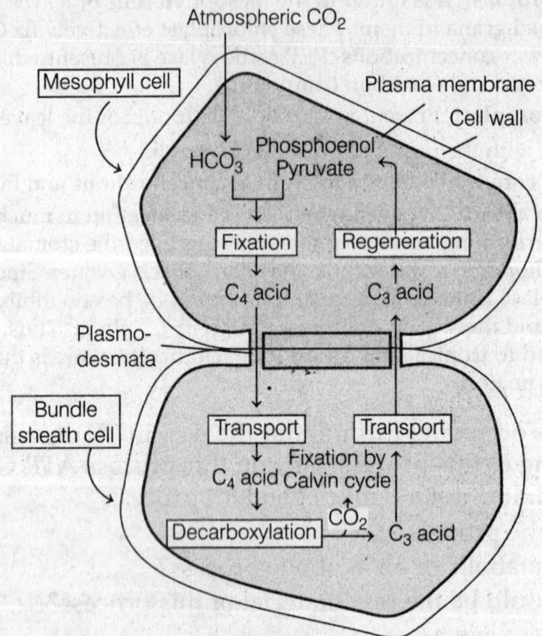

(a) Which group of plants exibit these two types of cells?

(b) What is the first product of C_4 cycle?

(c) Which enzyme is there in bundle sheath cells and mesophyll cells?

Ans. (a) Monocot plants belonging to Graminae/Poaceae family, *e.g.*, sugarcane, maize etc., possess these two types of cells. *i.e.*, bundle sheath and mesophyll cell (in kranz anatomy).

(b) A four carbon compound oxaloacetic acid is the first product of C_4 cycle.

(c) Mesophyll cells have PEP carboxylase to fix atmospheric CO_2 to form a 4-carbon compound oxalo acetic acid, whereas bundle sheath cells have RuBP carboxylase which fix CO_2 by this enzyme to form 3-carbon compound 3 PGA (3 phosphoglyceric acid).

Q. 19 A cyclic process is occurring in C_3 plant, which is light dependent and needs O_2. This process doesn't produce energy rather it consumes energy.

(a) Can you name the given process?

(b) Is it essential for survival?

(c) What are the end products of this process?

(d) Where does it occur?

Ans. (a) Photorespiration is the process, which do not produce energy rather consume it.

(b) It is not needed for the survival of C_3 plant.

(c) The end product of this process is phosphoglycolate, 3-phosphoglycerate and CO_2.

(d) This process occur in three cell organelles of the plant cell.

(i) Chloroplast (ii) Peroxisome (iii) Mitochondria

Long Answer Type Questions

Q. 1 Is it correct to say that photosynthesis occurs only in leaves of a plant? Besides leaves, what are the other parts that may be capable of carrying out photosynthesis? Justify.

Thinking Process Photosynthesis is a process of manufacturing food by plants. Many plant parts other than leaf also perform this function in some plants.

Ans. Photosynthesis is a process which mainly occurs in leaves of all green plants. The plants have designed their leaf in such a way that it is able to trap solar radiation and effectively convert solar/light energy to chemical energy.

But biology is science of exceptions. Some plants carry out photosynthesis in modified plant parts other then leaves. Few examples are as follows

1. **Root as Photosynthetic Organ**

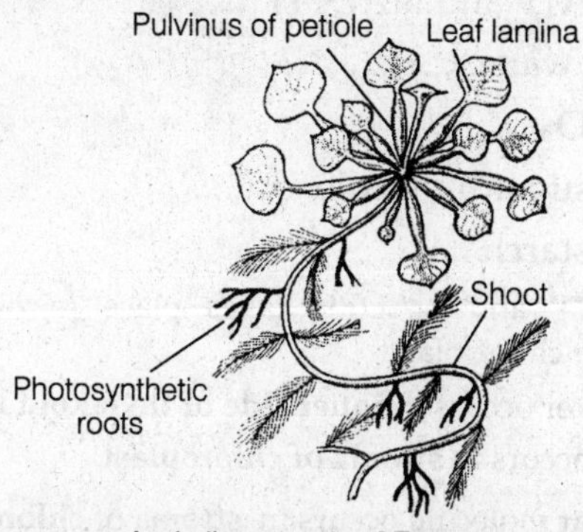

Assimilatory roots of *Trapa*

When roots develop chlorophyll and start photosynthesis, they are called assimilitory roots. *Trapa* is an example of assimilatory roots.

2. **Stem as Photosynthetic Organ**

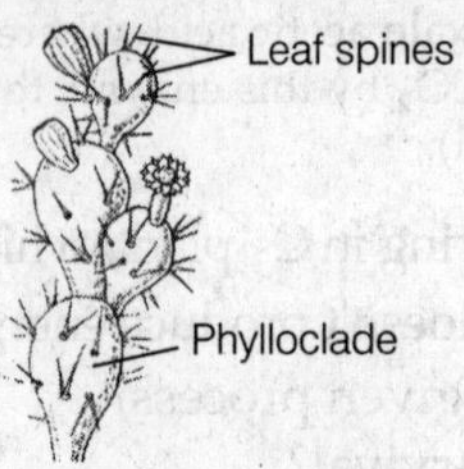

Phylloclade of *Opuntia*

In *Opuntia,* the stem gets modified to take up the function of leaves. It becomes flattened, thick and succulent and perform photosynthesis. Such structures are called phylloclade.

3. **Petiole as Photosynthetic Organ** In Australian *Acacia* the petiole takes the shape and function of photosynthesis because leaf lamina soon falls off after development.

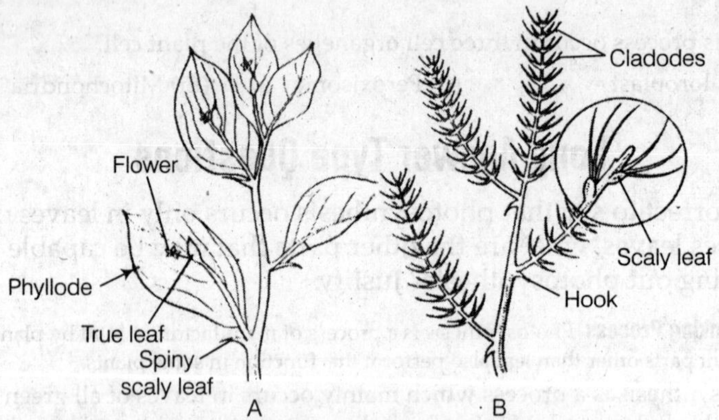

A. Phylloclade of *Ruscus* B. Cladode of *Asparages*

Q. 2 The entire process of photosynthesis consists of a number of reactions. Where in the cell do each of these take place?

(a) Synthesis of ATP and NADPH ....

(b) Photolysis of water ....

(c) Fixation of CO_2 ....

(d) Synthesis of sugar molecule ....

(e) Synthesis of starch ....

Ans. (a) Synthesis of ATP and NADPH takes place in outer side of **thylakoid membrane** of the chloroplasts.

(b) Photolysis of water occurs in **inner side of thylakoid membrane.**

(c) Fixation of CO_2 occurs in **stroma of chloroplast.**

(d) Synthesis of sugar molecule occurs in stroma of **chloroplast.**

(e) Synthesis of starch occurs in **stroma.**

Q. 3 Which property of the pigment is responsible for its ability to initiate the process of photosynthesis? Why is the rate of photosynthesis higher in the red and blue regions of the spectrum of light?

Thinking Process Plants are green because of the presence of the photosynthetic pigment called chlorophyll. They absorb all colours of light except green.

Ans. The chlorophyll pigments are present in the thylakoid membranes. They have the property of excitability and emits e^- in the excited stage. These electrons are used in the electron transport chain, which is crucial for photosynthesis.

Red and Blue Light have maximum energy which a chlorophyll pigment absorbs and get excited and initiate the process of photosynthesis. The wavelengths of red (around 660-700 nm) and blue (around 430-470 nm) fall within the Photosynthetically Active Radiation (PAR) range (400-700 nm). Therefore, these wavelengths are most effective for chlorophyll absorption.

Thus, the rate of photosynthesis is higher in blue and red light.

Q. 4 What can we conclude from the statement that the action and absorption spectrum of photosynthesis overlap? At which wavelength do they show peaks?

Ans. **Absorption Spectrum** This depicts the absorption of light of different wavelength by chlorophyll-*a*, *b*, xanthophyll and carotenoids.

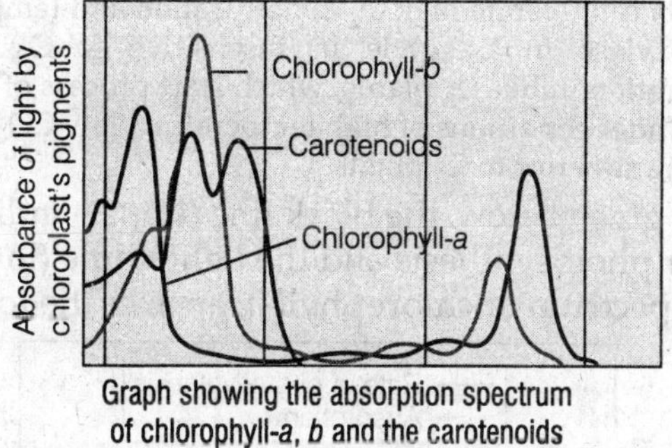

Graph showing the absorption spectrum of chlorophyll-*a*, *b* and the carotenoids

Action Spectrum This shows the rate of photosynthesis in the plant in the light of different wavelengths.

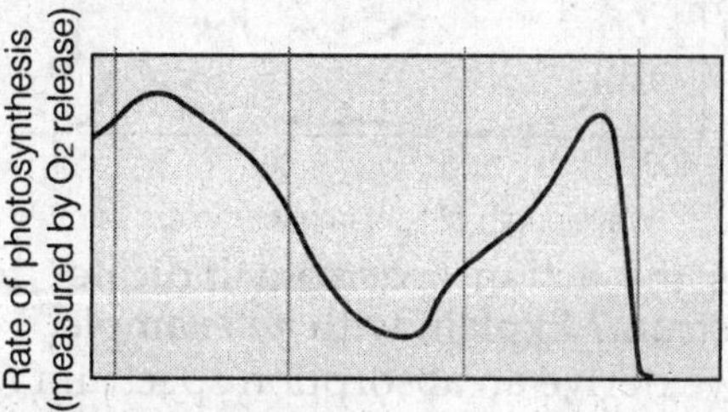

Graph showing action spectrum of photosynthesis

Super Imposed Absorption and Action Spectrum When we superimposed both action and absorption spectrum, it shows that in the region of red and blue light, the chlorophyll-*a* and *b* harness the maximum light energy and are the main photosynthetic pigments.

So, the rate of photosynthesis is high in these two regions. It shows maximum activity peak at wavelength 660-670 (red) and 430-470 nm (blue) and 390-430 nm (violet).

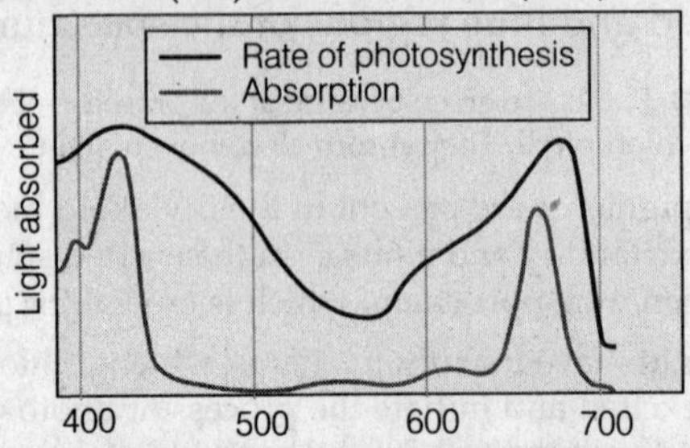

Graph showing action spectrum of photosynthesis superimposed on absorption spectrum of chlorophyll-*a*

Q. 5 Under what conditions are C_4 plants superior to C_3?

Thinking Process The different plants show different adaptations in carrying out photosynthesis. This process is important for autotrophs as these synthesise food for survival of plants and animals as well.

Ans. C_4 plants are advantageous over C_3 plants in following ways

(i) These plants can carry out photosynthesis even at low concentration of CO_2 in the atmosphere and in the shortage of water.

(ii) These plants can tolerate high O_2 concentration and temperature. The enzyme PEP carboxylase in C_4 cycle in insensitive to O_2 and do not show-photorespiration unlike C_3 plants, which start process of photorespiration and lose CO_2. Under conditions of high temperature, low CO_2 and water scarcity, C_4 plants are superior to C_3 plants.

Q. 6 In the figure given below, the black line (upper) indicates action spectrum for photosynthesis and the lighter line (lower) indicates the absorption spectrum of chlorophyll-*a*, answer the following

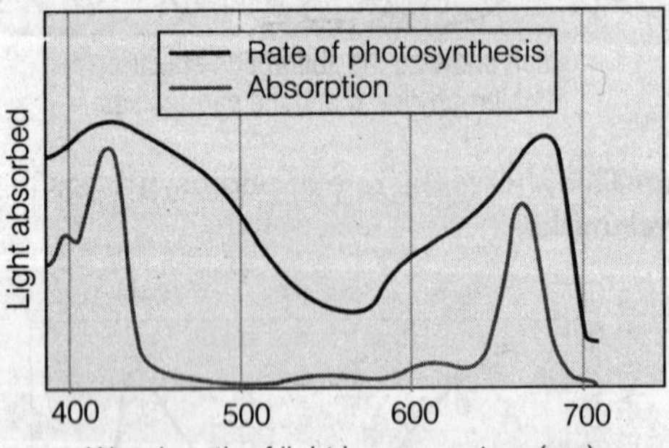

(a) What does the action spectrum indicate? How can we plot an action spectrum? Explain with an example.

(b) How can we derive an absorption spectrum for any substance?

Ans. (a) The action spectrum indicates the rate of photosynthesis at different wavelengths of light. It shows which colors of light are most effective in driving the process of photosynthesis.

To plot it, the rate of photosynthesis is measured (by O_2 release or CO_2 uptake) and then plotted on a graph with wavelength on the X-axis and rate of photosynthesis on the Y-axis.

In Engelman's experiment, a green alga was exposed to a specture of light and aerobic bacteria clustered in the blue and red regions, where the most oxygen was released. This indicated that photosynthesis was highest in blue and red light.

(b) Absorption of different wavelengths of light by a particular pigment is plotted and the graph is called the absorption spectra of that pigment.

Q. 7 What are the important events and end products of the light reaction?

Ans. The important events of light reaction are

(i) Excitation of chlorophyll molecule to emit a pair of electrons and use of their energy in the formation of ATP from ADP + Pi. This process is called photophosphorylation.

(ii) Splitting of water molecule ($2H_2O \longrightarrow 4H^+ + 4e^- + O_2 \uparrow$)

(iii) Reduction of $NADP^+$ ($NADP + 2H^+ \longrightarrow NADPH_2$)

End products of light reaction are NADPH and ATP.

ATP and $NADPH_2$ molecules which are used up in dark reaction, O_2 is evolved as a by product by the splitting of water.

Q. 8 In the diagram shown below label *A*, *B*, *C*. What type of phosphorylation is possible in this?

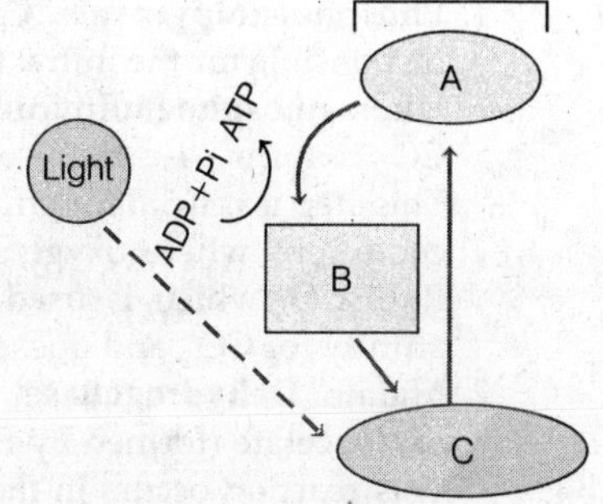

Ans. A–Electron acceptor

B–Electron transport system

C–Chlorophyll (photosystem I) P_{700}

The cyclic photophosphorylation is shown in the above figure.

Q. 9 Why is the RuBisCo enzyme more appropriately called RUBP carboxylase-oxygenase and what important role does it play in photosynthesis?

Thinking Process RuBisCo is the largest occurring enzyme on earth.

Ans. The enzyme RuBisCo has the remarkable property of fixing not only CO_2 but also O_2. Hence the name **RuBP carboxylase oxygenase** or RuBisCo short. RuBP carboxylase oxygenase has dual nature. It has affinity for both CO_2 and O_2 but has more affinity for CO_2 than O_2. Thus, the concentrations of two determines which of the two will bind to the enzyme.

RuBisCo play man important role in photosynthesis in following ways:

(i) In a normal condition when CO_2 and O_2 concentrations are normal, it acts as carboxylase and fix CO_2 by combining with ribulose bisphosphate and C_3 cycle operates normally, producing glucose molecule as an first product of photosynthesis.

(ii) If O_2 concentration goes up and CO_2 goes down, it starts acting as an oxygenase enzyme and C_2 cycle (photorespiration) starts where RuBP binds with O_2 to form phosphoglycolate.

(iii) C_4 plants have mechanisms to increase the concentration of CO_2 at enzyme site, and increasing the intracellular concentration of CO_2. Thus, here RuBisCo acts as carboxylase, minimising the affect of oxygenase.

Q. 10 What special anatomical features are displayed by leaves of C_4 plants? How do they provide advantage over the structure of C_3 plants?

Ans. **Kranz Anatomy**, is the feature exhibited by C_4 plant. These possess two types of chloroplast in their leaves. Agranal chloroplast found in bundle sheath cells whereas granal chloroplast is found in the mesophyll cells.

Bundle sheath cell perform C_3 cycle (dark reaction) where as mesophyll cell perform C_4 cycle. C_4 plants are more efficient even in high O_2 concentration and temperature as compared to C_3 plants. Many important crop plants (monocots) show C_4 cycle like maize, sorghum, sugarcane and millet.

Q. 11 Name the two important enzymes of C_4 pathway and explain their role in fixing CO_2.

Ans. The two important enzymes involved in the **C_4 pathway** of photosynthesis are:

1. **Phosphoenolpyruvate Carboxylase** (PEP carboxylase) PEP carboxylase is responsible for the initial fixation of CO_2 in C_4 plants. It catalyzes the reaction where **phosphoenolpyruvate** (PEP), a 3-carbon compound, combines with CO_2 to form a 4-carbon compound called oxaloacetate.
   This step is crucial for efficiently capturing CO_2 in C_4 plants, especially under conditions where oxygen is high and photorespiration is a concern. Unlike RuBisCO, which is used in the Calvin cycle, PEP carboxylase has a high affinity for CO_2 and does not catalyze the fixation of oxygen.
2. **Malate Dehydrogenase** Malate dehydrogenase is involved in converting **oxaloacetate** (formed by PEP carboxylase) into **malate**, a 4-carbon compound. This reaction occurs in the mesophyll cells. The malate is then transported to the bundle sheath cells, where it releases CO_2 for the Calvin cycle. This process is crucial for ensuring that CO_2 is efficiently delivered to the Calvin cycle without being lost through photorespiration.

Q. 12 Why is RuBisCo enzyme the most abundant enzyme in the world?

Ans. RuBisCo, also termed as RuBP carboxylase-oxygenase, is widely occurring enzyme because RuBisCo is used in the Calvin cycle to catalyse the first major step of carbon fixation. RuBisCO is thought to be the most abundant protein in the world since, it is present in every plant that undergoes photosynthesis through the Calvin cycle. It makes about 30-50% of the soluble protein in leaves It is estimated that every person on earth is there is 5 kg of RuBisCO of RuBisCo.

Q. 13 Why does photorespiration not take place in C_4 plants?

Ans. Photorespiration is associated with C_3 cycle, where plant lose CO_2 fixation because of the increase in concentration of O_2 and change the nature of activity of RuBP carboxylase-oxygenase. C_4 plants have evolved a mechanism to avoid loss of CO_2. There is not a direct contact of RuBP carboxylase-oxygenase as C_4 cycle operates in bundle sheath cells (where both temperature and oxygen level low). The CO_2 fixation is done by another enzyme PEP carboxylase in mesophyll cells and oxaloacetate is formed which is converted to malic acid and transported to bundle sheath cells. There, release CO_2 which is used in Calvin cycle, operating in bundle sheath cells of C_4 plants.

Chapter

14 Respiration in Plants

Multiple Choice Questions (MCQs)

Choose the correct answer from the given four options in the following questions :

Q. 1 The ultimate electron acceptor of respiration in an aerobic organism is

(a) cytochrome (b) oxygen (c) hydrogen (d) glucose

Thinking Process Oxygen is the driving force for respiration in aerobic conditions.

Ans. *(b)* Oxygen is the ultimate hydrogen acceptor in aerobic respiration because at the end of electron transport chain it accepts a pair of electron and combines with hydrogen atom to form water molecule.

Q. 2 Phosphorylation of glucose during glycolysis is catalysed by

(a) phosphoglucomutase (b) phosphoglucoisomerase

(c) hexokinase (d) phosphorylase

Ans. *(c)* **Hexokinase** catalyses the conversion of glucose into glucose 6-phosphate by the use of ATP molecule in phosphorylation reaction.

The other options are incorrect because

Phosphoglucomutase is an enzyme that transfers a phosphate group in D-glucose monomer from 1-to 6 position of carbon in forward direction (changes glucose 1-phosphate to glucose-6 phosphate).

Phosphoglucoisomerase catalyses conversion of glucose 6 phosphate to fructose 6 phosphate.

Phosphorylase is an enzyme which catalyses the addition of phosphate (PO_4^-) group from inorganic phosphate to an acceptor molecule.

Q. 3 Pyruvic acid, the key product of glycolysis can have many metabolic fates. Under aerobic condition it forms

(a) lactic acid (b) $CO_2 + H_2O$

(c) acetyl Co - A + CO_2 (d) ethanol + CO_2

Thinking Process Glycolysis occurs in the cytosol of the living cell and produces two pyruvic acid molecules from one glucose molecule

Ans. *(c)* Pyruvate, the product obtained through glycolysis, gets oxidised with the loss of its carboxy group as CO_2, to give acetyl Co-A, under aerobic condition. This acetyl Co-A is further completely oxidised to CO_2 and H_2O in citric acid cycle.

Other options are incorrect because:

Lactic acid is formed in muscles under anaerobic conditions.

Ethanol and CO_2 are products of anaerobic respiration in yeast cells.

CO_2 and H_2O are final and complete reaction products released at the end of cellular respiration.

Q. 4 Electron Transport System (ETS) is located in mitochondrial

(a) outer membrane (b) inter membrane space

(c) inner membrane (d) matrix

Ans. ***(c)*** Electron transport system is present in the inner mitochondrial membrane, which contain groups of proton (H^+) and electron (e^-) acceptors.

Q. 5 Which of the following exhibits the highest rate of respiration?

(a) Growing shoot apex (b) Germinating seed

(c) Root tip (d) Leaf bud

Thinking Process All metabolically active cells and tissues have high rate of respiration

Ans. ***(b)*** **Germinating seeds** have the highest rate of respiration. As soon as the water is imbibed by seeds, hydrolytic enzymes become active and mobilise the reserve food materials so the seeds show high metabolic activity and germinate into a tiny plant.

These processes require energy, which is derived from increased rate of respiration.

Q.6 Mitochondria are called powerhouses of the cell. Which of the following observations support this statement?

(a) Mitochondria synthesise ATP

(b) Mitochondria have a double membrane

(c) The enzymes of the Krebs' cycle and the cytochromes are found in mitochondria.

(d) Mitochondria are found in almost all plants and animal cells.

Ans. ***(a)*** Mitochondria are a double membrane bound structures and are the site of ATP production which is the energy currency of the cell.

The rest of the statements, though are correct but, does not verify and support the fact that mitochondria are the powerhouses of the cell.

Q. 7 The end product of oxidative phosphorylation is

(a) NADH (b) oxygen

(c) ADP (d) ATP + H_2O

Thinking Process Formation of ATP from ADP + Pi under certain set of enzymatically controlled reactions is called phosphorylation.

Ans. ***(d)*** Complete oxidation of glucose molecule produces 38 ATP molecules, water and carbon dioxide with the help of energy released during oxidation of reduced co-enzymes. This process is called oxidative phosphorylation.

Q. 8 Match the following columns.

	Column I		Column II
A.	Molecular oxygen	1.	α- ketoglutaric acid
B.	Electron acceptor	2.	Hydrogen acceptor
C.	Pyruvate dehydrogenase	3.	Cytochrome- *c*
D.	Decarboxylation	4.	Acetyl Co-A

Codes

	A	B	C	D		A	B	C	D
(a)	2	3	4	1	(b)	3	4	2	1
(c)	2	1	3	4	(d)	4	3	1	2

Ans. *(a)* **Molecular oxygen** ultimately combines with hydrogen to form water at the end of Electron Transport Chain (ETC).

Cytochrome-*c* is an electron acceptor in ETS.

Pyruvate dehydrogenase catalyses reaction converting pyruvic acid into acetyl Co- A. Decarboxylation of isocitrate forms α-**ketoglutaric acid** in a decarboxylation reaction.

Very Short Answer Type Questions

Q. 1 Energy is released during the oxidation of compounds in respiration. How is this energy stored and released as and when it is needed?

Thinking Process Adenosine Triphosphate (ATP) molecules are the energy currency of every living cell.

Ans. Complex organic food molecules such as sugars, fats and proteins are rich sources of energy for cells because much of the energy used to form these molecules is stored within the chemical bonds that hold them together. The cells release the stored energy through a series of oxidation reactions.

During each oxidation reaction involved in food breakdown, the product of reaction has a lower energy content than the donor molecule. At the same time, electron acceptor molecules capture some of the energy lost during oxidation and store it for later use. Cells convert the energy from oxidation reactions to energy-rich molecules such as ATP which can be used through out the cell to power metabolism and construct new cellular components.

Q. 2 Explain the term 'energy currency'. Which substance acts as energy currency in plants and animals?

Ans. The term energy currency refers to molecule which provides energy for cellular activities, whenever required. ATP is termed as energy currency because the energy is stored in the form of high energy bonds of ATP.

Other energy yielding molecules are GTP, CTP, UTP, etc.

Q. 3 Different substrates get oxidised during respiration. How does Respiratory Quotient (RQ) indicate which type of substrate, *i.e.*, carbohydrate, fat or protein is getting oxidised?

$$RQ = \frac{A}{B}$$

What do A and B stand for?

What type of substrates have RQ of 1, < 1 or > 1?

Ans. The ratio of the volume of CO_2 evolved to the volume of O_2 consumed in respiration is called the **Respiratory Quotient** (RQ) or respiratory ratio.

$$RQ = \frac{A}{B} = \frac{\text{Volume of } CO_2 \text{ evolved}}{\text{Volume of } O_2 \text{ consumed}}$$

Where :

A = Volume of CO_2 evolved

B = Volume of O_2 consumed

Substrates like carbohydrates have RQ =1 during, aerobic respiration.

Proteins and fats have RQ of < 1

Substrates like organic acids have RQ of > 1 under aerobic conditions.

Q. 4 F_0 - F_1 particles participate in the synthesis of ....

Ans. $F_0 - F_1$ particles present in the inner mitochondrial membrane are involved in the synthesis of ATP (Adenosine Triphosphate), the energy currency of the cell.

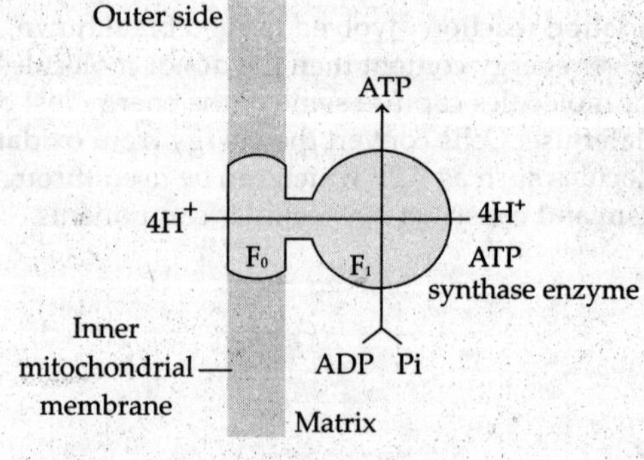

Q. 5 When does anaerobic respiration occur in man and yeast?

Thinking Process Anaerobic respiration is the form of respiration occurring in the deficiency or lack of oxygen.

Ans. (a) **In animals, anaerobic respiration** occurs in the deficiency of oxygen such as during heavy exercise, when pyruvic acid is reduced to lactic acid by the enzyme lactate dehydrogenase.

(b) **In yeast, the incomplete oxidation of glucose** occurs under anaerobic conditions, where pyruvic acid is converted to CO_2 and ethanol by the action of enzyme pyruvic acid decarboxylase and alcohol dehydrogenase.

Q. 6 Which of the following will release more energy on oxidation? Arrange them in ascending order.

(a) 1 gm of fat
(b) 1 gm of protein
(c) 1 gm of glucose
(d) 0.5 gm of protein + 0.5 gm glucose

Thinking Process Many biological organic molecules serve as substrate for cellular respiration and break down to produce energy in the form of ATP molecules

Ans. The ascending order of substrate that will release more energy on oxidation is be as follows

1gm fat <1 gm protein < 0.5gm protein + 0.5 gm glucose < 1 gm glucose

Q. 7 The product of aerobic glycolysis in skeletal muscle and anaerobic fermentation in yeast are respectively .... and ....

Ans. The product of aerobic glycolysis in skeletal muscles is lactic acid while in anaerobic fermentation in yeast, ethanol and CO_2 are produced.

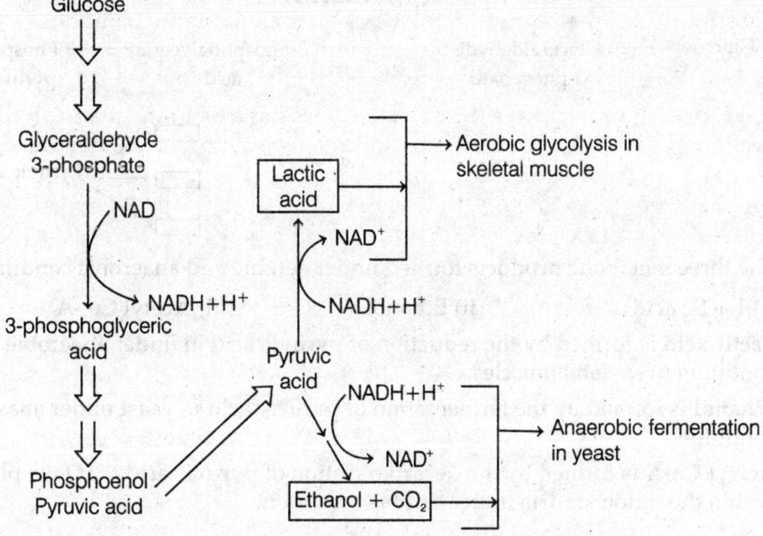

Glucose as substrate in aerobic and anaerobic respiration

Short Answer Type Questions

Q. 1 If a person is feeling dizzy, glucose or fruit juice is given immediately but not a cheese sandwich, which might have more energy. Explain.

Thinking Process Energy is required by every living cell to carry out its own metabolism and hence to stay alive.

Ans. The glucose is absorbed and reaches blood, giving instant energy. Whereas, cheese sandwich require time for digestion, and absorption. Sick person requires immediate energy supply, so glucose or fruit juices (contains glucose) are given to them.

Q. 2 What is meant by the statement 'aerobic respiration is more efficient'?

Thinking Process Aerobic respiration is the process that leads to the complete oxidation of organic substances in the presence of oxygen and release of CO_2, water and energy.

Ans. In the process of aerobic respiration, a single molecule of glucose can yield up to 38 ATP molecules. However, in fermentation or anaerobic respiration results in a net gain of only 2 molecules of ATP from each glucose molecule, which is comparatively much less than that of aerobic respiration.

Hence, aerobic respiration is a more efficient process.

Q. 3 Pyruvic acid is the end product of glycolysis. What are the three metabolic products of pyruvic acid under aerobic and anaerobic conditions? Write in the space provided in the diagram.

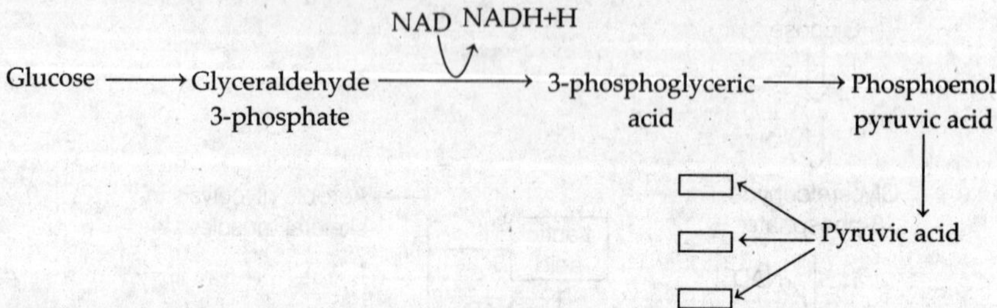

Ans. The three metabolic products formed under aerobic and anaerobic conditions are

(i) Lactic acid (ii) Ethanol (iii) Acetyl Co -A

Lactic acid is formed by the reduction of pyruvic acid in under anaerobic condition in skeletal muscles.

Ethanol is formed by the fermentation of pyruvic acid in yeast under anaerobic condition.

Acetyl Co-A is formed by the decarboxylation of pyruvic acid that take place within the mitochondria under aerobic condition.

$$\text{Pyruvic acid} + \text{Co - A} + NAD^+ \xrightarrow[\text{Pyruvate dehydrogenase}]{Mg^{2+}} \text{Acetyl Co - A} + CO_2 + NADH + H^+$$

Q. 4 **The energy yield in terms of ATP is higher in aerobic respiration than during anaerobic respiration. Why is there anaerobic respiration even in organisms that live in aerobic condition like human beings and angiosperms?**

Thinking Process Many metabolic pathway have evolved to give energy to metabolically active cells. Anaerobic respiration is one of them

Ans. Aerobic respiration occurs in normal conditions in human beings. Under intense conditions such as heavy excercises, muscles demand too much energy (ATP) and consume much more oxygen to produce that energy.

This high consumption leads to oxygen scarcity and the muscle cells begin to make lactic acid by anaerobic respiration to fulfill their energy needs. Similarly, yeast cells under deficient conditions of oxygen carry out anaerobic respiration, fermentation forming ethyl alcohol and CO_2. In such cases the organism switches to an aerobic respiration for providing energy quickly.

Q. 5 **Oxygen is an essential requirement for aerobic respiration but it enters the respiratory process at the end? Discuss.**

Ans. Aerobic respiration requires oxygen in order to generate ATP. Oxygen is highlyelectronegative element and acts as final acceptor in respiratory process.

It pulls e^- (electrons) and energy from the electron transport chain (ETC) and combine with protons (from medium) to form water.

Though O_2 enters in the respiratory process at the end, its presence is vital. It drives the process of aerobic respiration by removing electrons in the form of hydrogen from the system. Thus, acting as final hydrogen acceptor.

The energy is produced by the process of oxidative phosphorylation, utilising the energy of oxidation reduction reactions.

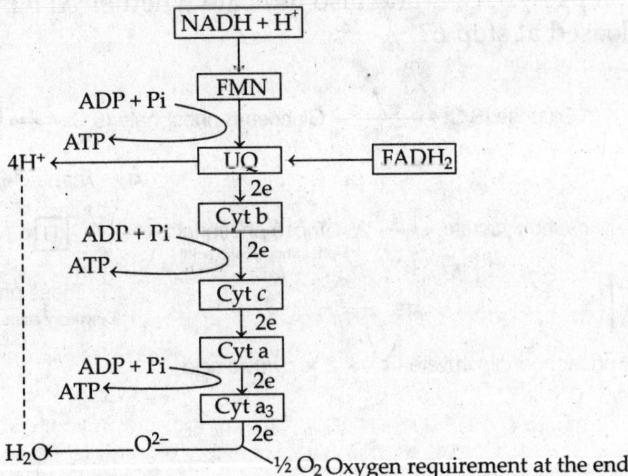

Q. 6 **Respiration is an energy releasing and enzymatically controlled catabolic process which involves a step-wise oxidative breakdown of organic substances inside living cells. In this statement about respiration explain the meaning of**

(a) Step-wise oxidative breakdown
(b) Organic substances (used as substrates).

Ans. (a) Respiration is a stepwise oxidation of organic molecules in a cell involving main three steps.

(i) Glycolysis

(ii) Krebs' cycle

(iii) Electron transport chain

In these steps glucose passes through series of enzymatically controlled reactions and is finally converted into H_2O + ATP + CO_2.

(b) **Organic substances** are the molecules normally found in living systems. They are usually composed of carbon atoms in rings or long chains to which other atoms such as hydrogen, oxygen and nitrogen are attached. *e.g.*, glucose, fatty acids, amino acids etc. These molecules used as substrate to produce energy through respiration.

Q. 7 Comment on the statement respiration is an energy producing process but ATP is being used in some steps of the process.

Thinking Process Energy is either produced or consumed in each metabolic reaction. Respiration involves many enzymatically controlled intermediate reactions

Ans. Although Respiration is a catabolic process which occurs stepwise to produce energy. Whenever biological system requires energy it is provided by hydrolysis of ATP molecule.

However in the initial steps of glycolysis ATP is required to activate glucose and its intermediates where 2 ATP molecules are used to phosphoxylate glucose and convert it into a more reactive form.

Q. 8 The figure given below shows the steps in glycolysis. Fill in the missing steps *A, B, C, D* and also indicate whether ATP is being used up or released at step *E*?

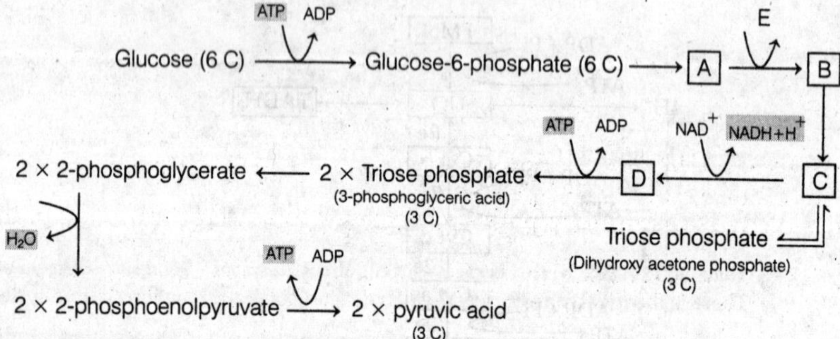

Ans. Process of glycolysis is summarised as follow

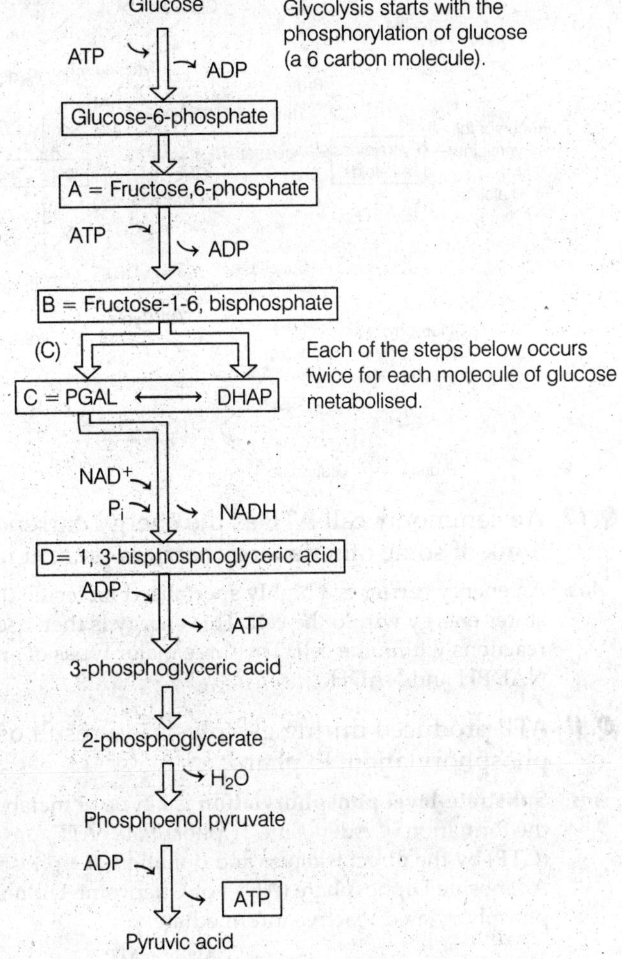

At step E-energy is being used up

Q. 9 Why is respiratory pathway referred to as an amphibolic pathway?

Thinking Process Krebs' cycle is amphibolic (Gk. *amphi – both, bole –throw)* Pathway. There is the involvement of both anabolic and catabolic reactions in this cycle.

Ans. Respiratory process involves the breaking down of substrate is catabolic proceses. During catabolism carbohydrates are first converted into glucose. Fats are broken down into glycerol and fatty acid which is further degraded into acetyl Co-A, while protein is degraded into, smaller units anino acids.

Sometime the fatty acid is required, then synthesis of it occurs by withdrawing acetly Co-A. This synthesising phase is the anabolic process.

Thus, respiratory pathway involves the catabolic process (break down) and anabolic pathway synthesis of molecules using respiratory intermediates front link, it is called as an amphibolic pathway.

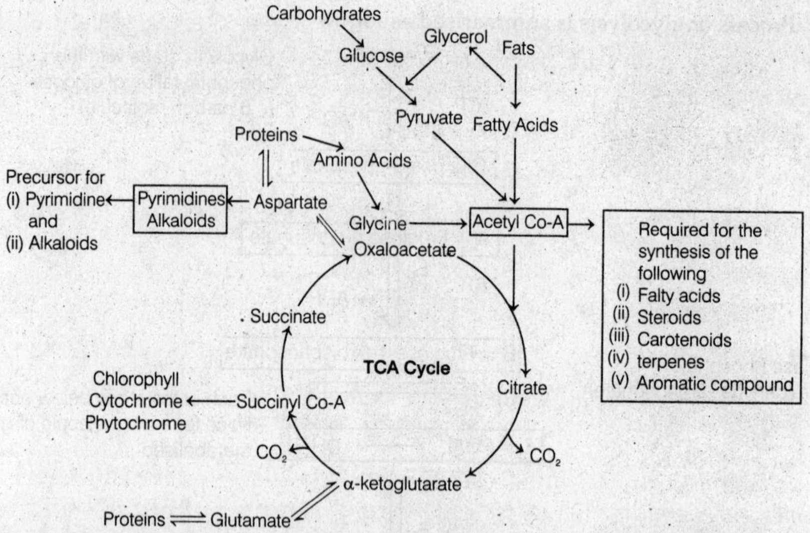

Q. 10 We commonly call ATP as the energy currency of the cell. Can you think of some other energy carriers present in a cell? Name any two.

Ans. An energy carrier is a highly specialised molecule that transfers, recieves and stores energy within the cell. This energy is then used to facilitate the chemical reactions within the cell. The three major types of energy carriers are ATP, NADPH and NADH.

Q. 11 ATP produced during glycolysis is a result of substrate level phosphorylation. Explain.

Ans. **Substrate-level phosphorylation** is a type of metabolic reaction that results in the formation of Adenosine Triphosphate (ATP) or Guanosine Triphosphate (GTP) by the direct transfer and donation of a phosphoryl (PO_3) group to Adenosine Diphosphate (ADP) or Guanosine Diphosphate (GDP) from a phosphorylated reactive intermediate.

$$\text{R-OPO}_3^{2-} \xrightarrow{\text{ADP} \quad \text{ATP}} \text{R-OH}$$

Substrate-level phosphorylation

In glycolysis substrate level phosphorylation occurs in following two reactions

(i) 2 molecules of 1, 3-biphosphoglyceric acid react with 2 molecules of ADP to form 2 molecules of 3-phosphoglyceric acid and 2 molecules of ATP.

$$\underset{\text{(2 molecules)}}{\text{1, 3 – biphosphoglyceric acid}} + 2\text{ ADP} \xrightarrow[\text{Mg}^{2+}]{\text{Phosphoglycerate kinase}} \underset{\text{(2 molecules)}}{\text{3 – phosphoglyceric acid} + 2\text{ ATP}}$$

(ii) 2 molecules of phosphoenolpyruvate reacts with 2 molecules of ADP to form molecules of pyruvic acid and 2 ATP.

$$\underset{\text{(2 molecules)}}{\text{2 – phosphoenolpyruvate acid}} + 2\text{ADP} \xrightarrow[\text{Mg}^{2+}]{\text{Pyruvate kinase}} \underset{\text{(2 molecules)}}{\text{Pyruvic acid} + 2\text{ATP}}$$

Q. 12 **Do you know any step in the TCA cycle where there is substrate level phosphorylation. Which one?**

Ans. In an intermediate reaction of TCA cycle, succinyl Co-A is converted to succinic acid and one GTP molecule is synthesised through substrate level phosphorylation.

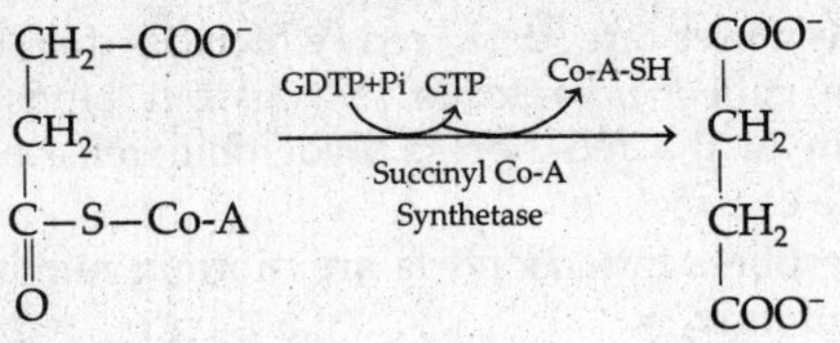

$$\underset{\text{(Succinyl Co-A)}}{\begin{matrix} CH_2-COO^- \\ | \\ CH_2 \\ | \\ C-S-Co\text{-}A \\ \| \\ O \end{matrix}} \xrightarrow[\text{Succinyl Co-A Synthetase}]{\text{GDTP+Pi} \;\; \text{GTP} \;\; \text{Co-A-SH}} \underset{\text{succinic acid}}{\begin{matrix} COO^- \\ | \\ CH_2 \\ | \\ CH_2 \\ | \\ COO^- \end{matrix}}$$

GTP formed in this reaction gives rise to ATP as follows

$$GTP + ADP \rightarrow GDP + ATP$$

Q. 13 **A process is occurring throughout the day, in 'X' organism. Cells are participating in this process. During this process ATP, CO_2 and water are evolved. It is not a light dependent process.**

(a) Name the process.

(b) Is it a catabolic or an anabolic process?

(c) What could be the raw material of this process?

Ans. (a) The process is **cellular respiration** (aerobic respiration).

(b) It is a **catabolic process**, as complex molecules like glucose are broken down into simpler molecules, releasing energy.

(c) The raw materials of this process are **glucose** (or other organic molecules) and **oxygen** (O_2)

Q. 14 **When a substrate is being metabolised, why does not all the energy that is produced get released in one step. It is released in multiple steps. What is the advantage of step-wise release?**

Ans. The process of aerobic respiration is divided into four phases glycolysis, oxidative decarboxylation TCA cycle, ETS or oxidative phosphorylation. The process of respiration and production of ATP in each phase takes place in a step-wise manner.

The product of one pathway forms the substrate of the other pathway and these substrates enter or withdrawn from the pathway according to the necessity, ATP gets utilised wherever required and enzymatic rates are generally controlled. Thus, the step-wise released of energy makes the system more efficient in extracting and storing energy.

Q. 15 **Respiration requires O_2. How did the first cells on the earth manage to survive in an atmosphere that lacked O_2?**

Ans. Respiration always does not require O_2. There are organisms which respire even in absence of O_2 through anaerobic respiration. The first cells of earth *i.e.*, chemosynthetic bacteria are the primitive organisms of early life on earth Obtained energy by breaking down inorganic molecules like H_2S, NO_2, etc. *e.g.*, chemosynthesis occured in sulphur bacteria in the following way

$$12H_2S + 6\,CO_2 \rightarrow C_6H_{12}O_6 + 6H_2O + 12S\downarrow$$

Q. 16 It is known that red muscle fibres in animals can work for longer periods of time continuously. How is this possible?

Ans. There are basically two kinds of muscle fibers

(i) Red muscles (ii) White muscles

Red muscles work for a longer time continuously because

(i) These muscle fibres are dark red which is due to the presence of red haemoprotein called **myoglobin**. Myoglobin binds and stores oxygen as **oxymyoglobin** in the red fibres. Myoglobin releases oxygen for utilisation during muscle contraction.

(ii) In red muscle fibres mitochondria are more in number, hence they work for long periods of time.

(iii) Red muscles have less sarcoplasmic reticulum.

(iv) They carry out considerable aerobic oxidation without accumulating much lactic acid. Thus, red muscle fibres can contract for a longer period without fatigue.

(v) These muscle fibres have slow rate of contraction for long periods. *e.g.*, extensor muscles of the human back.

Q. 17 The energy yield in terms of ATP is higher in aerobic respiration than during anaerobic respiration. Explain.

Thinking Process Respiration is a catabolic process occurring in all living cells providing them energy to stay alive and to remain metabolically active.

Ans. The energy yield in terms of ATP is higher in aerobic respiration than during anaerobic respiration is as given

Aerobic Respiration	Anaerobic Respiration
In aerobic respiration, there is complete oxidation of substrate molecules producing ATP molecules.	In anaerobic respiration there is incomplete oxidation of substrate molecules so the ATP produced are less in number.
Aerobic respiration of glucose produces 36 ATP molecules $+ H_2O + CO_2$.	Anaerobic respiration of glucose, when occurs in yeast, produces 2 ATP molecules+ ethyl alcohol + CO_2

Q. 18 RuBP carboxylase, PEP carboxylase, pyruvate dehydrogenase, ATPase, cytochrome oxidase, hexokinase, lactate dehydrogenase. Select/choose enzymes from the list above which are involved in

(a) Photosynthesis (b) Respiration

(c) Both in photosynthesis and respiration

Ans. RuBP Carboxylase This enzyme is a part of dark reaction of **photosynthesis**. It catalyses the fixing of CO_2 in C_3 cycle.

PEPcase This enzyme is a part of **photosynthesis** of C_4 plants. It catalyses the reaction of fixing of CO_2 to form first stable product oxaloacetate. 4 carbon compound.

Pyruvate dehydrogenase It is involved in **aerobic respiration** and catalyses the reaction of formation of acetyl Co-A from pyruvic acid. It requires the participation of NAD and Co-enzyme-A.

$$\text{Pyruvic acid} + \text{Co-A} + NAD^+ \xrightarrow[\text{Pyruvate dehydrogenase}]{Mg^{2+}} \text{Acetyl Co-A} + CO_2 + NADH + H^+$$

ATPase It is a part of both **respiration** and **photosynthesis**. Both these processes use electron transport chain and associated proton pump and ATP synthase as a key part of process. ETC uses the energy to pump hydrogen ions across a membrane.

The protons flow back through ATP synthase, driving the production of ATP.

Cytochrome Oxidase This is involved in both **respiration** and **photosynthesis**. It is an electron carrier in the electron transport chain.

Hexokinase This enzyme is also involved in, **respiration**. In glycolysis, it catalyses the first reaction, *i.e.*, formation of glucose -6- phosphate from glucose molecule. It uses one ATP molecule which transfers PO_4 group to glucose molecules.

The first step of glycolysis ⟶ Glucose (ATP → ADP, Mg^{2+}, Hexokinase) ⟶ Glucose-6-phosphate

Lactate Dehydrogenase

This enzyme is involved in **anaerobic respiration** in bacteria *Lactobacillus*. Pyruvic acid formed at the end of glycolysis is converted to lactic acid by lactic acid bacteria. Hydrogen from NADH molecule is transferred to pyruvate producing lactate leading to the formation of acid.

$$\underset{\text{Pyruvic acid}}{CH_3COCOOH} + NADH. \xrightarrow[\text{Dehydrogenase}]{\text{Lactate}} \underset{\text{Lactic acid}}{C_3H_6O_3} + NAD^+$$

Q. 19 How does a tree trunk exchange gases with the environment although it lacks stomata?

Thinking Process Gaseous exchange is an important phenomenon in plants. Plants take up CO_2 for photosynthesis and release O_2 as by product. They have devised structural adaptations in them to carry out this phenomenon.

Ans. Gaseous exchange is a vital process in plants. They take in CO_2 and releases O_2 as a by product in the process of photosynthesis. To facilitate this, tress have structural adaptations the outer layer tree trunk is covered by dead woody tissue called cork. The epidermal layers of such tree get ruptured and outer cortical cells are loosely arranged. These structures are called as **lenticels**.

These are the sites of gases exchange and transpiration.

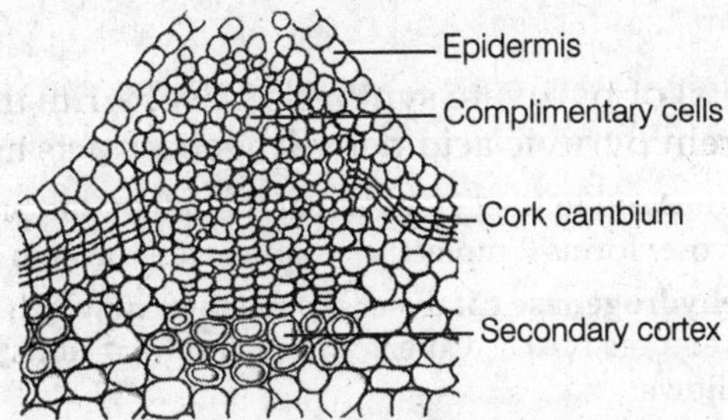

Q. 20 Write two energy yielding reactions of glycolysis.

Ans. The following figure shows the process of glycolysis, and sites for yielding energy during glycolysis

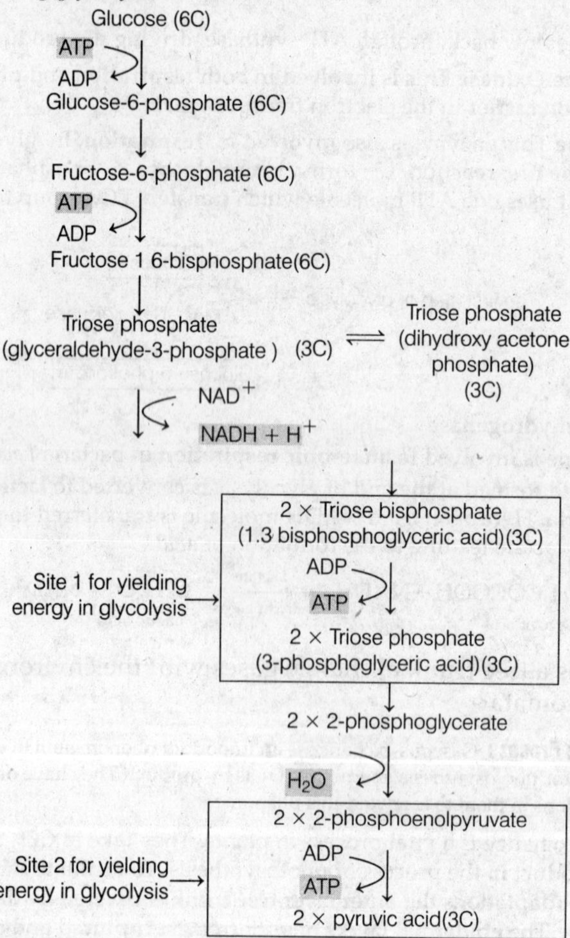

Thus, ATP is produced during Conversion of 1,3 biphosphoglyceric acid into 3-phosphoglyceric acid and during Conversion of 2-phosphoenol pyruvate into pyruvic acid.

Q. 21 Name the site(s) of pyruvate synthesis. Also, write the chemical reaction wherein pyruvic acid dehydrogenase acts as a catalyst.

Ans. **Pyruvate** is synthesised in the cytoplasm of the cell by the process of glycolysis. 1 molecule of glucose forms 2 molecules of pyruvate through a series of reactions.

Pyruvic acid dehydrogenase catalyses the reaction in which pyruvate forms acetyl Co-A. It requires NAD^+, Co-enzyme A and Mg^{2+} ions for its activity. The reaction is as follows

$$\text{Pyruvic acid} + \text{Co - A} + NAD^+ \xrightarrow[\text{Pyruvate Dehydrogenase}]{Mg^{2+}} \text{Acetyl Co-A} + NADH + H^+ + CO_2 \uparrow$$

Q. 22 Mention the important series of events of aerobic respiration that occur in the matrix of the mitochondrion as well as one that take place in inner membrane of the mitochondrion.

Ans. Krebs' cycle occurs in the matrix of mitochondria. It is depicted in the following series of reactions

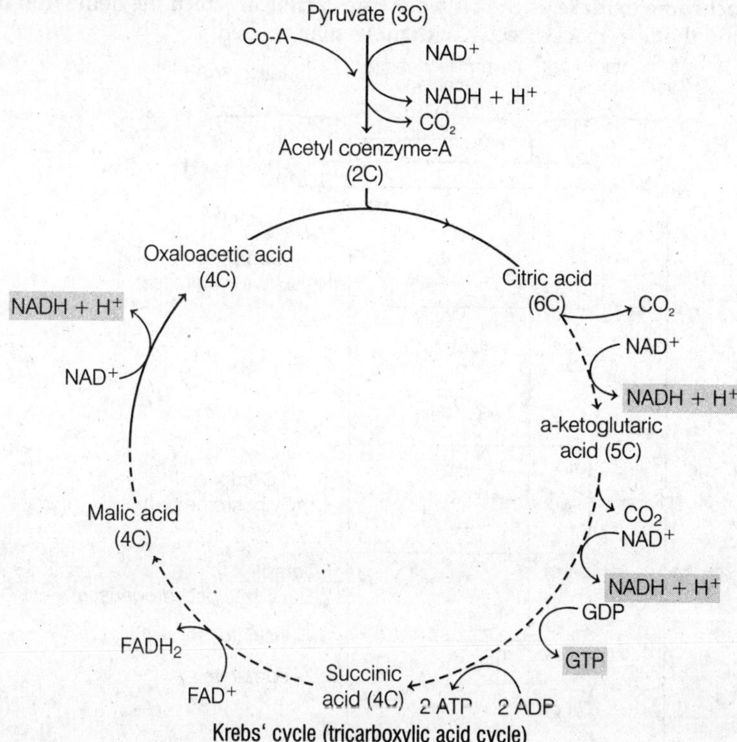

Krebs' cycle (tricarboxylic acid cycle)

Electron transport chain is carried out in the inner mitochondrial membrane

The inner mitochondrial membrane is specific about possessing proton (H^+) and electron (e^-) acceptors in a particular sequence called electron transport chain. It has four enzyme complexes.

The electrons either follow the pathway of complexes I, II, III and IV or II, III and IV depending upon the substrates from Krebs' cycle.

The transfer of electrons and hydrogen atoms takes place in the following way

Complex I Consists of flavoproteins of NADH dehydrogenase (FP_N) of which FMN is the prosthetic group. Combined with the flavoprotein is non-heme iron of NADH dehydrogenase. This complex spans inner mitochondrial membrane and is able to translocate protons across it from matrix side to outer side.

Complex II Consists of flavoprotein of succinate dehydrogenase, of which FAD is the prosthetic group. Combined with the flavoprotein is non-heme iron of succinate dehydrogenase.

Between complexes II and III is the **mobile carrier coenzyme-Q** (Co-Q) **or ubiquinone** (UQ).

Complex III Consists of cytochrome-*b* and cytochrome- c_1. Associated with cytochrome- *b* is non-heme iron of complex III. Between complexes III and IV, is the **mobile carrier cytochrome-c.**

Complex IV Consists of cytochrome-*a* and cytochrome- a_3, and bound copper that are required for this complex reaction to occur. This cytochrome also called **cytochrome oxidase**, is the only electron carrier in which the heme iron has a free ligand that can react directly with molecular oxygen.

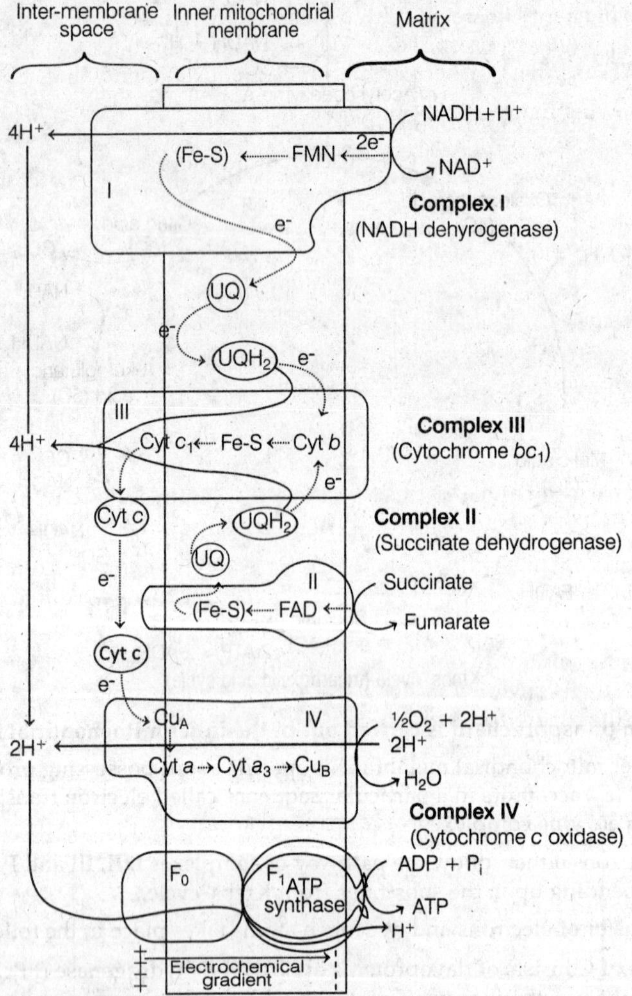

Thus, hydride ions are transferred from the substance to be oxidised to NAD$^+$. From NAD$^+$ the hydrogen atoms are transferred to FMN of flavoprotein 1 (Fp'N). After FMN the hydrogen atom undergoes ionisation, *i.e.,* it splits into an electron and a proton.

In further stages there is no longer a transfer of hydrogens but of electrons. The electron passes to co-enzyme- Q, and from co-enzyme Q to cytochromes- *b*, c_1, *c*, *a* and a_3. The proton is released free.

As the hydrogen atom or electron passes down by F_0-F_1 particle there is simultaneous oxidation of one coenzyme and reduction at another steps. Oxygen is able to diffuse inside the mitochondria.

It is converted to anionic form O_2^-, combines with $2H^+$ and forms metabolic water reduced co-enzyme NADH+H^+ helps in pushing out three pairs of H^+ to outer chamber while $FADH_2$ sends two pairs of H^+ to outer chamber.

Oxidative phosphorylation is the synthesis of energy rich ATP molecules, with the help of energy liberated during oxidation of reduced co-enzyme ($NADH_2$, d $FADH_2$) produced in respiration. The enzyme required for this synthesis is called ATP synthase present in inner mitochondrial membrane.

The following figures shows this process

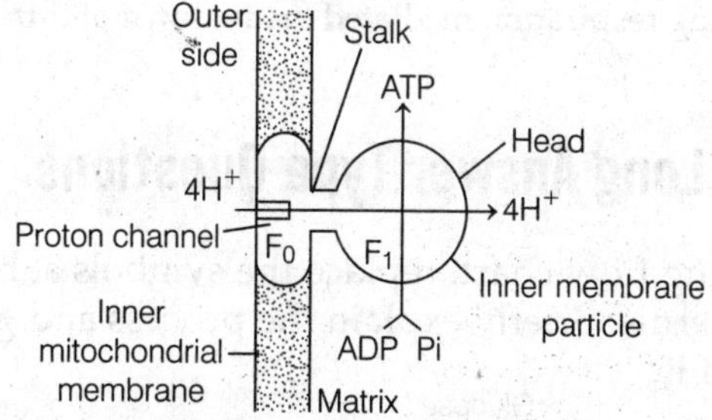

Showing the process of ATP synthesis

Q. 23 Respiratory pathway is believed to be a catabolic pathway. However, nature of TCA cycle is amphibolic. Explain.

Ans. Living cells obtain energy through respiration. It is the process of generating energy in the form of ATP molecules by breaking down food molecules like glucose, fats, etc.

The process starts with glycolysis which occurs in cytoplasm producing pyruvic acid. It is then converted to acetyl Co-A, which enters mitochondrial matrix. This initiates the tricarboxylic acid cycle.

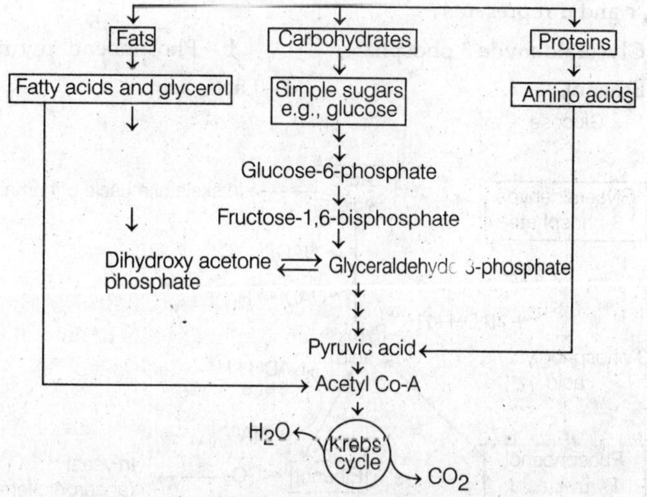

TCA cycle is said to be amphibolic because many intermediate compounds formed in this cycle act as precursors for biosynthesis of many important biological molecules, *i.e.*, co-enzymes, vitamins, hormones. Besides this, many molecules, *i.e.*, fatty acids, aminoacids, co-enzymes etc, can enter this cycle directly.

Acetyl Co-A is related to synthesis and breakdown of fatty acids, steroids, carotenoids terpenes and aromatic compounds. α- ketoglutarate and oxaloacetate are raw materials for synthesis of amino acids like glutamate and aspartate as well as pyrimidines and alkaloids. Succinyl-COA forms porphyrin compunds like cytochrome and chlorophyll.

So, it is the cycle where both breakdown and synthesis reactions keep on going simultaneously. The given figure shows interrelationship among metabolic pathway showing respiration mediated break down of different organic molecule.

Long Answer Type Questions

Q. 1 In the following flow chart, replace the symbols a, b, c and d with appropriate terms. Briefly explain the process and give any two application of it.

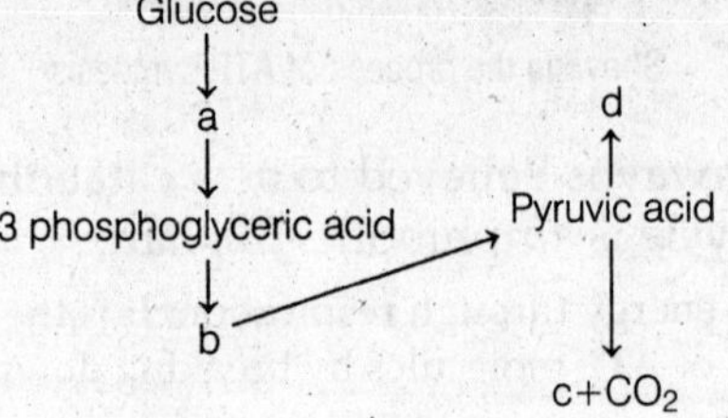

Thinking Process The pyruvic acid is the end product of glycolysis. It is further broken down depending on the circumstances and requirement of the cell .

Ans. The metabolic pathway given in the figure is **fermentation**. The products marked as a, b, c and d represents

a—Glyceraldehyde 3 phosphate, b—Phosphoenol pyruvic acid

c—Ethanol, d—Lactic acid

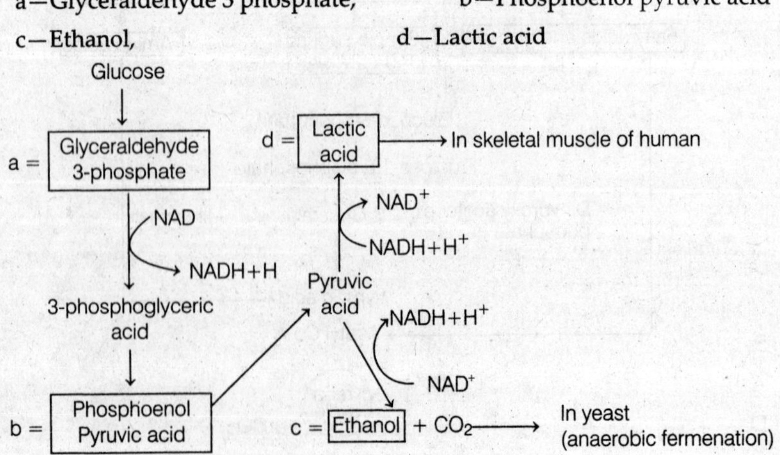

The fermentation is of two types

(i) **Alcohol Fermentation in Yeast** Alcohol fermentation is an incomplete oxidation of glucose under anaerobic condition. Alcohol fermentation in yeast occurs in 2 sets of reaction thus, converting pyruvic acid into ethanol and CO_2.

A. In the first step, pyruvic acid is decarboxylated (equation I), resulting in the formation of acetaldehyde and CO_2.

$$\underset{\text{Pyruvic acid}}{2CH_3COCOOH} \xrightarrow{\text{Pyruvic decarboxylase}} \underset{\text{Acetaldehyde}}{2CH_3CHO} \quad \text{...(i)}$$

B. In the second step acetaldehyde is reduced to alcohol by $NADH_2$ (equation (ii))

$$\underset{\text{Acetaldehyde}}{2CH_3CHO} \xrightarrow[\text{NADH}_2 \quad \text{NAD}]{\text{Alcohol dehydrogenase}} \underset{\text{Ethyl alcohol}}{2C_2H_5OH} + CO_2 \quad \text{.... (ii)}$$

(ii) **Lactic Acid Fermentation in Muscles**

In animal tissue like muscles, during exercise, when oxygen is inadequate for cellular respiration pyruvic acid is reduced to lactic acid by lactate dehydrogenase. The reducing agent is $NADH+H^+$ which is reoxidised to NAD^+ in the subsequent processes.

→ Applications of Fermentation:

(i) It helps in manufacture of ethyl alcohol.

(ii) It also helps in curdling of milk to make curd aided by bacteria *Lactobacillus.*

Q. 2 Given below is a diagram showing ATP synthesis during aerobic respiration, replace the symbols *A, B, C, D* and *E* by appropriate terms as given below.

F_1, particle, formation of Pi, $2H^+$, inner mitochondrial membrane, ATP, Fo particle, ADP.

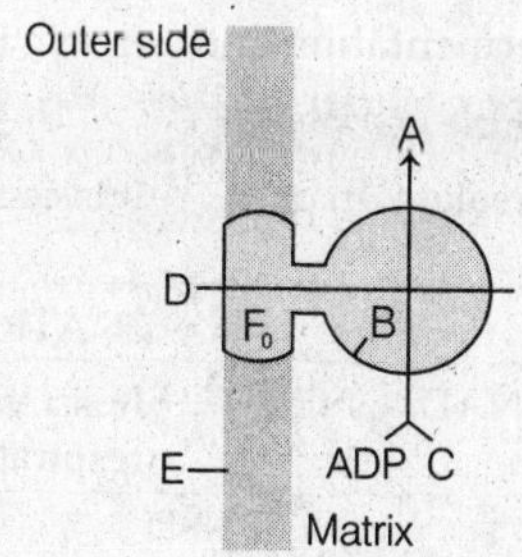

Thinking Process Phosphorylation of ATP from ADP + Pi is an important step occurring in every cell to obtain energy. This process takes place in the inner mitochondrial membrane

Ans. Symbol A, B, C, D and E in the diagram represents

A — ATP B — F_1 particle C — Pi

D — $4H^+$ E — Inner mitochondrial membrane.

Q. 3 Oxygen is critical for aerobic respiration. Explain its role with respect to ETS.

Ans. The respiration of glucose starts with glycolysis in cytoplasm, followed by in Krebs' cycle and finally Electron Transport Chain (ETC) in inner mitochondrial membrane. The requirement of O_2 is at the end of ETC. Where, it acts as final hydrogen acceptor. O_2 is responsible for removing electrons from the system. If oxygen is not available, electrons could not be passed through the co-enzymes, in turn proton pump will not be established and ATP will not be produced *via* oxidative phosphorylation. Thus Oxygen plays a critical role in aerobic respiration in mitochondrial matrix.

Q. 4 Enumerate the assumptions that we undertake in making the respiratory balance sheet. Are these assumptions valid for a living system? Compare fermentation and aerobic respiration in this context.

Ans. The calculations of the net gain of ATP for every glucose molecule oxidised can be made on the basis of following assumptions

(i) The metabolic pathway follows a sequential order, *i.e.*, glycolysis, TCA cycle and ETS in cytoplasm, mitochondrial matrix and inner mitochondrial membrane respectively.

(ii) NADH, synthesised in glycolysis enters in to ETC for phosphorylation.

(iii) None of the intermediates in the pathway are utilised to synthesise any other compound.

(iv) Glucose is the sole respiratory substrate.

These assumptions are not valid for a living system because of following reasons

(i) Metabolic pathways work simultaneously and do not take place one after the other.

(ii) ATP is utilised when needed.

(iii) Rate of enzyme actions is controlled by multiple factors.

Comparisan between fermentation and aerobic respiration are as follows

Fermentation	Aerobic Respiration
Fermentation is partial breakdown of glucose.	It is complete breakdown of glucose.
Net gain of only 2 ATP.	38 ATP are produced.
Oxidation of NADH to NAD^+ is slow process.	It is a vigorous reaction in aerobic respiration.

Q. 5 Give an account of glycolysis. Where does it occur? What are the end products? Trace the fate of these products in both aerobic and anaerobic respiration.

Ans. Glycolysis occurs in cytoplasm and involves the breakdown of one glucose molecule into 2 pyruvic acid molecules.

End Products of Glycolysis:

- Two molecules of pyruvic acid

- ~~Net~~ gain of 2ATP
- 2NADH moelcules

Fate of Pyruvic acid:

- **In Anaerobic Conditions** Pyruvic acid is reduced to ethanol and CO_2 in yeast and to lactic acid in muscles, with the net productionof 2ATP
- **In aerobic conditions** Pyruvic acid is converted to acetyl CoA and enters the Krebs cycle, leading to the production of 38 ATP

The steps of glycolysis are as follows

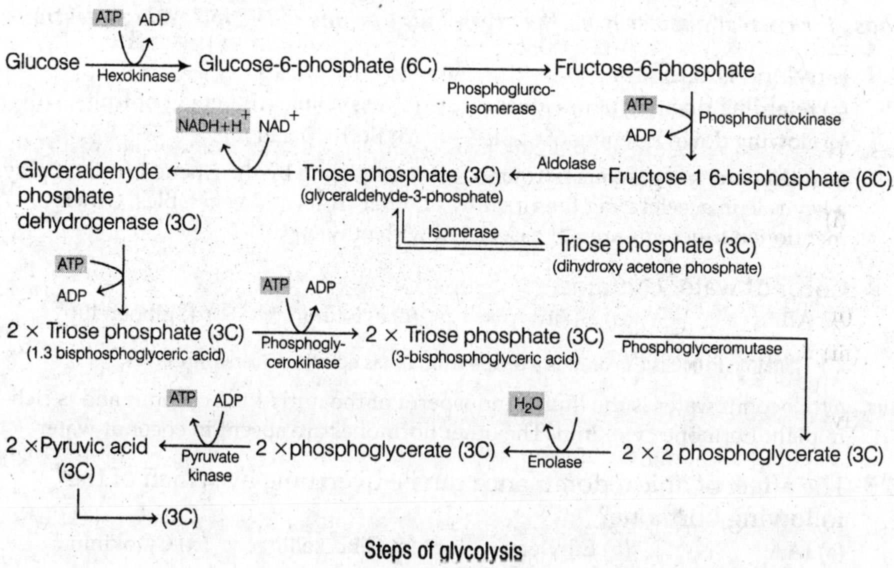

Steps of glycolysis

Chapter 15

Plant Growth and Development

Multiple Choice Questions (MCQs)

Choose the correct answer from the given four options in the following questions.

Q. 1 Ethylene is used for

(a) retarding ripening of tomatoes (b) hastening of ripening of fruits

(c) slowing down ripening of apples (d) Both (b) and (c)

Ans. ***(b)*** **Ethylene** is a gaseous hormone and is produced by the ripened fruits it plays a key role in accelerating the ripening of other fruits and vegetables. Other mentioned functions are not associated with ethylene.

Q. 2 Coconut water contains

(a) ABA (b) auxin (c) cytokinin (d) gibberellin

Thinking Process Coconut is a drupe fruit. It has edible endospermic layer.

Ans. ***(c)*** Coconut water is the liquid endosperm of the unripened coconut and is rich in plant hormone cytokinin. The other hormones are absent in coconut water.

Q. 3 The affect of apical dominance can be overcome by which of the following hormone?

(a) IAA (b) Ethylene (c) Gibberellin (d) Cytokinin

Thinking Process Various plant growth hormones are involved in the growth and development of the plant.

Ans. ***(d)*** Cytokinin is antagonistic to the action of auxin (IAA) and thus overcomes the phenomenon of apical dominance. Whereas, other options are incorrect because IAA, helps in apical dominance, ethylene in ripening of fruits and gibberellin in overcoming bud and seed dormancy.

Q. 4 Match the following.

Columm I	Column II
A. IAA	1. Herring sperm DNA
B. ABA	2. Bolting
C. Ethylene	3. Stomatal closure
D. GA	4. Weed-free lawns
E. Cytokinins	5. Ripening of fruits

Codes

	A	B	C	D	E
(a)	4	3	5	2	1
(b)	5	3	4	2	1
(c)	4	1	4	3	2
(d)	5	3	2	1	4

Ans. ***(a)***

A. **IAA-Weed free lawn** 2, 4- D and synthetic indole acetic acid kill the broad leaf weeds Thus, used as weedicides.

B. **ABA-Stomatal closure** ABA is a stress hormone. Under water stressed conditions, it shuts down stomata to reduce the rate of transpiration.

C. **Ethylene,** a gaseous hormone is responsible for ripening of fruits.

D. **GA** Gibberellic acid does the phenomenon of bolting, *i.e.,* when sprayed on the plant, it increases the internodal region of stem, thus making a plant extremely tall.

E. **Cytokinin** was isolated from herring sperm DNA, for the first time.

Q. 5 The term synergistic action of hormones refers to

(a) when two hormones act together but bring about opposite effects
(b) when two hormones act together and contribute to the same function
(c) when one hormone affects more than one function
(d) when many hormones bring about any one function

Thinking Process Growth and development of a plant is a complex process involving different plant hormones.

Ans. ***(b)*** Synergistic effect means when two hormones work together, they enhance each other's effect, leading to a stronger overall response.
Other options (a), (c) and (d) are stating incorrect statements about the synergistic action of hormones.

Q. 6 Apples are generally wrapped in waxed paper to

(a) prevent sunlight for changing its colour
(b) prevent aerobic respiration by checking the entry of oxygen
(c) prevent ethylene formation due to injury
(d) make the apples look attractive

Ans. ***(b)*** Apples have lenticels on their skin so, they respire. They are wrapped in wax paper after harvesting so as to prevent respiration and over ripening of the apples. Other options are incorrect because they do not support the reason for wrapping apple in waxed paper.

Q. 7 Growth can be measured in various ways. Which of these can be used as parameters to measure growth?

(a) Increase in cell number
(b) Increase in cell size
(c) Increase in length and weight
(d) All of these

Ans. ***(d)*** All the said statements are true for growth in a living organism.

Q. 8 Plasticity in plant growth means that

(a) plant roots are extensible
(b) plant development is dependent on the environment
(c) stems can extend
(d) None of the above

Thinking Process Plants have tremendous ability to adapt to the environment for their survival.

Ans. ***(b)*** The plants have the ability to change its phenotype according to the changes in environment. This ability to adapt is referred to as plasticity. Other option are incorrect because they cannot explain plasticity in plant growth.

Q. 9 To increase sugar production in sugarcanes, they are sprayed with
(a) IAA (b) cytokinin (c) gibberellin (d) ethylene

Ans. ***(c)*** Gibberellin spray on sugarcane induces the growth in the internodal area of the sugarcane plant, resulting in larger sugarcane with increased sugar content, as sucrose is the main constituent in the of sap of sugarcane stem.

Q. 10 ABA acts as antagonistic to
(a) ethylene (b) cytokinin (c) gibberellic acid (d) IAA

Thinking Process Sometimes some phytohormones act opposite to each other but this act could be beneficial for the plant.

Ans. ***(c)*** Abscisic acid (ABA) is stress hormone that induces seed dormancy in plants. Whereas, gibberellic acid breaks down seed dormancy and induces seed germination. Therefore they are antagonistic to each other. Option are incorrect because they are not antagonistic to ABA.

Q. 11 Monocarpic plants are those which
(a) bear flowers with one ovary (b) flower once and die
(c) bear only one flower (d) All of these

Ans. ***(b)*** Monocarpic plants flower once and die. The plants like *Bamboo* flower only once during their life cycle. Thus, these plants are called monocarpic plants.

Q. 12 The photoperiod in plants is perceived at
(a) meristem (b) flower (c) floral buds (d) leaves

Thinking Process A typical photoperiod exposer is the requirement of the plants for flowering however, for some plant it is not necessary.

Ans. ***(d)*** Fully developed leaves receive the stimulus of light. Photoperiodism is the effect of light and its duration on the growth and development of plants, especially flowering.

Even a single leaf is capable of inducing photoperiodism but very young leaves are insensitive to light. Other options are incorrect because meristem, flower and floral buds do not perceive the stimulus.

Very Short Answer Type Questions

Q. 1 Fill in the places with appropriate word/words.

(a) A phase of growth which is maximum and fastest is ....

(b) Apical dominance as expressed in dicotyledonous plants is due to the presence of more .... in the apical bud than in the lateral ones.

(c) In addition to auxin, a .... must be supplied to culture medium to obtain a good callus in plant tissue culture.

(d) ...... of a vegetative plants are the sites of photoperiodic perception.

Ans. (a) A phase of growth which is maximum and fastest is **exponential phase.**

(b) Apical dominance as expressed in dicotyledonous plants is due to the presence of more **auxins** in the apical bud than in the lateral ones.

(c) In addition to auxin, a **cytokinin** must be supplied to culture medium to obtain a good callus in plant tissue culture.

(d) Leaves of vegetative plants are the sites of photoperiodic perception.

Q. 2 Plant Growth Substances (PGS) have innumerable practical applications. Name the PGS you should use to

(a) increase yield of sugarcane

(b) promote lateral shoot growth

(c) cause sprouting of potato tuber

(d) inhibit seed germination

Thinking Process Pytohormones have their effect on various developmental and physiological functions of the plants.

Ans. (a) Gibberellic acid increases the yield of sugarcane.

(b) Cytokinin spray on plants promote lateral shoot growth.

(c) The effect of ethylene on potato causes its sprouting.

(d) ABA - Abscissic acid inhibit the seed germination.

Q. 3 A primary root grows from 5 cm to 19 cm in a week. Calculate the growth rate and relative growth rate over the period.

Ans. Growth rate is defined as an increase in growth per unit time. It is expressed as:

$$L_t = L_0 + rt$$

Where, l_t = length at time 't'

L_0 = length at time 'zero'

r = growth rate/elongation per unit time

$$\frac{L_t - L_0}{t} = r$$

$$\frac{19 - 5}{1} = r$$

$$r = 14 \text{ cm/week}$$

$$\text{Relative growth rate} = \frac{\text{Growth per unit time}}{\text{Initial size}} \times 100$$

$$= \frac{14}{5} \times 100$$

$$= 280\%$$

So, growth rate is 14 cm/week and relative growth rate is 280%.

Q. 4 Gibberellins were first discovered in Japan when rice plants were suffering from bakane (the foolish seedling disease) caused by a fungus *Gibberella fujikuroi*.

(a) Give two functions of this phytohormone.

(b) Which property of Gibberellin caused foolish seedling disease in rice?

Ans. (a) Two function phytohormone, gibberellin are

(i) Induce the phenomenon of bolting, *i.e.*, the growth of the internodal region of stem in rosette plants.

(ii) Promotes seed germination, break bud and seed dormancy.

(b) The fungus *Gibberella fujikuroi* produces excessive gibberellins, which leads to excessive elongation of the internodal region, causing the rice plants to grow abnormally tall, resulting in the "foolish seedling" appearance.

Q. 5 Gibberellins promote the formation of ...... flowers on genetically ..... plants in *Cannabis* whereas ethylene promotes formation of .... flowers on genetically ...... plants.

Ans. Gibberellin promotes the formation of male flower on genetically female plants while ethylene promotes formation of female flowers on genetically, male plants.

Q. 6 Classify the following plants into Long Day Plants (LDP), Short Day Plants (SDP) and Day Neutral Plants (DNP) *Xanthium*, henbane (*Hyoscyamus niger*), spinach, rice, strawberry, *Bryophyllum*, sunflower, tomato, maize.

Ans. **Long Day Plant** (LDP) Some plants require the exposure of light for a longer period exceeding a well defined critical duration of light. Among the above given plant LDP are for flowering henbane, *Bryophyllum* and spinach.

Short Day Plants (SDP) Some plants flower when and these can blossom throughout the year. exposed to light for a period less than well defined critical duration of light. *e.g.*, of SDP are. *e.g.*, *Xanthium*, rice, strawberry.

Day Neutral Plants (DNP) The exposure to light does not affect the flowering in certain plants, *e.g.*, DNP, are sunflower, tomato, maize.

Q. 7 A farmer grows cucumber plants in his field. He wants to increase the number of female flowers in them. Which plant growth regulator can be applied to achieve this?

Thinking Process Ethylene is a gaseous plant hormone. It is primarily responsible for ripening of fruits.

Ans. Ethylene is the plant growth regulator responsible for promoting the formation of female flowers in cucumbers. The farmer must spray ethylene hormone on this cucumber crop to produce female flowers and to increase the yield (number of fruits produced).

Q. 8 Where are the following hormones synthesised in plants?

(a) IAA (b) Gibberellins

(c) Cytokinins

Ans. (a) **IAA** Indole acetic acid is the chemical name of auxin. It is synthesised at the **growing apices of the plant**, *e.g.*, shoot tip, leaf primordia and developing seeds.

(b) **Gibberellins** It plays an important role in seed germination of plants and is synthesised in the **apical shoot buds**, young leaves, root tips and developing seeds.

(c) **Cytokinins** This plays an important role in actively dividing cells and are **synthesised mainly in roots**, but cytokinins also occurs in **endosperm of seeds**, growing embryo and seeds etc.

Q. 9 In botanical gardens and tea gardens, gardeners trim the plants regularly so that they remain bushy. Does this practice have any scientific explanation?

Ans. The apical buds present in tea and other plants prevents the growth of lateral buds in them by releasing auxin hormone. This phenomenon is called apical **dominance**. Trimming removes the apical bud and the Source of auxin is removed allowing the lateral buds to grow laterally and give plants a dense bushy appearance.

Q. 10 Light plays an important role in the life of all organisms. Name any three physiological processes in plants which are affected by light.

Ans. (i) **Photosynthesis** It is a totally light dependent process. Both quality and quantity affect the rate of the process resulting into total biomass accumulation by plants.

(ii) **Transpiration** It is loss of water by plant surface. Presence of light increases the temperature, thus affecting the rate of transpiration in plants.

(iii) **Flowering** The duration of light on plants affects flowering and this phenomenon is known as photo periodism. On the basis of photoperiodic response flowering plants are categorised as long day, short day and day neutral plants.

Q. 11 In the figure of sigmoid growth curve given below, label segments 1, 2 and 3.

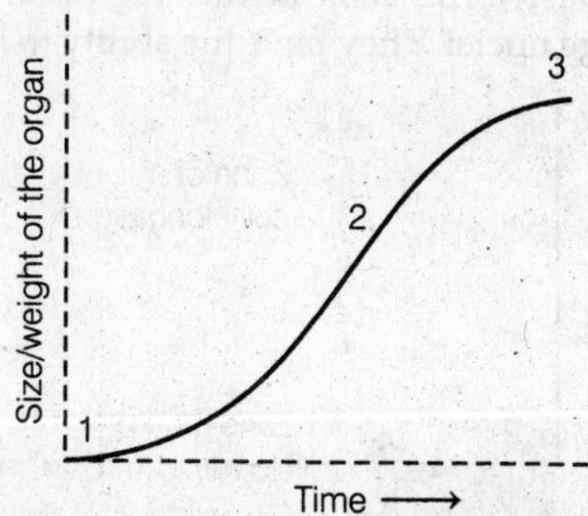

Ans. 1. Lag phase-Growth is slow in this phase.

2. Exponential phase-shows rapid growth and maintains maximum growth for sometime.

3. Stationany phase-Growth slows down and ultimately stops in this phase as the plant reach its carrying capacity.

Q.12 Growth is one of the characteristic of all living organism? Do unicellular organism also grow? If so, what are the parameters?

Ans. Growth is the main character which distinguish living organisms from non-living. All living organism grow in number and then accumulate biomass and grow in size as well. The growth is exhibited by all living organisms in terms of increase in number of cells as well as increase in size and length of each cell.

Yes, unicellular organisms also grow. In unicelluar organism, the growth is synchronous with reproduction. Unicellular organism when divide they produce offsprings (reproduction) *i.e.*, each cell accumulate (synthesise) protoplasm and increase in size but up to a limit and divide to from two cells.

Q. 13 The rice seedlings infected with fungus *Gibberella fujikuroi* is called foolish seedlings? What was the reason behind it?

Ans. The fungus *Gibberella fujikuroi* produces an excess of gibberllins, which causes excessive elongation of the internodes in rice plants, making them abnormally tall. This overgrowth is the reason behind the "foolish seedling" disease in rice.

Short Answer Type Questions

Q. 1 *Nicotiana tobacum*, a short day plant, when exposed to more than critical period of light fails to flower. Explain.

Ans. Short day plants are those plants that flower only when the photoperiod (exposure to duration of light) is shorter than a critical period. Tobacco, being a short day plant is unable to show flowering when exposed to light above than the critical period.

Q. 2 What are the structural characteristics of

(a) meristematic cells near root tip

(b) the cells in the elongation zone of the root

Ans. (a) **Meristematic cells near root tip** The cells of this region are called Root Apical Meristems (RAM) and are in active state of division, thus their number increases continuously. The cells in this region are thin walled with dense cytoplasm and large nuclei. They have the ability to divide and self perpetuate.

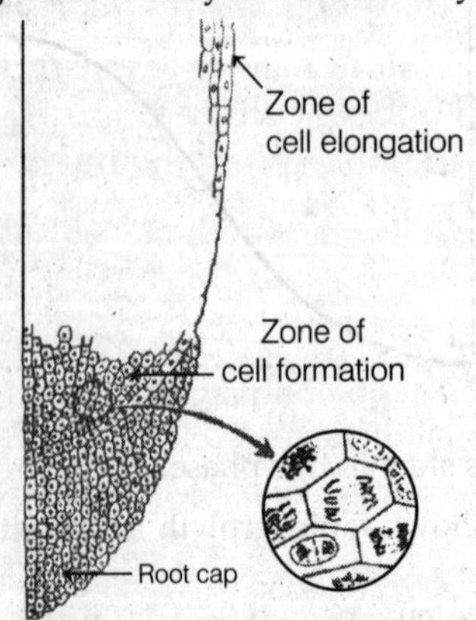

Root tip showing zone of cell formation

(b) **The Cells in the Elongation Zone of the Root** This region is situated just above the meristematic zone. In the cells of this zone, many small vacuoles develop and later these vacuoles fuse to form one large central vacuole filled with cell sap. The cells are elongated in this region.

Q.3 Does the growth pattern in plants differ from that in animals? Do all the parts of plant grow indefinitely? If not, name the regions of plant, which can grow indefinitely.

Ans. **Growth in plants** is indeterminate *i.e.*, plant grow through out their life due to presence of meristematic tissues in specific parts of plant such as apical, intercalary and lateral meristems. These tissue has ability to divide continuously and contribute to localised plant growth.

Growth in animals They have limited growth period after which further growth of their body stops.

All the parts of the plant do not grow indefinitely. The root apex and shoot apex having apical meristematic tissues keep growing, thus contributing to the elongation of plant axis (height).

Q.4 Explain in 2-3 lines each of the following terms with the help of examples taken from different plant tissues.

(a) Differentiation (b) De-differentiation

(c) Re-differentiation

Ans. (a) **Differentiation** is the process in which cells, tissues or organs become specialised in structure, composition and function. *e.g.*, cells distal to the root apical meristem differentiate into the root cap, cortex, endodermis and vascular tissues.

(b) **De-differentiation** is the process of despecialisation of differentiated cells so that they regain the ablility to divide. *e.g.*, in dicot stem, the cortical cells get de-differentiated and become meristematic to form cambium (interfascicular cambium, and fascicular cambiums).

(c) **Re-differentiation** after de-differentiation, cells can re-differentiate into specialized tissues. *e.g.*, cambium cells thus formed, again re-differentiate to form secondary cortex cells secondary xylem and phloem elements and phelloderm in case of secondary growth of woody dicot plants.

Q.5 Auxins are growth hormones capable of promoting cell elongation. They have been used in horticulture to promote growth, flowering and rooting. Write a line to explain the meaning of the following terms related to auxins.

(a) Auxins precursors (b) Anti-auxins

(c) Synthetic auxins

Ans. Auxin is an important plant phytohormone required for the growth and development of every plant in its life cycle.

(a) **Auxin Precursors** are raw materials required for the synthesis of auxins such as tryptophan, adenine compounds and derivatives of carotenoids.

(b) **Anti-Auxins** are compounds that inhibit action of auxins, *e.g.*, p-chlorophenoxy isobutyric acid (PCIB), TIBA.

(c) **Synthetic Auxin** These are synthesised not by plants but artificially by man, *e.g.*, 2-4 D (weedicide), NAA, dicamba and IBA, (Indole Butyric Acid) which are natural as well as synthetic auxin.

Q. 6 The role of ethylene and abscissic acid is both positive and negative. Justify the statement.

Ans.

Hormone	Positive Effects	Negative Effects
Ethylene	• Promotes horizontal growth. • Makes stem positively geotropic. • Promotes apical dominance. • Breaks seed and bud dormancy. • Enhances fruits ripening and stimulates root initiation.	• Inhibits longitudinal growth. • Decreases sensitivity to gravity. *i.e.*, root become apogeotropic • Enhances senescence of leaves and flowers, fruits. • Prolongs dormancy of lateral buds. • Mediates formation of ABA under water stressed conditions.
Abscissic Acid	• ABA act as an anti transpirant, by reducing water loss and during irrigation (by partial closure of stomata). • Also, induces flowering and root initiation in some plants. • Used in prolonging dormancy of buds and seeds. • Increases resistance of plants, to cold and other types of stresses thus also known as stress hormone.	• Promotes abscission of flower and fruits. • Stimulates senescence of leaves by stopping protein and RNA synthesis. • Promotes bud and seed dormancy. Retards cambial activity by stopping mitosis in vascular strands and cambium. • Act as antagonist to gibberellins and counteracts the effect of other growth hormones (IAA and cytokinin). • Inhibits seed germination and growth of embryos in them.

Q. 7 While experimentation, why do you think it is difficult to assign any affect seen to any single hormone?

Ans. **Phytohormones** are synthesised by plant cells themselves and individually. These are auxin, GA, ABA ethylene and cytokinin. There is not a separate system of their translocation in plants. So, their effects on plants are also inter mixed. *e.g.*, many effects of auxins and GA show the same function. Similarly, ethylene and ABA support each other for many roles in plants.

Secondly, effects of phytohormone *in vitro*, in controlled environment and *in vivo* in a living organism can be different.

Q. 8 What is the mechanism underlying the phenomenon by which the terminal/apical bud suppresses the growth of lateral buds? Suggest measures to overcome this phenomenon.

Ans. The phenomenon by which apical bud suppress the growth of lateral buds is known as **apical dominance**. It is caused by the release of plant hormone auxin from apical buds.

It can be overcome either by the spray of cytokinin, that promotes the growth of lateral buds or by trimming of bushes which remove apical buds and allow lateral buds to grow.

Q. 9 In animals, there are special glands secreting hormones, whereas there are no glands in plants. Where are plant hormones formed? How are the hormones translocated to the site of activity?

Ans. The plant hormones are synthesised by the plant cells as needed. Few hormones are specifically synthesised at a particular plant part, like auxin synthesised in growing shoot apices. Ethylene is emitted by ripened fruits. Cytokinin are found dividing cells. Unlike plants, animal are more advanced, and organised with proper hormone secreting glands and organs.

In both plant and animals these are transported through the transport system of their body. In plants, hormones are translocated via xylem and phloem to the site of activity or diffused to the other cells where these are being utilised.

Q. 10 Many discoveries in science have been accidental. This is true for plant hormones also. Can you justify this statement by giving an example? Also what term is used for such accidental findings?

Ans. Discovery of plant hormone gibberellins was accidental. In rice fields, a few plants of rice were observed, which were unusually taller than the normal ones. Scientific investigation revealed, that these were infected with a fungus, known as *Gibberella fufikuroi*.

This fungus releases a plant hormone gibberellic acid in excess concentrations which made the plant to grow unusually tall. This compound was later known as gibberellin which is a hormones present in all plants.

The term used for accidental finding is "serendipity" which means fortunate happenstance. It was coined by **Horace Walpole** in 1754. He explained it as making discoveries, by accident and sagacity of things that were not being actively sought.

Q. 11 To get a carpet-like grass lawns are mowed regularly. Is there any scientific explanation for this?

Thinking Process Apical dominance is overcome when apex of the growing plant is removed. It causes lateral branches of the plant to grow faster giving the plants a bushy appearance.

Ans. Regular mowing (cutting at apex) of lawn grass removes the apical portion of the plant which causes the lateral branches to grow faster. As the apical buds inhibits growth of lateral buds by releasing auxin, the phenomenon called **apical dominance**. Because of mowing of the grass, it becomes bushy and growth is faster. So, as to make evenness of the grass (carpet-like) in the lawn this practice is followed regularly to overcome the problem of apical dominance.

Q. 12 In a slide showing different types of cells can you identify which type of the cell may be meristematic and the one which is incapable of dividing and how?

Ans. The meristematic cells can be identified on the basis of the following characteristics

(i) Cell have thin cellulose wall and dense cytoplasm with large nucleus.

(ii) Plasmodesmal connections are more numerous among meristematic cells.

(iii) Cell division, *i.e.*, mitosis and its various stages are distinctly visible.

(iv) Chromosomes of cells replicate and divide into two homologous chromatids.

All these features contribute to open ended growth where structure is never completed in meristematic regions.

Whereas, cells incapable of divinding show features such as

(i) Attains particular shape, size and thickening.

(ii) Undergoes structural and physiological differentiation.

(iii) Different types of cell are formed such as epidermis, cortex, vascular tissues.

Q.13 A rubber band stretches and reverts back to its original position. Bubble gum stretches, but it would not return to its original position. Is there any difference between the two processes? Discuss it with respect to plant growth (hint elasticity (reversible) plasticity (irreversible).

Ans.

Elasticity	Plasticity
The elasticity is stretchability of the plant cells or products, *e.g.*, rubber or latex etc.	Different pathways in response to environment or phases of life to form different kinds of structure is called plasticity.
The elastic substances can revert back to its original form in relaxed state.	The plastic substances and phenomenon of plasticity are not reversible, *i.e.*, irreversible. *e.g.*, difference in shapes of leaves produced in air and those produced in water in buttercup. This is also known as heterophylly.
e.g., stretching of rubber.	

Q.14 Label the diagram

A. Which parts of a dicotyledonous plants are these?

B. If we remove part 1 from the plant, what will happen?

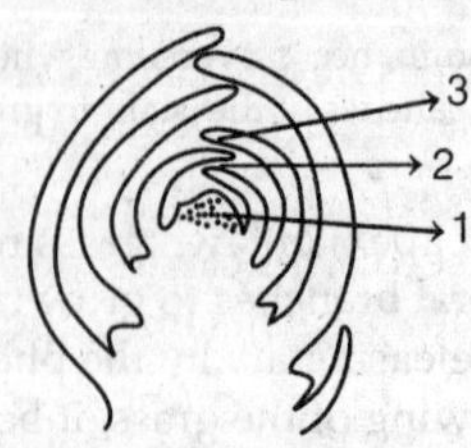

Ans. The labelling of the given diagram is as follows

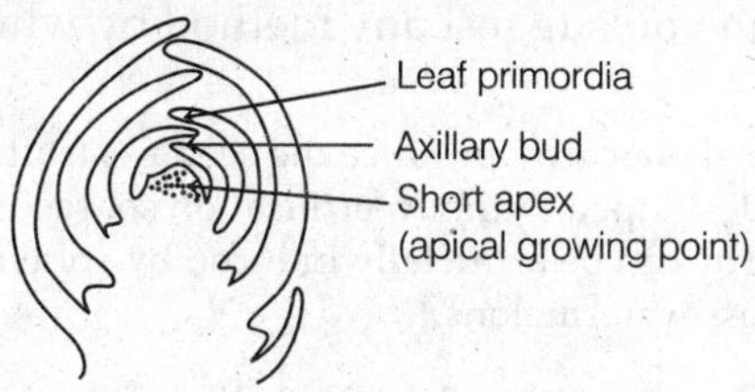

A. The plant part in the given diagram is growing shoot apex.

B. Removal of shoot apex will help to overcome the apical dominance. Thus, the lateral buds grow faster, giving rise to branches and give the plant a bushy appearance.

Q. 15 Both animals and plants grow. Why do we say that growth and differentiation in plants is open and not so in animals? Does this statement hold true for sponges also?

Ans. Growth and differentiation in plant and animals can be explained as follows

Growth in Plants	Growth in Animals
Plant growth is indeterminate, *i.e.*, cells can divide and enlarge continuously for life time.	Animal growth is determinate *i.e.*, till finite period, they mature and stop growing externally.
Growth is open due to presence of meristematic cells which keep dividing, *i.e.*, growing and replacing new organs.	Cell division is distributed through-out the body of organism to replace old and damaged cells, rather localised at specific regions.
Structure in plants at tips or meristematic zones is never complete, growing to open ended tips or apices. Plant growth is in a modular fashion, *i.e.*, grows longitudinally, laterally and in girth.	After a specific time period *i.e.*, embryonic, phase, the growth rate is reduced during juvenile phase and ceases in maturity.

Sponges are exception to this *i.e.*, growth is indeterminate. They show open growth as every cell of their body can give rise to an individual and their growth and differentiation is continuous is their life cycle.

Q. 16 Define parthenocarpy. Name the plant hormone used to induce parthenocarpy.

Thinking Process Seedless fruits are developed in some plants. Certain phytohormone induce development of fruit without fertilisation.

Ans. **Parthenocarpy** is the process in which fruit develop without fertilisation and as a result, they do not contain seed. This can be induced artificially by spraying auxin and gibberellins in certain plants like, grapes, papaya, etc.

Q. 17 While eating watermelons, all of us wish it was seedless. As a plant physiologist can you suggest any method by which this can be achieved.

Ans. The process of parthenocarpy produce the seedless fruits. This is a process in which fruits are developed without fertilisation so, seeds are not formed in the fruit. Parthenocarpy can be artificially induced by spraying auxin and gibberellin to produce seedless watermelons.

Q. 18 A gardener finds some broad-leaved dicot weeds growing in his lawns. What can be done to get rid of the weeds efficiently?

Ans. The broad-leaved dicot weeds can be killed and eliminated by the spray of weedicide 2-4 D, (which is a synthetic auxin). This herbicide will make the lawn free of weeds and help the gardener, to make the lawn weed free.

Q. 19 On germination a seed first produces shoots with leaves, flowers appear later,

A. Why do you think this happens?

B. How is this advantageous to the plant?

Ans. **A.** As soon as seed germinates, the plant enters into vegetative growth phase. This phase receives light stimulus (a critical length of light exposed to different plant, *i.e.*, photoperiod) and synthesise the florigen (a flowering hormone) which induce flowering.

B. The vegetative growth phase prepares the plant to bear reproductive structures like flower, fruits and seeds, and allows it to grow, mature and reproduce.

Q. 20 Fill in the blanks

A. Maximum growth is observed in ....phase.

B. Apical dominance is due to ....

C. .... initiate rooting .

D. Pigment involved in photoperception in flowering plants is......... .

Ans. A. Exponential B. Auxin

C. Auxin D. Phytochrome.

Long Answer Type Questions

Q. 1 Some varieties of wheat are known as spring wheat while others are called winter wheat. Former variety is sown and planted in spring and is harvested by the end of the same season. However, winter varieties, if planted in spring, fail to flower or produce mature grains within a span of a flowering season. Explain, why?

Thinking Process The chilling treatment to wheat seed prior to sowing reduces the vegetative growth period of wheat plant and induces flowering at an early time.

Ans. Some annual food plants such as wheat do not flower, unless they experience a low temperature. They remain vegetative during spring (warm period) but grow further to bear flowers and fruits after receiving low temperature (in winter).

The low temperature in winter prevents premature reproductive development in autumn, thus enabling the plant to reach vegetative maturity before reproductive phase. Thus, when spring varieties are planted in spring, they flower and bear fruits prior to end of growing season. But, if the winter varieties are planted in spring, they fail to flower and produce mature grains by the end of growing season, as they could not perceive low temperature of winters.

Q. 2 It is known that some varieties of wheat are sown in autumn but are harvested around next mid summer.

A. What could be the probable reason for this?

B. What term is used for this promotion of lowering under low temperature?

C. Which plant hormone can replace the cold treatment?

Ans. **A.** Annual winter wheat plants require an entire growing season for the completion of their vegetative growth period and then initiate flowers and fruits. After being planted in autumn, the seeds experience low temperature throughout winter, which enables them to reach vegetative maturity. They resume growth in spring and bear flowers and grains towards mid-summer.

B. The chilling or cold treatment of seeds to induce flowering is called vernalisation. It is a process of shortening of the juvenile or vegetative phase and hastening flowering by exposing the plant to cold treatment. This stimulus of vernalisation is perceived only by the meristematic cells. *e.g.*, shoot tip, embryo tip, root apex, developing leaves, etc.

C. GA or **gibberellic** acid can replace cold treatment and can induce flowering early by reducing the vegetative growth period in many long-day plants.

Q. 3 Name a hormone which

A. is gaseous in nature

B. is responsible for phototropism

C. induces femaleness in flowers of cucumber

D. is used for killing weeds (dicots)

E. induces flowering in long day plants.

Ans.

A. Ethylene is a hormone which is gaseous in nature.

B. Auxin (specifically synthetic auxin 2-4 D) is responsible for phototropism and geotropism in plants as it regulates cell elongation towards light and gravity.

C. Ethylene induces femaleness in flowers, particularly in plants like cucumber. External supply of very small quantity of ethylene can increase the number of female flowers there by promoting fruit production cucumber.

D. Synthetic auxin (2-4 D) kills broad leaved dicot weeds, hence used as weedicides.

E. Gibberellins, induces flowering in long-day plants.

Chapter 16

Digestion and Absorption*

Multiple Choice Questions (MCQs)

Choose the correct answer from the given four options in the following questions :

Q. 1 Select what is not true of intestinal villi among following

(a) they possess microvilli (b) they increase the surface area

(c) they are supplied with capillaries and the lacteal vessels

(d) they only participate in digestion of fats

Ans. *(d)* **Intestinal villi** are the numerous small finger-shaped projections which increase the absorptive surface area. They contain abundant blood capillaries and lymph vessels called **lacteals**. They also possess countless minute microvilli which further add to the absorptive surface.

They do not participate in the digestion of fats but helps in their **absorption** of various other substances such as **water, mineral, salts, amino acids, vitamins,** etc. Hence option (d) is incorrect.

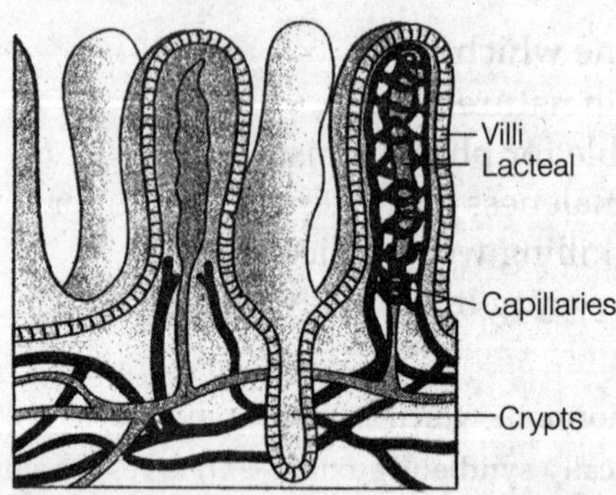

A section of small intestinal mucosa showing villi

Q. 2 Hepato-pancreatic duct opens into the duodenum and carries

(a) bile (b) pancreatic juice

(c) both bile and pancreatic juice (d) saliva

Ans. *(c)* The duct of **gall bladder** along with **hepatic duct** from the liver forms the **common bile duct**. The bile duct and the pancreatic duct open together into the duodenum as a common hepato-pancreatic duct which carries both **bile** and **pancreatic juice**.

Note (✱) *This chapter has been deleted from latest NCERT.*

The other options are incorrect because bile is secreted by the hepatic cells of liver and is stored further in a thin muscular sac called **gall bladder** while. Secretion of pancreatic juices takes place through the exocrine part of pancreas which consist of round lobules called **acini**. Saliva is mainly produced by the salivary glands.

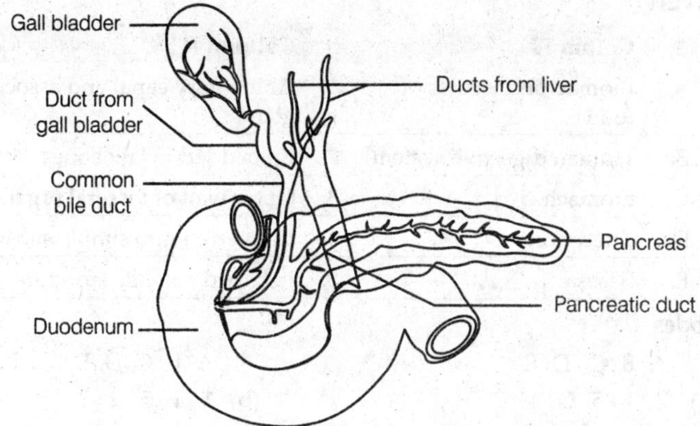

The duct systems of liver, gall bladder and pancreas

Q. 3 One of the following is not a common disorder associated with digestive system

(a) Tetanus (b) Diarrhoea (c) Jaundice (d) Dysentery

Ans. *(a)* **Tetanus** is a medical condition which is characterised by a prolonged contraction of skeletal muscle fibres. Hence, this disorder is not associated with digestive system. The other given disorders are associated with digestive system.

Diarrhoea is the abnormal frequency of bowel movement and increased liquidity of the faecal discharge. The food absorption is highly reduced in diarrhoea.

Jaundice represents one of the symptom of liver malfunctioning in which skin and eyes turn yellow due to the excess accumulation of bile pigments in the blood.

Dysentery is the inflammatory disorder of intestine, especially of the colon, resulting in severe diarrhoea containing blood and mucus in the faeces, abdominal pain and fever.

Q. 4 A gland not associated with the alimentary canal is

(a) pancreas (b) adrenal (c) liver (d) salivary glands

Ans. *(b)* **Adrenal gland** is not associated with the alimentary canal. This gland is present at the anterior part of each kidney acting as an endocrine gland, involve in regulation of metabolism, blood pressure, responsed to stress and other essential functions. The other gland are associated with alimentary canal.

Pancreas is located posterior to the stomach in the abdominal cavity. It is associated with the secretion of **alkaline pancreatic juices** which are essential in the digestion of starch, protein, fats and nucleic acid. **Pancreas** also produces hormones like glucagon, insulin, somatostatin are involved in glucose metabolism.

Liver is the largest gland of the body lying in the upper right side of the abdominal cavity just below the diaphragm. It is mainly involved in the production of bile which helps in the digestion of fats in small intestine by **emulsification process**.

Salivary glands are situated just outside the buccal cavity. They discharge their secretions (salivary juices) into the oral cavity, which help in the mastication of food.

Q. 5 Match the following columns and select the correct among options given

Column I	Column II
A. Biomacromolecules of food	1. Alimentary canal and associated gland
B. Human digestive system	2. Embedded in jaw bones
C. Stomach	3. Outer wall of visceral organs
D. Thecodont	4. Converted into simple substances
E. Serosa	5. J-shaped bag like structure

Codes

	A	B	C	D	E		A	B	C	D	E
(a)	2	1	5	3	4	(b)	4	1	5	2	3
(c)	1	2	3	4	5	(d)	1	3	2	4	5

Ans. *(b)* **Biomacromolecules of food** like carbohydrates, fats, proteins and nucleic acid are converted into simpler monomers during the digestion process.

Human digestive system consists of alimentry canal and its associated gland.

Stomach is the widest organ of the alimentry canal. It is a J-shaped bag like structure, and plays an important role in digestion.

Thecodont are teeth that are embedded in the sockets of the jaw bones.

Serosa is an another name for **serous membrane,** forming outer wall of the visceral organs.

Q. 6 Match the following columns.

Column I	Column II
A. Duodenum	1. A cartilaginous flap
B. Epiglottis	2. Small blind sac
C. Glottis	3. 'U' shaped structure emerging from the stomach.
D. Caecum	4. Opening of wind pipe.

Codes

	A	B	C	D		A	B	C	D
(a)	1	2	3	4	(b)	4	3	2	1
(c)	3	1	4	2	(d)	2	4	1	3

Ans. *(c)* **Duodenum** is a 'U'-shaped structure emerging from the stomach.

Epiglottis is a **cartilaginous flap** that prevents the entry of food into the glottis.

Glottis is the opening of the wind pipe.

Caecum is a small blind sac which hosts some symbiotic microorganisms that helps in the digestion process.

Q. 7 Match the enzyme with their respective substrate and choose the right one among options given

	Column I		Column II
A.	Lipase	1.	Carbohydrates
B.	Nuclease	2.	Fats
C.	Carboxypeptidase	3.	Nucleic acids
D.	Glycosidases	4.	Proteins, peptones and proteoses

Codes

	A	B	C	D		A	B	C	D
(a)	2	3	1	4	(b)	3	4	2	1
(c)	3	1	4	2	(d)	2	3	4	1

Ans. ***(d)*** **Lipase** is a fat digestive enzyme.

Nuclease is the enzymes that digest nucleic acid.

Carboxypeptidases are the enzymes involved in the digestion of proteins, peptones and proteases.

Glycosidases act on carbohydrates.

Q. 8 Dental formula in human beings is

(a) $\frac{3223}{3223}$ (b) $\frac{2123}{2123}$

(c) $\frac{1232}{1232}$ (d) $\frac{2233}{2233}$

Ans. ***(b)*** An adult human has 32 permanent teeth which are of four different types, namely **Incisors** (I), **Canine** (C), **Premolar** (PM) and **Molar** (M). Arrangement of teeth in each half of the upper and lower jaw in the order I,C,PM,M is represented by a dental formula, which is $\frac{2123}{2123}$.

Q. 9 Liver is the largest gland and is associated with various functions, choose one which is not correct.

(a) Metabolism of carbohydrate

(b) Digestion of fat

(c) Formation of bile

(d) Secretion of hormone called gastrin

Thinking Process Liver is the largest gland of body. It lies in the upper right side of the abdominal cavity just below the diaphragm.

Ans. ***(d)*** Liver is involved in the production of bile (hepatic bile pH is 8.6). Bile helps in the digestion of fats in the small intestine by the **emulsification process** (conversion of large fat droplets into small ones).

Liver also plays a critical role in regulating glucose metabolism by maintaining glucose concentration in normal range.

Gastrin is secreted by G-cells in pyloric region of stomach. It stimulates gastric glands to secrete and release gastric juices. Hence option (d) is incorrect.

Q. 10 Mark the right statement among the following

(a) Trypsinogen is an inactive enzyme

(b) Trypsinogen is secreted by intestinal mucosa

(c) Enterokinase is secreted by pancreas

(d) Bile contains trypsin

Ans. *(a)* **Trypsinogen** is an inactive pencreatic enzyme secreted by pancreas. It is activated, by enterokinase, (an enzyme secreted by intestinal mucosa). Active form of trypsinogen is called trypsin, which in turn activates other enzymes present in the pancreatic juice. Bile does not contain trypsin, it contain bile pigments salts etc. It does not have any enzymes.

Very Short Answer Type Questions

Q. 1 The food mixes thoroughly with the acidic gastric juice of the stomach by the churning movements of its muscular wall. What do we call the food then?

Ans. The food is stored in stomach for 4-5 hours, and it gets thoroughly mixed with the acidic gastric juice of stomach by the churning movements of its muscular wall. The food at this stage is called as **chyme**.

Q. 2 Trypsinogen is an inactive enzyme of pancreatic juice. An enzyme, enterokinase, activates it. Which tissue/cells secrete this enzyme? How is it activated?

Thinking Process Secretion of pancreatic juice takes place through the exocrine part of pancreas. The juice contains inactive enzymes *i.e.*, **trypsinogen, chymotrypsinogen, procarboxypeptidase, amylase, lipases** and **nucleases**.

Ans. **Trypsinogen** is activated to trypsin by the enzyme **enterokinase**. This enzyme is secreted by the **intestinal mucosa**.

Q. 3 In which part of alimentary canal does absorption of water, simple sugars and alcohol takes place?

Ans. The absorption of water primarily occurs in the large intestine. The absorption of alcohol and simple sugars does occur in the small intestine. But a small portion of water, simple sugar and a significant portion of alcohol are also obsorbed in the stomach.

Q. 4 Name the enzymes involved in the breakdown of nucleotides into sugars and bases?

Ans. The enzymes **nucleotidases** and **nucleosidases** are involved in the breakdown of nucleotides into sugars and bases.

$$\text{Nucleotides} \xrightarrow{\text{Nucleotidases}} \text{Nucleosides} \xrightarrow{\text{Nucleosidases}} \text{Sugars} + \text{Bases}$$

Q. 5 Define digestion in one sentence.

Ans. The process of conversion of complex food substances in to simple absorbable forms by mechanical and biochemical methods is called **digestion**.

Q. 6 What do we call the type of teeth attachment to jaw bones in which each tooth is embedded in a socket of jaw bone?

Ans. The type of attachment where teeth are embedded in the socket of jaw bone is called **thecodont**.

Q. 7 Stomach is located in upper left portion of the abdominal cavity and has three major parts. Name these three parts.

Ans. The three major parts of stomach are as follows.

(a) **Cardiac** into which the oesophagus opens.

(b) **Fundus** which is commonly filled with air or gases.

(c) **Pylorus** which opens into small intestine (posterior part of stomach).

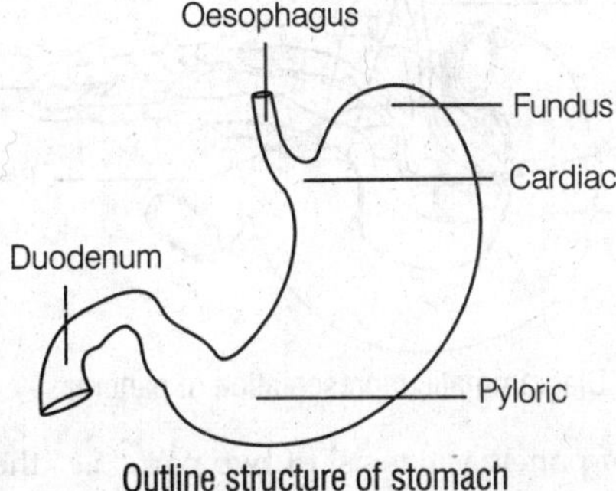

Outline structure of stomach

Q. 8 Does gall bladder make bile?

Ans. **Gall bladder** is not associated with the bile formation rather it is involved in the storage of bile. Bile is secreted by the hepatic cells of the liver.

Q. 9 Correct the following statements by deleting one of entries (given in bold).

(a) Goblet cells are located in the intestinal mucosal epithelium and secrete **chymotrypsin/mucus.**

(b) Fats are broken down into di-and monoglycerides with the help of **amylase/lipases.**

(c) Gastric glands of stomach mucosa have **oxyntic cell/chief cells** which secrete HCl.

(d) Saliva contains enzymes that digest **starch/protein**

Ans. (a) Goblet cells are located in the intestinal mucosal epithelium and secrete **mucus.**

(b) Fats are broken down into di and monoglycerides with the help of **lipases.**

$$\text{Fats} \xrightarrow{\text{Lipases}} \text{Diglycerides} \longrightarrow \text{Monoglycerides.}$$

(c) Gastric glands of stomach mucosa have **oxyntic cells** which secrete HCl

(d) Saliva contains enzymes that digest **starch**.

$$\text{Starch} \xrightarrow[\text{pH 6.8}]{\text{Salivary amylase}} \text{Maltose} + \text{Isomaltose} + \alpha\text{–dextrins}$$

Short Answer Type Quesations

Q. 1 What is pancreas? Mention the major secretions of pancreas that are helpful in digestion.

Ans. The **pancreas** is a compound (both exocrine and endocrine) and elongated organ, situated between the limbs of 'U' shaped duodenum.

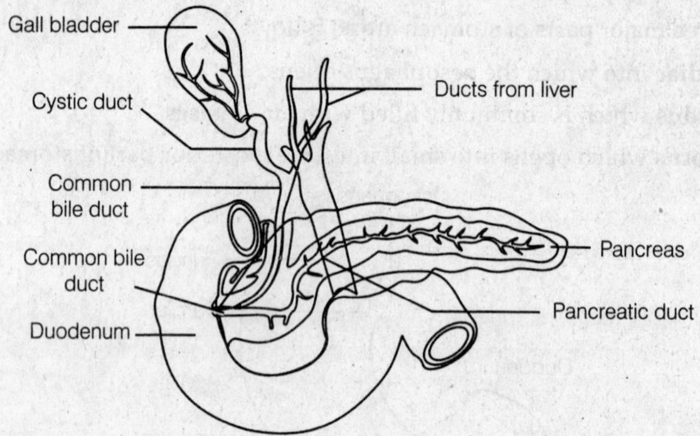

Diagrammatic representation of pancreas

Internal structure of pancreas consist of two parts, *i.e.*, the exocrine and endocrine part.

(i) **Exocrine part** consists of rounded lobules called acini that are involved in the secretion of alkaline pancreatic juice of pH 8.4. The pancreatic juice is mainly involved in the digestion of starch, proteins, fats and nucleic acids.

(ii) **Endocrine part** is involved in the secretion of hormones like, insulin and glucagon that regulate glucose metabolism.

Q. 2 Name the part of the alimentary canal where major absorption of digested food takes place. What are the absorbed forms of different kinds of food materials?

Ans. Small intestine is the principal organ for the absorption of nutrients. The process of digestion is complete here and the final products of digestion are absorbed through the mucosa into the blood stream.

The absorbed form of different food materials is

Food Material	Absorbed Form
Carbohydrates	Glucose
Proteins	Amino acids
Fats	Fatty acids

Q. 3 List the organs of human alimentary canal and name the major digestive glands with their location.

Ans. **Human digestive system** consists of two main parts: alimentary canal and digestive glands.

Alimentary canal comprises of following parts

(i) Mouth (ii) Pharynx (iii) Oesophagus
(iv) Stomach (v) Small intestine (vi) Large intestine
(vii) Rectum (viii) Anus

Digestive glands include

(i) **Salivary glands** are situated just outside the buccal cavity and secrete salivary juice into it.

(ii) **Liver** is the largest gland in the body, situated in the abdominal cavity just below the diaphragm and has two lobes. It secretes bile which helps in the digestion of fats.

(iii) **Pancreas** is the compound organ situated between the limbs of U-shaped duodenum and act as both endocrine and exocrine organ. The exocrine portion secretes pancreatic juice whereas endocrine portion secretes hormones like insulin and glucagon.

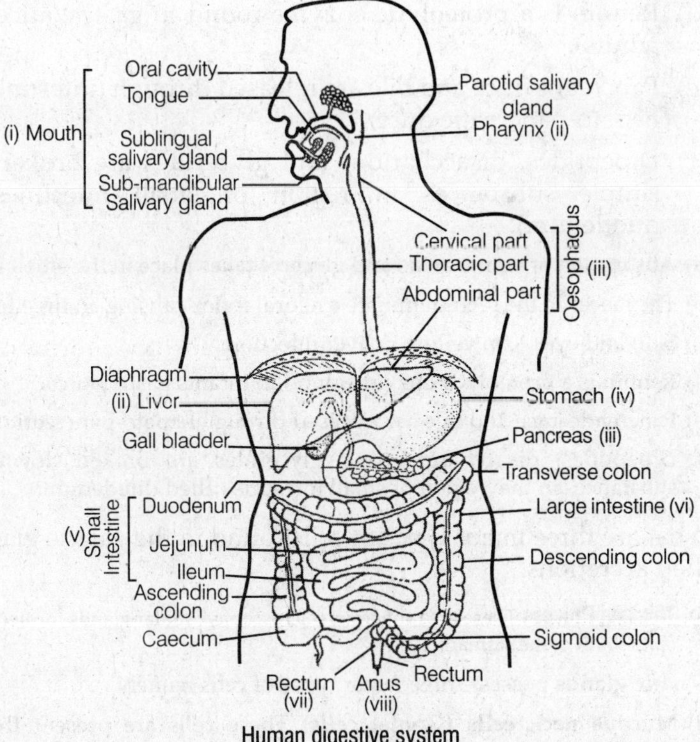

Human digestive system

Q. 4 What is the role of gall bladder? What may happen if it stops functioning or is removed?

Ans. **Gall Bladder** is a pear-shaped sac-like structure, attached to the posterior surface of the liver by a **connective tissue**. The bile secreted by the hepatic cells of liver, passes through the hepatic ducts and gets stored and concentrated in the gall bladder.

Non-functioning and removal of gall bladder results in bile simply run in the continuous stream from the liver into the intestine. It would not be as concentrated as the bile stored in gall bladder. The body gradually adjust to it but a low fat diet is recommended because fat digestion is significantly reduced after gall bladder removal.

Q. 5 Correct the statements given below by the right option shown in the bracket against them.

(a) Absorption of amino acids and glycerol takes place in the (small intestine/ large intestine).

(b) The faeces in the rectum initiate a reflex causing an urge for its removal (neural/ hormonal).

(c) Skin and eyes turn yellow in infection (liver/stomach).

(d) Rennin is a proteolytic enzyme found in gastric juice in (infants/ adults).

(e) Pancreatic juice and bile are released through (intestine pancreatic/ hepato-pancreatic duct).

(f) Dipeptides, disaccharides and glycerides are broken down into simple substances in region of small intestines (jejunum/ duodenum).

Ans. (a) Absorption of amino acids and glycerol takes place in the small intestine.

(b) The faeces in the rectum initiate a neural reflex causing an urge for its removal.

(c) Skin and eyes turn yellow in liver infection.

(d) Rennin is a proteolytic enzyme found in infants gastric juice.

(e) Pancreatic juice and bile are released through hepato-pancreatic duct.

(f) Dipeptides, disaccharides and glycerides are broken down into simple substances in the region of small intestine called duodenum.

Q. 6 What are three major types of cells found in the gastric glands? Name their secretions.

Thinking Process These are numerous microscopic, tubular glands formed by the epithelium of the stomach.

Ans. **Gastric glands** possess three major types of cells namely

(i) **Mucous neck cells (Goblet cells)** These cells are present throughout the epithelium of gastrointestinal tract and are involved in the secretion of mucus.

(ii) **Peptic or Chief cells (Zymogenic cells)** These cells are usually basal in location and are involved in the secretion of gastric digestive enzymes such as proenzymes **pepsinogen** and **prorennin**.

(iii) **Parietal or Oxyntic cells** These cells are large and most numerous present on the side walls of the **gastric glands**. They are involved in the secretion of HCl and Castle's Intrinsic Factor (CIF) which is essential for the absorption of vitamin-B_{12} in ileum.

Q. 7 How is the intestinal mucosa protected from the acidic food entering from stomach?

Ans. The mucus secreted by the goblet cells along with bicarbonates from the pancreas play an important role in **lubrication** and **protection** of the mucosal epithelium from excoriation by the highly concentrated hydrochloric acid.

Q. 8 How are the activities of gastro-intestinal tract regulated?

Ans. The activities of the **Gastro-Intestinal Tract** (GIT) are under **neural** and **hormonal** control for proper coordination among different parts. The gastrointestinal tract is innervated by intrinsic nerves as well as by **extrinsic nerves.**

The intrinsic neural system, also called the **enteric neural system** consists of
(i) **Meissner's plexus** situated in the submucosa and
(ii) **Auerbach's plexus** situated in the muscular layer.
The enteric neural system controls most of the gastrointestinal functions like secretion and motility.

The extrinsic innervation of the gut consists of **parasympathetic** and **sympathetic nerves** which can modify the activity of intrinsic neural system in response to reflex activity initiated by GIT or from other body parts.

The sight, smell and the presence of food in the oral cavity can stimulate the secretion of the **saliva** through vagus nerve. Gastric and intestinal secretions are also stimulated by **neural signals**. The muscular activity of different parts of the alimentry canal can also be moderated by neural mechanisms, both local and through CNS. Hormonal control of the secretions of digestive juice is carried out by the local hormones produced by the **gastric** and **intestinal mucosa**. These include **gastrin** (stimulate release of gastric juice), **enterogastrone** (inhibits gastric secrection and motility), **secretin** (decreases gastric secretion), **duodocrinin** (stimulate Brunner's gland) etc.

Q. 9 Distinguish between constipation and indigestion. Mention their major causes.

Ans. **Constipation** is characterised by small amounts of hard, dry bowel movements usually fewer than three times a week. In constipation, the faeces are retained within the rectum as the bowel movement occurs irregularly. The causes of constipation involve water deficiency, lack of roughage in diet, spasm of colon, lack of exercise, emotional stress and certain drugs.

Indigestion is the condition in which the food is not properly digested leading to a feeling of fullness. The cause of indigestion are inadequate enzyme secretion, anxiety, food poisoning, over eating and spicy food consumption.

Q. 10 Describe the enzymatic action on fats in the duodenum.

Ans. Fats are broken down by lipases with the help of bile into di-and monoglycerides and further into fatty acids and glycerol in the duodenum. The reaction involved in this process are as follows

$$\text{Fats} \xrightarrow{\text{Lipases}} \text{Diglycerides} \longrightarrow \text{Monoglycerides}$$

$$\text{Di and Monoglycerides} \xrightarrow{\text{Lipases}} \text{Fatty acids+Glycerol.}$$

Long Answer Type Questions

Q. 1 A person had roti and dal for his lunch. Trace the changes in those during its passage through the alimentary canal.

Thinking Process **Carbohydrates, fats, proteins** and **nucleic acids** occur in food in the form of large and complex insoluble macromolecules or polymers. When these polymers are made to react with water in the presence of enzymes, they break down into simpler monomers. This process is called digestion.

Ans.

1. **Digestion of Roti** (Carbohydrates)

(a) **Digestion of Carbohydrates in the Oral Cavity**

In oral cavity, the roti is mixed with saliva. The saliva contains an enzyme salivary amylase (ptyalin) which converts starch in roti into maltose, isomaltose and small dextrins called α-dextrin. About 30% of starch is hydrolysed in the oral cavity.

$$\text{Starch} \xrightarrow[\text{pH 6.8}]{\text{Salivary Amylase}} \text{Maltose} + \text{Isomaltose} + \text{a -Dextrin}$$

(b) **Digestion of Carbohydrates in the Small Intestine**

The passage of partially digested roti from oral cavity to oesophagus and then to stomach is regulated by peristalsis (the successive waves of muscular contraction in oesophagus). The stomach stores the food for 4-5 hours. The gastric juice does not contain carbohydrate digesting enzyme.

The partially digested food is now called **chyme.** In intestine, following action occurs.

(i) **Action of Pancreatic Juice** Carbohydrates in the chyme are hydrolysed by pancreatic amylase into disaccharides:

$$\text{Polysaccharides (starch)} \xrightarrow{\text{Amylase}} \text{Disaccharides}$$

(ii) **Action of Intestinal Juice** Intestinal juice contain maltase, isomaltase, sucrase (invertase), lactase and α-dextrinase.These enzymes act on food and converting it into simpler compounds like glucose, fructose, galactose, etc.

$$\text{Maltose} \xrightarrow{\text{Maltase}} \text{Glucose} + \text{Glucose}$$

$$\text{Isomaltose} \xrightarrow{\text{Isomaltase}} \text{Glucose} + \text{Gucose}$$

$$\text{Sucrose} \xrightarrow{\text{Sucrase}} \text{Glucose} + \text{Fructose}$$

$$\text{Lactose} \xrightarrow{\text{Lactase}} \text{Glucose} + \text{Galactose}$$

$$\alpha\text{-Dextrins} \xrightarrow{\text{a-dextrinose}} \text{Glucose}$$

2. **Digestion of Protein**

Proteins are made up of amino acids. Proteins are broken down to amino acid during the process of digestion.

Saliva does not contain any protein digesting enzyme. So, protein digestion starts in stomach.

(a) **Digestion of Protein in Stomach** The stomach normally stores food for 4-5 hours. The gastric glands of the stomach secrete gastric juice. Which contains HCl, proenzymes like- pepsinogen and prorennin. Various reactions in stomach are discussed below

$$\text{Pepsinogen} \xrightarrow{\text{HCl}} \underset{\text{(Proenzyme)}}{\text{Pepsin}}$$

$$\text{Proteins} \xrightarrow{\text{Pepsin}} \text{Peptones and proteoses}$$

$$\text{Prorennin} \xrightarrow{\text{HCl}} \underset{\text{(Proenzyme)}}{\text{Rennin}}$$

(b) **Digestion of Protein in Small Intestine** Digestion of protein in small intestine is completed in following steps.

(i) **Action of Pancreatic Juice** The enzymes trypsinogen, chymotrypsinogen and procarboxypeptidase in pancreatic juice are all concerned with the protein digestion.

Some reactions are given below

$$\text{Trypsinogen} \xrightarrow{\text{Enterokinase}} \text{Trypsin}$$

$$\text{Proteins} \xrightarrow{\text{Trypsin}} \text{Dipeptides}$$

$$\text{Chymotrypsinogen} \xrightarrow{\text{Trypsin}} \text{Chymotrypsin}$$

$$\text{Peptones} \xrightarrow{\text{Chymotrypsin}} \text{Dipeptides}$$

$$\text{Procarboxypeptidase} \xrightarrow{\text{Trypsin}} \text{Carboxypeptidases}$$

$$\text{Proteoses} \xrightarrow{\text{Carboxypeptidases}} \text{Dipeptides}$$

(ii) **Action of Intestinal Juice** Intestinal juice contain enzymes enterokinase, amino peptidase and dipeptidase and their actions are given below

$$\text{Peptides} \xrightarrow{\text{Amino peptidase}} \text{Amino acid}$$

$$\text{Dipeptides} \xrightarrow{\text{Dipeptidase}} \text{Amino acid}$$

The macromolecules that are broken down into simpler components are the products of roti and dal (carbohydrates and proteins) which are further absorbed by the villi in intestine and the rest of the undigested food is removed in the form of faeces.

Q. 2 What are the various enzymatic types of glandular secretions in our gut helping digestion of food? What is the nature of end products obtained after complete digestion of food?

Ans. Several enzymatic secretions play crucial roles in the digestion of food in human digestive system. These include gastric juice, pancreatic juice, bile and intestinal juice. Gastric juice is released in stomach whereas the bile, pancreatic juice and the intestinal juice are the secretions released into the small intestine. Pancreatic juice and bile juice are released through the hepato-pancreatic duct. Gastric juice contains hydrochloric acid and proenzyme - pepsinogen and prorennin. HCl maintains a strongly acidic pH which converts these proenzymes into pepsin and rennin (in infants) respectively. These enzymes act on proteins and convert them into simpler form, peptones. The pancreatic juice contains inactive enzymes trypsinogen, chymotrypsinogen, procarboxypeptidases, amylases, lipases and nucleases.

Trypsinogen is activated by an enzyme, enterokinase, (secreted by the intestinal mucosa) into active trypsin, which in turn activates the other enzymes in the pancreatic juice.

The bile released into the duodenum contains bile pigments (billirubin and billiverdin), bile salts, cholesterol and phospholipids but no enzymes. Bile helps in emulsification of fats, *i.e.*, breaking down of the fats into very small micelles. Bile also activates lipases.

The secretions of the brush border cells of the mucosa along with the secretions of the goblet cells constitute the intestinal juice or succus entericus.

This juice contains a variety of enzymes like disaccharidases (*e.g.*, maltase), dipeptidases, lipases, nucleosidases, etc. The mucus along with the bicarbonates from the pancreas protects the intestinal mucosa from acid as well as provide an alkaline medium (pH 7.8) for enzymatic activities. Sub-mucosal glands (Brunner's glands) also help in this process.

Various reactions involved in this process are as follows

(i) Pepsinogen $\xrightarrow{\text{HCl}}$ Pepsin

Proteins $\xrightarrow{\text{Pepsin}}$ Peptones

(ii) Peptones $\xrightarrow[\text{Carboxypeptidase}]{\text{Trypsin/Chymotrypsin}}$ Dipeptides

Dipeptides $\xrightarrow{\text{Dipeptidases}}$ Amino acids

(iii) Carbohydrates $\xrightarrow{\text{Amylase}}$ Disaccharides

Maltose $\xrightarrow{\text{Maltase}}$ Glucose + Glucose

Lactose $\xrightarrow{\text{Lactase}}$ Glucose + Galactose

Sucrose $\xrightarrow{\text{Sucrase}}$ Glucose + Fructose

(iv) Fats $\xrightarrow{\text{Lipases}}$ Diglycerides $\longrightarrow$ Monoglycerides

Di and Monoglycerides $\xrightarrow{\text{Lipases}}$ Fatty acids + Glycerol

(v) Nucleic acids $\xrightarrow{\text{Nucleases}}$ Nucleotides $\xrightarrow{\text{Nucleotidases}}$ Nucleosides

Nucleosides $\xrightarrow{\text{Nucleosidases}}$ Sugars + Bases

The end products of digestion are simpler molecules like amino acids, fatty acids, glucose, nitrogenous bases etc. These are absorbed by the body for energy, growth and repair.

Q. 3 Discuss mechanisms of absorption.

Thinking Process Absorption is the process by which the end products of digestion pass through the intestinal mucosa into the blood or lymph, It is carried out by passive, active or facilitated transport mechanism.

Ans. **Mechanism of absorption for different molecules is as follow**

(i) Small amounts of **monosaccarides** like **glucose, amino acids** and some **electrolytes like chloride ions** are generally absorbed by simple diffusion. The passage of these substances into the blood depends upon the concentration gradient.

(ii) Fructose and some amino acids are absorbed with the help of carrier ions like Na^+. This mechanism of transport is called **facilitated transport** (if no energy is required).

(iii) Transport of water depends on **osmotic gradient**.

(iv) Fatty acids and glycerol being **insoluble,** cannot be absorbed into the blood. They are first incorporated into **micelles** (small droplets) which move into intestinal mucosa. Further, they are reformed into protein coated **fat globules** called **chylomicrons** which are transported to the lymph vessels in the villi. These lymph vessels ultimately release the absorbed substances into the blood stream.

Q. 4 Discuss the role of hepato-pancreatic complex in digestion of carbohydrate, protein and fat components of food.

Ans. The bile duct (from gall bladder and liver) and the pancreatic duct (from pancreas) releases pancreatic juice and bile into the duodenum through the common hepato-pancreatic duct which is guarded by a sphincter called sphincter of Oddi.

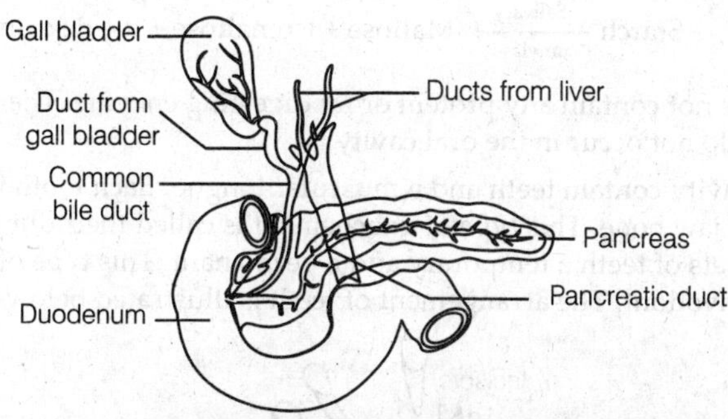

The duct system of liver, gall bladder and pancreas

The pancreatic juice contains inactive enzymes, *i.e.,* **trypsinogen, chymotrypsinogen, procarboxypeptidase, amylase, lipases** and **nucleases.**

The action of hepato-pancreatic secretion on digestion on carbohydrate, proteins and fats are summarised below

(i) Carbohydrates in the chyme are hydrolysed by pancreatic amylase into disaccharides.

$$\text{Polysaccharides (starch)} \xrightarrow{\text{Pancreatic amylase}} \text{Disaccharides}$$

(ii) Fats are emulsified by bile then broken down by lipases into di and monoglycerides.

$$\text{Triglycerides} \xrightarrow{\text{Bile}} \text{Emulsified triglycerids} \xrightarrow{\text{Lipase}} \text{Diglycerides}$$
$$\longrightarrow \text{Monoglycerides}$$

(iii) Proteins in the chyme reaching the intestine are acted upon by the proteolytic enzymes of pancreatic juice. Which break then down into smaller peptides.

$$\left.\begin{matrix}\text{Proteins}\\ \text{Peptones}\\ \text{Proteoses}\end{matrix}\right. \xrightarrow[\text{Carboxy peptidase}]{\text{Trypsin/Chymotrypsin}} \text{Dipeptides}$$

Q. 5 Explain the process of digestion in the buccal cavity with a note on the arrangement of teeth.

Ans. The buccal cavity performs two major functions *i.e.,* mastication of food and facilitation of swallowing

Firstly, food gets mixed with saliva which lubricates and softens the food and chewing process breaks the food into smaller pieces.
Buccal cavity is also involved in the digestion of carbohydrates.

Digestion of carbohydrates starts in the buccal cavity. The food is mixed with saliva which contains salivary amylase. This enzyme converts starch into maltose, isomaltose and α –dextrins. About 30% of the starch in food is hydorlysed in the buccal cavity.

$$\text{Starch} \xrightarrow[\text{amylase}]{\text{Salivary}} \text{Maltose} + \text{Isomaltose} + \alpha - \text{dextrins}$$

Saliva does not contain any protein or fat digesting enzyme. Therefore, their digestion do not occur in the oral cavity.

The oral cavity contain teeth and a muscular tongue. Each tooth is embedded in a socket of jaw bone. This type of attachement is called thecodont. The human have two sets of teeth a temporary and a permanant. This type of dentition is called diphyodont. The arrangement of teeth is illustrated below.

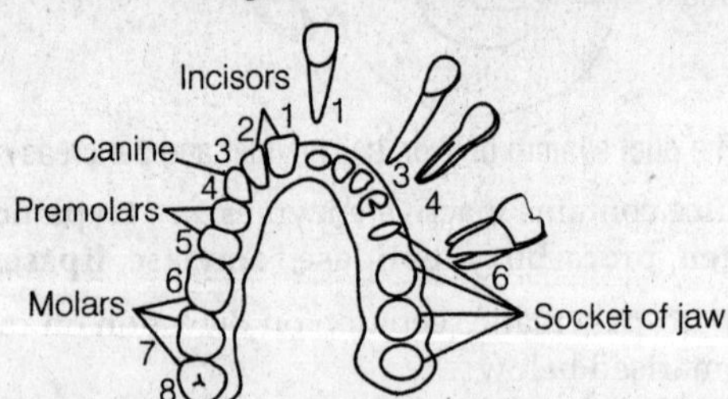

Arrangement of different types of teeth in the jaws on one side the sockets on the other side

Chapter

17 Breathing and Exchange of Gases

Multiple Choice Questions (MCQs)

Q. 1 Respiration in insects is called direct because

(a) the cells exchange O_2/CO_2 directly with the air in the tubes

(b) the tissues exchange O_2/CO_2 directly with coelomic fluid

(c) the tissues exchange O_2/CO_2 directly with the air outside through body surface

(d) tracheal tubes exchange O_2/CO_2 directly with the haemocoel which then exchange with tissues

Ans. ***(a)*** Insects have a network of tubes (tracheal tubes) to transport atmospheric air within the body. They have small openings called spiracles that lead to trachae. The cells exchange O_2/CO_2 directly with the air in the spiracles present in insect's body.

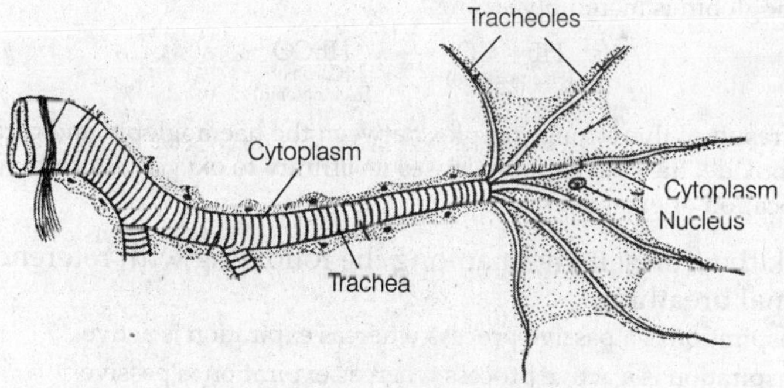

Trachea and tracheoles in insects

Q. 2 Regarding the functions of our respiratory system, mark the wrong entry.

(a) Humidifies the air

(b) Warms up the air

(c) Exchange of gases

(d) Cleans up the air

Ans. ***(d)*** While the respiratory system does have mechanisms to filter and remove particles (such as through the nose and mucous membranes), the primary function of "cleaning up the air" is more accurately attributed to the upper respiratory system, particularly the nose and trachea, and not a core function of the entire respiratory system.

Other options are key functions of respiratory system.

Q. 3 A person suffers punctures in his chest cavity in an accident, without any damage to the lungs. Its effect could be

(a) reduced breathing rate
(b) rapid increase in breathing rate
(c) no change in respiration
(d) cessation of breathing

Ans. *(d)* The movement of air into and out of the lungs is carried out by creating a pressure gradient between the lungs and the atmosphere. The pressure within the lungs is less than the atmospheric pressure so there is a negative pressure in the lungs with respect to atmospheric pressure.

A puncture in the chest cavity affects this pressure gradient maintained by the lungs and thus may cause cessation of breathing.

Q. 4 It is known that exposure to carbon monoxide is harmful to animals because

(a) it reduces CO_2 transport
(b) it reduces O_2 transport
(c) it increases CO_2 transport
(d) it increases O_2 transport

Thinking Process The reaction between haemoglobin and CO_2 is reversible, whereas it is irreversible in case of CO.

Ans. *(b)* Haemoglobin consist of a protein globin and pigment heme. The four portion of iron in the haemoglobin molecule combine with molecule of oxygen. It is an easy reversible reaction to form oxyhaemoglobin

$$Hb + O_2 \rightleftharpoons HbO_2$$

Whereas, the complex formed by the reaction of carbon monooxide and haemoglobin is incredibly strong

$$\underset{\text{(Haemoglobin)}}{Hb} + CO \longrightarrow \underset{\text{(Carboxy haemoglobin)}}{HbCO}$$

As a result of this strong complex between the haemoglobin and carbon monooxide, the haemoglobin looses its affinity to oxygen which may lead to suffocation or even death.

Q. 5 Mark the true statement among the following with reference to normal breathing

(a) inspiration is a passive process whereas expiration is active
(b) inspiration is a active process whereas expiration is passive
(c) inspiration and expiration are active processes
(d) inspiration and expiration are passive processes

Ans. *(b)* Inspiration is a active process whereas expiration is a passive process. Inspiration occur when the muscles of diaphragm contract to increase the overall volume of thoracic cavity.

This causes the pressure within the lungs (intra-pulmonary pressure) to become less in comparison to the atmospheric pressure, *i.e.*, there is a negative pressure in the lungs with respect to atmospheric pressure forcing the air to move into the lungs. As the muscles use energy for contraction, inspiration is called an active process.

Whereas, during the expiration diaphragm muscles relax without the use of energy this increases the intra pulmonary pressure and it becomes higher than the atmospheric pressure and air rushes out. Thus, it is a passive process.

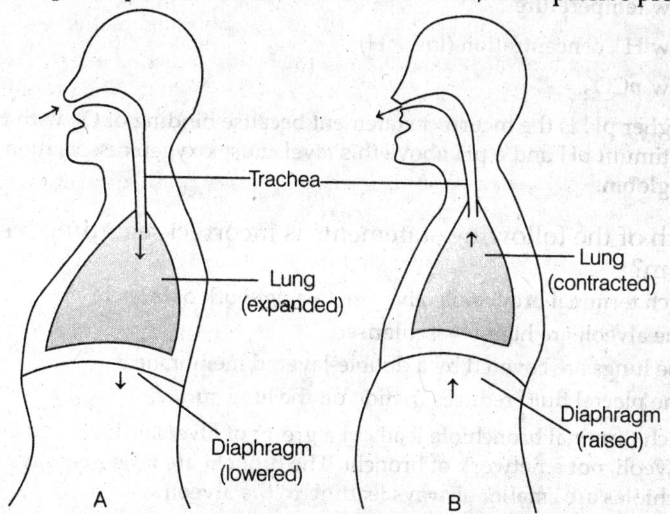

Mechanism of breathing A. Inspiration (chest cavity enlarged)
B. Expiration (chest cavity reduced)

Q. 6 A person breathes in some volume of air by forced inspiration after having a forced expiration. This quantity of air taken in is

(a) total lung capacity

(b) tidal volume

(c) vital capacity

(d) inspiratory capacity

Ans. *(c)* The maximum volume of air that a person can breathe in after forced expiration or the maximum volume of air that a person can breathe out after forced inspiration is called vital capacity

VC = IRV (Inspiratory reserve volume) + ERV (Expiratory reserve volume) + TV (Tidal volume)

The value of vital capacity varies from 4000 mL to 4800 mL.

On the other hand, tidal volume is the air inspired or expired during normal breathing.

Total lung capacity is the volume of air present in lungs and respiratory passage after maximum inspiration. Whereas, inspiratory capacity is total volume of air that a person can inspire after normal inspiration.

Q. 7 Mark the incorrect statement in context to O_2 binding to Hb

(a) higher pH

(b) lower temperature

(c) lower pCO_2

(d) higher pO_2

Ans. ***(a)*** There are various factors which affect the binding of O_2 with Hb.

These factors are

(i) Low temperature

(ii) Low H^+ concentration (low pH)

(iii) Low pCO_2

So, higher pH is the incorrect statement because binding of O_2 with Hb require an optimum pH and a pH above this level cause oxygen dissociation from hemoglobin.

Q. 8 Which of the following statements is incorrect regarding respiratory system?

(a) Each terminal bronchiole give rise to a network of bronchi

(b) The alveoli are highly vascularised

(c) The lungs are covered by a double-layered membrane

(d) The plecral fluid reduces friction on the lung surface

Ans. ***(a)*** Each terminal bronchiole leads to a group of alveolar ducts and eventually to the alveoli, not a network of bronchi. The bronchi are larger airways while the branchioles are smaller airways leading to the alveoli.

The other statement are correct regarding respiratory system.

Q. 9 Incidence of emphysema a respiratory disorder is high in cigarette smokers. In such cases

(a) the bronchioles are found damaged

(b) the alveolar walls are found damaged

(c) the plasma membrane is found damaged

(d) the respiratory muscles are found damaged

Ans. ***(b)*** **Emphysema** is a chronic disorder where the alveolar walls are damaged due to the infection or irreversible and abnormal distension. It is a respiratory disorder caused by cigarette smoking and inhalation of other smoke or toxic substances over a period of time.

Q. 10 Respiratory process is regulated by certain specialised centres in the brain. One of the following listed centres can reduce the inspiratory duration upon stimulation.

(a) Medullary inspiratory centre (b) Pneumotaxic centre

(c) Apneustic centre (d) Chemosensitive centre

Ans. ***(b)*** **Pneumotaxic Centre** Located in the dorsal part of pons varolii in the brain can reduce the duration of inspiration and thus alter the respiratory rate.

Whereas Apneustic Centre is located in the lower part of pons varolii is responsible for promoting inspiration process.

Chemosensitive Centre is situated adjacent to the rhythm centre which is highly sensitive to CO_2 and hydrogen ions. Increase in CO_2 and H^+ in body and activates this centre for the elimiration of CO_2 and H^+

Medullary Inspiratory Centre is a specialised region present in medulla of the brain. and is primarily responsible for regulating the respiratory rhythm.

Q. 11 CO_2 dissociates from carbaminohaemoglobin when

(a) pCO_2 is high and pO_2 is low
(b) pO_2 is high and pCO_2 is low
(c) pCO_2 and pO_2 are equal
(d) None of the above

Thinking Process CO_2 is carried by haemoglobin as carbamino haemoglobin. This binding is related to the partial pressure of CO_2.

Ans. ***(b)*** When, the pCO_2 is low and pO_2 is high (as in the lung alveoli) dissociation of CO_2 from carbamino-haemoglobin takes place, CO_2 which is bound to haemoglobin, from the tissue, is delivered at the alveoli, to be exhaled.

Exchange of gases takes place between tissue capillary and body tissue. Capillary cells with high pO_2 causes diffusion of O_2 into tissue cells *via* tissue fluid on the other hand high pCO_2 in the body tissue cells causes diffusion of CO_2 into tissue capillary *via* tissue fluid.

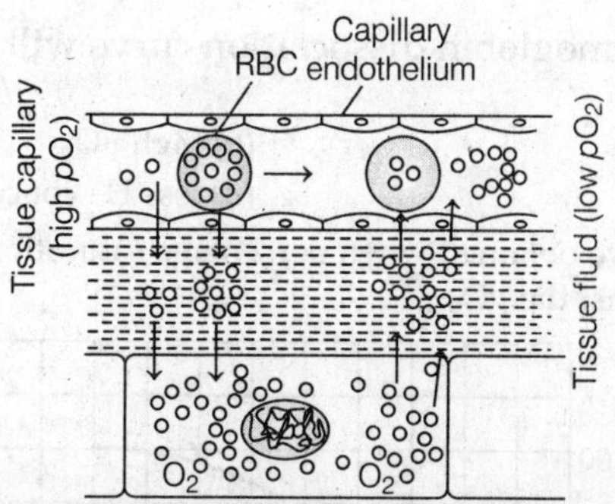

Cell showing low pO_2 high pCO_2

Q. 12 In breathing movements, air volume can be estimated by

(a) stethoscope
(b) hygrometer
(c) sphygmomanometer
(d) spirometer

Ans. ***(d)*** **Spirometer** is the device used to measure the volume of air involved in breathing movements and it also helps in clinical assessment of pulmonary functions.

On the other hand stethoscope is a medical device used for listening the internal sounds of an animal or human body.

Hygrometer is a device used for measuring the moisture content in the atmosphere, *i.e.*, humidity.

Sphygmomanometer is a device that is used to measure **blood pressure**.

Q. 13 From the following relationships between respiratory volume and capacities, mark the correct option.

(i) Inspiratory Capacity (IC) = Tidal Volume + Residual Volume

(ii) Vital Capacity (VC) = Tidal Volume (TV) + Inspiratory Reserve Volume (IRV) + Expiratory Reserve Volume (ERV).

(iii) Residual Volume (RV) = Vital Capacity (VC) – Inspiratory Reserve Volume (IRV)

(iv) Tidal Volume (TV) = Inspiratory Capacity (IC) – Inspiratory Reserve Volume (IRV)

Codes

(a) (i) Incorrect, (ii) Incorrect, (iii) Incorrect, (iv) Correct
(b) (i) Incorrect, (ii) Correct, (iii) Incorrect, (iv) Correct
(c) (i) Correct, (ii) Correct, (iii) Incorrect, (iv) Correct
(d) (i) Correct, (ii) Incorrect, (iii) Correct, (iv) Incorrect

Ans. (b) (i) **Inspiratory Capacity** (IC) = Tidal Volume + Inspiratory Reserve Volume (TV + IRV).

(ii) **Vital Capacity** (VC) = Tidal Volume + Inspiratory Reserve Volume + Expiratory Reserve Volume. (TV + ERV + IRV)

(iii) **Residual Volume** (RV) Volume of air remaining in the lungs after a forcible expiration.

(iv) **Tidal Volume** (TV) Volume of air inspired or expired during a normal respiration.

Q.14 The oxygen-haemoglobin dissociation curve will show a right shift in case of

(a) high pCO_2
(b) high pO_2
(c) low pCO_2
(d) less H^+ concentration

Ans. ***(a)*** A **sigmoid curve** obtained when percentage saturation of haemogblobin with O_2 is plotted against the pO_2.

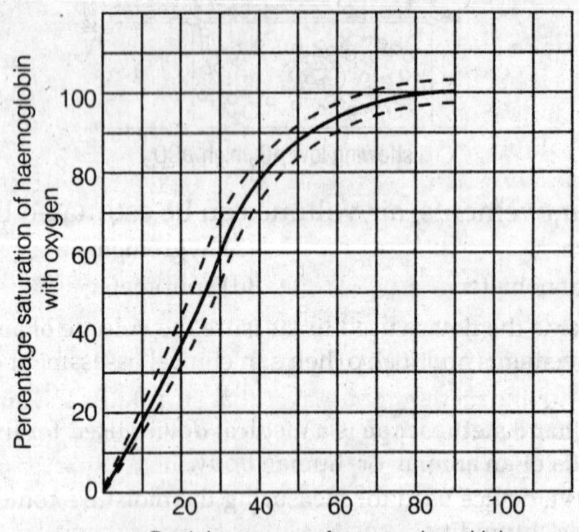

Oxygen dissociation curve

The oxygen haemoglobin dissociation curve is shifted to right under following condition.

(i) Decrease in partial pressure of oxygen.
(ii) Increase in partial pressure of carbondioxide.
(iii) Increase in hydrogen concentration.
(iv) Decrease in pH.
(v) Increased body temperature.

Mistake Alert! *Be cautious when identifying factors that cause a right shift in the oxygen-hemoglobin dissociation curve. A right shift indicates that hemoglobin releases oxygen more readily, and it's influenced by factors like increased* pCO_2*,* H^+ *concentration (acidity), and temperature.*

Q.15 Match the following columns.

	Column I		Coulmn II
A.	Earthworm	1.	Moist cuticle
B.	Insects	2.	Gills
C.	Fishes	3.	Lungs
D.	Birds/Reptiles	4.	Trachea

Codes

	A	B	C	D		A	B	C	D
(a)	2	1	4	3	(b)	1	4	2	3
(c)	1	3	2	4	(d)	1	2	4	3

Ans. ***(b)*** Earthworm respire through their moist cuticle and insects respire through trachea. Fishes respire through **gills,** and birds/reptiles respire through **lungs**.

Very Short Answer Type Questions

Q. 1 Define the following terms?

(a) Tidal volume (b) Residual volume (c) Asthma

Thinking Process The quantity of air that lung can receive, hold or expel under different condition is called pulmonary volume. Combination of two or more pulmonary volume is called pulmonary capacities.

Ans. (a) **Tidal Volume** (TV) is the volume of air inspired or expired during normal breath. This is about 500 mL, *i.e.*, a healthy man inspire or expire about 6000 to 8000 mL of air per minute.

(b) **Residual Volume** (RV) is the volume of air remaining in the lungs even after a forcible expiration. It is about 1100 mL to 1200 mL.

(c) **Asthma** It is a chronic disease caused by an allergic reaction to foreign substances. The major symptoms are difficulty in breathing, wheezing and coughing due to the inflammation of bronchi and bronchioles.

Q. 2 A fluid filled double membranous layer surrounds the lungs. Name it and mention its important function.

Ans. A fluid filled double membranous layer that surrounds the lungs is called **pleura**, and fluid between these layers is pleural fluid. The outer pleural membrane is in close contact with the thoracic lining whereas, the inner pleural membrane is in contact with the lung surface. These collectively reduce friction during lung movement allowing the lungs to expand and contract smoothly.

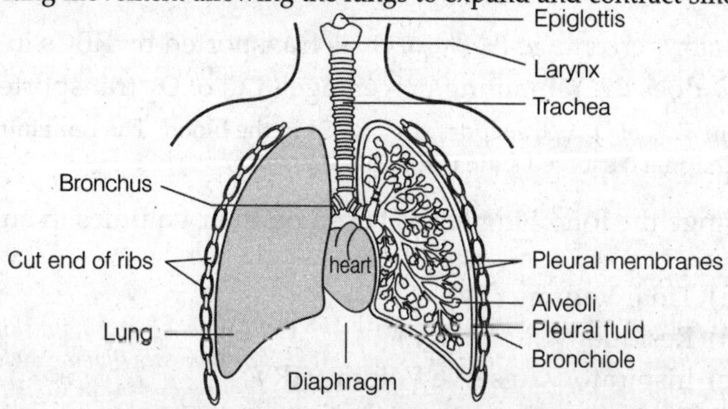

Diagrammatic view of human respiratory system of man

Q. 3 Name the primary site of exchange of gases in our body?

Ans. The primary site for the exchange of gases in our body is **alveoli**. There are approximately 300 millions of alveoli collectively in both the lungs. These alveoli have very thin wall made of squamous epithelium, with an extensive network of blood capillaries.

The proximity of these blood capillaries to the alveolar walls facilitates the easy exchange of gases. Each alveolus is also called as miniature lung due to its essential role in gas exchange.

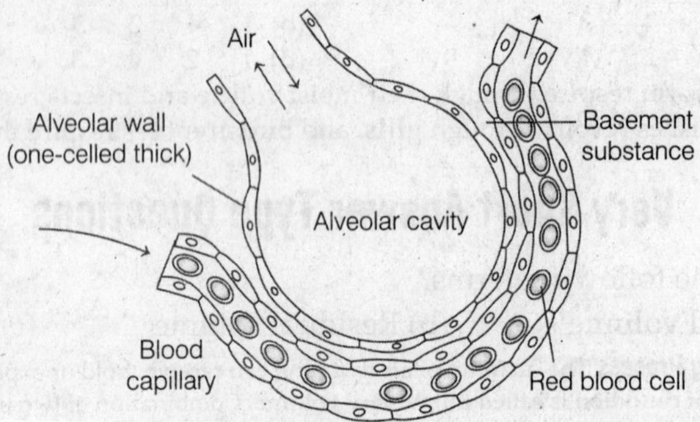

A diagram of a section of an alveolus with a pulmonary capillary

Q. 4 Cigarette smoking causes emphysema. Give reason.

Ans. Emphysema is a chronic disorder of respiratory system, where inflation or abnormal distension of the alveoli and damage of alveolar wall occurs. Cigarette smoking and the inhalation of toxic substances over the time causes the damaging of septa between the alveoli. This damage results in the breakdown of elastic tissue in the lungs.

Hence, the respiratory surface decreases, thus leading to the **emphysema**. Which causes shortness of breath, production of sputum, chronic bronchitis, etc.

Q. 5 What is the amount of O_2 supplied to tissues through every 100 mL of oxygenated blood under normal physiological conditions?

Ans. Every 100 mL of oxygenated blood can deliver around 5 mL of O_2 to the tissue under normal physiological conditions.

Q. 6 A major percentage (97%) of O_2 is transported by RBCs in the blood. How does the remaining percentage (3%) of O_2 transported?

Ans. About 97% of O_2 is transported by RBCs in the blood. The remaining 3% of O_2 is carried in a dissolved state through the plasma.

Q. 7 Arrange the following terms based on their volumes in an ascending order.

(a) Tidal Volume (TV)

(b) Residual Volume (RV)

(c) Inspiratory Reserve Volume (IRV)

(d) Expiratory Capacity (EC)

Ans. The ascending order is TV < RV < EC < IRV

(i) **Tidal Volume (TV)** = 500 ml

(ii) **Residual Volume (RV)** = 1100 ml to 1200 ml

(iii) **Expiratory Capacity (EC)**

$$EC = TV + ERV$$
$$= 500 + (1100 \text{ to } 1200) \text{ ml.} = 1600 \text{ to } 1700 \text{ ml.}$$

(iv) **Inspiratory Reserve Volume** (IRV) = 2500 to 3000 ml.

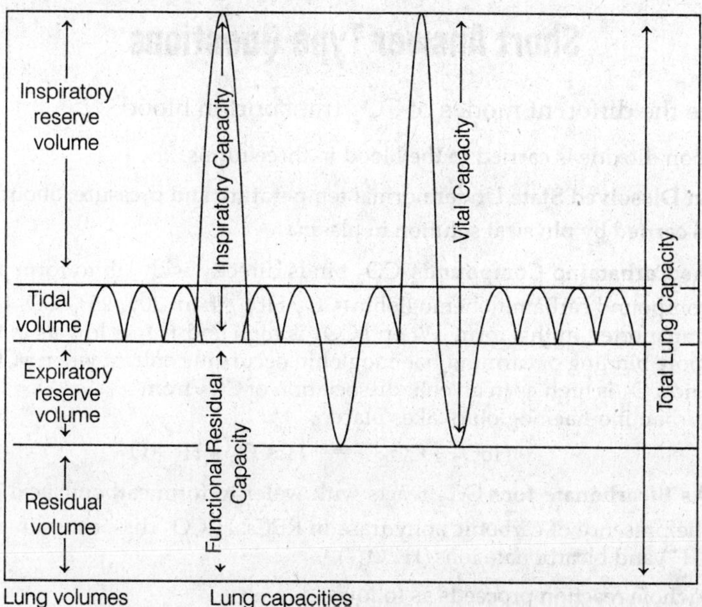

Diagram depicting pulmonary volume and pulmonary capacities

Q. 8 Complete the missing terms

(a) Inspiratory Capacity (IC) = ... + IRV

(b) ... = TV + ERV

(c) Functional Residual Capacity (FRC) = ERV + ...

Ans. **(a)** Inspiratory Capacity (IC) = (TV) + (IRV) [Tidal Volume + Inspiratory Reserve Volume]

(b) Expiratory Capacity (EC) = (TV + ERV) [Tidal Volume + Expiratory Reserve Volume]

(c) Functional Residual Capacity (FRC) = ERV + RV [Expiratory Reserve Volume + Residual Volume]

Q. 9 Name the organs of respiration in the following organisms.

(a) Flatworm .... (b) Birds ....

(c) Frog .... (d) Cockroach ....

Thinking Process Mechanism of breathing vary among different groups of animals depending on their habitats and levels of organisation.

Ans. (a) **Flatworm** General body surface (b) **Birds** Lungs

(c) **Frog** Lungs and moist skin (d) **Cockroach** Tracheal tubes

Q. 10 Name the important parts involved in creating a pressure gradient between lungs and the atmosphere during normal respiration.

Ans. The diaphragm and a specialised set of **external** and **internal intercostals muscles (located** between the ribs) are responsible for the generation of pressure gradient during normal respiration.

Short Answer Type Questions

Q. 1 State the different modes of CO_2 transport in blood.

Ans. Carbon dioxide is carried in the blood in three forms, *i.e.*,

(i) **In Dissolved State** Under normal temperature and pressure, about 7% of CO_2 is carried by physical solution in plasma.

(ii) **As Carbamino Compounds** CO_2 binds directly with Hb to form an unstable compound carbaminohemoglobin (CO_2 Hb) About 20%-25% CO_2 is transported in this form. When pCO_2 is high and pO_2 is low as in the tissues, more binding of carmino-haelmoglobin occurs in contrast when pCO_2 is low and pO_2 is high as in alveoli, dissociation of CO_2 from carbamino-haemoglobin takes place.

$$HbO_2 + CO_2 \rightleftharpoons HbCO_2 + H^+ + O_2$$

(iii) **As Bicarbonate Ions** CO_2 reacts with water to form carbonic acid (H_2CO_3) in the presence of carbonic anhydrase in RBCs. H_2CO_3 dissociates into hydrogen (H^+) and bicarbonate ions (HCO_3^-).

The whole reaction proceeds as follows

$$CO_2 + H_2O \underset{\text{Anhydrase}}{\overset{\text{Carbonic}}{\rightleftharpoons}} \underset{\text{Carbonic acid}}{H_2CO_3}$$

$$\underset{\text{Carbonic acid}}{H_2CO_3} \rightleftharpoons \underset{\text{Hydrogen ion}}{H^+} + \underset{\text{Bicarbonate ion}}{HCO_3^-}$$

The reaction mainly occur in RBCs as they contain high concentration of enzyme carbonic anhydrase. A small amount of this reaction also occurs in plasma.

Q. 2 Compared to O_2, diffusion rate of CO_2 through the diffusion membrane per unit difference in partial pressure is much higher. Explain.

Thinking Process Diffusing capacity can be defined as the volume of gas, that diffuses through the membrane per minute for a pressure difference of 1 mm Hg. It is further dependent on the solubility of the diffusing gases.

Ans. Since, the solubility rate of CO_2 is 20-25 times higher than that of O_2, the amount of CO_2 that can diffuse through the diffusion membrane per unit difference in a partial pressure is much higher compared to that of O_2. This explains why CO_2 diffuses more rapidly than O_2 across alveolar membrane.

Q. 3 For completion of respiration process, write the given steps in sequential manner.

(a) Diffusion of gases (O_2 and CO_2) across alveolar membrane.
(b) Transport of gases by blood.
(c) Utilisation of O_2 by the cells for catabolic reactions and resultant release of CO_2.
(d) Pulmonary ventilation by which atmospheric air is drawn in and CO_2 rich alveolar air is released out.
(e) Diffusion of O_2 and CO_2 between blood and tissues.

Ans. The correct sequence of events in the process of respiration is as follows:

(a) Diffusion of gases (O_2 and CO_2) across alveolar membrane.
(b) Transport of gases by blood.
(c) Utilisation of O_2 by the cells for catabolic reactions and resultant release of CO_2.
(d) Pulmonary ventilation by which atmospheric air is drawn in and CO_2 rich alveolar air is released out.
(e) Diffusion of O_2 and CO_2 between blood and tissues.

Q. 4 Differentiate between

(a) Inspiratory and expiratory reserve volume
(b) Vital capacity and total lung capacity.
(c) Emphysema and occupational respiratory disorder.

Ans. Difference between these are as follows

(a)

Inspiratory Reserve Volume	Expiratory Reserve Volume
It is an additional volume of air, a person can inspire by a forcible inspiration. It ranges between 2500 mL to 3000 mL.	It is an additional volume of air a person can expire by a forcible expiration. It ranges between 1000 mL to 1100 mL.

(b)

Vital Capacity	Total Lung Capacity
Vital capacity is the maximum volume of air a person can breathe in after a forced expiration. This includes ERV, TV and IRV or the maximum volume of air a person can breathe out after a forced inspiration. *i.e.*, VC = ERV + IRV + TV	Total lung capacity is the total volume of air accommodated in the lungs at the end of a forced inspiration. This includes RV, ERV, TV and IRV or vital capacity + residual volume. *i.e.*, TLC = RV + (ERV +IRV +TV) or VC +RV

(c)

Emphysema	Occupational Respiratory Disorder
Emphysema is a chronic disorder of respiratory system, in which alveolar walls are damaged due to which respiratory surface is decreased. Cause of emphysema is cigarette smoking.	It is caused by the long-term exposure to dust produced by stone grinding or breaking which result to inflammation, leading to fibrosis and serious lung damage. Protective masks are provided to workers in such industries to reduce the risk of exposure.

Long Answer Type Questions

Q. 1 Explain the transport of O_2 and CO_2 between alveoli and tissue with diagram.

Ans. **Transport of O_2 and CO_2 between alveoli and tissues:**

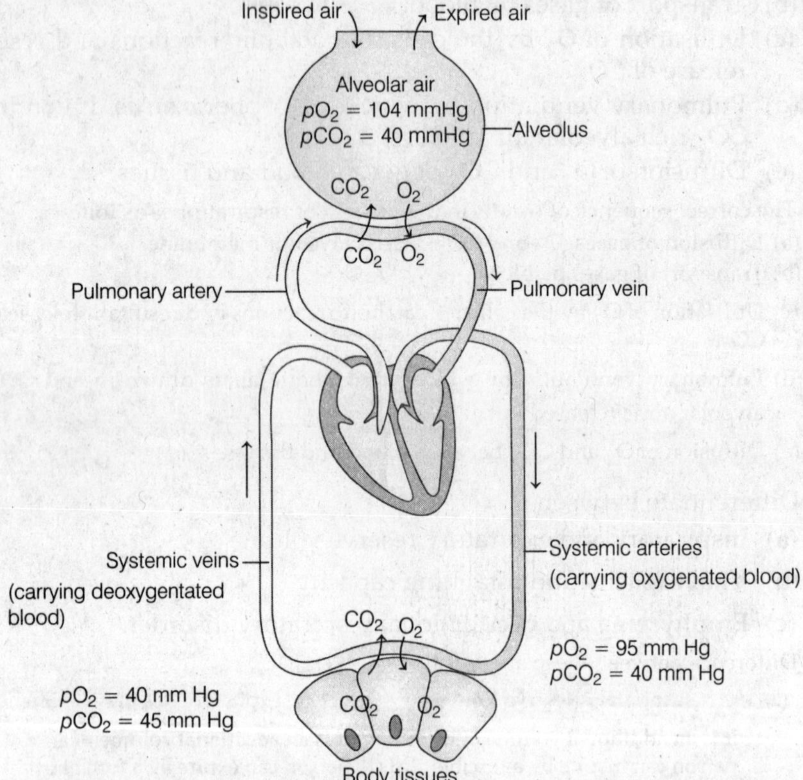

Diagrammatic representation of exchange of gases at the alveolus and the body tissue with blood and transport of oxygen and carbon dioxide

(i) In the alveoli (lungs):

- **Oxygen (O_2)** Oxygen from the inhaled air diffuses across the thin walls of the alveoli into the capillaries, where it binds to hemoglobin in red blood cells.
- **Carbon dioxide (CO_2)** CO_2 which is produced by cellular metabolism, diffuses from the blood into the alveoli, to be exhaled.

(ii) **In the bloodstream**

- **Oxygen transport** Once oxygen enters the bloodstream, it binds to haemoglobin in red blood cells to form oxyhemoglobin. This allows oxygen to be transported throughout the body.
- **Carbon Dioxide transport** CO_2 is carried in three ways: dissolved in plasma, bound to hemoglobin as carbaminohemoglobin and in the form of bicarbonate ions (HCO_3^-) in plasma. The majority of CO_2 is transported as bicarbonate ions.

(iii) **In the tissues**

- **Oxygen release** When blood reaches the tissues, the lower oxygen level cause oxygen to dissociate from hemoglobin and diffuse into the tissues for cellular respiration.
- **Carbon dioxide uptake** As cells produce CO_2 during metabolism, it diffused into the blood, where it is carried back to the lungs for exhalation.

Q. 2 Explain the mechanism of breathing with neat labelled sketches.

Ans. **Mechanism of Breathing**

Breathing involves two phase :

- **Inspiration** (inhalation) and **expiration** (exhalation)
- **Inspiration** During inspiration, the diaphragm contracts and flattens, increasing the volume of the thoracic cavity. Simultaneously, the external intercostal muscles contract, causing the ribs to lift and expand the chest. As the volume of the thoracic cavity increases, the air pressure inside the lungs decreases, causing air to move from the higher pressure (atmosphere) into the lungs (air flows from higher pressure to low pressure).
- **Expiration** During expiration, the diaphragm relaxes and moves upward and the intercostal muscles also relaxes, which reduces the volume of thoracic cavity. This increases the pressure inside the lungs, forcing air out into the atmosphere.

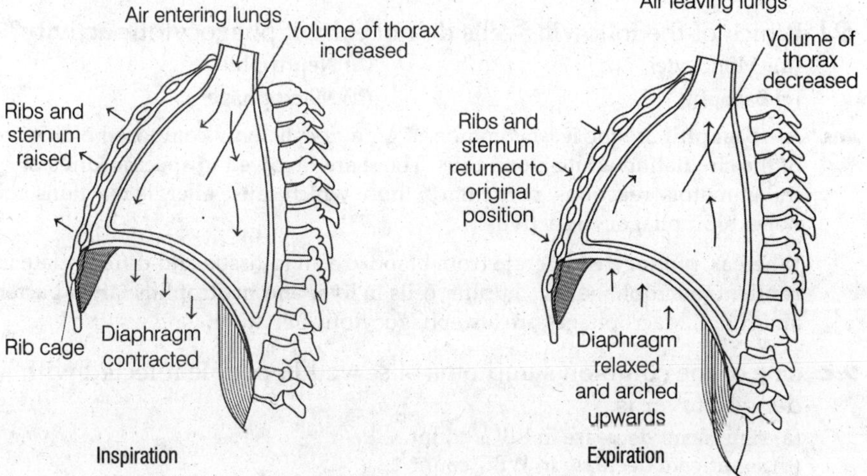

Q. 3 Explain the role of neural system in regulation of respiration.

Ans. Human beings have a significant ability to maintain and moderate the respiratory rhythm to suit the demands of the body tissue. This is achieved through the neural system. Respiration can be regulated by neural system in following ways

(i) A specialised centre present in the medulla region of the brain called **respiratory rhythm centre** is primarily responsible for regulating respiration process. Another centre present in the pons region of the brain called **pneumotaxic centre**, can modify the functions of the respiratory rhythm centre. Neural signal from pneumotaxic centre, can reduce the duration of inspiration and thereby alter the respiratory rate.

(ii) A **chemosensitive area** is situated adjacent to the rhythm centre is highly sensitive to CO_2 and hydrogen ions. Increase in the concentration of these substances activates this area, which in turn signals the rhythm centre to make necessary adjustments in the respiratory process by which these substances can be eliminated.

(iii) Receptors associated with aortic arch and carotid artery also recognise changes in CO_2 and H^+ concentration and send necessary signals to the rhythm centre for remedial action. The role of oxygen in the regulation of respiratory rhythm is relatively less significant compared to CO_2 and H^+ levels.

Chapter

18 Body Fluids and Circulation

Multiple Choice Questions (MCQs)

Q.1 Which of the following cells do not exhibit phagocytotic activity?

(a) Monocytes
(b) Neutrophil
(c) Basophil
(d) Macrophage

Ans. *(c)* **Basophil** are the least common of granulocyte, only composed of 0.5% to 1% of the circulating white blood cells. These are involved in specific kinds of inflammatory reactions, particularly those which cause allergic reactions and do not exhibit phagocytic activity.

Whereas, **monocytes** migrate from bloodstream to tissue and differentiate into resident macrophage, *e.g.*, kupffer cells in liver and neutrophils target bacteria and fungi. Macrophages are also phagocytotic in nature.

Q.2 One of the common symptoms observed in people infected with dengue fever is

(a) significant decrease in RBCs count
(b) significant decrease in WBC count
(c) significant decrease in platelets count
(d) significant increase in platelets count

Ans. *(c)* The low platelet count leads to life threatening condition and is one of the most common symptoms observed in people infected with dengue fever whereas, other options are not the symptoms of dengue fever.

Q.3 Which among the following is correct during each cardiac cycle?

(a) The volume of blood pumped out by the Rt and Lt ventricles is same
(b) The volume of blood pumped out by the Rt and Lt ventricles is different
(c) The volume of blood received by each atrium is different
(d) The volume of blood received by the aorta and pulmonary artery is different

Ans. ***(a)*** **Cardiac Cycle** is one cycle of contraction and relaxation of the cardiac muscle. The contraction phase is called the systole while the relaxation phase is called the diastole.

The purpose of cardiac cycle is to effectively pump the blood. The right ventricle pumps the volume of deoxygenated blood to the lungs through pulmonary artery. After the oxygenation of blood the volume of blood carried through pulmonary vein is pumped through left ventricle into the aorta and transferred to the entire body.

This pumping of blood, is about the same and any mismatch in volumes ejected by the ventricles (*i.e.*, right ventricle pump more blood than left or *vice versa*) can result in the heart failure. Thus, all the other options are wrong.

Q.4 Cardiac activity could be moderated by the autonomous neural system. Tick the correct answer.

(a) The parasympathetic system stimulates heart rate and stroke volume
(b) The sympathetic system stimulates heart rate and stroke volume
(c) The parasympathetic system decreases the heart rate but increase stroke volume
(d) The sympathetic system decreases the heart rate but increase stroke volume

Ans. ***(b)*** Neural signals through the sympathetic nerves can increase the rate of the heart beat, the strength of ventricular contraction and thereby stimulating the cardiac output. Hence, sympathetic system is involved in stimulating heart rate and stroke volume. Therefore, other options are wrong.

Q.5 Mark the pair of substances among the following which is essential for coagulation of blood.

(a) Heparin and calcium ions
(b) Calcium ions and platlet factors
(c) Oxalates and citrates
(d) Platelet factors and heparin

Ans. ***(b)*** Certain factors released by the tissues at the site of injury can initiate coagulation process.

Calcium ions and platelet factor play a role in the first step of coagulation which is as follows

(i) At the site of an injury, the blood platelets disintegrate and release a phospholipid, called platelet factor 3 (platelet thromboplastin).
(ii) Injured tissues also release a tissue factor called thromboplastin.
(iii) These two factors combine with calcium (Ca^{2+}) ions and certain proteins of the blood plasma to form an enzyme called pro-thrombinase.
(iv) Prothrombinase catalyzes prothrombin into active protein called thrombin.
(v) Thrombin further converts inative fibrinogens into fibrin in the blood plasma.
(vi) Then the long fibres of fibrin form a dense network upon wound and trap blood corpuscles RBCs, WBCs and platelets) to form a clot.

And the other options are wrong.

Q.6 ECG depicts the depolarisation and repolarisation processes during the cardiac cycle. In the ECG of a normal healthy individual one of the following waves is not represented.

(a) Depolarisation of atria (b) Repolarisation of atria

(c) Depolarisation of ventricles (d) Repolarisation of ventricles

Ans. ***(b)*** A normal ECG represents P-wave atrial depolarisation, QRS complex-ventricular depolarisation and T-wave ventricular repolarisation. Therefore, atrial repolarisation is not represented in an electrocardiogram (ECG).

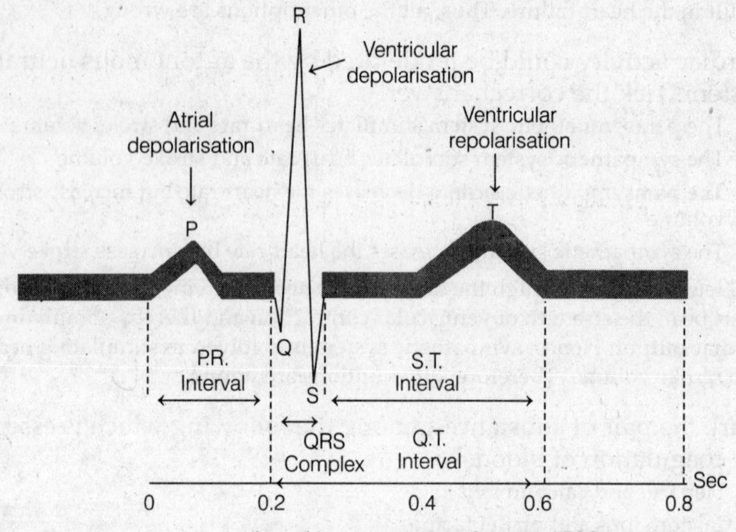

A graphic representation of a normal ECG

Q.7 Which of the following type of cells lack nucleus in humans?

(a) Erythrocytes (b) Neutrophils

(c) Eosinophils (d) Monocytes

- **Concept Insight** In humans, certain blood cells lack a nucleus, which is a characteristic feature of erythrocytes (red blood cells). This absence helps maximize space for hemoglobin, enhancing oxygen transport. On the other hand, most white blood cells, such as neutrophils, eosinophils and monocytes, retain nucleus.

Ans. ***(a)*** The erythrocytes on the RBCs (Red Blood Corpuscles) in humans lack nucleus. Absence of nucleus in the cell reduces the O_2 consumption by the cell in various cellular activities. Therefore, the cell is able to transport maximum amount of O_2 to other cells of the body.

Other cells like neutrophils, eosinophils and monocytes possess nucleus of varied shape and size as shown below.

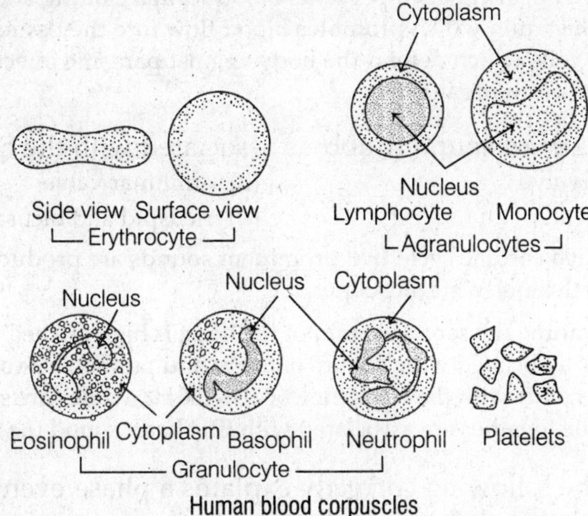

Human blood corpuscles

Q.8 Which one of the following blood cells is involved in antibody production.

(a) B-lymphocytes (b) T-lymphocytes
(c) RBC (d) neutrophils

Thinking Process Lymphocytes are of two major types, i.e., 'B and T' lymphocytes. Both B and T lymphocytes are responsible for immune responses in the body.

Ans. *(a)* **B-lymphocytes** Their principal function is to make antibodies against soluble antigens that are important in regulating humoral immunity. On the other hand RBCs transport oxygen, T-lymphocytes play central role in cell mediated immunity and neutrophils acts as phagocytes.

Q.9 The cardiac impulse is initiated and conducted further upto ventricle. The correct sequence of conduction of impulse is

(a)	SA Node	AV Node	Purkinje fiber	AV Bundle
(b)	SA Node	Purkinje fiber	AV Node	AV Bundle
(c)	SA Node	AV Node	AV Bundle	Purkinje fiber
(d)	SA Node	Purkinje fiber	AV Bundle	AV Node

Ans. *(c)* **SA Node** It is situated in the walls of the right auricle near the opening of the superior vena cava. In myogenic heart the contraction is initiated by SA node.

AV Node The wave of contraction reaches AV node which is stimulated to emit an impulse of contraction spreading to the ventricular muscle *via* the **atrio ventricular bundle** and then to the **Purkinje fibres** stimulating heart beat.

Q.10 The cells involved in inflammatory reactions are

(a) basophils (b) neutrophils (c) eosinophils (d) lymphocytes

Thinking Process Alteration in cells and tissue as a result of disease includes degenerative and infiltrative changes and all are involved in inflammatory reactions.

Ans. *(d)* Lymphocytes are white blood cells responsible for immune response of the body. These cells recognise and react with antigens. Basophils contain anticoagulant heparin which pervents blood form a clotting and also contain vasodilator histamin which promotes blood flow into the tissues. Eosinophils are white blood cells which defend the body against parasitic infections. Neutrophils phagocytose forign organisms.

Q.11 The second heart sound (dubb) is associated with the closure of

(a) tricuspid valve
(b) semilunar valve
(c) bicuspid valve
(d) tricuspid and bicuspid valve

Ans. *(b)* During each cardiac cycle two prominent sounds are produced which can be easily heard through a **stethoscope**.

Semilunar value The second sound of the heart is high pitched 'DUB' It is caused by vibrations associated with closure of aortic and pulmonary valves. It lasts for an about 0.12 seconds with the frequency of 100-150 Hz, while tricuspid value and bicuspid value together are associated with first heart sound (*i.e.*, lubb).

Q.12 Which of the following correctly explains a phase/event in cardiac cycle in a standard electrocardiogram?

(a) QRS complex indicates atrial contraction.
(b) QRS complex indicates ventricular contraction.
(c) Time between S and T represents atrial systole.
(d) P-wave indicates beginning of ventricular contraction.

Ans. *(b)* **QRS Complex** begins after a fraction of second after the P wave. It begins as a small downward deflection (Q) and continuous as a large upright (R) and triangular wave, ending as downward wave (S) at its base.

This represents ventricular depolarisation (ventricular contraction). Thus, the other options are wrong.

P_{wave} – represent atrial depolarisation

T_{wave} – represent ventricular repolarisation

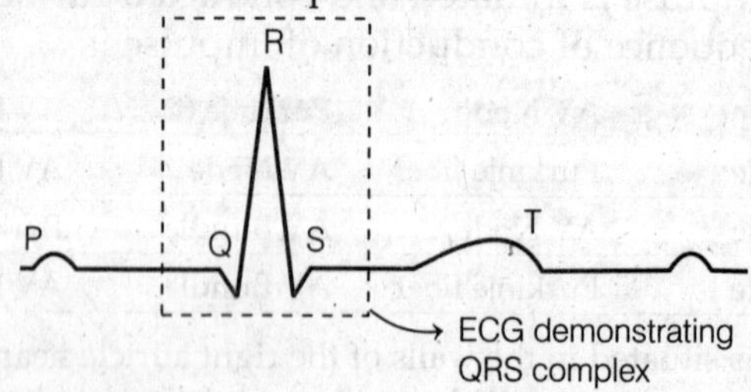

Q.13 Which of the following statements is incorrect?

(a) A person of 'O' blood group has anti 'A' and anti 'B' antibodies in his blood plasma.
(b) A person of 'B' blood group can't donate blood to a person of 'A' blood group.
(c) Blood group is designated on the basis of the presence of antibodies in the blood plasma.
(d) A person of AB blood group is universal recipient.

Thinking Process Blood Groups is determined by I gene. There are three alleles I^A, I^B, I^o of this gene. Protein produced by I^A and I^B alleles are called A antigen and B antigen respectively.

Ans. *(c)* ABO blood grouping in human is based on the presence or absence of two surface antigens on the RBCs namely A and B. Similarly, the plasma of different individuals contain two natural antibodies. This distribution of antigens and antibodies results in the four groups of blood *A, B, AB* and *O*, which are as follows

Blood Groups and Donors Compatibility

Blood Group	Antigens on RBCs	Antibodies in Plasma	Donor's Group
A	A	anti-B	A, O
B	B	anti-A	B, O
AB	A, B	nil	AB, A, B, O
O	nil	anti-A, B	O

Thus blood group O is universal donor and blood group AB in universal recipient and the other options are correct.

Q.14 What would be the cardiac output of a person having 72 heart beats per minute and a stroke volume of 50 mL?

(a) 360 mL (b) 3600 mL (c) 7200 mL (d) 5000 mL

Ans. *(b)* **3600 ml Cardiac Output**

The volume of blood pumped by left ventricle per minute is called the cardiac output.

It is determined by multiplying the heart rate with the volume of blood pumped out by each ventricle during each beat, which is called as **stroke volume.**

Cardiac output = Heart rate × Stroke volume = 72 × 50 = 3600 ml

Q.15 Match the following columns.

	Column I		Column II
A.	Lymphatic system	1.	Carries oxygenated blood
B.	Pulmonary vein	2.	Immune response
C.	Thrombocytes	3.	To drain back the tissue fluid to the circulatory system
D.	Lymphocytes	4.	Coagulation of blood

Codes

	A	B	C	D		A	B	C	D
(a)	2	1	3	4	(b)	3	1	4	2
(c)	3	1	2	4	(d)	2	1	3	4

Ans. *(b)* The correct matching is as listed below

	Column I		Column II
A.	Lymphatic system	3.	To drain back the tissue fluid to the circulatory system
B.	Pulmonary vein	1.	Carries oxygenated blood
C.	Thrombocytes	4.	Coagulation of blood
D.	Lymphocytes	2.	Immune response

Q.16 Read the following statements and choose the correct option.

Statement I Atria receive blood from all parts of the body and lungs which subsequently flows to ventricles.

Statement II Action potential generated at sino-atrial node passes from atria to ventricles.

(a) Action mentioned is statement I is dependent on action mentioned in Statement II

(b) Action mentioned in statement II is dependent on action mentioned in Statement I

(c) Action mentioned in statement I and II are independent of each other.

(d) Action mentioned in statement I and II are synchronous.

Ans. *(d)* The superior vena cava pours venous blood into right atria where as left atria receive blood from lungs. This blood then flows into ventricles. The contraction of muscles of atria arise from SA nodes and passes to AV node and then to the Purkinje fibres.

Therefore, action mentioned in statement I and II are synchronous, while the other options are wrong.

Very Short Answer Type Questions

Q.1 Name the blood component which is viscous and straw coloured fluid.

Ans. **Plasma** is a straw coloured, viscous fluid constituting of nearly 55 % of the blood, 90-92% of plasma is water and proteins contributes approx 6-8% . The plasma proteins contains **fibrinogen, globulins** and **albumins.**

Q.2 Complete the missing word in the statement given below

(a) Plasma without .... factors is called serum.

(b) .... and monocytes are phagocytic cells.

(c) Eosinophils are associated with .... reactions.

(d) .... ions play a significant role in clotting.

(e) One can determine the heart beat rate by counting the number of .... in an ECG.

Ans. (a) Plasma without **clotting factors** is called serum.

(b) **Neutrophils** and monocytes are phagocytic cells.

(c) Eosinophils are associated with **allergic** reactions.

(d) **Calcium** ions play a significant role in clotting.

(e) One can determine the heart beat rate by counting the number of **QRS complex** in an ECG.

Q.3 Given below is the diagrammatic representation of a standard ECG. Label its different peaks.

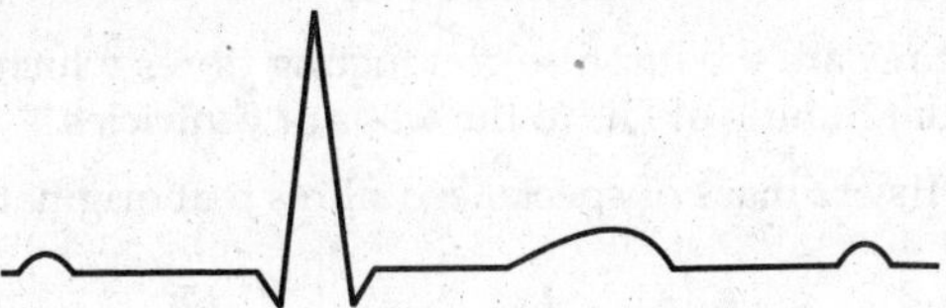

Ans. The representation of a standard ECG diagram

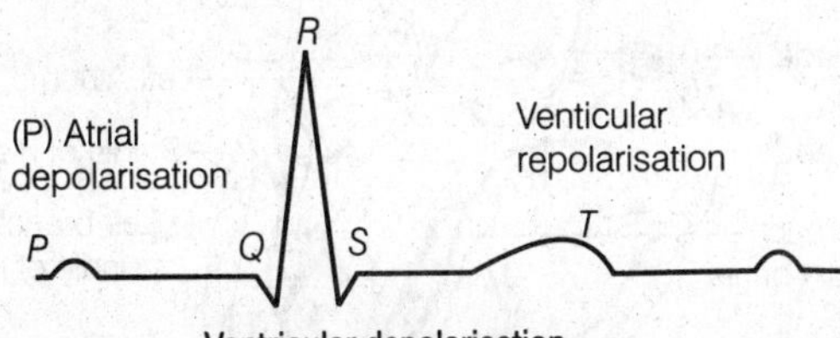

P = Electrical excitation (depolarisation)
Q = Initial phase of ventricular depolarisation
R = Ventricular depolarisation repolarisation
S = Completion of ventricular depolarisation
T = Return of ventricles from excited to normal state

Q.4 Name the vascular connection that exists between the digestive tract and liver.

Ans. The unique vascular connection that, exists between the digestive tract and liver is called **hepatic portal system**.

Q.5 Given below are the abnormal conditions related to blood circulation. Name the disorders

(a) Acute chest pain due to failure of O_2 supply to heart muscles

(b) Increased systolic pressure

Ans. (a) **Angina** also called as 'angina pectoris'. A symptom of acute chest pain that appears when there is no enough oxygen is reaching to the heart muscle. Angina can occur in men and women of any age but it is more common among the middle aged and elder people. It occurs due to condition that affect the blood flow (hypertension etc.)

(b) **High Blood Pressure** (hypertension) is the term for blood pressure that is higher than normal (120/80). In this measurement 120 mm Hg is the systolic, or pumping pressure and 80 mm Hg is the diastolic or resting pressure. Increased systolic pressure, *i.e.*, 140/80 or 150/80, shows hypertension. High blood pressure leads to heart diseases and also affects vital body organs like brain and kidney.

Q.6 Which coronary artery diseases is caused due to narrowing of the lumen of arteries?

Ans. **Atherosclerosis** is the coronary artery disease caused due to the narrowing of the lumen of arteries. The narrowing of arteries occurs due to deposition of calcium, fat, cholesterol and fibrous tissue affecting the supply of blood to the heart muscles.

Q.7 Define the following terms and give their location?
(a) Purkinje fibre (b) Bundle of His

Ans. (a) **Purkinje fibres** are the impulse conducting fibres which relay the contraction impulses from Bundle of His to the walls of ventricles.

(b) **Bundle of His** are mass of specialised fibres that originates from the AV node.

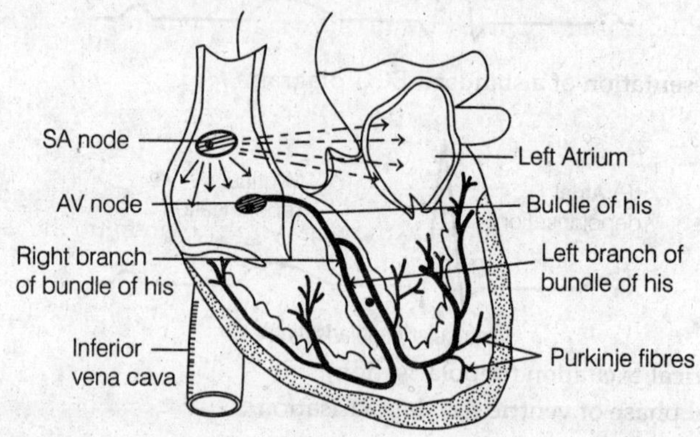

Diagram depicting purkinje fibre and bundle of his in heart

Q.8 State the functions of the following in blood
(a) fibrinogen (b) globulin
(c) neutrophils (d) lymphocytes

Ans. (a) **Fibrinogens** are inactive components of blood plasma. Under the action of enzyme thrombin it is converted into insoluble fibrin threads which form a clot in which dead and damaged elements of blood are trapped.

(b) **Globulins** are primarily involved in immunity, *i.e.*, defence mechanisms of the body.

(c) **Neutrophils** are phagocytic cells which destroy foreign organisms entering the body.

(d) **Lymphocytes** are specialised cells which are responsible for the immune responses in the body. Two major types of lymphocytes, that are involved in this process are B and T-lymphocytes.

Q.9 What physiological circumstances lead to erythroblastosis foetalis?

Ans. A protein named as **rhesus factor** (Rh antigen), is present on the surface of red blood corpuscles. Individual having this protein are called **Rh positive** (Rh^+) while others who do not have this protein are known as **Rh negative** (Rh^-) (dominant).

Erythroblastosis Foetalis occurs due to Rh incompatibility between the foetus and mother during pregnancy. Rh antigen of the foetus do not get exposed to the Rh^- blood of the mother in the first pregnancy. However, during the delivery of the first child, there is a possibility of exposure of the maternal blood to small amounts of the Rh^+ blood from the foetus. In such cases, the mother starts preparing antibodies against Rh antigen in her blood and during her subsequent pregnancies the Rh antibodies from the mother (Rh^-) leak into the blood of the foetus (Rh^+) resulting in the destruction of foetal RBCs. This could be fatal to the foetus or could cause severe anaemia and jaundice , even may lead to the death of the foetus.

Q.10 Explain the consequences of a situation in which blood does not coagulate.

Ans. Blood exhibits coagulation or clotting in response to an injury or trauma.

Coagulation prevents excessive loss of blood from the body. In its absence there could be huge loss of blood, which can be fatal.

In case of decrease in platelets count, the coagulation process can be affected, resulting in blood loss, in case of injury

Q.11 What is the significance of time gap in the passage of action potential from sino-atrial node to the ventricle?

Ans. The time gap in the passage of action potential from sino-atrial node to the ventricles allows atria to contract and empty their blood into the ventricles before ventricular contraction begin.

Q.12 How will you interpret an electrocardiogram (ECG) in which time taken in QRS complex is higher?

Ans. **Electrocardiogram** (ECG) is a graphical representation of the electrical activity of the heart during a cardiac cycle. A patient is connected to the machine with three electrical leads (one to each wrist and one to the left ankle) that continuously monitor the heart activity. For a detailed evaluation of the heart functions multiple leads are attached to the chest region.

The **QRS complex** represents the depolarisation of the ventricles, which initiates the ventricular contraction. The contraction starts shortly after Q and marks the beginning of the systole. The time taken in QRS complex is 0.12 second in normala ECG.

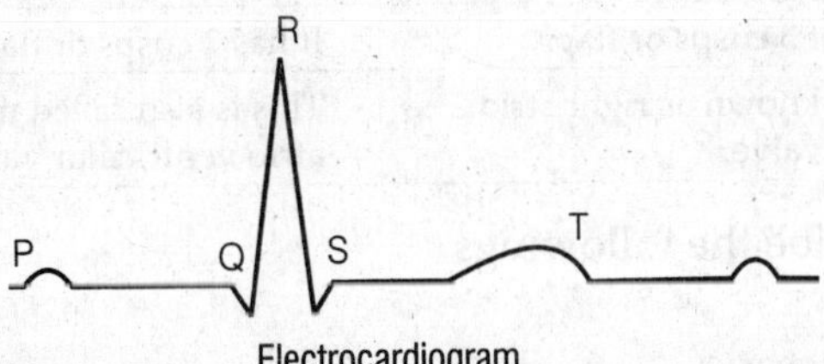

Electrocardiogram

If the QRS complex takes longer than normal on an ECG, it typically indicates delay in ventricular contraction.

Short Answer Type Questions

Q.1 The walls of ventricles are much thicker than atria. Explain.

Ans. The structure of heart of fishes, reptiles, birds and mammals show many structures of evolutionary significance. Thicker walls of **ventricles** is one of them.

Ventricles have thick walls because these are mainly involved in pumping the blood to the body parts with considerable pressure.

The walls of the left ventricle is about 3 times thicker from the right ventricle, while the atria acts as a collecting chambers for the blood returning to the heart and they only have to force the blood into the ventricles that lies just below them thus atria have thin walls.

Q.2 Differentiate between
(a) blood and lymph
(b) basophils and eosinophils
(c) tricuspid and bicuspid valve

Ans. (a) Difference between blood and lymph are as follows

Blood	Lymph
Blood is a connective tissue which have erythrocytes, leucocytes and platelets present in fluid called plasma.	Lymph is also a connective tissue which is devoid of RBC but has large number of WBC (leucocytes) in plasma.
It flows through the blood vessels.	It flows only through lymphatic system and is also found extracellularly inside the tissue.

(b) Difference between basophils and eosinophils are as follows

Basophils	Eosinophils
Secrete histamine, serotonin, heparin, included in immune response and inflammation.	Contains enzymes that can resist infections and allergic reactions.
These are normally 0.5-1% is the blood.	These are 2-3% is the blood.

(c) Difference between tricuspid valve and bicuspid valve are as follows

Tricuspid Valve	Bicuspid Valve
This valve separate the right atria from right ventricle.	This valve separates the left atria from left ventricle.
It is made of 3 cusps or flaps.	It has 2 cusps or flaps.
This is also known as right atrio ventricular valve.	This is also called mitral valve or left atrio ventricular valve.

Q.3 Briefly describe the followings
(a) anaemia
(b) angina pectoris
(c) atherosclerosis
(d) hypertension
(e) heart failure
(f) erythroblastosis foetalis

Ans. (a) **Anaemia** is a condition in which there is decrease in the number of RBC than the normal amount or **haemoglobin** than the normal value in blood leading to a reduced capacity to carry oxygen to fissues. This is the most common disorder of the blood.

(b) **Angina Pectoris** ocurs when there is blockage in coronary artery, thus insufficient supply of blood reaches to heart muscles. This results in chest pain, anxiety, pale skin, profuse sweating and vomitting. The anginal pain usually starts in the centre of the chest and spreads down to the left arm which last for only few second.

(c) **Atherosclerosis** is the deposition of cholesterol in the inner lining of arteries called atherosclerotic plaque. Sometimes arteries are completely blocked, this result in stroke or heart attack.

(d) **Hypertension** is sometimes also called as arterial hypertension. The blood pressure in the arteries gets elevated. It can be classified into primary hypertension which has no obvious medical reason and secondary hypertension which is caused by various conditions which affect kidneys, arteries heart or endocrine system.

(e) **Heart Failure** is the state of heart when it does not pump blood effectively enough to meet the needs of the body.

(f) **Erythroblastosis foetalis** is a haemolytic disease of new borns. It is an allo-immune condition that develops in foetus when IgG antibodies produced by mother pass through placenta and attack the fetal RBC causing reticulocytosis and anaemia. It develops due to Rh incompatibility between the mother and fetus. In a man with RH^+ blood and women with Rh^-, blood the second pregnancy foetus may have this problem due to IgG accumulation in women during first child development and delivery.

Q.4 Explain the advantage of the complete partition of ventricle among birds and mammals and hence leading to double circulation.

Ans. The birds and mammals have evolutionary advancement as far as structure of heart is concerned. They need more oxygen to live in terrestrial habitat.

In these animals, the blood received by left and right auricles is oxygenated and deoxygenated respectively. It passes towards the left and right ventricles and thus the oxygenated and deoxygenated blood is not mixed. The ventricles pump oxygenated deoxygenated blood without mixing. Thus, two separate circulatory pathways are found. This type of blood circulation is called as **double circulation,** which include **systemic** and **pulmonary circulation**. Both pathway ensures that oxygen is efficiently delived to the tissues.

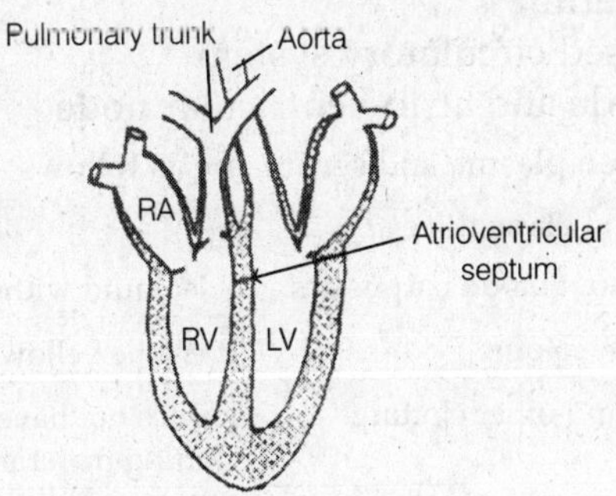

Heart of Bird and Mammal

Q.5 What is the significance of hepatic portal system in the circulatory system?

Ans. There is special vascular connection that exists between the digestive tract and liver in all chordates and is called as **hepatic portal system.** This system carries blood from intestine to the liver before it is delivered to the **systemic circulation.**

Significance of hepatic portal system in circulatory system

(i) Blood that comes from alimentary canal contain glucose, amino acids and other nutrients. The liver absorbs excess of fats and glucose to be used at the time of starvation when blood passess through liver.

(ii) Harmful nitrogenous wastes like ammonia is converted into urea which is later removed by kidney.

(iii) Liver produces proteins which are transported through blood circulation *(e.g.,* fibrinogen for blood clotting).

Mistake Alert! *Don't confuse the hepatic portal system with general circulation; its role is to direct nutrient-rich blood from the digestive organs to the liver for processing and detoxification, rather than distributing it throughout the body.*

Q.6 Explain the functional significance of lymphatic system?

Ans. **Human Lymphatic System** comprises of lymph, lymphatic capillaries, lymphatic vessels, lymphatic ducts and lymphatic nodes.

Functional significance of lymphatic system

(i) It removes CO_2 and other metabolic waste from the tissue where blood vessels cannot reach.

(ii) Lymphatic blood capillaries in the intestine are called lacteals, which help in absorption of fats.

(iii) Lymph filters out through lymph nodes where phagocytotic WBC and macrophages are present in a good number which destroys harmful microorganisms and remove foreign particles from the body fluid.

(iv) Collects excess interstitial fluid and returns it the blood stream preventing fluid build up in the tissues, mainting fluid balance in the body.

Q.7 Write the features that distinguish between the two

(a) plasma and serum

(b) open and closed circulatory system

(c) sino-atrial node and atrio-ventricular node

Ans. (a) Difference between plasma and serum are as follows

Blood Plasma	Blood Serum
It is the fluid without blood corpuscles.	It is liquid without clotting elements.
It is faint yellow in colour.	It is pale yellow.
It has fibrinogen and other clotting materials.	It does not have fibrinogen and other clotting materials.
It takes part in blood clotting.	It does not take part in blood clotting.

(b) Difference between open and closed circulatory system are as follows

Open Circulatory System	Closed Circulatory System
Open circulation occurs in arthropods and molluscs.	It occurs in annelids (earthworms), some molluscs and all vertebrates.
The blood is not completely enclosed within vessels, the heart pumps blood through arteries into large cavities or sinuses, where it mixes with the interstitial fluid and bathes the cells of the body.	In closed circulatory system, materials move between the blood and interstitial fluid through thin walls capillaries.
Circulation is **slower** in an open system, because some of the blood pooled in sinuses and, the heart is unable to build up enough pressure to make the blood flow rapidly.	Blood flows at a **high pressure** in a closed circulatory system.
Respiratory pigment, if present, is dissolved in the plasma, no red corpuscles are present.	Respiratory pigment is present which may be dissolved in the plasma but is usually contained red blood corpuscles.

(c) Difference between sino atrial node and atrio-ventricular node are as follow

SA Node	AV Node
It is the small mass of specialised muscle cells in the wall of right atrium near the opening of vena cava.	It is situated near the fibrous ring between the right atrium and right ventricle of the heart.
It initiates and maintains the heart beat.	It is the pathway through which electrical impulses can pass.

Q.8 Thrombocytes are essential for coagulation of blood. Comment.

Ans. Blood is a connective tissue. It has many cellular components. Thrombocytes or platelets are one of them. Thrombocytes or platelets are found in blood. They are formed in bone marrow and their life span is 7-10 days. These are essential for clotting.

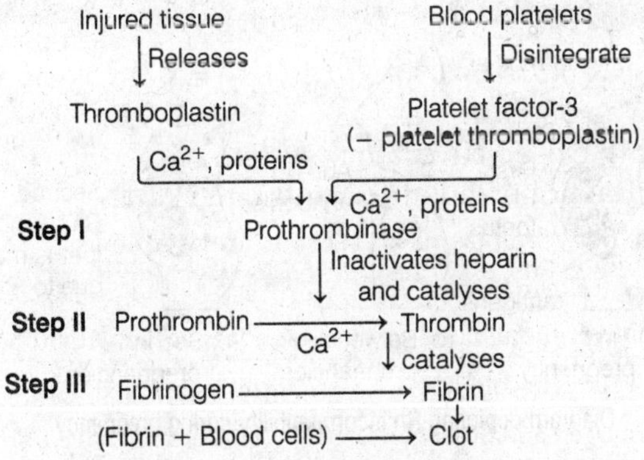

Role of thrombocytes in blood coagulation

When an injury is caused in the blood vessel, bleeding starts, and the platelets are disintegrated to release the clotting factor 3 called thromboplastin. This in presence of Ca^{2+} ions activate prothrombinase. A series of reactions ultimately occurs which causes blood to clot and plug the injured blood vessel thus preventing further loss of blood.

Q.9 Answer the following

(a) Name the major site where RBCs are formed.

(b) Which part of heart is responsible for initating and maintaining its rhythmic activity?

(c) What is specific in the heart of crocodiles among reptilians?

Ans. **(a)** Red Bone marrow

(b) SA Node (Sino Atrial Node)

(c) Reptile have 3 chambered heart with an exception of crocodile which possess 4 chambered heart, due to the partial division of ventricle through a septum.

Long Answer Type Questions

Q.1 Explain Rh-incompatibility in humans.

Ans. Rh antigen is observed on the surface of RBCs of majority (nearly 80%) of humans. Such individuals are called Rh positive (Rh^+) and those individuals where this antigen is absent are called Rh negative (Rh^-).

Both Rh^+ and Rh^- individuals are phenotypically normal. The problem in them arises during blood **transfusion** and **pregnancy**.

(i) **Incompatibility During Blood Transfusion** The blood transfusion of Rh^+ blood to the person with Rh^- blood causes an immune reaction and destruction of the red blood corpuscles of the donor.

(ii) **Incompatibility During Pregnancy** When the Rh-ve mother is pregnant with a Rh + ve foetus it leads to Rh incompatibilty. The Rh antigens of the foetus do not get exposed to the Rh^- ve blood of the mother in the first pregnancy as the two bloods are well separated by the placenta.

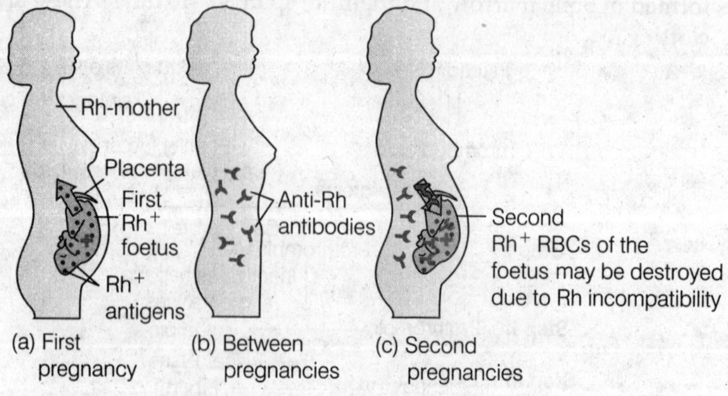

Diagram depicting Rh incompatibility during pregnancy

But in the subsequent, pregnancy the anti Rh factors (antibodies) of the mother destroy the foetal red blood corpuscles.

This result in the **Haemolytic Disease of the New Born** (HDN), called as **erythroblastosis foetalis**. In some cases new born may survive but will be anaemic and may also suffer with jaundice. This condition can be avoided by administering anit-Rh antibodies to the mother immediately after the delivery of the first child.

Q.2 Describe the events in cardiac cycle. Explain 'double circulation'.

Ans. The cardiac cycle consist of one cycle of contraction and relaxation place in the cardiac muscles. During the heart beat there is a contraction and relaxation of atria and ventricles. The contraction phase is referred as **systole** while the relaxation phase is called as **diastole.**

The successive events of the cardiac cycle are briefly described as below

(i) **Atrial Systole** The atria contract due to the wave of contraction, stimulated by the SA node. The blood is forced into the ventricles as the bicuspid and tricuspid valves are open.

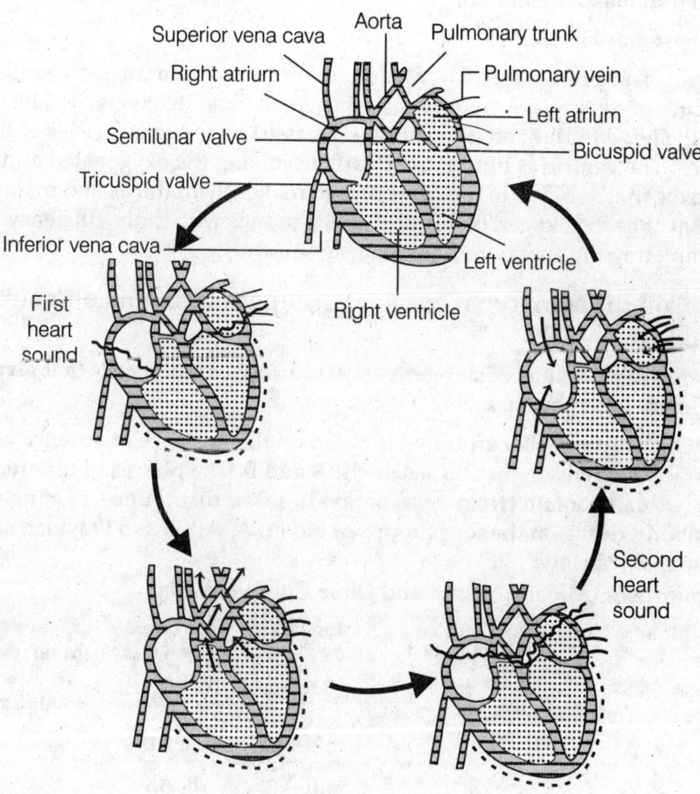

(ii) **Beginning of Ventricular Systole** The contraction of ventricles begin due to the wave of contraction stimulated by AV node. This led to the closing of bicuspid and tricuspid valve producing first heart sound, *i.e.*, lub.

(iii) **Complete Ventricular Systole** After ventricular contraction, the blood flows into the pulmonary trunk and aorta as the semilunar valves open.

(d) **Beginning of the Ventricular Diastole** The ventricles relax and the semilunar valves are closed. This cause the second heart sound, *i.e.*, dub.

(e) **Complete Ventricular Diastole** The opening of tricuspid and bicuspid valves due to fall in pressure of ventricles and blood flows from the atria into the ventricles. Contraction of the heart does not cause this blood to flow, backward direction, due to the fact that the pressure within the relaxed ventricles is less than that of the atria and veins.

The duration of **cardiac cycle** last for 0.8 sec.

In double circulation, the blood passes twice through the heart during one complete cycle. *Double circulation is carried out by two ways*

(i) Pulmonary circulation

(ii) Systemic circulation

Significance of Double Circulation In birds and mammals, two separate circulatory pathways are present. Oxygenated and deoxygenated blood received by the left and right atria respectively passes on to the ventricles of the same sides. The ventricles pump it out without mixing the oxygenated and deoxygenated blood in the heart, which makes them (birds and mammals) more efficient as the oxygen is supplied to the tissues with more efficiency, thus completing the energy requirement significantly.

Q.3 Explain different types of blood groups and donor compatibility by making a table.

Ans. There are more than 30 antigens on the surface of blood cells that give rise to different blood groups.

ABO Grouping ABO grouping is based on the presence or absence of two surface antigens on the RBCs namely, A and B. The plasma of different individuals contain two natural antibodies. The distribution of antigen and antibody results in the four groups of blood, A, AB, B and O which are explained in the table below.

Human ABO Blood Groups and their Compatibility

Blood Group	Antigens on Red Blood Corpuscles	Antibodies in Blood Plasma	Recipient group (can give blood to	Donor's group (can receive blood from)
A	A	Anti-B	A, AB	A, O
B	B	Anti-A	B, AB	B, O
AB	AB	None	AB	AB, A, B, O
O	None	Anti-A, Anti-B	AB, A, B, O	O

From the above table it is evident that group 'O' blood can be donated to persons with any other blood group and hence 'O' group individuals are called **'Universal donors'**. Person with 'AB' blood can accept blood from persons with AB, as well as the other groups of blood. Therefore, such persons are called **'Universal recipients'**.

Q.4 Write short note on the following.
(a) Hypertension (b) Coronary Arteries Disease

Ans. (a) **Hypertension** Commonly known as high blood pressure is a condition in which blood pressure in the arteries is consistenly elevated. The high blood pressure can harm heart, brain, kidneys and eyes. High blood pressure is most common disease affecting the heart and blood vessels. Blood pressure is considered normal at 120/80. When it goes beyond 140 mm Hg and 90 mm Hg it is called hypertension or high blood pressure.

Causes of Hypertension

(i) Blockage in the coronary heart vessels.

(ii) Tobacco smoking speeds up heart rate. It constricts the blood vessels and raises blood pressure.

(b) **Coronary Artery Disease** (CAD) It is caused due to the deposition of fatty substances on the arterial wall causing **atherosclerotic plaques**. The lumen of artery decreases, thus obstructing the blood flow and sometimes completely blocks the artery resulting into heart attack.

Q.5 In the diagrammatic presentation of heart given below, mark and label. SAN, AVN, AV bundles, bundle of His and Purkinje fibres.

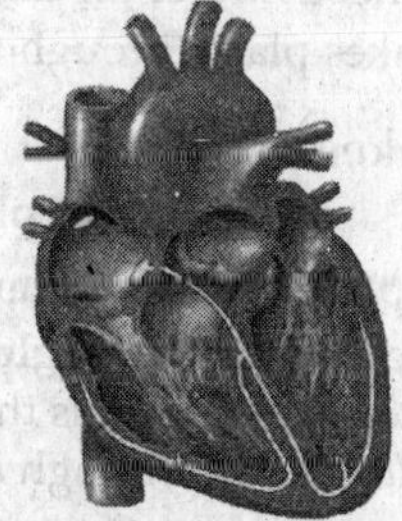

Ans. The diagrammatic presentation of heart with labelled SAN, AVN, AV bundles bundle of His and purkinje fibres in heart is show as follows

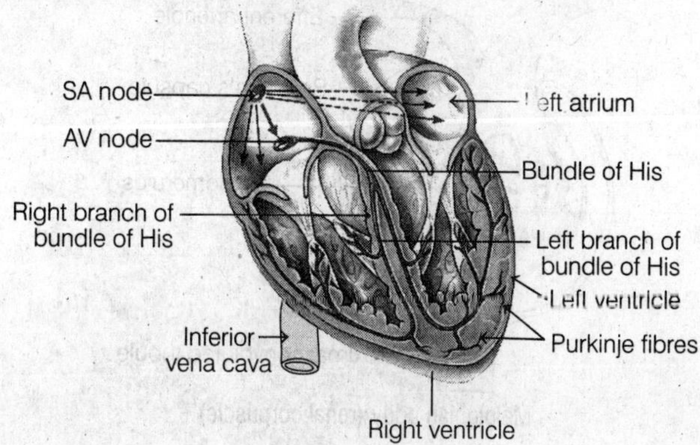

Chapter
19

Excretory Product and their Elimination

Multiple Choice Questions (MCQs)

Choose the correct answer from the given four options in the following questions :

Q. 1 The following substances are the excretory products in animals. Choose the least toxic form among them.

(a) Urea (b) Uric acid (c) Ammonia (d) Carbon dioxide

Thinking Process Nitrogenous waste such as ammonia, urea and uric acid are produced during protein metabolism according to the species. Their excretory form produced in the animals body depends on the availability of water.

Ans. *(b)* **Uric acid** is the least toxic substance. Insects, land tortoises, lizards and birds converts most of their nitrogenous waste into uric acid. It is the least toxic because it is insoluble in water as these are in solid form, thus, contains the least water. In birds, uric acid mixes with undigested food to form the bird dropping.

Other options are incorrect because

Urea moves to blood get filtered and eliminated with water in urine *via* kidneys.

Ammonia is very toxic and needs water for diffusion.

Carbon dioxide excretion takes place through the lungs.

Q. 2 Filtration of the blood takes place at

(a) PCT (b) DCT (c) Collecting ducts (d) Malpighian body

Ans. *(d)* Filtration of blood takes place at **Malpighian body.**

Malpighian body or corpuscle comprises of **glomerulus** and **Bowman's capsule.** Filtration of blood takes place in glomerulus through glomerular filtration in which blood enters in the glomerules through an afferent arteriole and leaves it through efferent arteriole.

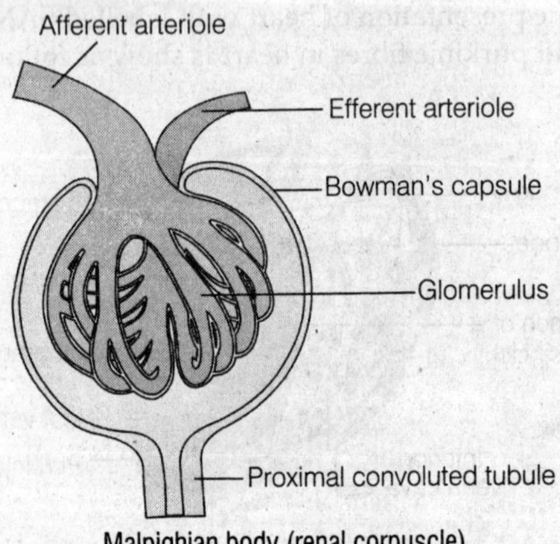

Malpighian body (renal corpuscle)

Proximal Convoluted Tubule (PCT), is lined by cuboidal epithelium cells bearing brush border and allows the reabsorption of salts by active transport.

Distal Convulated Tubule (DCT), allows conditional reabsorption of Na^+ and water as well as selective secretion of H , K^+, NH_3 to maintain pH and Na – K balance in blood.

Collecting Duct extends from cortex of kidney to the inner part of medulla. Large amount of water is reabsorbed from this region to produce the concentrated urine.

Q. 3 Which of the following statement is incorrect?

(a) ADH prevents conversion of angiotensinogen in blood to angiotensin
(b) Aldosterone facilitates water reabsorption
(c) ANF enhances sodium reabsorption
(d) Renin causes vasodilation

Ans. ***(b)*** Aldosterone, secreted by the adrenal cortex, promotes the reabsorption of sodium ions in the distal tubules and collecting duct of the nephron. Water follows sodium due to osmosis, thus indirectly facilitating water reabsorption.

Q. 4 A large quantity of one of the following is removed from our body by lungs.

(a) CO_2 only (b) H_2O only
(c) CO_2 and H_2O (d) ammonia

Thinking Process CO_2 and water both are metabolic wastes produced during oxidation of food in the cells.

Ans. ***(c)*** Our lungs remove large amounts of CO_2 (18L /day) and also significant amount of water everyday.

While respiration, CO_2 alone can not be eliminated from the body and the same holds true for H_2O. Ammonia is highly toxic, and is not found in free NH_3^+ form in our body, thus it is immediately converted to non-toxic of urea.

Q. 5 The pH of human urine is approximately

(a) 6.5 (b) 7 (c) 6 (d) 7.5

Thinking Process The urine is a light yellow coloured watery fluid, which is slightly acidic and has a characteristic odour.

Ans. ***(c)*** The pH of human urine is approximately 6.0. Other options are not correct for the pH of urine.

Q. 6 Different types of excretory structures and animals are given below. Match them appropriately and mark the correct answer from among those given below

	Excretory Structure/Organ		Animals
A.	Protonephridia	1.	Prawn
B.	Nephridia	2.	Cockroach
C.	Malpighian tubules	3.	Earthworm
D.	Green gland or antennal gland	4.	Flatworms

Codes

	A	B	C	D		A	B	C	D
(a)	4	3	2	1	(b)	2	3	1	2
(c)	4	3	1	2	(d)	2	3	2	4

Thinking Process Animal kingdom possess a variety of excretory structures for excretion.

Ans. *(a)*

1. Prawn possesses **green glands** or **antennal glands** as their excretory structures.
2. Cockroach possesses **Malpighian tubules** as their excretory structures.
3. Earthworm possesses **nephridia as** their excretory structures.
4. Flatworm possesses **protonephridia** as their excretory structures.

Q. 7 Which one of the following statements is incorrect?

(a) Birds and land snails are uricotelic animals
(b) Mammals and frogs are ureotelic animals
(c) Aquatic amphibians and aquatic insects are ammonotelic animals
(d) Birds and reptiles are ureotelic

Thinking Process Animals secreting urea as their excretory product are called ureotelic animals. Animals secreting uric acid and ammonia are called uricotelic and ammonotelic respectively.

Ans. *(d)* **Birds** and **reptiles** are uricotelic (not ureotelic) as they excrete nitrogenous waste uric acid in the form of pellet or paste with a minimum loss of water. Rest of the other statement are correct.

Q. 8 Which of the following pairs is wrong?

(a) Uricotelic .... Birds
(b) Ureotelic .... Insects
(c) Ammonotelic .... Tadpole
(d) Ureotelic .... Elephant

Ans. *(b)* Insects excrete nitrogenous wastes as **uric acid** hence are **uricotelic.**

Ureotelic animals involve **mammals**, terrestrial **amphibians** and elasmobranchs.

Whereas, other options are correct birds are uricotelic and tadpoles exerete ammonia. Elephant being a mammal is ureotelic.

Q. 9 Which one of the following statement is incorrect?

(a) The medullary zone of kidney is divided into a few conical masses called medullary pyramids projecting into the calyces
(b) Inside the kidney, the cortical region extends in between the medullary pyramids as renal pelvis
(c) Glomerulus along with Bowman's capsule is called the renal corpuscle
(d) Renal corpuscle, Proximal Convoluted Tubule (PCT) and Distal Convoluted Tubule (DCT) of the nephron are situated in the cortical region of kidney

Thinking Process Inside the kidney, there are two zones, an outer cortex and an inner medulla.

Ans. ***(b)*** Inside the kidney, the cortical region extends in between the medullary pyramids as renal columns are called **Columns of Bertini,** not as renal pelvis. Rest other statements are true.

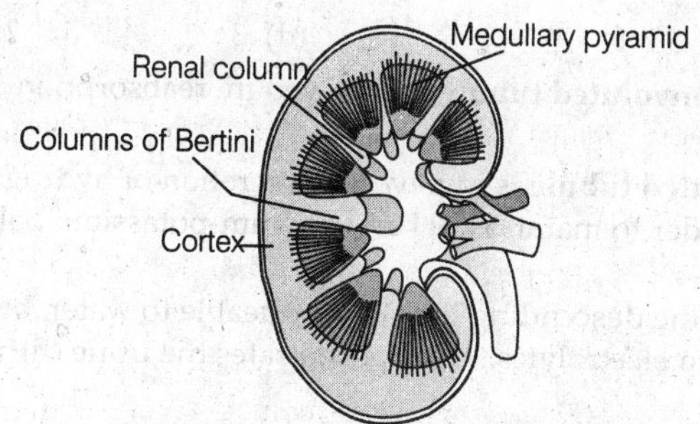

Diagrammatical representation of kidney

Q. 10 The condition of accumulation of urea in the blood is termed as

(a) renal calculi
(b) glomerulonephritis
(c) uremia
(d) ketonuria

Ans. ***(c)*** **Uremia** is accumulation of urea in blood . It occurs due to malfunctioning of kidney.

Other options are wrong because. **Renal calculi** refers to the formation of stones or insoluble mass of crystallised salts (oxalates, etc) with in the kidney. **Glomerulonephritis** is the inflammation of glomeruli of kidney.

Ketonuria is a medical condition in which ketone bodies are present in the urine. It is seen during starvation or more commonly in **type 1 diabetes mellitus.**

Q. 11 Which one of the following is also known as antidiuretic hormone?

(a) Oxytocin
(b) Vasopressin
(c) Adrenaline
(d) Calcitonin

Ans. ***(b)*** Vasopressin is also known as **Antidiuretic Hormone** (ADH). It is secreted from the **neurohypophysis** of pituitary and facilitates water reabsorption from latter parts of the tubule, thereby preventing diuresis.

Other options are wrong because. **Oxytocin** is a mammalian neurohypophysial hormone produced by the hypothalamus and is stored and secreted by the posterior pituitary gland. Oxytocin stimulates contractions of uterus at the end of pregnancy and also contractions of mammary glands the help in flow of milk. Adrenaline is relesed by adrenal medulla at the time of emergency, hence has a role in 'fight or flight' reaction.

Calcitonin is produced in humans primarily by the parafollicular cells of the thyroid. It acts to reduce blood calcium (Ca^{2+}), level opposing the effect of **parathyroid hormone.**

Q. 12 Match the following columns.

	Column I		Column II
A.	Proximal convoluted tubule	1.	Formation of concentcrated urine
B.	Distal convoluted tubule	2.	Filtration of blood
C	Henle's loop	3.	Reabsorption of 70-80% of electrolytes
D.	Counter current mechanisms	4.	Ionic balance
E.	Renal corpuscle	5.	Maintenance of concentration gradient in medullary interstitium.

Codes

	A	B	C	D	E		A	B	C	D	E
(a)	3	5	4	2	1	(b)	3	4	1	5	2
(c)	1	3	2	5	4	(d)	3	1	4	5	2

Ans. *(b)* **Proximal convoluted tubule** is involved in reabsorption of 70-80% of electrolytes.

Distal convoluted tubule is involved in secretion of hydrogen, potassium ions and NH_3 in order to maintain pH and sodium-potassium balance in blood (ionic balance).

Henle's loop (the descending limb) is permeable to water, but almost impermeable to electrolytes. This concentrates the urine (filtrate) as it moves down.

Counter current mechanisms helps to maintaining a concentration gradient in the medullary interstitium of kidney.

Renal corpuscle involves filtration of blood *via* **glomerulus** and **Bowman's capsule.**

Q. 13 Match the following columns.

Column I	Column II
A. Glycosuria	1. Accumulation of uric acid in joints
B. Renal calculi	2. Inflammation in glomeruli
C. Glomerular nephritis	3. Mass of crystallised salts within the kidney
D. Gout	4. Presence of glucose in urine

Codes

	A	B	C	D		A	B	C	D
(a)	1	3	2	4	(b)	3	2	4	1
(c)	4	3	2	1	(d)	4	2	3	1

Ans. *(c)* **Glucosuria** is the presence of glucose in the urine.

Renal calculi is the formation of mass of crystallised salts within the kidney.

Glomerular nephritis is the inflammation of glomeruli of kidney.

Gout is the accumulation of uric acid crystals in joints causing inflammation.

Q.14 We can produce a concentrated/dilute urine. This is facilitated by a special mechanism. Identify the mechanism.

(a) Reabsorption from PCT

(b) Reabsorption from collecting duct

(c) Reabsorption/Secretion in DCT

(d) Counter current mechanism in Henle's loop/vasa recta

Ans. *(d)* Counter current mechanism in Henle's loop and vasa recta helps to maintain concentration gradient in the **medullary interstitum**. Presence of such interstitial gradient helps an easy passage of water from the collecting tubule thereby **concentrating the urine**. Other options are wrong because they cannot produce concentrated urine.

PCT helps in maintaining pH and ionic balance of the body fluid by the secretion of H^+, ammonia and potassium ions and reabsorbing 70-80% of electrolytes and water.

Collecting duct helps in reabsorption of water to produce concentrated urine and in maintaining osmolarity. It also plays a vital role in maintaining pH and ionic balance in blood by secreting H^+ and K^+ ion.

DCT reabsorb Na^+ and water along with HCO_3^-, maintaining pH and sodium-potassium/ionic balance in blood by the selectively secreting hydrogen and potassium ions.

Q. 15 Dialysing unit (artificial kidney) contains a fluid which is almost same as plasma except that it has

(a) high glucose (b) high urea
(c) no urea (d) high uric acid

Thinking Process Dialysis is a process for removing waste and excess water from the blood and is used primarily as an artificial replacement for lost kidney function in people with renal failure.

Ans. *(c)* The dialysing unit (fluid) has the same composition as that of plasma except the nitrogenous waste (urea). Which is the waste product that needs to be removed from the blood during dialysis.

Other options are wrong, as dialysing unit will not have high glucose, high urea or high uric acid.

Very Short Answer Type Questions

Q. 1 Where does the selective reabsorption of glomerular filtrate take place?

Ans. The selective reabsorption of glomerular filtrate takes place in Proximal Convoluted Tubules (PCT) and Distal Convoluted Tubules (DCT).

In PCT all essential elements like nutrients, such as glucose, amino acids, 70-80% of electrolytes and water is absorbed whereas, Distal Convoluted Tubule (DCT) is involved in conditional reabsorption of Na^+ and water.

Q. 2 What is the excretory product from kidneys of reptiles?

Thinking Process Animals accumulate ammonia, urea, uric acid, carbon dioxide, water and ions like Na^+, K^+, Cl^-, phosphate, sulphate, etc., either by metabolic activities or by other means like excess ingestion. The waste products are removed in the form of nitrogenous wastes.

Ans. Reptiles excrete nitrogenous wastes as uric acid in the form of pellet or paste with a minimum loss of water and are called **uricotelic** animals.

Q. 3 What is the composition of sweat produced by sweat glands?

Thinking Process Perspiration (sweating) is the production of sweat and secretion by the sweat glands in the skin of mammals.

Ans. Sweat produced by sweat glands is a watery fluid **containing NaCl, small amounts of urea, lactic acid,** trace amounts of ammonia and uric acid. Its primary function is to facilitate a cooling effect on the body surface and also to helps in removal of waste.

Q. 4 Identify the glands that perform the excretory function in prawns.

Ans. In prawns, the excretory organs are known as **antennary glands or green glands.** These glands are opaque-white pea sized structures, enclosed in the coxa of each 2nd antenna. They mainly excrete ammonia.

Q. 5 What is the excretory structure in *Amoeba*?

Thinking Process *Amoeba* is a protozoan which forms the simplest of all organism in the animal kingdom. Inspite of being unicellular, it is physiologically balanced and performs all the essential processes of an animal.

Ans. Contractile vacuole is the excretory organ in *Amoeba*. It is also involved in osmoregulation.

Q. 6 The following abbreviations are used in the context of excretory functions, what do they stand for?

(a) ANF (b) ADH
(b) GFR (d) DCT

Ans. (a) **ANF** Atrial Natriuretic Factor
(b) **ADH** Antidiuretic Hormone
(c) **GFR** Glomerular Filteration Rate
(d) **DCT** Distal Convoluted Tubule

Q. 7 Differentiate glycosuria from ketonuria.

Ans. Difference between glycosuria and ketonuria is as follows

Glycosuria	Ketonuria
The presence of glucose in urine is known as glycosuria. It occurs in **diabetes mellitus.**	Presence of abnormally high ketone bodies in urine is termed as ketonuria. Increase ketones in urine usually occurs at the time of **longtime fasting**. or in diabetic ketoacidosis.

Q. 8 What is the role of sebaceous glands?

Ans. Sebaceous glands are involved in the elimination of certain substances like cholesterol, squalene, triglycerides wax and esters through sebum. This secretion provides oily covering to the skin.

Q. 9 Name two actively transported substances in glomerular filtrate.

Ans. The substances that are actively transported in the glomerular filtrate are glucose and amino acids.

Q. 10 Mention any two metabolic disorders, which can be diagnosed by analysis of urine.

Ans. Metabolic disorders that can be diagnosed by analysis of urine are

(i) **Hematuria** It is the presence of blood or blood cells in the urine, which could be a sign of kidney stone or a tumor in urinary tract.

(ii) **Albuminuria** It is the presence of albumin in urine and occurs in **nephritis** *i.e.,* inflammation of glomeruli. In this condition the size of filtering slits becomes enlarged.

Q. 11 What are the main processes of urine formation?

Ans. Urine formation includes **glomerular filteration** (ultra filteration), **selective reabsorption** and **tubular secretion** that takes place in different parts of the nephron.

Glomerular filteration involves the filteration of blood, which is carried out by glomerulus.

Selective reabsorption is the absorption of filtrate through renal tubules either actively or passively.

Tubular secretion involves secretion through tubular cells in order to maintain ionic and acid-base balance of body fluids.

Q. 12 Sort the following into actively or passively transported substances during reabsorption of GFR. *e.g.*, glucose, amino acids, nitrogenous wastes, Na^+, water.

Thinking Process The tubular epithelial cells in different segments of nephron perform reabsorption either by active or passive mechanism.

Ans. **Actively transported** substances during reabsorption of GFR- Glucose, amino acids, Na^+.

Passively transported substances during reabsorption of GFR– Nitrogenous wastes, water.

Q. 13 Complete the following

(a) Urinary excretion = tubular reabsorption + tubular secretion –

(b) Dialysis fluid = plasma –

Ans. (a) **Urinary excretion** = tubular reabsorption + tubular secretion – filtration

(b) **Dialysis fluid** = plasma – nitrogenous wastes. (mainly urea and creatinine)

Q. 14 Mention the substances that exit from the tubules in order to maintain a concentration gradient in the medullary interstitium.

Ans. The concentration gradient in medullary interstitium is established primarily by renal tubules of loop of Henle and the blood vessels surrounding them (vasa recta) in a process called countercurrent exchange.

The substances that exit from tubules for maintenance of such gradient are mainly sodium chloride (NaCl), water and urea (contaning H^+, K^+ and NH_3^+).

Q. 15 Fill in the blanks appropriately

Organ	Excretory wastes
(a) Kidneys	....
(b) Lungs	....
(c) Liver	....
(d) Skin	....

Ans.

Organ	Excretory wastes
(a) Kidneys	Urine
(b) Lungs	CO_2
(c) Liver	Urea
(d) Skin	Sweat

Short Answer Type Questions

Q. 1 Show the structure of a renal corpuscle with the help of a diagram.

Ans. Representing the structure of a renal corpuscle

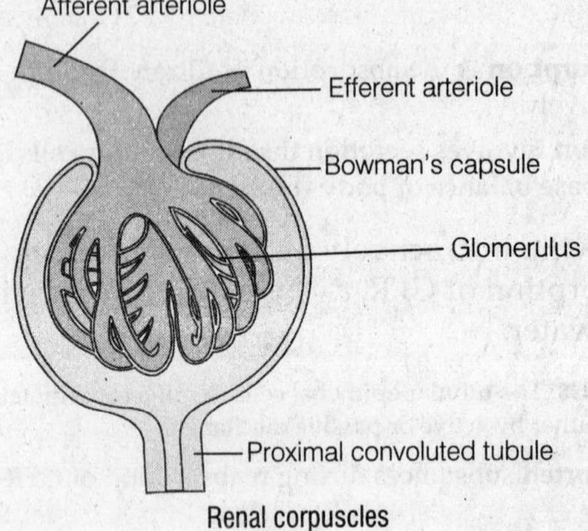

Renal corpuscles

Q. 2 What is the role played by renin-angiotensin in the regulation of kidney function?

Thinking Process The functioning of kidney is efficiently monitered and regulated by hormonal feedback mechanisms involving the hypothalamus, JGA and to certain extent, the heart

Ans. Renin is released from the Juxta-Glomerular Apparatus (JGA) when there is a fall in the glomerular blood pressure/flow. Renin converts angiotensinogen in blood to angiotensin I and further to angiotensin II. Angiotensin II, being a powerful vasoconstrictor, increases the glomerular blood pressure and thereby Glomerular Filteration Rate (GFR).

Angiotensin II also activates the adrenal cortex to release aldosterone. Aldosterone promotes the reabsorption of Na^+ and water from the distal parts of the tubule. This also, leads to an increase in blood pressure and GFR. This complex mechanism is generally known as **Renin Angiotensin Aldosterone System** or RAAS.

Q. 3 Aquatic animals generally are ammonotelic in nature whereas terrestrial forms are not. Comment.

Ans. The process of excreting ammonia is called **ammonotelism**. Many bony fishes, aquatic amphibians and aquatic insects are **ammonotelic**. Ammonia, is readily soluble in water and is excreted by diffusion across body surface or through gill surfaces (in fishes) as **ammonium ions**.

Since ammonia is highly soluble in water and requires large amount of water to be excreted from the body. Such a mode of excretion is thus suitable for aquatic organisms which have a constant access to water.

Terrestrial adaptation requires the production of lesser toxic nitrogenous wastes like urea, and uric acid. Urea is less toxic and less soluble in water. This is important adaptation for water conservation in animals body. Mammals, many terrestrial amphibians and marine fishes mainly excrete urea and are called **ureotelic** animals.

In most insects, land snails, reptiles etc., uric acid is excreted, hence they are called uricotelic animals. Conversion of ammonia to uric acid and its elimination requires less water, thus it is very essential for terrestrial forms that do not have constant water supply.

Q. 4 The composition of glomerular filtrate and urine is not same. Comment.

Ans. The composition of **glomerular filtrate** and **urine** is not same. Glomerular filtrate contains a large amount of water and other dissolved substances such as urea, uric acid, creatinine, amino-acid, glucose, sodium, potassium, vitamins, etc.

Urine on the other hand is a transparent, light yellow fluid, which is formed after rigorous reabsorption and secretion from the filterate. It constitute about 95% water and 5% of other organic and inorganic substances.

Organic substances in urine includes nitrogen, urea, creatine, ammonia, uric acid, oxalic acid, vitamins, hormones and enzymes.

Whereas inorganic substance in urine include chloride, phosphate, sulphate, potassium, sodium, calcium, magnesium, iodine, arsenic and lead. Glucose is not found in urine normally. Hence, composition of glomerular filtrate and urine is different due to processes of selective reabsorption and secretion.

Q. 5 What is the procedure advised for the correction of extreme renal failure? Give a brief account of it.

Thinking Process Malfunctioning of kidneys can lead to the accumulation of urea in blood (uremia), which is highly harmful and may lead to kidney failure.

Ans. **Kidney transplantation** is the ultimate method for the correction of acute/extreme renal failure (kidney failure). A functional kidney is used as a transplant from a donor, preferably a close relative, to minimise its chances of rejection by the immune system of the host. Modern clinical procedures have increased the success rate of such a complicated technique.

Q. 6 How have the terrestrial organisms adapted themselves for conservation of water?

Ans. **Terrestrial organisms** have evolved various strategies to conserve water. Many mammals and terrestrial amphibians necessitated the production of lesser toxic nitrogenous wastes like urea and uric acid for the **conservation of water**. Mammals and many terrestrial amphibians mainly excrete urea and are called uriotelic animals.

Ammonia produced by metabolism is converted into urea in the liver of these animals and released into the blood, which is filtered and excreted out by the kidneys.

Some urea is retained in kidney in order to maintain osmolarity. Reptiles, birds, land snails and insects excrete nitrogeneous waste, as **uric acid** in the form of pellet or paste with a minimum loss of water and are called **uricotelic animals.** Conversion of ammonia to uric acid and its subsequent elimination requires lesser amount of water.

Hence, due to less availability of water on land, and in order to minimise water loss, terrestrial organism adapted themselves accordingly.

Q. 7 Label the parts in the following figure.

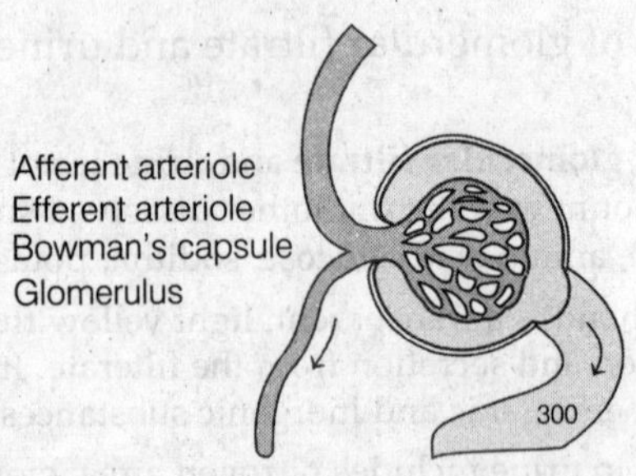

Ans. The labelling part of the given figure are as listed

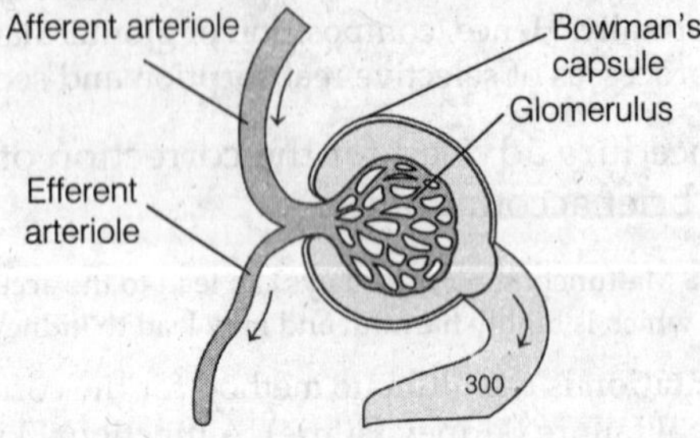

Q. 8 Explain, why a haemodialysing unit called artificial kidney?

Ans. **Haemodialysis** This method is a boon for thousands of uremic (accumulation of urea in blood) patients all over the world.

Haemodialysing unit is called an artificial kidney because it performs the function of kidney in removing wastes products such as urea from patients blood. In this process blood is drained from artery and pumped into a dialysing unit after the addition of an anticoagulant like **heparin**.

Inside the unit, blood passed through a coiled cellophane tube surrounded by a dialysing fluid having the same composition as that of plasma except nitrogenous waste. The porous cellophane membrane of the tube allows the passage of molecules based on concentration gradient.

Due to the absence of nitrogenous wastes in dialysing fluid these substances freely move out, thereby clearing the blood.

In the end the cleared blood is pumped back to the body through a vein after the addition of anti-heparin to it thereby completing the process.

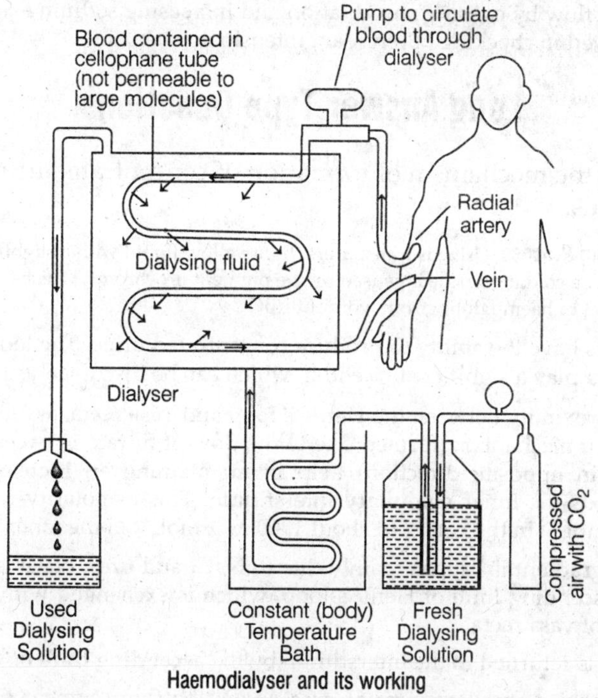

Haemodialyser and its working

Q. 9 Comment upon the hormonal regulation of selective reabsorption.

Ans. The hormonal regulation of selective reabsorption in the kidney involves following. **Antidiuretic Hormone** (ADH), **Juxtaglomerular Apparatus** (JGA) and **Atrial Natriuretic Factor** (ANF).

(a) **Antidiuretic Hormone** (ADH) or vasopressin secreted by neurohypophysis, facilitates water reabsorption from latter parts of tubule, *i.e.,* **distal convoluted tubule** and **collecting duct** by increasing the permeability to water and salt and by accelerating water and ion transfer in a direction determined by the osmotic gradient.

(b) The **Renin-Angiotensin-Aldosterone System (RAAS)** involves the secretion of **renin** by **the Juxtaglomerular Apparatus (JGA).** JG cells secrete an enzyme, **renin**, which, changes plasma protein called **angiotensinogen** to a peptide called angiotensin I and further to **angiotensin II,** which works as a hormone.

Angiotensin II, being a powerful **vasoconstrictor** increases the glomerular blood pressure and thereby GFR. It also stimulate's soduim absorption by proximal tubules.

(c) Angiotensin II also activates the adrenal cortex to release aldosterone. **Aldosterone** induces the distal convoluted tubule to absorb more Na^+ and water.

(d) **Atrial Natriuretic Factor** (ANF) is produced by the atria of heart. It regulates blood flow by causing vasodilation and increasing sodium excretion. It is also involved in checking of renin-angiotensin mechanism.

Long Answer Type Questions

Q. 1 Explain the mechanism of formation of concentrated urine in mammals.

Thinking Process Urine is transparent, light yellow liquid with a slightly acidic pH (6.0). The colour of urine is caused by the pigment urochrome, which is a breakdown product of haemoglobin from wornout RBCs.

Ans. Mammals have the ability to produce concentrated urine. The loop of Henle and vasa recta play a significant role in it, which can be discussed as follows

(i) The proximity between the **Henle's loop** and **vasa recta**, as well as the counter current mechanism (formed due to the flow of filtrate in two limb's of Henle's loop in opposite direction) help in maintaining an **increasing osmolarity** towards the inner medullary interstitium, This osmolarity ranges from 300 $mOsmoL^{-1}$ in the cortex to about 1200 $mOsmoL^{-1}$ in the inner medulla.

(ii) This gradient is caused mainly due to **NaCl** and **urea**. NaCl is transported by the ascending limb of Henle's loop, which is exchanged with the descending limb of vasa recta.

(iii) NaCl is returned to the interstitium by the **ascending limb** of vasa recta.

(iv) Similarly, a small amount of urea enters the thin segment of the **ascending limb** of Henle's loop, which is transported back to the interstitium by the **collecting tubule.**

(v) This special arrangement of Henle's loop, and vasa recta, is called the **counter current mechanism.**

(vi) The countercurrent exchange reduces the rate of dissipation of the osmotic gradient. This, in turn reduces the amount of Na^+ that must be pumped to maintain any given gradient.

(vii) Presence of such interstitial gradient helps the easy passage of water from the collecting tubule thereby concentrating the filtrate (urine).

(viii) Human kidneys can produce urine nearly four times concentrated than the initial filtrate formed.

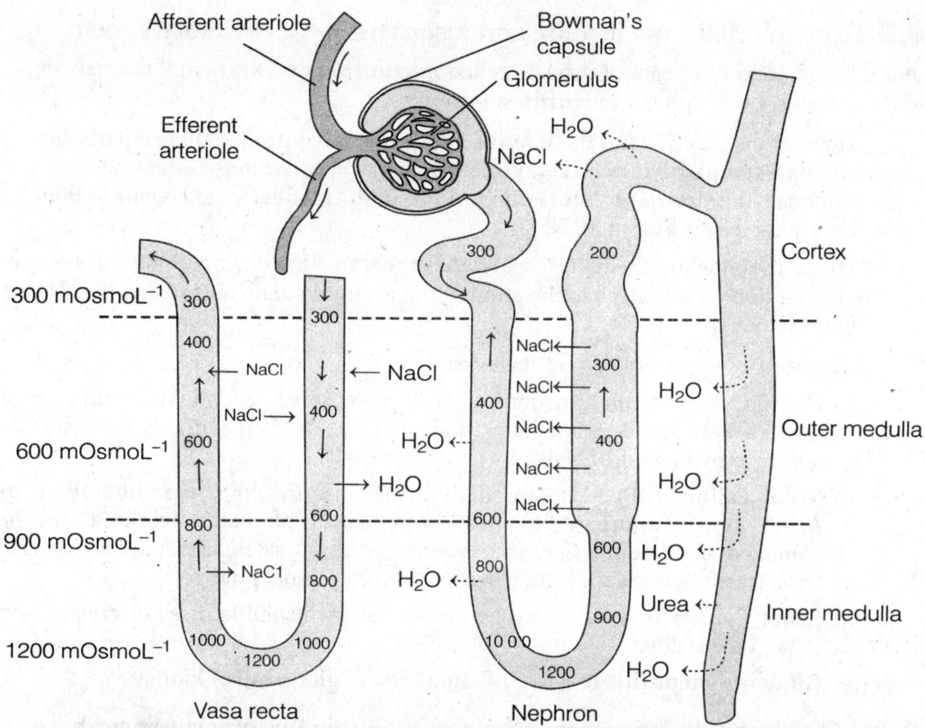

Diagrammatic representation of a nephron and vasa recta showing counter current mechanism

Q. 2 Draw a labelled diagram showing reabsorption and secretion of major substances at different parts of the nephron.

Ans. A diagram showing reabsorption and secretion of major substances at different parts of the nephron are as follows

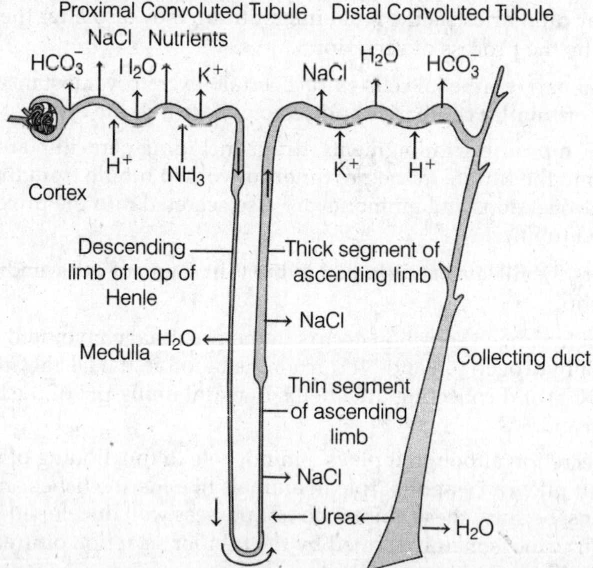

Q. 3 Explain briefly, micturition and disorders of the excretory system.

Ans. The process of release of urine is called **micturition** and the neural mechanism. causing it is called the **micturition reflex.**

The urinary bladder and the internal sphincter are controlled by **sympathetic** and **parasympathetic** nervous systems of autonomic nervous system. In response, the stretch receptors on the walls of the bladder send signals to the Central Nervous System (CNS).

The CNS sends motor signals to initiate the contraction of smooth muscles of the bladder and simultaneous relaxation of the urethral sphincter causing the release of urine.

Disorders of excretory system includes

(i) **Uremia** It is the malfunctioning of kidneys, which leads to accumulation of urea in blood and results in kidney failure. In such patients urea can be removed by **haemodialysis.**

(ii) **Renal Failure** (RF) It is caused by a decrease in glomerular filteration. In Acute Renal Failure (ARF) both kidneys abruptly stop working due to damaged renal tubules, kidney stones, antibiotics, etc. Haemodialysis and renal transplant are the only ways to overcome renal failure.

(iii) **Renal Calculi** It is the formation of stones or insoluble mass of crystallised salts in the kidney.

(iv) **Glomerulonephritis** It is the inflammation of glomeruli of kidney.

Q. 4 How does tubular secretion help in maintaining ionic and acid-base balance in body-fluids?

Thinking Process Tubular secretion is an important step in urine formation as it helps in the maintenance of ionic and acid base balance of body fluid.

Ans. In addition to the role of Proximal Convoluted Tublues (PCT) in selective reabsorption of materials from the glomerular filtrate back into the blood of peritucular capillaries *via* the renal interstitium, they also alter the composition of filtrate by the process of **secretion.**

In its distal part, epithelial cells extract certain excretory substances from the blood of peritubular capillaries and secrete these into the filtrate.

Creatinine, hippuric acid, pigments, drugs including penicillin are actively secreted into the filtrate in the proximal convolued tubule from the interstitial fluid. Hydrogen ions and ammonia are also secreted into the proximal convoluted tubules.

Urea enters the filtrate *via* diffusion in the thin segment of ascending limb of Henle's loop.

Significant hydrogen secretion occurs in the proximal convoluted tubules, but removal of hydrogen ion and NH_3 from the blood in the Distal Convoluted Tubule (DCT) and collecting duct helps in maintaining pH of the blood, *i.e.*, between 6 and 8.

Tubular secretion although it plays a minor role in functioning of the human kidney, but plays an essential role in animals like marine fishes and desert amphibians, because these animal do not possess well developed glomeruli hence their urine is mainly formed by the tubular secretion of **urea, creatinine** and **mineral ions.**

Q. 5 The glomerular filtrate in the loop of Henle gets concentrated in the descending and then gets diluted in the ascending limbs. Explain.

Ans. The **glomerular filtrate** in the loop of Henle is concentrated in the descending loop and then diluted in the ascending limb. The thin wall of **descending** limb of **Henle's loop** is permeable to water, but not to the solutes. The isotonic tubular fluid flows down the limb. It gradually looses its water by the **exosmosis** due to increasing osmolarity of medullary interstitium through which the limb extends.

Thus, the filtrate becomes hypertonic to blood plasma. The **ascending limb of loop** of **Henle** is impermeable to water, but permeable to ions like K^+, Cl^-, Na^+ and it is partially permeable to urea. Thus, in the thick ascending limb of the loop of Henle, Na^+, K^+, Ca^{2+}, Mg^{2+} and Cl^- are reabsorbed, making the filtrate **hypotonic** to blood plasma and diluted as compared to descending limb.

Q. 6 Describe the structure of a human kidney with the help of a labelled diagram.

Thinking Process In humans, the excretory system consists of a pair of kidneys, one pair of ureters, a urinary bladder and a urethra.

Ans. **Human kidney** are reddish-brown, bean-shaped organs situated between the last thoracic and third lumbar vertebra close to the dorsal inner wall of the abdominal cavity. Each kidney of an adult human measures 10-12 cm in length, 5-7 cm in width, 2-3 cm in thickness with an average weight of 120-170 gm.

The kidneys is covered by a fibrous connective tissue, the renal capsule, which protect the kidney. Internally, it consists of renal cortex and an renal medulla, both containing nephron (structural and functional units of kidney).

The median concave border of a kidney contains a notch called hilum. Through which ureter blood vessels and nerves pass. The renal cortex is granular in apperance and contains convoluted tubules and Malpighian corpuscles. The renal medulla is lighter in color and contains loop of Henle, collecting ducts and tubules.

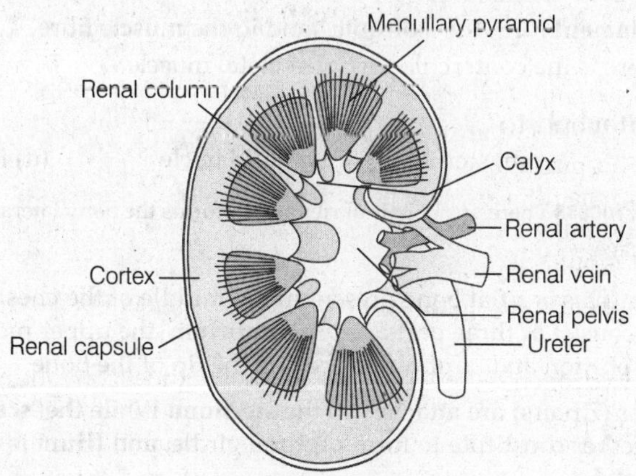

LS of human kidney

Medulla is divided into conical masses, the medullary pyramids which further form papillae.The papillae form calyces, which join to renal pelvis leading to ureter. Between the medullary pyramids, cortex extends into medulla and forms renal columns which are called as column of Bertini.

Chapter 20

Locomotion and Movement

Multiple Choice Questions (MCQs)

Choose the correct answer from the given four options in the following questions :

Q. 1 Match the following columns.

	Column I		Column II
A.	Fast muscle fibres	1.	Myoglobin
B.	Slow muscle fibres	2.	Lactic acid
C.	Actin filament	3.	Contractile unit
D.	Sarcomere	4.	I-band

Codes

	A	B	C	D		A	B	C	D
(a)	1	2	4	3	(b)	2	1	3	4
(c)	2	1	4	3	(d)	3	2	4	1

Ans. (c) 1. **Fast muscle fibres** contract spontaneously and reach anaerobic conditions in shorter time, so accumulate lactic acid faster in the muscles.

2. **Slow muscle fibres** have better ability to endure, as they are more resistant to fatigue and contract slowly, it is because, of accumulation, of large amount, of myoglobin in them.
3. **Actin filament** form the isotropic band in the muscle fibre.
4. **Sarcomere** is the contractile unit of skeletal muscle.

Q. 2 Ribs are attached to

(a) scapula (b) sternum (c) clavicle (d) ilium

Thinking Process There are 12 pair of ribs which forms the bony lateral walls of the thoracic cage.

Ans. (b) **Sternum** This is a flat bone present in the middle of the chest. It is about 15 cm long. It consist of three parts, i.e., **manubrium** the upper most part, **body** the middle portion and **xiphoid process** is the tip of the bone.

The true ribs (7 pairs) are attached to the **sternum**. While the, **scapula** and clavicle together constitute to form pectoral girdle, and **Ilium** is a part of **pelvic girdle**.

Q. 3 What is the type of movable joint present between the atlas and axis?

(a) Pivot (b) Saddle (c) Hinge (d) Gliding

Thinking Process The structural arrangement of tissues by which bones are joined together are called joints.

Ans. *(a)* **Pivot joint** is the joints found between the atlas and axis and between the radius and ulna just below the elbow .This joint allows the movement in only one plane. In a pivot joint, rounded or pointed bone fits into a shallow depression of another bone.

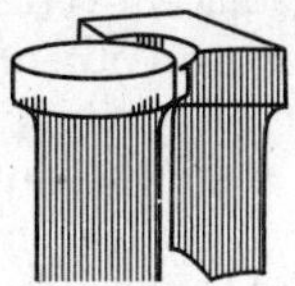

Pivot joint

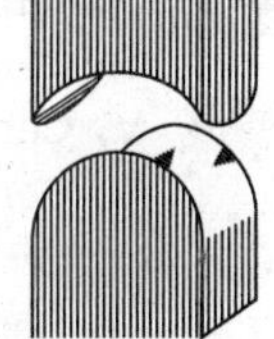

Saddle joint

Whereas, **saddle joint** provides free movement in two planes back-forth and side to side. The projection of one bone fits in saddle-shaped depression of another bone. The joint between the carpel and metacarpel of thumb in the hand is an example of saddle joint.

Hinge joint allows movement primarily in one plane. In a hinge joint reel (spoon) like surface of one bone fits into the concave surface of another bone for example the elbow, the knee, ankle etc.

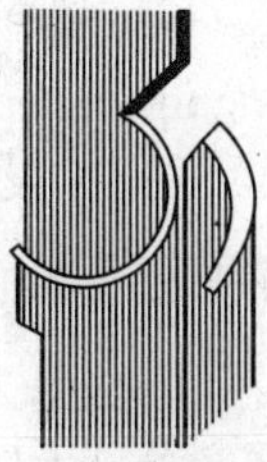

Hinge joint

Gliding joint also known as plane joint, it is a common type of synovial joint formed between bones that meet at flat or nearly flat articulating surface examples of gliding joint include carpel bones of the wrist and joint between metacarpels of the palm.

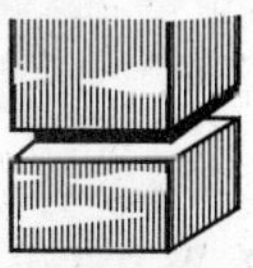

Gliding joint

Q. 4 ATPase of the muscle is located in

(a) actinin (b) troponin (c) myosin (d) actin

Ans. *(c)* The globular head of **myosin** in muscle fibres is an active ATPase enzyme having binding sites for ATP and active site for actin.

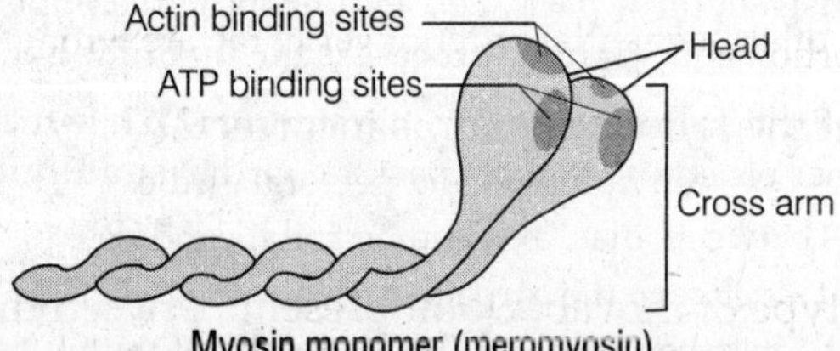

Myosin monomer (meromyosin)

While the ATPase is not found in actinin, troponin or actin of muscle fibre.

Q. 5 Intervertebral disc is found in the vertebral column of
(a) birds (b) reptiles (c) mammals (d) amphibians

Ans. *(c)* **Intervertebral disc** is found in the vertebral column of **mammals**. These are present between the bodies of adjacent vertebrae from second cervical vertebra to the sacrum. Each disc consist of an outer fibrous ring made up of fibrocartilage and an inner soft pulpy, highly elastic substance. These disc are majorly involved in formation of strong joints that permits various movements of the **vertebral column** and absorb **vertical shockes**. Intervertebral disc is not found in the vertebral column of birds reptiles and amphibians.

Q. 6 Which one of the following is showing the correct sequential order of vertebrae in the vertebral column of human beings?
(a) Cervical — lumbar — thoracic — sacral — coccygeal
(b) Cervical — thoracic — sacral — lumbar — coccygeal
(c) Cervical — sacral — thoracic — lumbar — coccygeal
(d) Cervical — thoracic — lumbar — sacral — coccygeal

Thinking Process Our vertebral column is formed by 26 serially arranged units called vertebrae, there are dorsally placed, extending from the base of the skull and constitutes the main frame work of the trunk.

Ans. *(d)* The correct sequence showing the vertebral column of human being is
Cervical — thoracic — lumbar — sacrals — coccygeal

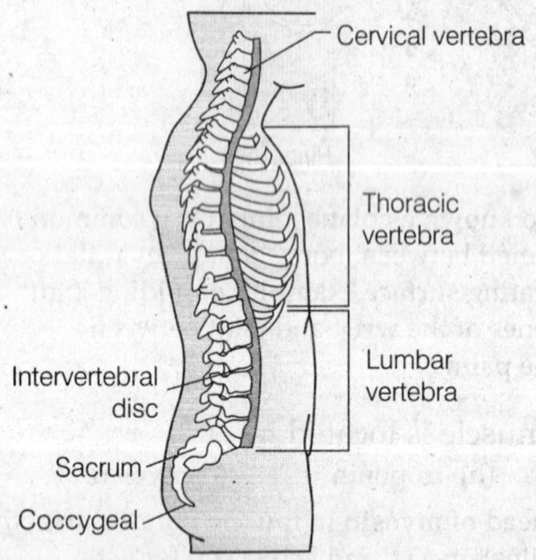

Vertebral column (right lateral view)

Whereas, the other sequential order of vertebrae are wrong.

Q. 7 Which one of the following pair is incorrect?
(a) Hinge joint – between humerus and pectoral girdle
(b) Pivot joint – between atlas, axis and occipital condyle
(c) Gliding joint – between the carpals
(d) Saddle joint – between carpel and metacarpals of thumb

Thinking Process Joints are points of contact between two bones or between bones and cartilages.

Ans. *(a)* The joint present between humerus and pectoral girdle is ball and socket joint. Hinge joint is present between humerus and radius ulna (elbow joint) not between humerus and pectoral girdle. The elbow, knee, ankle and interphalangeal joints are the examples of hinge joints. (*Also, refer to* Q. 3)
Rest of the pair are correct regarding to the presence of joints.

Q. 8 Knee joint and elbow joints are examples of

(a) saddle joint
(b) ball and socket joint
(c) pivot joint
(d) hinge joint

Ans. *(d)* Knee joint and elbow joints are examples of **hinge joints,** allowing movement primarily in one plane.
(*Also, refer to* Q. 3 *and* 7)

Q. 9 Macrophages and leucocytes exhibit

(a) ciliary movement
(b) flagellar movement
(c) amoeboid movement
(d) gliding movement

Thinking Process In some cells, microfilaments are involved in showcasing amoeboid movement.

Ans. *(c)* Some specialised cells in blood like macrophages and leucocytes exhibit amoeboid movement. They have the ability to reach the interstitial fluid by squeezing through the thin walls of blood vessels, whereas ciliary movement, flageller movement or gliding movement are not shown by macrophages and leucocytes.

Q. 10 Which one of the following is not a disorder of bone?

(a) Arthritis (b) Osteoporosis (c) Rickets (d) Atherosclerosis

Ans. *(d)* Atherosclerosis also known as **ateriosclerotic vascular disease**, where arteries wall get thickens as a result of accumulation of WBC, containing both livings active WBCs (white blood cells) and remnants of dead WBC's along with **cholesterol** and **triglycerides.** Remaining diseases, *i.e.,* arthritis, osteoporosis and rickets are all bone related disorders.

Q. 11 Which one of the following statement is incorrect?

(a) Heart muscles are striated and involuntary
(b) The muscles of hands and legs are striated and voluntary
(c) The muscles located in the inner walls of alimentary canal are striated and involuntary
(d) Muscles located in the reproductive tracts are unstriated and involuntary

Thinking Process The walls of internal organs such as the **blood vessels, stomach and intestine** contain **smooth muscles.**

Ans. *(c)* Smooth muscles are **'involuntary'** and **non-striated** as they cannot be controlled directly like that of skeletal muscles which are voluntary, controlled and possess striations. The inner walls of alimentary canal contain smooth muscles (non-striated and involuntary muscles). Rest other statements are correct.

Q. 12 Which one of the following statements is true?

(a) Head of humerus bone articulates with acetabulum of pectoral girdle.
(b) Head of humerus bone articulates with glenoid cavity of pectoral girdle.
(c) Head of humerus bone articulates with a cavity called acetabulum of pelvic girdle.
(d) Head of humerus bone articulates with a glenoid cavity of pelvic girdle.

Ans. *(b)* Head of humerus bone articulates with the glenoid cavity of pectoral girdle. This articulation results in the formation of ball and socket joints, *e.g.*, shoulder joint and hip joint while other statement are incorrect.

Q. 13 Muscles with characteristic striations and involuntary are

(a) muscles in the wall of alimentary canal
(b) muscles of the heart
(c) muscles assisting locomotion
(d) muscles of the eyelids

Ans. *(b)* Cardiac muscle fibres are supplied with **autonomic nervous system** and are not under the control of the will of the **animal,** *i.e.*, they are involuntary. These muscles possess striation as the myofibrils of heart have transverse faint dark and light bands which alternate with each other giving them striped appearence.

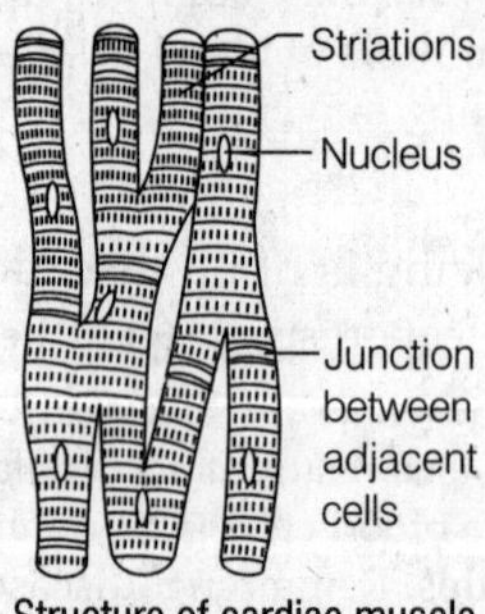

Structure of cardiac muscle

While muscles of the wall of alimentary canal are smooth muscle, *i.e.*, non-striated and involuntary, muscle assisting locomotion, *i.e.*, skeletal muscles are striated and voluntary and muscles of eyelid are voluntary and striated. Thus the other options are wrong.

Q. 14 Match the following columns.

	Column I		Column II
A.	Sternum	1.	Synovial fluid
B.	Glenoid cavity	2.	Vertebrae
C.	Freely movable joint	3.	Pectoral girdle
D.	Cartilagenous joint	4.	Flat bones

Codes

	A	B	C	D		A	B	C	D
(a)	2	1	3	4	(b)	4	3	1	2
(c)	2	1	4	3	(d)	4	1	2	4

Ans. *(b)* A. → (4) B. → (3) C. → (1) D. → (2).

Sternum is a flat bone present in the middle of the front of the chest.

Glenoid Cavity is the depression which articulates with the head of the humerus to form the ball and socket joint in pectoral girdle.

Freely Movable Joints are characterised by the presence of a fluid filled synovial cavity between the articulating surface of the two bones. This fluids represents the **synovial fluid,** *e.g.,* in gliding and hinge joints.

Cartilagenous Joints are present between the adjacent vertebrae in the vertebral column.

Very Short Answer Type Questions

Q. 1 Name the cells/tissues in human body which
(a) exhibit amoeboid movement (b) exhibit ciliary movement

Thinking Process Cells of the human body exhibit three main types of movements, namely amoeboid, ciliary and muscular.

Ans. (a) **Macrophages** and **leucocytes** in blood exhibit **amoeboid movement**. Cytoskeletal elements like microfilaments are also involved in amoeboid movement.

(b) **Ciliary Movement** This types of movements occurs mostly in the internal organs, lined by the **ciliated epithelium**. *e.g.,* cilia in the trachea helps in removing dust particle and foreign substances inhaled along with atmospheric air. Passage of ova through the female reproductive tract is also facilitated by the **ciliary movement** due to the presence of ciliated epithelium in the Fallopian tube.

Q. 2 Locomotion requires a perfect coordinated activity of muscular .... systems.

Ans. Locomotion requires a prefect coordinated activity of muscular, skeletal and neural systems.

Q. 3 Sarcolemma, sarcoplasm and sarcoplasmic reticulum refer to particular type of cell in our body. Which is this cell and to what parts of that cell do these names refer to?

Thinking Process Mechanism of contraction in our body occurs through skeletal muscles made of a number of muscle bundles. Each muscle bundle contains a number of muscle fibres.

Ans. These parts belongs to the **muscle fibre**, which is encased by the plasma membrane called **sarcolemma**. Muscle fibres are syncytial because **sarcoplasm** (the cytoplasm) of muscle fibre contains mutiple nuclei and **sarcoplasmic reticulum** is the endoplasmic reticulum of the muscle fibre and serve as the store house of calcium ions.

Q. 4 Label the different components of actin filament in the diagram given below

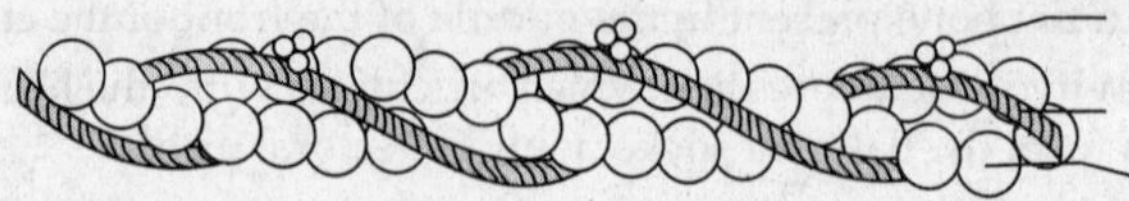

💡 **Thinking Process** Each actin filament is made of two 'F' (filamentous) actins helically wound to each other and each 'F' actin is a polymer of monomeric 'G' (globular) actins.

Ans. Labelled diagram representing different component of actin filament is given below:

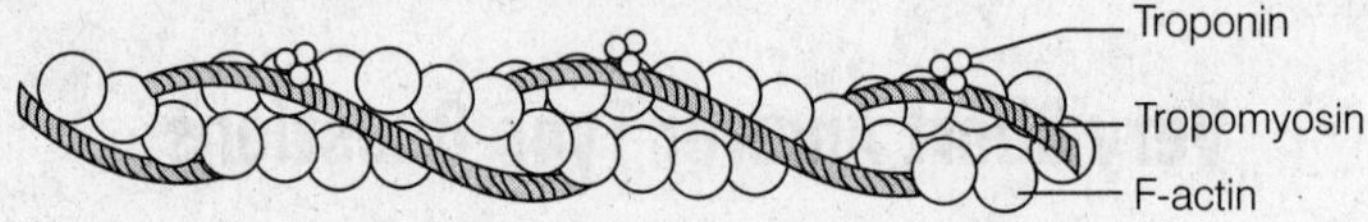

Q. 5 The three tiny bones present in middle ear are called ear ossicles. Write them in correct sequence beginning from ear drum.

Ans. Each middle ear contains three tiny bones, *i.e.*, malleus, incus and stapes which are collectively called as **ear ossicles.**

Q. 6 What is the difference between the matrix of bones and cartilage?

Ans. Difference between the matrix of bones and cartilage are as follows

Matrix of Bones	Matrix of Cartilage
Matrix of bones has an inflexible material, called **ossein**.	Matrix of cartilage has a flexible material, called **chondrin**.
Matrix of **bones** also contains **calcium salts**.	Calcium salts may or may not be present in matrix.

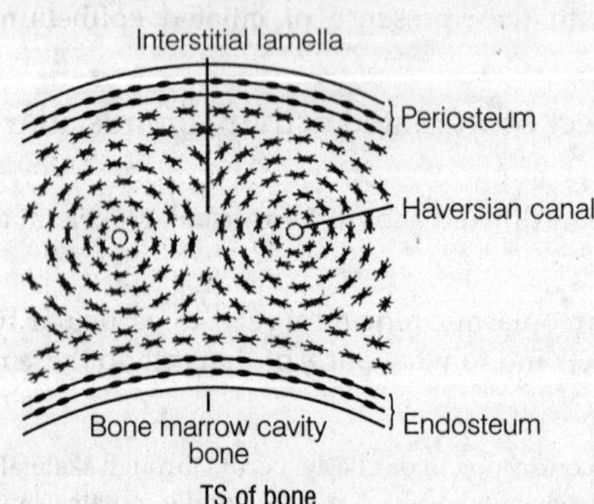

TS of bone

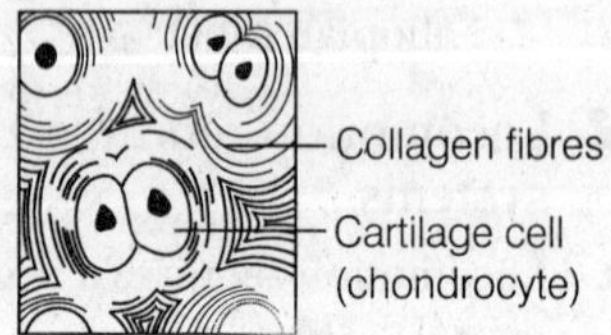

TS of cartilage

Q. 7 Which tissue is afflicted by myasthenia gravis? What is the underlying cause.

Ans. **Myasthenia gravis** is an autoimmune disorder that affects the skeletal muscle, particularly neuromuscular junction, and leads to fatigue, weakening and paralysis of the **skeletal muscle**. In this condition, the body produces antibodies that block or destroy the acetylcholine receptors at neuromuscular junction.

Q. 8 How do our bone joints function without grinding noise and pain?

Ans. The presence of **synovial fluid**, between the articulating surface of two bones, enclosed within synovial cavity of synovial joints, allows our joints to function without grinding noise and pain.

Q. 9 Give the location of a ball and socket joint in a human body

Ans. **Ball and socket joint** allows free movement of bone in all direction. e.g., shoulder joints (where humerus bone fits into the socket of pectoral girdle) and hip joints (where femur bone fits into the socket of pelvic girdle).

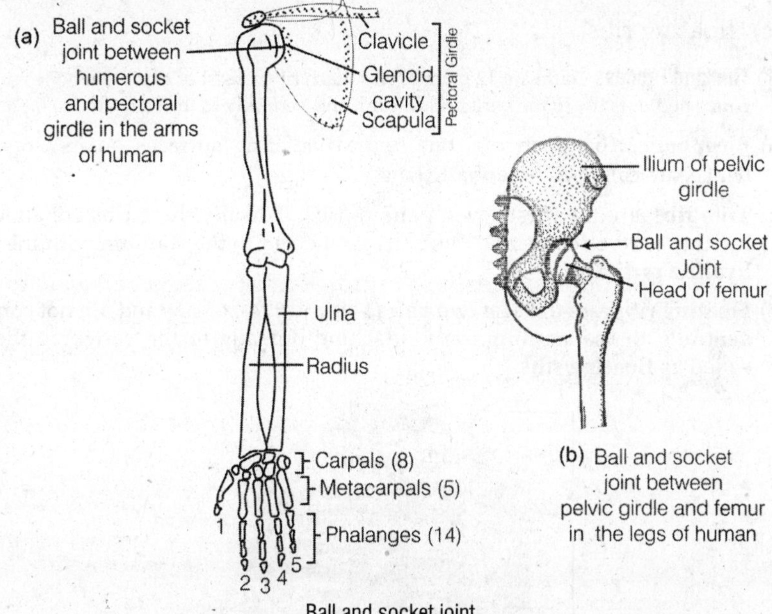

Ball and socket joint

Q. 10 Our forearm is made of three different bones. Comment.

Ans. Our arm is made of three bones, *i.e.*, humerus, radius and ulna. Humerus is present in the upper arm. The forearm consists of the radius and ulna, humerus connects them at the elbow joint and plays a key role in the arm's over all function. These bones are shown in following figure

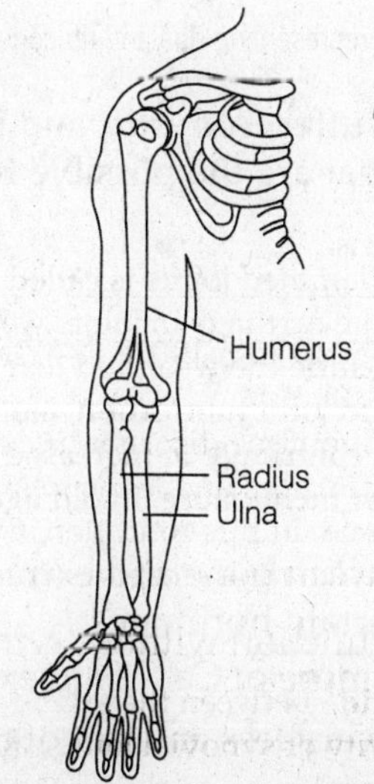

Diagram illustrating forearm bones

Short Answer Type Questions

Q. 1 With respect to rib cage, explain the following

(a) bicephalic ribs (b) true ribs

(c) floating ribs

Thinking Process There are 12 pairs of ribs. Each rib consist of a thin flat bone connected dorsally to the vertebral column and ventrally to the sternum.

Ans. (a) **Bicephalic ribs,** each ribs has two articulating surfaces on its dorsal end hence, are called as **bicephalic ribs.**

(b) **True ribs** are the first seven pairs of ribs. Dorsally these ribs are attached to the thoracic vertebrae and ventrally connected to the sternum with the help of **hyaline cartilage.**

(c) **Floating ribs** are the last two pair (11th and 12th) of ribs and are not connected ventrally to the sternum, only attaching dorsally to the vertebrae therefore, called as **floating ribs.**

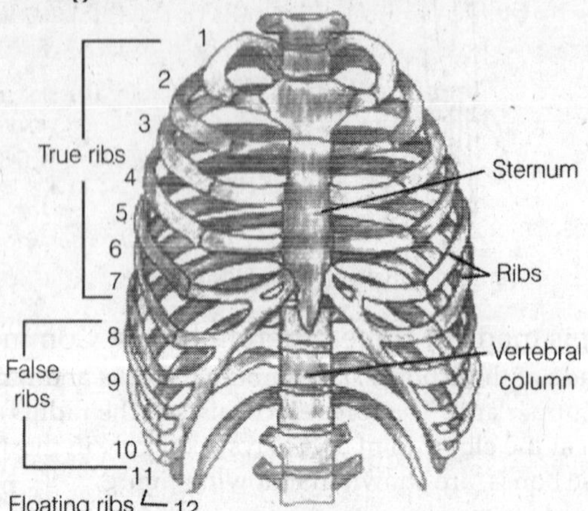

Diagram representing ribe and rib cage

Q. 2 In old age, people often suffer from stiff and inflamed joints. What is this condition called? What are the possible reasons for these symptoms?

Ans. The condition of stiff and inflammed joints is called as **osteoarthritis.** It is an age-related disorder where the cartilage in joints wears down, causing pain and stiffness. Possible reasons include the wear and tear of joints over time, reduced cartilage repair, and decreased joint lubrication, along with hormonal changes. Decreased levels of estrogen contribute to increased risk or progression of osteoarthritis in females after menopause, in old aged females.

Q. 3 Exchange of calcium between bone and extracellular fluid takes place under the influence of certain hormones

(a) What will happen if more of Ca^{++} is in extracellular fluid?

(b) What will happen if very less amount of Ca^{++} is in the extracellular fluid?

Thinking Process Parathyroid and thyroid glands, functions under the feed back control of blood calcium level.

Ans. (a) More Ca^{2+} concentration in extracellular fluid is associated with **hyperparathyroidism.** It causes **demineralisation, resulting** in **softening** and **bending** of the bones. This condition leads to **osteoporosis.**

(b) Very less amount of Ca^{2+} in extracellular fluid is associated with **hypoparathyroidism**. This increases the excitability of nerves and muscles, causing cramps, sustained contraction of the muscles of larynx, face, hands and feet. This disorder is called **parathyroidtetany.**

Q. 4 Name atleast two hormones which result in fluctuation of Ca^{2+} level.

Ans. **Parathyroid** hormone and calcitonin results in the fluctuation of Ca^{2+} level. **Parathyroid Hormone** (PTH) increases the Ca^{2+} levels in the blood. PTH acts on the bones and stimulates the process of bone resorption (dissolution/demineralisation).

PTH also stimulates reabsorption of Ca^{2+} by the renal tubules and increases Ca^{2+} absorption from the digested food.

Calcitonin is a **32-amino acid linear polypeptide hormone**, that is produced in humans primarily by the parafollicular cells of the thyroid. It acts by reducing blood calcium (Ca^{2+}) levels, opposing the effect of Parathyroid Hormone (PTH).

Q. 5 Rahul exercises regularly by visiting a gymnasium. Of late he is gaining weight. What could be the reason? Choose the correct answer and elaborate.

(a) Rahul has gained weight due to accumulation of fats in body

(b) Rahul has gained weight due to increased muscle and less of fat

(c) Rahul has gained weight because his muscle shape has improved

(d) Rahul has gained weight because he is accumulating water in the body

Ans. *(b)* Rahul has gained weight due to increased muscle mass and decreased fat. Regular exercise causes the enlargement of muscles due to increase in the amount of sarcoplasm as well as size and number of myofibrils. Due to which excess fat is burnt. This is the reason that led him gain the mass and size of body muscle and reduction in fat content.

Q. 6 Radha was running on a treadmill at a great speed for 15 minutes continuously. She stopped the treadmill and abruptly came out. For the next few minutes, she was breathing heavily/fast. Answer the following questions.

(a) What happened to her muscles when she did strenuously exercised?

(b) How did her breathing rate change?

Ans. (a) During to continuous exercise, her muscles got fatigued because of the accumulation of lactic acid. Pain is also oftenly experienced in the fatigued muscles.

(b) Her breathing rate changes from normal to high during exercise, as her body muscle require more oxygen for the ATP production, than the normal value. Hence, her breathing enhances, to take most oxygen from the atmosphere.

Q. 7 Write a few lines about gout.

Ans. **Gout** is a disease, caused by a defect in **purine metabolism**. Leading to accumulation of excess of uric acid crystals in the joints. This results in **gouty arthritis**. The excess of uric acid in blood can also lead to the formation of stones in the kidneys.

Q. 8 What is the source of energy for muscle contraction?

Ans. **ATP** (Adenosine Triphosphate) is the primary source of energy for muscle contraction. The head of each myosin molecule contains an enzyme called myosin ATPase.

In the presence of this enzyme along with Ca^{2+} and Mg^{2+} ions, the ATP molecule breaks down into ADP and inorganic phosphate, thus releasing energy in the head of myosin.

$$\text{ATP} \longrightarrow \text{ADP} + \text{Pi} + \text{Energy}$$

Energy from ATP causes energised myosin to form cross bridges with actin, initiating muscle contraction.

Q. 9 What are the points for articulation of pelvic and pectoral girdles?

Thinking Process Pectoral and pelvic girdle help in the articulation of bones of the upper and the lower limbs respectively with the axial skeleton.

Ans. **Pectoral girdle** Each half of the pectoral girdle consist of a clavicle and a scapula. The dorsal flat, triangular body of scapula has a slightly elevated ridge called the spine that projects as a flat expanded process called the acromion and the clavicle articulats with it. Below the acromion there is a depression called the glenoid cavity which articulates with the head of the humerous to form the **shoulder joint**. **Pelvic girdle** consist of two coxal bones each, formed by the fusion of three bones, **ilium, ischium** and **pubis**. It articulates with femur through a cavity called **acetabulum**, forming hip joint.

Long Answer Type Questions

Q. 1 Calcium ion concentration in blood affects muscle contraction. Does it lead to tetany in certain cases? How will you correlate fluctuation in blood calcium with tetany?

Thinking Process Concentration of **calcium ion** (Ca^{2+}) in body fluid mainly affects the muscle contraction, as the binding of contractile proteins **actin** and **myosin** depends on it.

Ans. For the muscle fibre to contract, the binding site on thin filaments must be uncovered. This occurs when Ca^{2+} bind to another set of regulatory proteins, called troponin complex which control the position of tropomyosin on the thin filament. The calcium binding rearranges the tropomyosin-troponin complex, exposing the myosin-binding sites on the thin filament. When Ca^{2+} is present in the cytosol, the thin and thick filament slide part each other resulting in muscle contraction. Similarly, when the Ca^{2+} concentration falls, the binding sites get covered and contraction stops.

In case of **tetany** there occur low calcium levels in body fluid due to diminished function of **parathyroid gland**. This gland is mainly involved in the secretion of **parathyroid hormone** which is associated in regulating calcium levels in blood. Tetany results in periodic painful muscular spasm (wild contraction) and tremors.

Q. 2 An elderly women slipped in the bathroom and had severe pain in her lower back. After X-ray examination doctors told her it is due to a slipped disc. What does that mean? How does it affect our health?

Ans. The intervertebral discs are present between the bodies of adjacent vertebrae from the **second cervical vertebra** to the **sacrum**. These discs form strong joints that permit various movements of vertebral column and absorbs vertical shock. Slipped disc is a medical condition in which spine is affected due to wear and tear in the outer fibrous ring (anulus fibrosus) of an **intervertebral disc**, allowing the soft, central portion to bulge out beyond the damaged outer rings.

The cause of slip disc can be due to general wear and tear of intervertebral disc during performing various jobs, that require constant sitting and squatting. The slipped disc or herniation occurs in two regions of body, *i.e.,* **cervical disc** and **lumber disc**.

Slip disc in lower back, lead to sharp pain in one part of leg due to sciatica, (disturbance in sciatic nerve) along with hip discomfort and cause numbness in other lower parts of the body.

Slip disc in neck region (cervical disc) leads to pain while moving neck, especially near or over the shoulder bone Pain also occurs while moving forearm, or fingers. It also causes numbness in shoulder, elbow, forearm and finger area.

Hence, slipped disc affect the upper and lower body parts, thus, influencing life style and health.

Q. 3 Explain sliding filament theory of muscle contraction with neat sketches.

Thinking Process The contraction of muscle fibre takes place by the sliding of the thin filaments over thick filaments.

Ans. **Sliding filament theory** is applicable to smooth, cardiac and skeletal muscles. The essential features of this theory are as follows

(i) During muscle contraction, **thin myofilaments** slide past the thick filament narrowing the **H-zone**.

(ii) The sarcomere, the basic unit of muscle contraction, shortens, without changing the length of thin and thick myofilaments.

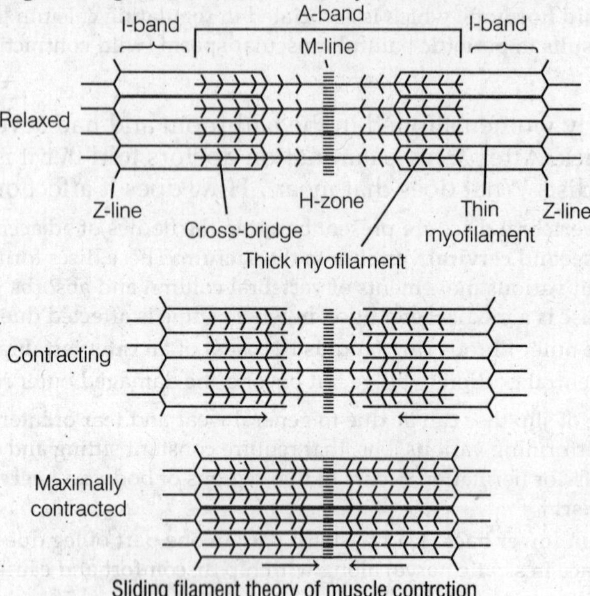

Sliding filament theory of muscle contrction

(iii) The cross arm of the thick myofilaments connect with the portions of actin of the thin myofilaments to form cross-bridge. These cross-bridge move on the surface of the thin myofilaments, resulting in the sliding of thin and thick myofilaments over each other.

(iv) A muscle fibre maintains a resting potential under resting conditions just like a nerve fibre. As soon as a nerve impulse reaches the terminal end of the axon, small sacs called **synaptic vesicles** fuse with the axon membrane and release a chemical transmitter,called **acetylcholine**.

It diffuses across the **synaptic cleft** (the space between the axon membrane and the motor end plate) and binds to the receptor sites of the motor end plate.

(v) As soon as depolarisation of the motor end plate reaches a certain level, it creates an **action potential**. After this, an enzyme **cholinesterase** present along with the receptor sites for acetylcholine, breaks down acetylcholine into acetate and choline.

A portion of the choline diffuses back to the axon and is reused to synthesise more acetylcholine for the transmission of subsequent impulses.

(vi) The action potential triggers the release of calcium ions from sarcoplasmic reticulum.

(vii) **Calcium** plays a key regulatory role in muscle contraction. The Ca^+ ions bind to troponin causing a change in its shape and position. This in turn alters the shape and position of tropomyosin.

This shift exposes the **active sites** on the **F-actin** molecules and myosin cross-bridges are then able to bind to these active sites.

(viii) The head of each myosin molecule contains an enzyme **myosin ATPase**. In the presence of myosin ATPase, and Mg^{2+} ions, ATP breaks down into ADP and inorganic phosphate as

$$\text{ATP} \xrightarrow[\text{Mg}^{2+}]{\text{Myosin ATPase}} \text{ADP} + \text{P}_i + \text{Energy}$$

(ix) Energy from ATP causes energised myosin head to bind to actin to form cross-bridge. The energised cross-bridge move, causing the thin myofilaments to slide along the thick myofilaments. This movement is like the movement of the oars of a boat.

(x) As stated earlier, there is no shortening of thin and thick myofilaments. However, the sarcomere shortens, due to the sliding of the thin myofilaments produced by cross-bridge movements. The H-zone and I-band shorten, but the width of the A-band remains constant.

Q. 4 How does a muscle shorten during its contraction and return to its original form during relaxation?

Ans. Formation of cross-bridge between the actin and myosin filament help muscle to contract.

(i) An ATP molecule joins the active site on myosin head of myosin myofilament. These heads contains an enzyme, **myosin ATPase** that along with Mg^{2+} ions catalyses the breakdown of ATP.

$$ATP \xrightarrow[Mg^{2+}]{\text{Myosin ATPase}} ADP + P_i + Energy$$

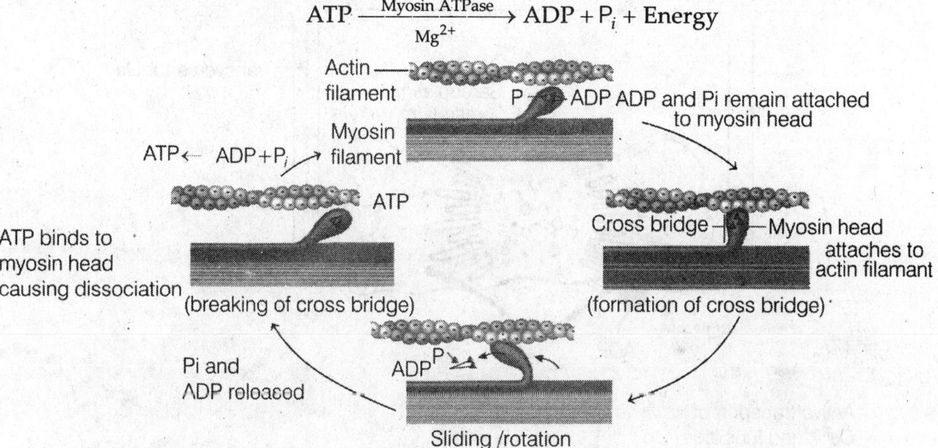

Stages in cross-bridge formation, rotation of head and breaking of cross-bridge

(ii) The energy is transferred to myosin head which energises and straightens to join an active site on actin myofilament, forming a cross-bridge.

(iii) The energised cross-bridges move, causing the attached actin filaments to move towards the centre of A-band. The Z-line is also pulled inwards causing shortening of sarcomere, *i.e.*, contraction. During contraction A-bands retain the length, while I-bands get reduced.

(iv) The myosin head releases ADP and Pi, relaxes to its low energy state. The head detaches from actin myofilaments when new ATP molecule joins it and cross-bridge are broken.

(v) In repeating cycle, the free head cleaves the new ATP. The cycles of cross-bridge formation and breakage are repeated causing further sliding.

(vi) Muscle relaxation occurs after contraction when the calcium ions are pumped back to the sarcoplasmic cisternae, blocking the active sites on actin myofilaments. The Z-line returns to original position, *i.e.*, relaxation.

Q. 5 Discuss the role of Ca^{2+} ions in muscle contraction. Draw neat sketches to illustrate your answer.

Ans. Calcium plays a key regulatory role in muscle contraction. These ions bind to troponin, causing change in its shape and position. This, in turn alters the shape and position of tropomyosin. This shift exposes the active sites on the F-actin molecules, allowing myosin head able to bind to these **active sites.**

The head of each myosin molecule contains an enzyme called **myosin ATPase.** In the presence of myosin ATPase and Mg^{2+} ions, ATP breaks down into ADP and inorganic phosphate,

$$\text{ATP} \xrightarrow[\text{Mg}^{2+}]{\text{Myosin ATPase}} \text{ADP} + \text{P}_i + \text{Energy}$$

Energy from ATP causes energised myosin cross-bridges to bind with actin. The complete process is outlined in the figure given below:

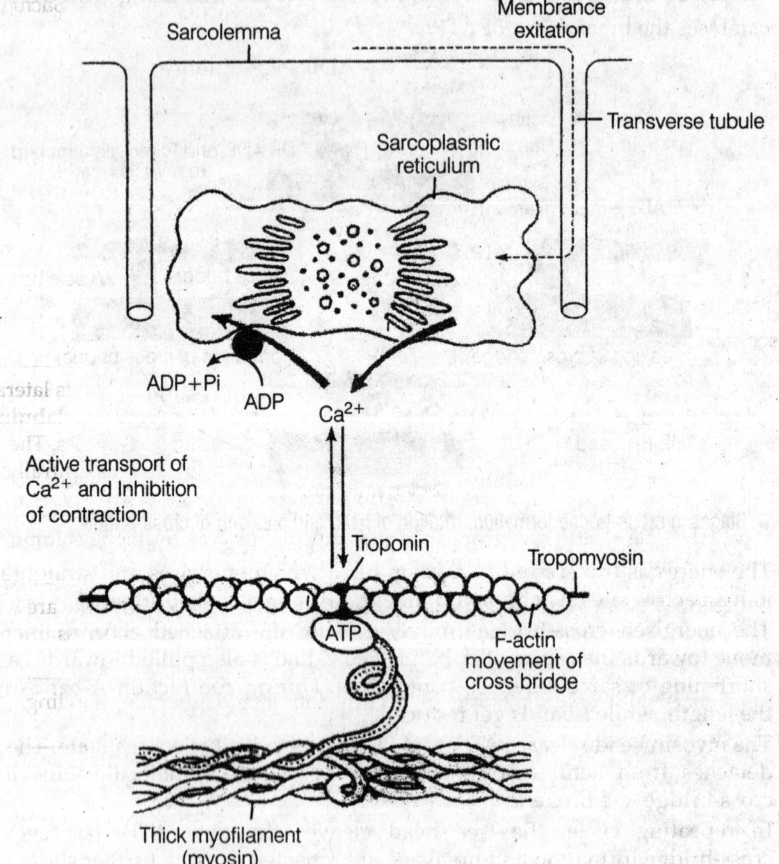

Q. 6 Differentiate between pectoral and pelvic girdle.

Ans. The pectoral and pelvic girdle are responsible in providing support to the upper and lower body portions. The different between them are as follows.

Pectoral Girdle	Pelvic Girdle
It occurs in the shoulder region, hence also called as **shoulder girdle**.	It occurs in the hip region, hence also called as **hip girdle**.
Pectoral girdles contain two bones, *i.e.*, one clavicle and one scapula. 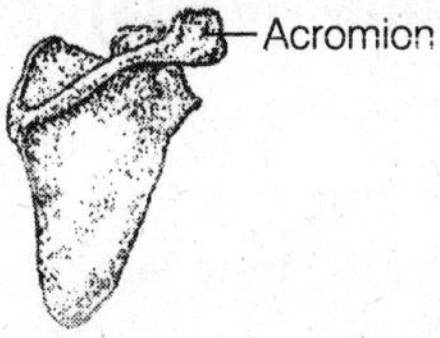 **Scapula** 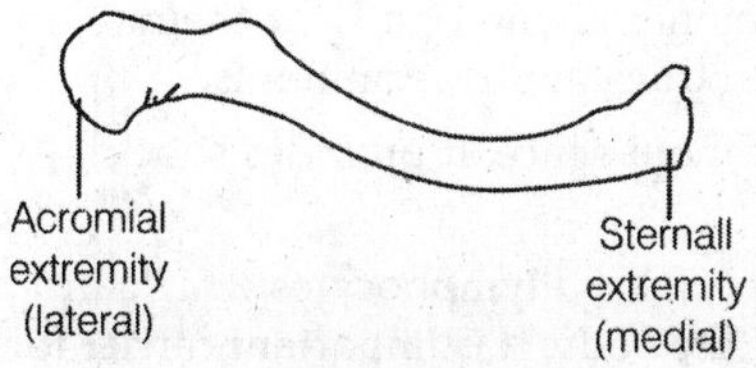 **Clavicle**	There is one pelvic girdle, which is formed by two, innominate bones. Each bone consist of three parts. *i.e.*, ilium, ischium and pubis. 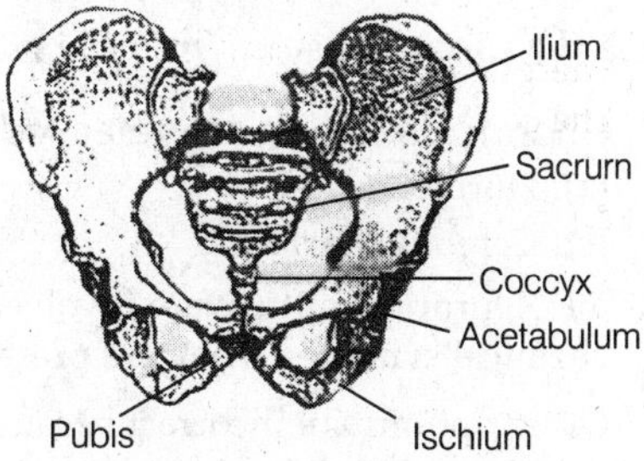 **Human pelvis from anterior aspect**
Clavicle and scapula helps in articulate the upper limb with axial skeleton.	The innominate at the middle of its lateral surface has a deep, cup shaped **acetabulum**. where head of the femur articulates. The two halves of the pelvic girdle meet ventrally to form public symphysis.
It has no articulation with the vertebral column.	It has articulation with vertebral column.
Bones associated with pectoral girdle are light, as they are not subjected to much stress.	Bones associated with pelvic girdle are hard as they are subjected to much stress
Its functions include holding, lifting	Its functions includs running, standing, jumping.

Chapter 21

Neural Control and Coordination

Multiple Choice Questions (MCQs)

Choose the correct answer from the given four options in the following questions :

Q. 1 Chemicals which are released at the synaptic junction are called

(a) Hormones (b) Neurotransmitters

(c) Cerebrospinal fluid (d) Lymph

Ans. ***(b)*** Neurotransmitters are involved in the transmission of impulses at the chemical synapses. They are present in the synaptic vesicles at axon terminals.

Other options are incorrect because, hormones are non-nutrient chemicals which act as intercellular messengers and are produced in trace amounts.

Cerebrospinal fluid is present in subarachnoid space. It provides shock resistance to brain

Lymph is a colourless fluid containing specialised lymphocytes which are responsible for the immune responses of the body. It is important carrier for nutrients, hormones, etc. Fats are absorbed through lacteals (lymph vessels) present in microvilli of intestine.

Q. 2 Potential difference across resting membrane is negatively charged. This is due to differential distribution of the following ions.

(a) Na^+ and K^+ ions (b) CO_3^{2-} and Cl^- ions

(c) Ca^{2+} and Mg^{2+} ions (d) Ca^{4+} and Cl^- ions

Thinking Process Neurons are called excitable cells because their membranes are in a polarised state. Different types of ion channels are present on the neural membrane. These ion channels are selectively permeable to different ions.

Ans. ***(a)*** The ion gated channels on the neurolemma control the movement of Na^+ and K^+ ions across the inner and outer side of nerve cell membrane.

Other options are incorrect because Ca^{2+}, CO_3^{2-}, Mg^{2+} and Ca^{4+} ions are not related with nerve excitation rather are involved in other biological functions. Ca^{2+} ions are related to muscle contraction where Mg^{2+} ions act as a cofactor in some reactions.

Cl^- ion channels play an important role in setting the resting membrane potential, and regulating salt transport.

Q. 3 Resting membrane potential is maintained by

(a) hormones (b) neurotransmitters

(c) ion pumps (d) None of these

Thinking Process The electrical potential difference across the resting plasma membrane is called as the **resting potential.**

Ans. *(c)* The ionic gradients across the resting membrane are maintained by the active transport of ions through sodium-potassium pumps (or ion pumps) which transport 3 Na^+ out of the cell for every $2K^+$ ions pumped.

Q. 4 The function of our visceral organs is controlled by

(a) sympathetic and somatic neural system
(b) sympathetic and parasympathetic neural system
(c) central and somatic nervous system
(d) None of the above

Ans. *(b)* Sympathetic and parasympathetic neural system control all the visceral organs of the body. Other options are incorrect because somatic neural system is a part of peripheral nervous system and is not involved in regulation of visceral organs. Similarly CNS is not concerned with it.

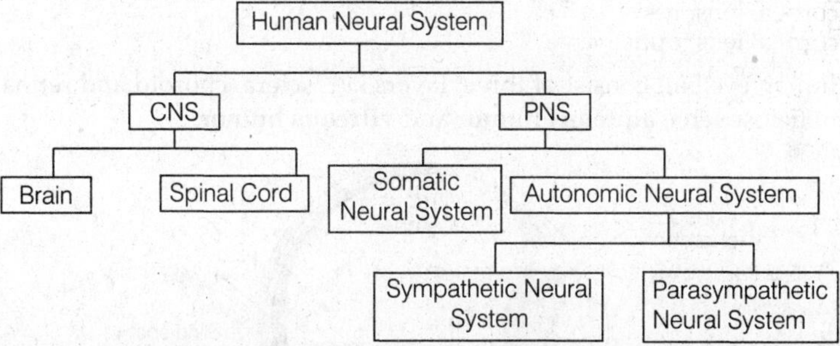

Q. 5 Which of the following is not involved in knee-jerk reflex?

(a) Muscle spindle (b) Motor neuron (c) Brain (d) Inter neurons

Thinking Process Reflex action is a form of animal behaviour in which the stimulation of a sensory organ results in the activity of some organs without the intervention of brain.

Ans. *(c)* Brain is not involved in any reflex action (*e.g.*, knee-jerk reflex) which is a simple reflex, while the muscle spindle, inter neuron and motor neuron are the part of reflex arch.

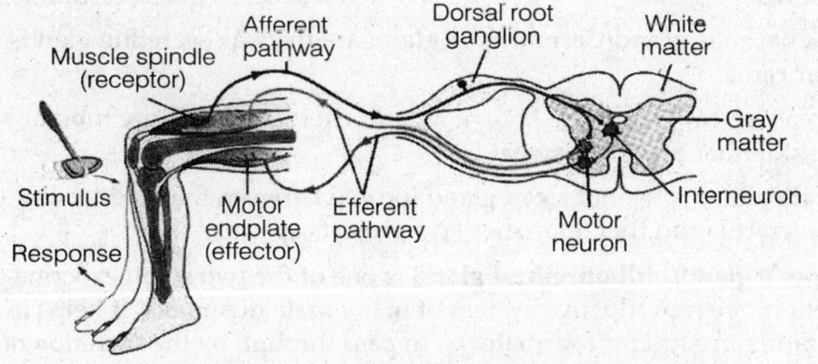

Diagrammatic presentation of reflex action (showing knee jerk reflex)

Q. 6 An area in the brain which is associated with strong emotions is

(a) cerebral cortex
(b) cerebellum
(c) limbic system
(d) medulla

Ans. *(c)* The **limbic lobe or limbic system**, along with the hypothalamus, is involved in the regulation of emotions (*e.g.*, excitement, pleasure rage and fear) and as well as motivation states.

Q. 7 Mark the vitamin present in rhodopsin
(a) vit-A (b) vit-B (c) vit-C (d) vit-D

Ans. *(a)* The rods contain a purplish red protein called the rhodopsin. It is a photosensitive compound in eye that is composed of opsin (a protein) and retinal (an aldehyde of vitamin-A), whereas vitamin-B, C and D not directly involved in vision.

Q. 8 Human eyeball consists of three layers and it encloses
(a) lens, iris, optic nerve
(b) lens, aqueous humor and vitreous humor
(c) cornea, lens, iris
(d) cornea, lens, optic nerve

Ans. *(b)* Human eye ball consist of three, layers *i.e.*, sclera, choroid and retina. These layer enclose **lens, aqueous humor** and **vitreous humor**.

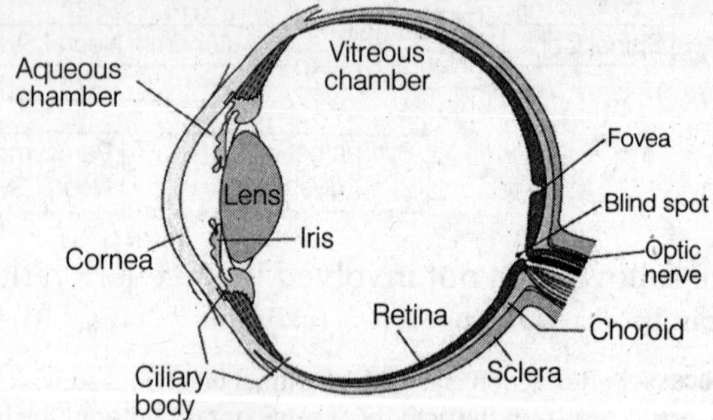

Diagram showing parts of an eye

Q. 9 Wax gland present in the ear canal is called
(a) sweat gland (b) prostate gland
(c) Cowper's gland (d) sebaceous gland/ceruminous gland

Ans. *(d)* **Sebaceous gland/Ceruminous gland** are the wax secreting glands present in the ear canal.

Whereas, **sweat gland** also known as sudoriferous glands are tubular structures of the skin that **produces sweat.**

Prostate gland is walnut sized gland located between the bladder and the penis and secretes fluid that nourishes and protects sperms.

Cowper's gland/bulbourethral gland is one of the two small exocrine glands present in the reproductive system of many male mammals. It helps in lubricating urethra for spermatozoa to pass through by the secretion of viscous fluid known as **pre-ejaculate.** Other options are incorrect because they do not secrete wax.

Q. 10 The part of internal ear responsible for hearing is

(a) cochlea
(b) semicircular canal
(c) utriculus
(d) sacculus

Ans. *(a)* **Cochlea** is the part of internal ear responsible for hearing. It is connected with saccule and is a spirally coiled structure that resembles a snail shell in appearance.

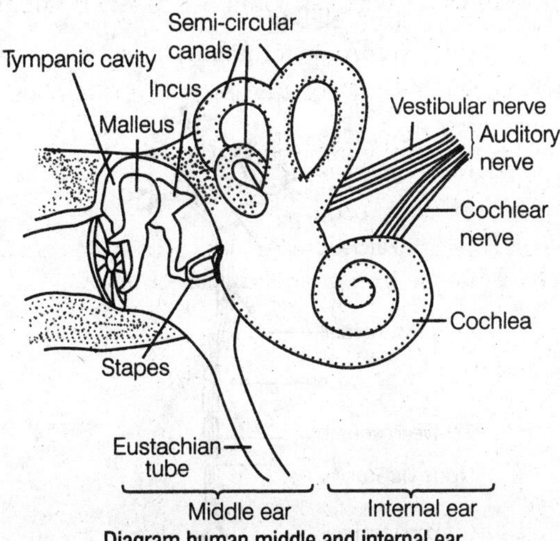

Diagram human middle and internal ear

Semicircular canal are membranous canal suspended in the perilymph of the bony canals and are the structures of equilibrium (balancing). Whereas, utriculus and **sacculus** are the parts of the balancing apparatus located within the vestibule of the bony labyrinth. These have small stones and a viscous fluid to stimulate **hair cells** to detect **motion** and **orientation**. Other options are incorrect because they are not responsible for hearing.

Q. 11 The organ of corti is a structure present in

(a) external ear
(b) middle ear
(c) semi circular canal
(d) cochlea

Ans. *(d)* The organ of Corti is a structure present in cochlea. Cochlea contains the canal called scala media, which has an upper membrane, the **Reissner's membrane** and a lower membrane, **basilar membrane**. Organ of corti are present on the sensory ridge of **basilar membrane.** Other options are incorrect because organ of corti is not present in them.

Very Short Answer Type Questions

Q. 1 Rearrange the following in the correct order of involvement in electrical impulse movement. Synaptic knob, Dendrites cell body. Axon terminal and axon.

Thinking Process Neurons are exitable cells because their membranes are in a polarised state.

Ans. The correct order of involvement in electrical impulse movement.

(i) Dendrites (ii) Cell body
(iii) Axon (iv) Axon terminal
(v) Synaptic knob

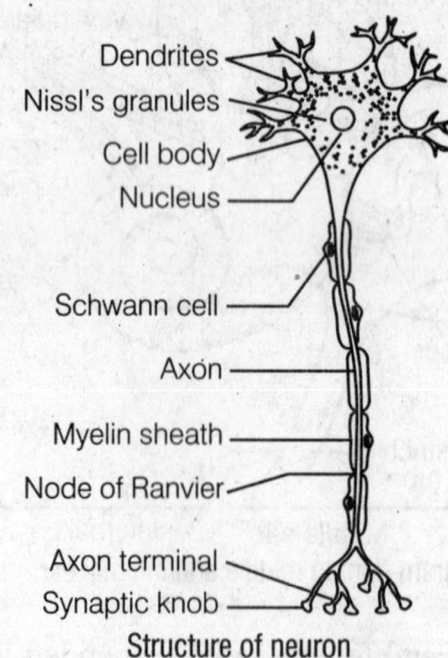

Structure of neuron

Q. 2 Comment upon the role of ear in maintaining the balance of the body and posture.

Ans. The vestibular system is the sensory apparatus of the inner ear that helps the body maintain its postural equilibrium.

There are two sets of organs in inner ear, or labyrinth
(i) The semicircular canals which respond to rotational movements; and
(ii) The utricle and saccule within the vestibule, respond to changes in the position of the head with respect to gravity.

Each semicircular canal contains hair cells. Rotation of the head causes a flow of fluid, which in turn causes displacement of the top portion of hair cells embedded in jelly-like capula. Utricle and saccule called otolithic organs contain hair cells blanketed with tiny stones called otoconia. When the head is tilted or body position is changed, the displacement of stones causes the hair cells to bend, sending signals to the brain regarding the body's position.

Q. 3 Which cells of the retina enable us to see coloured objects around us?

Thinking Process There are two types of photoreceptor cells, namely rods and cone. These cells contain the light sensitive proteins called the photopigments.

Ans. Cone cells of retina enable us to see the colours. There are three types of cones which possess their own characteristic photopigments that respond to red, green and blue light. Whereas, rod handle low-light vision.

Q. 4 Arrange the following in the order of reception and transmission of sound wave from the ear drum. Cochlear nerve, external auditory canal, ear drum, stapes, incus, malleus, cochlea.

Ans. External auditory canal → Eardrum → Malleus → Incus → Stapes → Cochlea → Cochlear nerve.

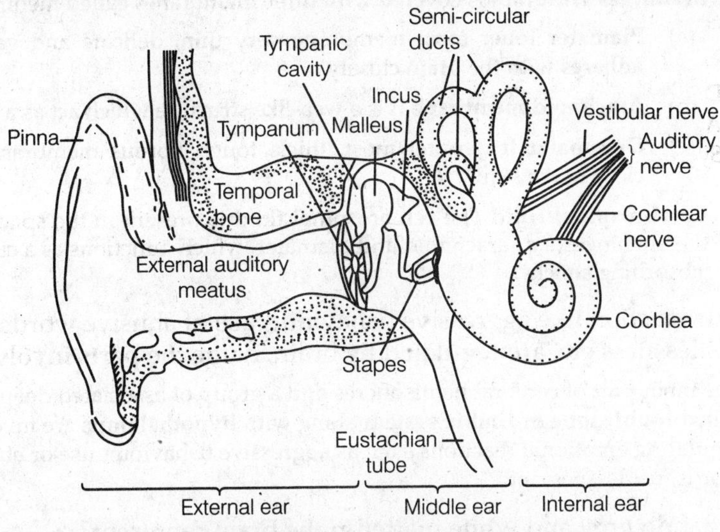

Diagrammatic representation of human ear

Q. 5 During resting potential, the axonal membrane is polarised, indicate the movement of +ve and –ve ions leading to polarisation diagrammatically.

Ans.

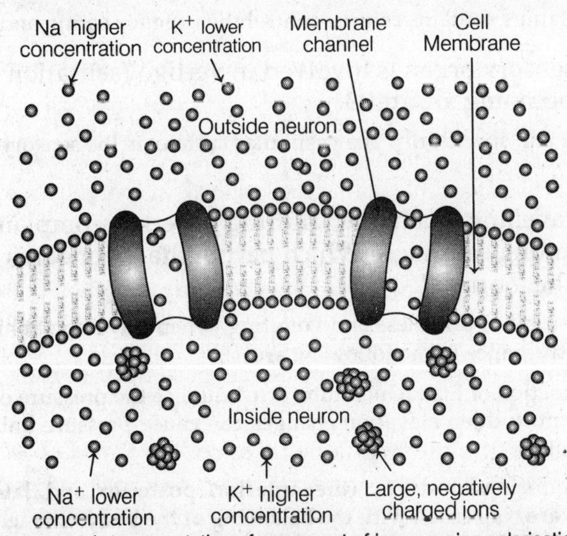

Diagrammatic representation of movement of ions causing polarisation of axonal membrane

Q. 6 Name the structures involved in the protection of the brain.

Ans. The following structures are involved in the protection of brain in animals

(i) **Cranium** There are 8 cranial bones which form a hard protective outer covering, cranium for the brain.

(ii) **Meninges** The brain is covered with three membranes called meninges.

(a) **Piamater** Inner most membrane very thin, delicate and vascular and adheres with the brain closely.

(b) **Arachnoid membrane** It is a web-like structure which act as a cushion.

(c) **Duramater** It is outer most, thick, tough fibrous membrane adhering close to the skull.

(iii) **Cerebrospinal fluid** The cerebrospinal fluid is present in the spaces between the meninges, *i.e.*, arachnoid and piamater, which functions as a cushion, absorbing shocks.

Q. 7 Our reaction like aggressive behaviour, use of abusive words, restlessness etc. are regulated by brain, name the parts involved.

Ans. The inner part of cerebral hemispheres and a group of associated deep structures called **limbic lobe or limbic system** along with **hypothalamus** are involved in regulating emotional reactions such as aggressive behaviour, use or abusive words, restlessness, etc.

Q. 8 What do grey and white matter in the brain represent?

Ans. Grey matter is consists of neural cell bodies, dendrite, unmyelinated axons, glial cells and capillaries. White matter consists mostly of glial cell and myelinated axons which facilitate communication between different parts of the brain.

Q. 9 Where is the hunger centre located in human brain?

Ans. Hypothalamus contains centres control the urge for eating and drinking.

Q. 10 Which sensory organ is involved in vertigo (sensation of oneself or objects spinning around)?

Ans. The inner ear, specifically the vestibular system, is the sensory organ involved in vertigo.

Q. 11 While travelling at a higher altitude, a person complains of dizziness and vomiting sensation. Which part of the inner ear is disturbed during the journey?

Ans. The symptoms of dizziness and vomiting, when travelling at higher altitude are due to disturbance in the following areas :

(i) The function of Eustachian tube is to equalise the pressure on both sides of the eardrum; sudden elevation changes can cause pressure imbalance, leading to discomfort.

(ii) The semicircular ducts, **(the anterior, posterior** and **lateral semicircular)** ducts) are concerned with the balancing of the body, Change in altitude brings changes in the reorientation and adjustments in these structures of internal ear causing confusion in balance and contributing to dizziness and vomiting.

Q. 12 Complete the statement by choosing appropriate match among the following.

	Column I		Column II
A.	Resting potential	1.	Chemicals involved in the transmission of impulses at synapses.
B.	Nerve impulse	2.	Gap between the pre synaptic and post synaptic neurons.
C.	Synaptic cleft	3.	Electrical potential difference across the resting neural membrane.
D.	Neurotransmitters	4.	An electrical wave like response of a neuron to a stimulation.

Ans. A. → (3) B. → (4) C. → (2) D. → (1)

	Column I	Column II
A.	Resting potential	3. Electrical potential difference across the resting neural membrane.
B.	Nerve impulse	4. An electrical wave like response of a neuron to a stimulation.
C.	Synaptic cleft	2. Gap between the pre-synaptic and pos-synaptic neurons.
D.	Neurotransmitters	1. Chemicals involved in the transmission of impulses at synapses.

Short Answer Type Questions

Q. 1 The major parts of the human neural system are depicted below. Fill in the empty boxes with appropriate words.

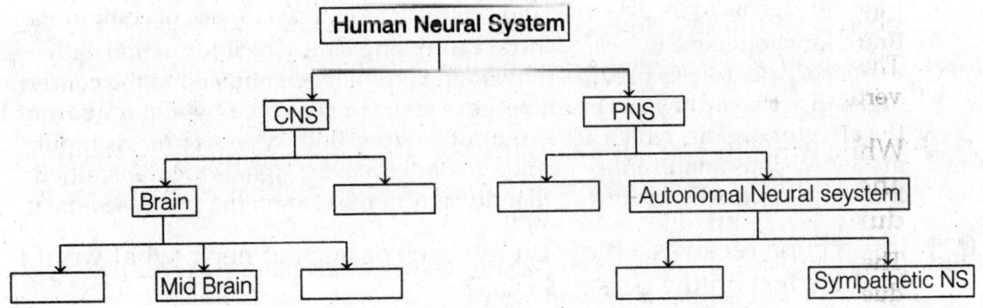

Ans. The major parts of the human neural system are filled in the boxes with appropriate words

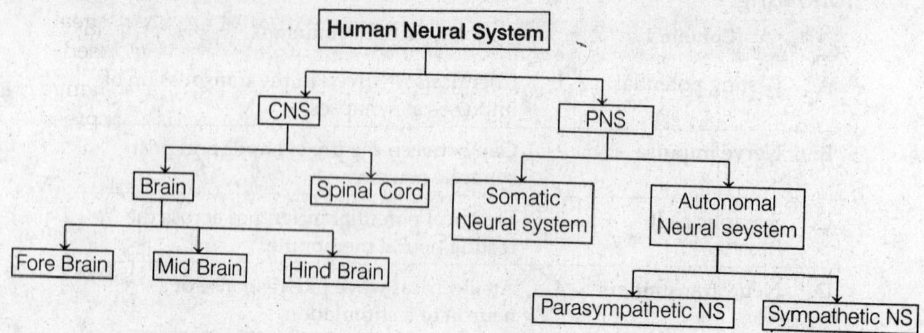

Q. 2 What is the difference between electrical transmission and chemical transmission?

Ans. Differences between electrical transmission and chemical transmission are as given below

Electrical Transmission	Chemical Transmission
It occurs at electric synapse.	It occurs at chemical synapse.
Synaptic cleft may or may not be present.	Synaptic cleft is always present.
At electrical synapses, electrical current can flow directly from one neuron into the other across these synapses.	At chemical synapse, neurotransmitter from pre-synaptic neurons transfer to post-synaptic neurons, leading to transmission of impulse.
Impulse transmission is faster.	Impulse transmission is slower.

Q. 3 Neuron system and computers share certain common features. Comment in five lines. (Hint : CPU, input-output divices)

Ans. The **sensory neurons** present in various organs sense the environment and transmit signals to the brain. So, it is equivalent to input device of computers. **Brain** function like CPU, *i.e.*, Central Processing Unit. The information gathered by sensory neurons is processed by brain and it gives command to the concerned organ to act accordingly. This message is taken or conveyed by **motor neurons to the effector organs,** which act as output devices. Both systems process input, make decisions and produce output. In both systems, signals are transmitted through a network of pathway that direct action based on the processed data.

Q. 4 If someone receives a blow on the back of neck, what would be the effect on the person's CNS?

Thinking Process The central nervous system, that includes brain and spinal cord, are the actual command centre for entire body and any damage, or abnormality in these can lead to non-functioning of body parts and organs.

Ans. If a person receives a blow on the back of neck, then it will lead in an impairment of cognitive abilities or physical functioning. Such an injury can damage the brainstem or spinal cord, leading to loss of motor or sensory function. It can also result in the disturbance of behavioural or emotional functioning. Cervical injuries often lead to quadriplegia (paralysic of all four limbs).

Q. 5 What is the function ascribed to Eustachian tube?

Ans. The **Eustachian tube** connects the middle ear cavity to the pharynx. It helps in equalising air pressures on either sides of the ear drum. At the pharyngeal opening of the Eustachian tube, is a valve which normally remains closed.

The valve opens during yawning, swallowing and during an abrupt change in altitude, when air enters or leaves the tympanic cavity to equalise the pressure of air on the two sides of the tympanic membrane.

Q. 6 Label the following parts in the given diagram using arrow.

(a) Aqueous chamber

(b) Cornea

(c) Lens

(d) Retina

(e) Vitreous chamber

(f) Blind spot

Ans. Representation of the following parts of eye is given below:

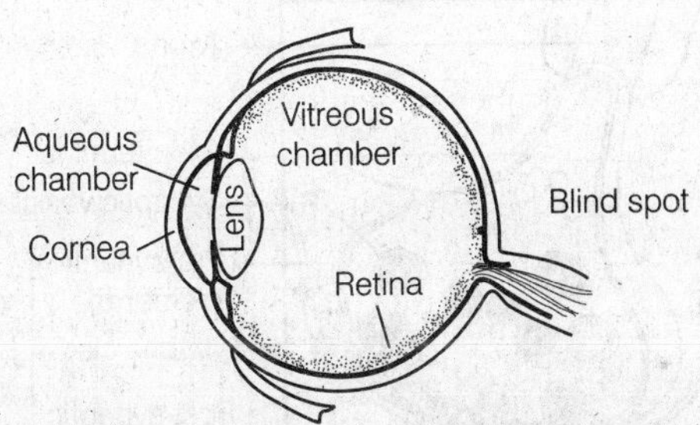

Long Answer Type Questions

Q. 1 Explain the process of the transport and release of a neurotransmitter with the help of a labelled diagram showing a complete neuron, axon terminal and synapse.

Ans. A neuron has three main parts

(i) Cell body (ii) Axon

(iii) Dendrites

Any stimulus or nerve impulse passes along a neuron *via* axon. This nerve impulse is wave of bioelectric or electrochemical disturbance that passes along neuron during conduction of an excitation.

Transport and release of a neurotransmitter occurs within a synapse. At a chemical synapse, the membranes of the pre- and post-synaptic neurons are separated by a fluid-filled space called synaptic cleft.

Neurotransmitters are involved in the transmission of impulses at these synapses. The axon terminals contain vesicles filled with these neurotransmitters.

When an impulse (action potential) arrives at the axon terminal, it stimulates the movement of the synaptic vesicles towards the membrane, where they fuse with the plasma membrane and release their neurotransmitters in the synaptic cleft.

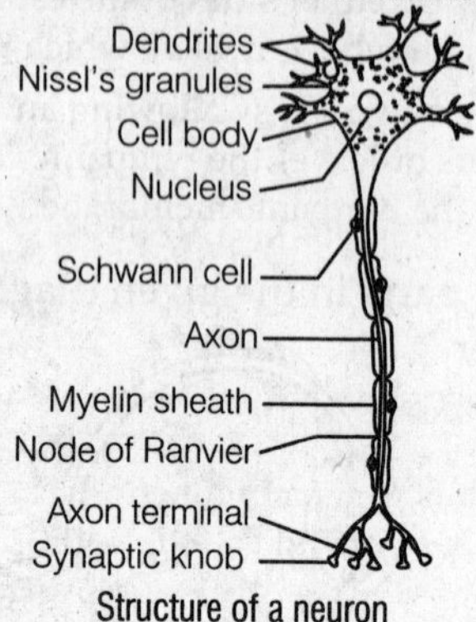

Structure of a neuron

The released neurotransmitters bind to their specific receptors, on the post-synaptic membrane. This binding opens ion channels allowing the entry of ions which can generate a new action potential in the post-synaptic neuron.

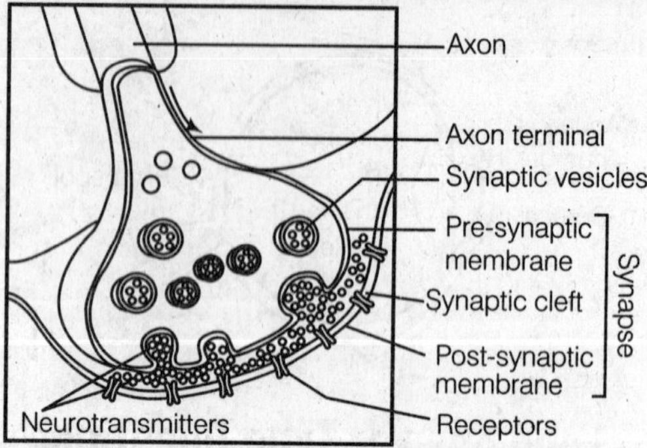

Transmission of a nerve impulse at chemical synapse

Q. 2 Name the parts of human forebrain indicating their respective functions.

Thinking Process The brain is the central information processing organ of our body and act as the 'command and control system'.

Ans. The forebrain is the largest part of the brain most of which is **cerebrum**. Other important structures include the **thalamus, hypothalamus** and the **limbic system**.

The cerebrum is divided into two cerebral hemisphere connected by a mass of white matter known is **corpus callosum**. Each hemispere is split into four lobes. The surface of each hemisphere is made up of grey matter known as the cerebral cortex that is folded to increase the surface area.

Various structures of forebrain are given below

Brain Region	Structure	Function
Diencephalon	Thalamus	Organising sensory information
Diencephalon	Hypothalamus	Endocrine system, thermoregulation
Telencephalon	Cerebral cortex	Consciousness, language, etc
Telencephalon	Limbic system	Memory, motivation, emotions
Telencephalon	Olfactory bulb /lobes	Smell

Thalamus The thalamus has many functions, including processing and relaying sensory information selectively to various parts of the cerebral cortex, transmitting signals to the cerebral cortex and also regulating states of sleep and wakefulness. The thalamus plays a major role in regulating arousal levels of consciousness and levels of activity.

Hypothalamus

The function of the hypothalamus is mainly involved regulation of the endocrine system and is closely related to the pituitary gland.

Cerebral Cortex The cerebral cortex is essential for memory, attention, awareness, thought, language and consciousness. The cerebral cortex is connected to structures such as the thalamus and the basal ganglia, sending information to them along efferent connections and receiving information from them *via* afferent connections.

Motor Cortex

The motor cortex areas in both hemispheres of the brain are responsible for controlling voluntary movements, especially fine movements.

Sensory Areas

The sensory areas are the areas that receive and process information from the sensory inputs. Inputs from thc thalamus are relayed to the primary sensory areas, where vision, hearing and touch are processed. The two hemispheres of the cerebral cortex receive information from the opposite (contralateral) side of the body.

The association areas of the brain function to produce a perception of the world enabling an animal to interact with their environment effectively. The frontal lobe or prefrontal association complex is involved in planning actions and movement.

Limbic System

The limbic system is principally responsible for emotions and the various types of emotion can affect the activity of the Autonomic Nervous System (ANS) and this is facilitated by the hypothalamus.

Olfactory Bulb

The olfactory bulb is responsible for olfaction concerned with sense of smell.

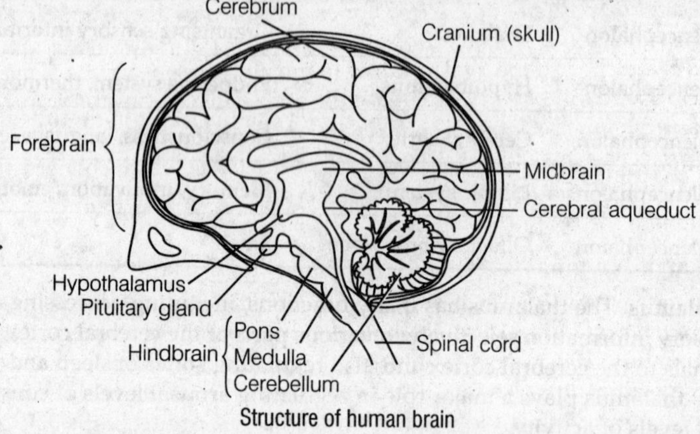

Structure of human brain

Q. 3 Explain the structure of middle and internal ear with the help of diagram.

Ans. Ears are a pair of **statoacoustic organ** meant for both balancing and hearing. In most mammals, the external ear is a flap of tissue also called pinna. It is a part of auditory system. The human ear consists of three main parts: external ear, middl e, ear and internal ear.

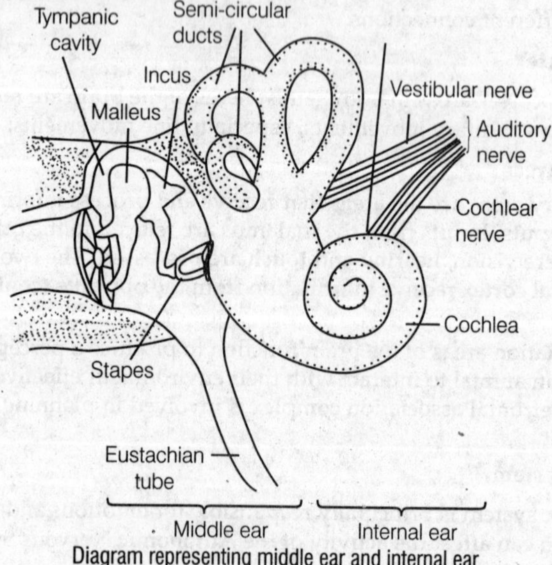

Diagram representing middle ear and internal ear

Structure of Middle Ear

The middle ear contains three bones or ossicles–the **malleus** (hammer), **incus** (anvil) and **stapes** (stirrup). These bones are attached to one another in a chain-like fashion. The malleus is attached to the tympanic membrane and the stapes is attached to the oval window (a membrane beneath the stapes) of cochlea. These three ossicles increase the efficiency of transmission of sound waves to the inner ear.

The middle ear also opens into the **Eustachian tube**, which connects with the pharynx and maintains the pressure between the middle ear and the outside atmosphere,

Structure of Internal Ear

The inner ear consists of a **labyrinth** of fluid-filled chambers within temporal bone of the skull. The labyrinth consists of two parts, *i.e.*, the **bony labyrinth** and **membranous labyrinth**.

The bony labyrinth is a series of channels. Inside these channels, membranous labyrinth lies, which is surrounded by a fluid called **perilymph**. The membranous labyrinth is filled with a fluid called **endolymph**. The coiled portion of the labyrinth is called **cochlea.**

The cochlea has two large canals the upper vestibular canal (scala vestibuli) and a lower tympanic canal (scala tympani). These are separated by a small **cochlear duct** (scala media). The vestibular and tympanic canals contain **perilymph** and the cochlear duct is filled with **endolymph.**

Chapter 22

Chemical Coordination and Integration

Multiple Choice Questions (MCQs)

Choose the correct answer from the given four options in the following questions :

Q. 1 Select the right match of endocrine gland and their hormones among the options given below

Column I		Column II	
A.	Pineal	1.	Epinephrine
B.	Thyroid	2.	Melatonin
C.	Ovary	3.	Estrogen
D.	Adrenal medulla	4.	Tetraiodothyronine

Codes

	A	B	C	D		A	B	C	D
(a)	4	2	1	3	(b)	2	4	1	3
(c)	3	2	1	4	(d)	2	4	3	1

Thinking Process Endocrine glands lack ducts, hence are called ductless glands. Their secretion are called hormones.

Ans. *(d)* **Pineal gland** secretes a hormone called **melatonin**. It is involved in regulating biological rhythm and sleep-wake cycle.

Thyroid gland secretes a hormone called **tetraiodothyronine**. It primarily regulates metabolism of body.

Ovary secretes **estrogen** which is involved in growth and **stimulation** of female secondary sex organs and also in the development of growing ovarian follicles.

Adrenal medulla secretes **epinephrine** and **norepinephrine** in response to stress or in any kind of emergency situations.

Q. 2 Which of the following hormones is not secreted by anterior pituitary?

(a) Growth hormone
(b) Follicle stimulating hormone
(c) Oxytocin
(d) Adrenocorticotrophic hormone

Thinking Process The pituitary gland is divided anatomically into two parts, *i.e.,* adenohypophysis or **Anterior pituitary** and a neurohypophysis or **Posterior pituitary** which are involved in secretion of different hormones accordingly.

Ans. *(c)* **Oxytocin** is the hormone of posterior pituitary in origin. It acts on the smooth muscles of uterus and stimulates their contraction and also plays role in milk secretion.

Follicle stimulating hormone stimulates growth of ovarian follicles in the female and spermatogenesis in the male.

Growth Hormone stimulates body growth by promoting the synthesis and deposition of proteins in tissues and also in the growth of bones and muscles.

Adrenocorticotrophic Hormone stimulates adrenal cortex of adrenal gland to produce glucocorticoid and mineralocorticoid.

Q. 3 Mary is about to face an interview. But during the first five minutes before the interview she experiences sweating, increased rate of heart beat, respiration, etc. Which hormone is responsible for her restlessness?

(a) Estrogen and progesterone
(b) Oxytocin and vasopressin
(c) Adrenaline and noradrenaline
(d) Insulin and glucagon

Thinking Process Adrenaline hormone is responsible for "flight or fight" response in our body.

Ans. ***(c)*** Mary, during her first five minutes, before interview experiences sweating, increased heart rate and respiration because she is having stress which leads to release of **emergency hormones** or **hormones of flight** and **fight**, *i.e.*, adrenaline and noradrenaline. These hormones stimulate the breakdown of glycogen resulting in increase concentration of glucose in blood.

Estrogen and progesterone Estrogen regulates growth and development of female sex organs, female secondary sexual characters, mammary gland development and progestrone supports pregnancy.

Oxytocin and vasopressin Oxytocin is involved in contraction of smooth muscles of uterus at the time of child birth in females and acts mainly on mammary gland for milk ejection. Vasopressin stimulates the absorption of water and electrolytes by distal tubules in kidney and also reduces loss of water.

Insulin and glucagon are the peptide hormones. **Insulin** decreases blood glucose level and **glucagon** is involved in increasing normal glucose levels in the blood.

Q. 4 The steroid responsible for balance of water and electrolytes in our body is

(a) insulin
(b) melatonin
(c) testosterone
(d) aldosterone

Thinking Process In humans steroid hormones are derived from cholesterol. Cholesterol is stored and produced in liver and is transported in cells as High Density Lipoprotein or HDL and Low Density Lipoprotein (LDL).

Ans. ***(d)*** **Aldosterone** acts at the renal tubules stimulating the reabsorption of Na^+, water and excretion of K^+ and phosphate ion. Thus, it helps in the maintenance of electrolytes, body fluid volume, osmotic pressure and blood pressure.

Insulin is a peptide hormone, that plays an important role in maintaining the normal blood glucose levels.

Testosterone is the male sex hormone, stimulating male features like muscular growth, growth of facial and axial hair, aggressiveness, low pitch of voice, etc, and spermatogenesis.

Melatonin hormone has a very important role in regulating 24 hours (diurnal) rhythm of our body.

Q. 5 Thymosin is responsible for

(a) raising the blood sugar level
(b) raising the blood calcium level
(c) differentiation of T-lymphocytes
(d) decrease in blood RBCs

Ans. *(c)* **Thymosins** play a major role in the differentiation of T-lymphocytes, which provide cell mediated immunity. It also promotes antibody production to provide **humoral immunity**.

Q. 6 In the mechanism of action of a protein hormone, one of the second messengers is

(a) Cyclic AMP (b) Insulin (c) T_3 (d) Gastrin

Ans. *(a)* **Cyclic AMP** is one of the second messengers involved in the action of a protein hormone. The other three options are incorrect as

Insulin regulates glucose homeostasis.

T_3 (Triiodothyronine) regulates the metabolic rate of the body and thus, helps in maintaining Basal Metabolic Rate (BMR).

Gastrin is a peptide hormone, that stimulates the secretion of **hydrochloric acid** and **pepsinogen** in the stomach.

Q. 7 Leydig cells produce a group of hormones called

(a) androgens (b) estrogens (c) aldosterone (d) gonadotropins

Ans. *(a)* The **Leydig cells** or **interstitial cells**, which are present in the interstitial spaces of testis produce a group of hormones called **androgens** mainly **testosterone.**

Estrogen is secreted by growing follicles in ovaries and stimulates growth and development of female secondary sex organs.

Aldosterone is secreted by adrenal gland, helps in maintaining electrolytes in the body fluid, volume, osmotic pressure and blood pressure.

Gonadotropins are secreted by anterior pituitary and stimulate the gonadal activity. These include LH and FSH.

Q. 8 Corpus luteum secretes a hormone called

(a) prolactin (b) progesterone (c) aldosterone (d) testosterone

Ans. *(b)* **Corpus luteum** secretes a hormone called as **progesterone** which supports pregnancy and stimulates development of the **mammary gland** for the milk production in female.

Prolactin also known as luteotropic hormone, its a protein hormone that is involved in production of milk in females. The source for prolactin secretion is anterior pituitary gland.

Testosterone stimulates muscular growth, growth of facial and axillary hair, aggressiveness, low pitch of voice, etc in males. The source for the secretion of testosterone is **Leydig cells** or **interstitial cells.**

Aldosterone is secreted by adrenal cortex and plays a role in reabsorption of sodium ions, etc.

Q. 9 Cortisol is secreted from

(a) pancreas (b) thyroid (c) adrenal (d) thymus

Ans. *(c)* **Cortisol** is secreted from the adrenal gland. The **zona fasciculata** region of adrenal cortex secretes **cortisol, corticosterone** and **cortisone**. These hormones are involved in maintaining glucose homeostasis.

Pancreas is a composite gland which secretes insulin, glucagon and somatostatin.

Thyroid gland secretes thyroxin or tetraiodothyronine (T_4) and triodothyronine (T_3) which regulate the metabolic rate of the body and maintain basal metabolic rate. It also secretes calcitonin.

Thymus secretes thymosin, involved in providing cell mediated immunity to the body.

Q. 10 A hormone responsible for normal sleep-wake cycle is

(a) epinephrine (b) gastrin (c) melatonin (d) insulin

Ans. *(c)* **Melatonin** hormone plays a very important role in maintaining the normal rhythms of sleep-wake cycle.

Gastrin is secreted by the endocrine cells present in the gastrointestinal tract and stimulates the secretion of hydrochloric acid and pepsinogen.

Epinephrine is secreted from the adrenal gland and acts as a stress relieving hormone at the time of stress condition in the body.

Insulin secreted from pancreas is involved in maintaining glucose homeostasis.

Q. 11 Hormones are called chemical signals that stimulate specific target tissues. Their action depends on the presence of receptors on the respective target tissues. Which is the correct location of these receptors in of protein hormones?

(a) Extra cellular matrix (b) Blood

(c) Plasma membrane (d) Nucleus

Thinking Process Hormones produce their effects on target tissue by binding to specific proteins called hormone receptor.

Ans. *(c)* Hormone receptors are located in the target tissue only and protein receptors are present on the plasma membrane/cell membrane of the target cell.

Q. 12 Choose the correct option among the following options

	Column I		Column II
A.	Epinephrine	1.	Stimulates in muscle growth
B.	Testosterone	2.	Decrease in blood pressure
C.	Glucagon	3.	Breakdown of in liver glycogen
D.	Atrial natriuretic factor	4.	Increases heart beat

Codes

	A	B	C	D		A	B	C	D
(a)	2	1	3	4	(b)	4	1	3	2
(c)	1	2	3	4	(d)	1	4	2	3

Ans. *(b)* **Epinephrine** increases heart beat and also called as **stress hormone.**

Testosterone stimulates muscle growth, as a secondary sex-character in males.

Glucagon leads to breakdown of the glycogen content in liver. It is secreted from pancreas.

Atrial Natriuritic Factor decrease blood pressure by vasodilation

Q. 13 Which of the following organs in mammals does not consist of a central in calcium balance in the human body?

(a) Vitamin-D (b) Parathyroid hormone
(c) Thyrocalcitonin (d) Thymosin

Ans. *(d)* **Thymosin hormone** has no role in regulation of blood calcium homeostasis. It plays a major role in the differentiation of T-lymphocytes, which provides cell mediated immunity. While, vitamin-D, thyrocalcitonin and parathyroid hormone plays a vital role in maintaining calcium homeostasis by regulating blood calcium levels.

Q. 14 Which of the following organs in mammals does not consist of a central 'medullary' region surrounded by a cortical region.

(a) ovary (b) adrenal (c) liver (d) kidney

Ans. *(c)* **Liver,** the largest gland of body surrounded by the abdominal cavity, is the only organs from the above mentioned options that does not consist of a central 'medullary' region, surrounded by a cortical region.

Rest three options, *i.e.,* ovary, adrenal and kidney bear a prominent 'medullary and cortical region'.

Q. 15 Which of the following conditions is not linked to deficiency of thyroid hormone?

(a) Cretinism (b) Goitre (c) Myxoedema (d) Exophthalmia

Ans. *(d)* **Exophthalmia,** is a condition, that is not linked to deficiency of thyroid hormone but to oversecretion of thyroid hormone. In this condition there is a bulging of the eye anteriorly out of the orbit.

Cretinism, goitre and myxoedema are the diseases linked to thyroid deficiency.

Very Short Answer Type Questions

Q. 1 There are many endocrine glands in human body. Name the glands which is absent in male and the one absent in female.

Ans. In males a pair of testis is present in the scrotal sac. Testes perform dual functions as **a primary sex organ** as well as an **endocrine gland**. This gland is absent in females.

In females a pair of ovaries is present which are located in the abdomen. Ovary is the primary female sex organ which produces ovum during menstrual cycle and act as an endocrine gland in producing hormone like **estrogen** and **progesterone.** This gland is absent in males.

Q. 2 Which of the two adrenocortial layers, zona glomerulosa and zona reticularis lies outside enveloping the other?

Ans. **Zona glomerulosa** (outer layer) envelops zona reticularis (inner layer) from the outside.

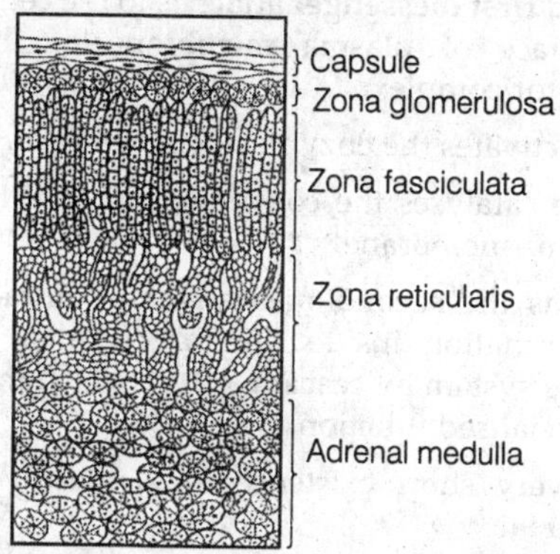

Diagram depicting different zones in adrenal gland

Q. 3 What is erythropoiesis? Which hormone stimulates it?

Ans. **Erythropoiesis** is the process of formation of RBC. Peptide hormone **erythropoietin** secreted from the juxtaglomerular cells of kidney stimulates erythropoiesis.

Q. 4 Name the only hormone secreted by pars intermedia of the pituitary gland.

Ans. **Pars intermedia** of pituitary gland secretes only one hormone called Melanocyte Stimulating Hormone (MSH). This hormone causes dispersal of pigment granules in the pigment cells, thereby darkening the colour in certain animals like fishes and amphibians.

Q. 5 Name the endocrine gland that produces calcitonin and mention the role played by this hormone.

Ans. Calcitonin (also known as thyrocalcitonin) is a 32 amino acid, linear polypeptide hormone that is produced in humans primarily by the **parafollicular cells** of the **thyroid gland**. It checks excess Ca^{2+} and phosphate in plasma by decreasing mobilisation from bones.

Q. 6 Name the hormone that helps in cell-mediated immunity.

Ans. Thymosins play a major role in the development and differentiation of **T-lymphocytes**, which provide cell-mediated immunity.

Q. 7 What is the role of second messenger in the mechanism of protein hormone action?

Ans. The hormones that are derivatives of polypeptides or proteins are called peptide hormones. These being insoluble in lipids can not enter the target cell.

These act at the surface of target cell as primary messengers and bind to the cell-surface receptor forming the hormone-receptor complex. This process activates a second messenger such as cyclic AMP (*c*AMP), to transmit the signal inside the cell. It involves following steps

(i) Hormone called **first messenger** attaches to the cell surface receptor protein on the outer surface of plasma membrane of the target cell, forming a hormone-receptor complex.

(ii) This complex activates the enzyme adenyl cyclase.

(iii) Adenyl cyclase catalyses the conversion of ATP to cyclic AMP on the inner surface of plasma membrane.

(iv) ***c*AMP** serves as the **second messenger** or intracelluar hormonal mediator delivering information inside the target cells. This activates appropriate cellular enzyme system by **cascade effect** which induces the cell machinery to perform its specialised function.

(v) *c*AMP has a very short existence. It is rapidly degraded by the enzyme **phosphodiesterase.**

Water soluble hormones, such as amines, peptides, proteins and glycoproteins exert their control through the cyclic AMP. These hormones act quickly and produce immediate effect.

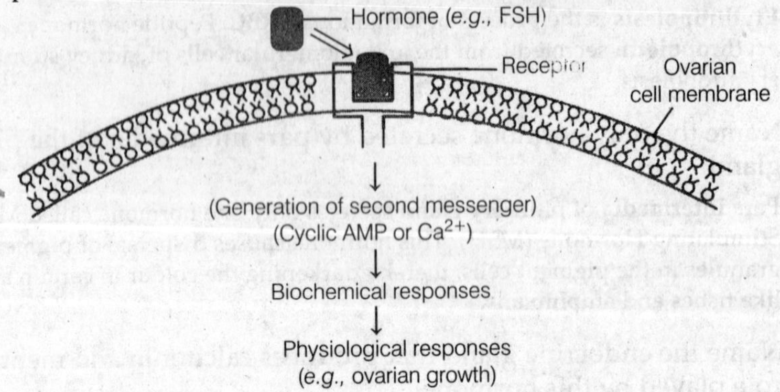

Q. 8 State whether true or false

(a) Gastrointestinal tract, kidney and heart also produce hormones.

(b) Pars distalis produces six trophic hormones.

(c) B-lymphocytes provide cell-mediated immunity.

(d) Insulin resistance results in a disease called diabetes mellitus.

Ans. (a) **Gastrointestinal tract, kidney** and **heart** also produce hormones other than endocrine glands hence, the statement is **True**. GI tract secretes hormones such as gastrin, secretin, cholecystokinin etc., Kidney secretes renin and erythropoietin. Heart secretes anti-natriuretic factor

(b) **Pars distalis** produces six trophic hormones, *i.e.,* Growth Hormone (GH) Prolactin (PRL), Thyroid Stimulating Hormone (TSH), Adrinocorticotrophic Hormone (ACTH), Luteinising Hormone (LH) and Follicle Stimulating Hormone (FSH) hence, the statement is **True**.

(c) **T-lymphocytes** are involved in providing cell-mediated immunity not **B-lymphocytes** hence, the statement is **False**. B-lymphocytes are responsible for antibody production in humoral immunity.

(d) Insulin resistance leads to type 2 Diabetes mellitus, a condition in which the body does not respond properly to insulin, leading to high blood glucose level. In contrast, the Insulin Dependent Diabetes Mellitus (IDDM) is caused by the failure of beta cells to produce adequate amount of insulin hence, results in a disease called Type 1 **Diabetes mellitus**. So, the statement is True.

Q. 9 A patient complains of constant thirst, excessive passing of urine and low blood pressure. When the doctor checked the patients' blood glucose and blood insulin level, the level were normal or slightly **low**. The doctor diagnosed the condition as diabetes insipidus. But he decided to measure one more hormone in patients blood. Which hormone does the doctor intend to measure?

Ans. The doctor is likely to measure antidiuretic hormone (ADH), also known as **vasopressin**, in the patient's blood. Diabetes insipidus is caused by a deficiency of ADH or the kidney's inability to respond to ADH, leading to excessive urination and thirst. Unlike diabetes melitus, where blood glucose is high, insipidus is characterised by normal or low blood glucose.

Q. 10 Correct the following statements by replacing the term **underlined**.

(a) Insulin is a **steroid** hormone.

(b) TSH is secreted from the **corpus luteum**.

(c) **Tetraiodothyronine** is an emergency hormone.

(d) The **pineal gland** is located on the anterior part of the kidney.

Ans. **(a)** Insulin is a **peptide** hormone

(b) TSH is secreted from the **pars distalis region of pituitary.**

(c) **Adrenaline** is an **emergency hormone**. Tetraiodothyronine is an essential hormone.

(d) The **adrenal gland** is located on the anterior part of the kidney.

Q. 11 Rearrange the following hormones in column I so as to match with their chemical nature in column II.

	Column I		Column II
A.	Oxytocin	1.	Amino acid derivative
B.	Epinephrine	2.	Steroid
C.	Progesterone	3.	Protein
D.	Growth hormone	4.	Peptide

Ans. The correct matching is as follows

	Column I	Column II
A.	Oxytocin	Peptide
B.	Epinephrine	Amino acid derivative
C.	Progesterone	Steroid
D.	Growth hormone	Protein

Short Answer Type Questions

Q. 1 What is the role-played by luteinising hormones in males and females respectively?

Thinking Process LH and FSH stimulate gonadal activity and hence are called gonadotropins.

Ans. **In males**, luteinising hormone (LH) stimulates the synthesis and secretion of hormones called **androgens** from testis. Androgens along with FSH (Follicle Stimulating Hormone) regulate **spermatogenesis** (the production of sperm).

In females, LH induces ovulation of fully mature follicles (Graafian follicles) and maintains the corpus luteum, which is formed from the remnants of the Graafian follicles after ovulation. The corpus luteum secretes progesterone.

Q. 2 What is the role of second messenger in hormone action?

Ans. *Refer to Q.* 7 of very short answer type questions.

Q. 3 On an educational trip to Uttaranchal, Ketki and her friends observe that many local people were having swollen necks, Please help Ketki and her friends to find out the solutions to the following questions.

(a) which probable disease are these people suffering from?

(b) How is it caused?

(c) What effect does this condition have on pregnancy?

Ans. (a) People with swollen necks are suffering from **goitre due to deficiency of iodine** in the their diet.

(b) **Iodine** is essential for the synthesis of thyroid hormones (T_3 and T_4) which are iodinated forms of tyrosine. Deficiency of **iodine** in our diet results in hypothyroidism and enlargement of the thyroid gland (goitre) occurs.

(c) **Hypothyroidism** during pregnancy causes developmental abnormalities in growing baby like stunted growth (cretinism) mental retardation, low intelligence quotient (IQ), abnormal skin, deaf mutism, etc.

Q. 4 George comes on a vacation to India from US. The long journey disturbs his biological system and he suffers from jet lag. What is the cause of his discomfort?

Thinking Process The melatonin hormone secreted by the pineal gland is also called as 'sleep hormone' as it promotes sleep-wake cycle.

Ans. Jet lag is caused by the disruption of the body's internal clock as it is out of synchronisation because of the unfamiliar time zone of the destination. The body experiences different patterns of light and dark conditions, which disrupts the natural sleep-wake cycle.

Melatonin is a hormone that plays a key role in body rhythms and causes jet lag. After the sun sets, eyes perceive darkness and alert the hypothalamus to stimulate the release melatonin, which promotes sleep. Conversely, when the eyes perceive sunlight, they tell the hypothalamus to inhibit melatonin production.

However, the hypothalamus can not readjust its schedule instantly and it may take several days, to overcome this problem.

Q. 5 Inflammatory responses can be controlled by a certain steroid. Name the steroid, its source and also its other important functions.

Ans. **Glucocorticoids,** particularly cortisol, produce anti-inflammatory reactions and suppress the immune response. The source for glucocorticoids is the middle zone, which is the widest of three zones, in adrenal cortex called zona fasciculata.

The functions of glucocorticoids as the name suggests is that they affect carbohydrate metabolism and metabolism of proteins and fats. They stimulate gluconeogenesis (formation of glucose from non sugar sources), lipolysis (break down of lipids) and proteolysis (break down of proteins).

They also inhibit cellular uptake and utilisation of amino acids. Cortisol is also called **stress** hormone as it copes with stress.

Q. 6 Old people have weak immune system. What could be the reasons?

Thinking Process Thymus plays a major role in the development of the immune system.

Ans. The thymus gland is a lobular structure located on the anterior side of the heart and the aorta. It is derived from the endoderm of the embryo. Thymus secretes a hormone named thymosin which stimulates the development of White Blood Cells (WBCs), involved in immune function.

As people age, the thymus undergoes atrophy (degeneration), resulting in decreased production of thymosin. As result the immune system becomes weak, in old people.

Q. 7 What are the effects of hypothyroidism (observed during pregnancy) on the development and maturation of a growing baby?

Ans. **Hypothyroidism** during pregnancy cause defective development and maturation of the growing baby leading to a stunted growth (cretinism), mental retardation, low intelligence Quotient (IQ), abnormal skin, deaf mutism, and other developmental defects.

Q. 8 Mention the difference between hypothyroidism and hyperthyroidism.

Thinking Process Thyroid gland is the largest endocrine gland located in the neck region. The hormones secreted by thyroid gland are involved in variety of functions.

Ans. Differences between hypothyroidism and hyperthyroidism are as follows

Hypothyroidism	Hyperthyroidism
It is the insufficient secretion of thyroid hormones causing cretinism in children and myxoedema in adults	This syndrome arises as the body tissues are exposed to excessive levels of T_3 and T_4. The main effects are due to increased metabolic rate. The gland enlarges and may develop single or multiple hormone secreting nodule such as in Grave's disease and toxic nodular goitre

Hypothyroidism	Hyperthyroidism
Cretinism is associated with the retarded mental and physical development. The child receives hormones from the mother before birth, so appears normal at first, but within a few weeks or months, it becomes evident that physical and mental development is retarded. Symptoms are disproportionately short limbs, a large protruding tongue, coarse dry skin, poor abdominal muscle tone and an umbilical hernia.	**Exophthalmic goitre** (Grave's disease) is the most common cause of thyrotoxicosis in adults. It affects, women more commonly than men. High levels of thyroxine are secreted, which are not subjected to the normal secretion of TRH from the hypothalamus and TSH from the anterior pituitary. **Exophthalamus** (Protrusion of the eyeballs) due to the deposition of excess fat and fibrous tissue behind the eyes, is often present in Grave's disease. In severe cases, the eyelids may not completely cover the eyes during blinking of the conjuctiva and thus, predisposed to infection.
Myxedema (Gull's disease), this conditions is common in adults and five times more common in females than in males. It results in an abnormally low metabolic rate and lack of response to demand for increased energy, by muscles, during exercise. Mental and physical processes become slower, skin become coarse, the hair lacks lustre, becomes brittle and tends to fall out.	**Toxic nodular goitre** (Plummer's disease) is associated with excess secretion of thyroxine leading to the general effects of increased metabolic rate.

Q. 9 You have learnt that a characteristic feature of endocrine system is the presence of feed back loops. By this what is meant if hormone *A* stimulates gland '*X*' to secrete hormone *B*, the production of '*A*' could be modified when the level of *B* changes in our blood. An example is the relation between hormones LH and estrogen (E_2).

An old woman exhibits the following features. High levels of LH in blood but low levels of E_2 in the blood. Another woman exhibits high level of LH in blood and also high level of E_2 in the blood. Where is the defect in both these women? Provide suitable diagram to support this answer.

Ans. When the secretion of hormone is under the control of factors or other hormones it is called **feedback control.**

Negative feedback control If there is a high concentration of a hormone *B* in the blood then it will have an inhibitory effect on the secretion of hormone *A*. Decreased secretion of *A* will eventually result in a decrease in the production of hormone *B*. This is negative feedback control.

Positive feedback control If there is low concentration of hormone *B* in our blood then it will have a stimulatory effect on the secretion of hormone *A*. Increased secretion of *A* will eventually result in an increase in production of hormone *B*. This is positive feedback control.

Case Analysis

1. **Old Woman (High LH, Low E_2)** Low level of E_2 should have positive feedback control on secretion of LH resulting in increase in production of E_2. But old woman shows low level of E_2 and high level of LH hormone, this means. LH is not stimulating gland X to secrete hormone E_2.
2. **Young Woman (High LH, High E_2)** High level of E_2 should have negative feedback control on secretion of LH resulting in decrease in production of E_2. But young woman shows high level of both E_2 and LH, this means there is some defect in the negative feedback loop.

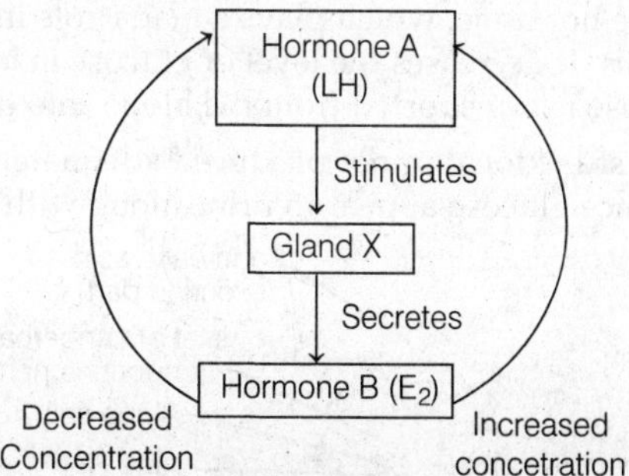

Long Answer Type Questions

Q. 1 A milkman is very upset one morning as his cow refuses to give any milk. The milkman's wife gets the calf from the shed. On feeding by the calf, the cow gave sufficient milk. Describe the role of endocrine gland and pathway associated with this response?

Ans. Suckling by the calf creates a **neuroendocrine reflex** which results in the increased secretion of oxytocin from the neurohypophysis. Oxytocin is synthesised in the hypothalamus in specific nuclei, the paraventricular nucleus and the supraoptic nucleus (a cluster of nerve cells in the brain is often called a nucleus).

Neurons in this region (hypothalamic nuclei) synthesise the oxytocin precursor and package it into vesicles. The oxytocin concentration in the blood normally, gets increased within 1-2 min, after the udder stimulation.

It brings about contraction of smooth muscles of the udder resulting in the milk flow. A direct intra-udder function of oxytocin like hormone would perform the same function.

It can be summarised as follows

Udder (suckling stimulus) $\rightarrow$ Brain (hypothalamus) $\rightarrow$ Neurohypophysis $\rightarrow$ Blood (oxytocin) $\rightarrow$ Udder (smooth muscles) $\rightarrow$ Milk flow.

Q. 2 A sample of urine was diagnosed to contain high content of glucose and ketone bodies. Based on this observation, answer the following

(a) which endocrine gland and hormone is related to this condition?

(b) name the cells on which this hormone acts

(c) what is the condition called and how can it rectified?

Thinking Process Pancreas is a composite gland which acts both as exocrine and endocrine gland. It plays a role in maintaining blood glucose levels.

Ans. (a) The pancreas is associated with this condition and the related hormone is insulin.

The pancreas consists of 'islets of Langerhans. The two main type of cells in the islets of Langerhans are α-cells and β-cells. α-cells secrete **glucagon** while β-cell secrete **insulin.**

Insulin is a peptide hormone, which plays a major role in the regulation of glucose homeostasis. It decreases the level of glucose in blood by increasing the rate at which glucose is transported from the blood into the cell.

When insulin is dysfunctional or not produced adequately glucose uptake is hampered' and hence glucose appear in urine along with ketone bodies.

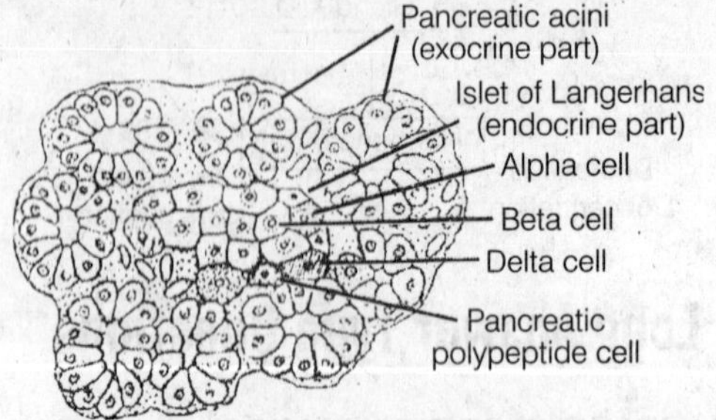

Section of Pancreaf

(b) Insulin hormone mainly acts on hepatocytes cells (liver cells) and adipocytes cells (cells of adipose tissue) and enhances cellular glucose up take and utilisation.

(c) Prolonged hyperglycemic condition leads to a complex disorder called **diabetes mellitus** which is associated with loss of glucose through urine and formation of harmful compounds known as ketone bodies due to fat metabolism.

Diabetic patients are successfully treated with **insulin therapy.** It lowers the blood glucose levels and give relief to the patients.

Q. 3 Calcium plays a very important role in the formation of bones. Write the role of endocrine glands and hormones responsible for maintaining calcium homeostasis.

Ans. The endocrine glands and hormones responsible for maintaining calcium homeostasis, are **thyroid** and **parathyroid glands** and their associated hormones are **calcitonin** and **Parathyroid Hormone (PTH).**

(i) **Parathyroid glands** are the glands developed from the endoderm of the embryo. The cells of parathyroid glands are of two types, *i.e.*, **chief cells** and **oxyphil cells**. The chief cells of the parathyroid glands secrete parathyroid hormone (PTH).

This hormone (PTH) is involved in regulating calcium and phosphate balance between the blood and other tissue. It mobilises the release of calcium into the blood from bones. PTH increases calcium reabsorption by the body organs like intestine and kidneys.

(ii) **Thyroid gland** is the largest endocrine gland located anterior to the thyroid cartilage of the larynx in the neck. This gland plays a vital role in maintaining calcium homeostasis. It releases thyrocalcitonin (also called calcitonin) hormone produced by the parafollicular cells, also called 'C' cells.

This hormone is secreted when the calcium level in blood gets high. It is a 32 amino acid peptide hormone that lowers the calcium level by suppressing release of calcium ions from the bones. Thus, calcitonin has an action opposite to that of the parathyroid hormone on calcium homeostasis.

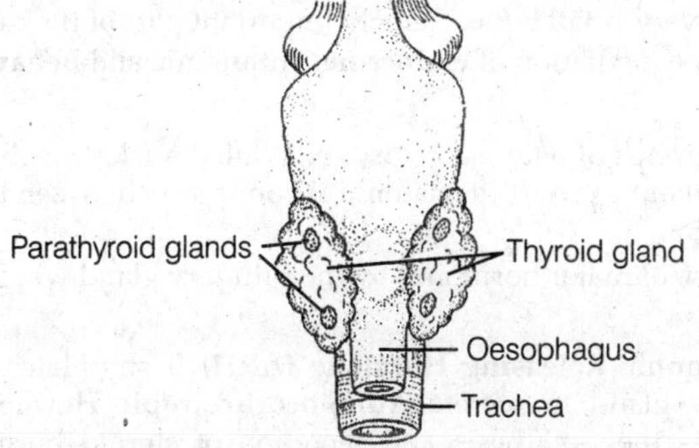

Diagram illustrating parathyroid glands and thyroid gland
(Occupying the posterior surface of thyroid gland)

Q. 4 Illustrate the differences between the mechanism of action of a protein and a steroid hormone.

Ans. Differences between the mechanism of action of a peptide and a steroid hormone are as follows

Peptide Hormone Action	Steroid Hormone Action
Peptide hormones interact with membrane bound receptors.	They interact with intracellular receptors to form hormone receptor complex
They generate second messengers (*e.g.* cyclic AMP, IP_3, Ca^{2+}, etc.)	They regulate gene expression or chromosomes function by the interaction of hormone receptor complex with the genome.
The second messengers regulate cellular metabolism.	Cumulative biochemical actions results in physiological and development effects.

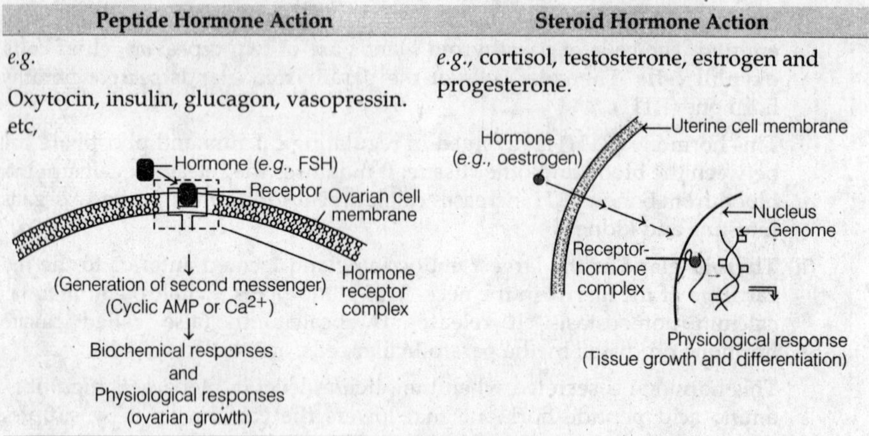

Q. 5 Hypothalamus is a super master endocrine gland. Elaborate.

Ans. **Hypothalamus** is a very small but extremely important part of the diencephalon that is involved in the mediation of **endocrine, autonomic** and **behavioural function.**

It contains several groups of neurosecretory cells called nuclei which produce hormones. Hypothalamus provides anatomical connection between the nervous and endocrine system.

It controls the release of major hormones by the pituitary gland which are summarised below

(i) **Adrenocorticotrophic Releasing Hormone (ARH)** It stimulates the anterior lobe of pituitary gland to secrete **Adrenocorticotropic Hormone** (ACTH). **ACTH** stimulates the synthesis and secretion of steroid hormones called glucocorticoids by adrenal glands.

(ii) **Thyrotropin Releasing Hormone (TRH)** It stimulates the anterior lobe of pituitary gland to release **Thyroid Stimulating Hormone** (TSH).

(iii) **Growth Hormone Releasing Hormone (GHRH)** It stimulates the anterior lobe of the pituitary gland to release growth hormone or (GH) somatostatin.

(iv) **Gonadotropin Releasing Hormone (GnRH)** It stimulates the anterior lobe of the pituitary gland to release gonadotropic hormones **(FSH and LH)**.

(v) **Prolactin Releasing Hormone (PRH)** It stimulates the anterior lobe of the pituitary gland to secrete **prolactin.**

(vi) **MSH Releasing Hormone (MSH-RH)** It stimulates the intermediate lobe of the pituitary gland to secrete **Melanocyte Stimulating Hormone (MSH)**

(vii) **Somatostatin** : This hormone prevent the secretion of several other hormones including growth hormone, TSH, cholecystokinin (in small intestine) and insulin.

These hormones released from hypothalamus are involved in the process like temperature regulation, control of water balance in body, sexual behaviour and reproduction, control of daily cycles in physiological state, behaviour and emotional responses. Hence, hypothalamus is called as **super master endocrine gland** of the body.